Modern Indian Poetry in English

Modern Indian Poetry in English

Revised Edition

BRUCE KING

OXFORD
UNIVERSITY PRESS

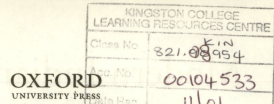

OXFORD
UNIVERSITY PRESS

YMCA Library Building, Jai Singh Road, New Delhi 110 001

Oxford University Press is a department of the University of Oxford. It furthers the
University's objective of excellence in research, scholarship, and education
by publishing worldwide in

Oxford   New York

Athens   Auckland   Bangkok   Bogota   Buenos Aires   Cape Town
Chennai   Dar es Salaam   Delhi   Florence   Hong Kong   Istanbul   Karachi
Kolkata   Kuala Lumpur   Màdrid   Melbourne   Mexico City   Mumbai
Nairobi   Paris   São Paulo   Shanghai   Singapore   Taipei   Tokyo   Toronto   Warsaw

with associated companies in   Berlin   Ibadan

Oxford is a registered trade mark of Oxford University Press
in the UK and in certain other countries

Published in India
By Oxford University Press, New Delhi

ISBN 019 565616 4

Typeset in Garamond (11/12) by Eleven Arts, Delhi 110 035
Printed in India by Rekha Printers Pvt. Ltd., New Delhi 110 020
Published by Manzar Khan, Oxford University Press
YMCA Library Building, Jai Singh Road, New Delhi 110 001

Preface to the Revised Edition

This book consists of the original *Modern Indian Poetry in English*, first published in 1987 and slightly updated in 1989 along with five new chapters. Written in 1999, the new chapters, really a mini-book in themselves, survey developments in the previous decade. The Chronology has also been brought up to date in this edition.

Along with discussions of recent books by established poets, major new anthologies, and changes in publishing and the literary scene, the main new features are a long essay on Agha Shahid Ali, who has emerged as a major poet, and two chapters on significant new poets and what they represent. Many will regard these as the controversial chapters of the book, but there is continuity as some of the poets, such as Agha Shahid Ali, Meena Alexander and Bibhu Padhi were already mentioned in the first edition but were not discussed there for reasons of space or because they had not published enough.

Since *Modern Indian Poetry in English* first appeared, Arvind Krishna Mehrotra, Eunice de Souza and Makarand Paranjape have compiled important anthologies which have brought new poets to attention or revised the canon. As I read reviews of poets by poets, read poets who have won awards, and discussed with poets their impression of the work of others, a pattern emerged. Finally, however, any book such as this depends on subjective choices. There were poets whose work I thought excellent, others who seemed to me to express previously unpublished areas of social or cultural experience, and they had to be brought into the book. I do not claim that these are the only good or interesting new poets in India. There are a few poets I began to write about but eventually decided not to include as I did not like their work and no poet was willing to convince me I was wrong. Others can write about them. In some cases, I have, reluctantly, decided to pass over several young poets whose work is excellent but who have not yet published a volume of poetry and who are in no major anthologies. Future critics can have the pleasure of introducing such discoveries.

I decided against any alterations in the original *Modern Indian Poetry in English*, which forms the first part of this book. Even to update the three charts would require revising the text and the entire book would have needed rewriting for the sake of consistency. I preferred to write a small new book, a Part II, surveying the past decade. I had already discussed Nissim Ezekiel, A.K. Ramanujan, and Dom Moraes at greater length in *Three Indian Poets* (Oxford University Press, 1991). Readers who know that small book will probably understand my reluctance to revise the original *Modern Indian Poetry in English*. To include that material along with the five new chapters would have made for an unwieldy, impossibly long book. The present double-decker seemed the more elegant solution.

Bruce King

Preface to the First Edition

In this introduction to the English-language poetry of India since national independence I will first be concerned with its history, how its canon of significant authors, books and texts is being formed, the social background of the poets, their market and readers, and the main aesthetics of their work. Subsequently I will discuss the most significant poets, Nissim Ezekiel, R. Parthasarathy, A.K. Ramanujan, Kamala Das, Adil Jussawalla, Arvind Krishna Mehrotra, Jayanta Mahapatra, G.S. Sharat Chandra, Gieve Patel, Arun Kolatkar, Dilip Chitre, Eunice de Souza, Santan Rodrigues, Manohar Shetty, Saleem Peeradina, Melanie Silgardo, Vikram Seth and others, before offering a chronology of publications, journals and events. This is the first comprehensive study of modern Indian poetry in English and my approach is historical, cultural, sociological and literary.

My research and some of the writing took place in India during 1984 on a fellowship from the American Institute of Indian Studies. Without their ten-month grant I could not have started. I am also happy to acknowledge that a period as a scholar in residence at the Rockefeller Foundation Research Center in Bellagio, Italy, allowed me to write or revise some chapters in extremely pleasant surroundings. A National Endowment for the Humanities summer stipend in 1985 allowed me to complete my manuscript. Finally, I am indebted to the Indian poets, including some who are not mentioned in the following pages, their friends, publishers and several Indian academics for information, aid, photocopies, books, journals and hospitality. While my debts of this kind are so immense that I dare not attempt to list the many names here, I must particularly thank Nissim Ezekiel, Jayanta Mahapatra, Adil Jussawalla, Arvind Krishna Mehrotra, Manohar Shetty and Ayyappa Paniker for their friendship as well. This book is dedicated to them.

Contents

PART
1

Introduction

Modern Indian English-language poetry is one of the many 'new literatures' which began to emerge at the end of the Second World War after the end of colonialism. Unlike the creative writing of Africa and the Caribbean, modern Indian poetry in English has been neglected by most critics, foreign readers and intellectuals for it has no obvious direct relationship to the cultural movements which led to national independence; by 1947 the situation had changed and with it the concern of the new poets became their relationship to and alienation from the realities of their society. In particular, they faced a challenge from older nationalist intellectuals and from regionalists who demanded a renaissance of the culture of the pre-colonial languages of India.

The only answer to those who claimed that Indians could not write authentic poetry in the English in which they had been educated was to write poetry as good as that of British, American and Irish poets, but to write it about Indian lives and conditions. This in itself became the basis of a still continuing conflict as cultural conservatives, nationalists and political radicals wanted a literature about traditional culture or the poor and the rural Hindu masses, whereas the poets were more likely to be well educated, middle class and part of or aware of the modern westernized culture of the cities, universities and professional classes. They often had been raised in families where English was one of the languages spoken, attended good English-language schools, early fallen in love with the English language and its literature, and been either brought up in a cultured environment or by their university days had friends with an interest in the arts and ideas. The supposedly traditional culture of the Hindi-speaking masses, or of their Parsi or Goan Catholic families, was either irrelevant to them or, in some cases, was part of the restrictions against which they were rebelling.

Many of the poets left India for study and travel abroad, or out of dissatisfaction. In this they were no different from previous generations of Indian intellectuals and writers, including the leaders of the independence movement. Similar to previous generations, some of the writers settled abroad, while others returned, having made a significant choice which would be central to their subsequent history and the development of Indian poetry in English. Among the early poets Nissim Ezekiel, Kersey Katrak, Srinivas Rayaprol and Keshav Malik returned, while Dom Moraes remained abroad for many years. Such poets as Deb Kumar Das, R. Bartholomew and Lawrence Bantleman were, for one reason or another, to become permanent exiles. Later the process would be repeated when Adil Jussawalla and R. Parthasarathy would study in England with the intention of residing there, only to return disillusioned to India, while G. S. Sharat Chandra and A. K. Ramanujan would become American residents.

By the early 1960s the pioneering of Ezekiel and others, centred first on the magazines *Illustrated Weekly of India* and *Quest*, had borne fruit in Writers Workshop volumes of poetry and the journal *Miscellany*. P. Lal, the editor, was one of the early poets; for the first time there was a publisher of volumes of Indian poetry and another devoted promoter and publicist besides Ezekiel.

By the later '60s English-language poetry in India had a handful of now classic volumes, not necessarily published by Writers Workshop, and established significant writers, including Ramanujan, Kamala Das, Gieve Patel, Ezekiel and Jussawalla; it was gaining recognition from those with an interest in poetry and culture both in India and abroad. Other significant writers had begun to appear, including Parthasarathy, Arvind Krishna Mehrotra, Arun Kolatkar and Dilip Chitre, along with Pritish Nandy. A few years later Keki Daruwalla, Shiv Kumar and Jayanta Mahapatra were becoming names to those with an interest in poetry. By now the modern Indian English poets formed a sufficiently large group to have different tastes, aesthetics, standards and styles, with the result that Lal and Nandy were not considered by many of the more serious poets to be of their number. This partly reflected the rapidity with which the poetry was evolving towards international standards as well as differing notions of the art. By 1980, when Keki Daruwalla published the most recent of the major anthologies of modern Indian English verse, eighteen poets were considered worthy of serious attention, and since then others, such as Manohar Shetty, Santan Rodrigues, Vikram Seth and Melanie Silgardo have appeared, as has a small but rapidly increasing body of critical studies in books and academic journals on the poetry.

Despite continuing attacks on the Indian English poets, their place in modern Indian culture is recognized. Their poetry is part of the process of modernization which includes urbanization, industrialization, mobility, independence, social change, increased communication (in the form of films, television, radio, journals and newspapers), national and international transportation networks, mass education and the resulting paradox that as an independent national culture emerges it also participates in the international, modern, usually westernized world. Unless some new radical change occurs, Indian social and economic progress is linked to the same processes of modernization which, for historical and political reasons, have become wedded to the spread of the English language and the evolution of an English-language culture alongside Hindi and the regional languages. Although presently the language of only some four per cent of the population and with no regional base, English is the language of those who govern, communicate, produce and make decisions at the national level. As the language of upward mobility and modern consumer tastes, its use is likely to spread further and as it does it will increasingly become Indianized, a process already noticeable in magazines and in English-language poetry—in such features as the syntax, word order, lexis, idioms, pronunciation, intonation and stress patterns. This reflects a change in mentality. English is no longer the language of colonial rulers; it is a language of modern India in which words and expressions have recognized national rather than imported significances and references, alluding to local realities, traditions and ways of feeling. Such Indianization has been proceeding for several generations and is prominent in the poetry of Kamala Das and Pritish Nandy, and present, although more nuanced, in the work of Keki Daruwalla; it is more likely to be felt in terms of voice and stress in the verse of Ezekiel and Jayanta Mahapatra, or in the kind of rapidly expressed ironies found in the poetry of Ramanujan.

The poets as a group tend to be marginal to traditional Hindu society not only by being alienated by their English-language education but also, more significantly, by coming from such communities as the Parsis, Jews and Christians, or by being rebels from Hinduism and Islam, or by living abroad. Many of the poets come from families that have already been partly wester- nized or that moved extensively during their childhood; several were sent to boarding schools. They often do not have local roots, or have been brought up in urban centres or studied or travelled abroad while still in their formative years. Their pers- pective is modern rather than traditional. Unlike many of the colonial clerks and the bourgeoisie who attempted to imitate the British, there is no other authentic mentality for the poets except that of the modern world and its concerns, which they may express or criticize but of which they are a part, as are an increas- ing number of Indians.

Since Ezekiel published his first book (1952) and the *Illustrated Weekly* and *Thought* began publishing English- language poetry, a history of publication, major works, journals, events, personalities and awards has already developed. There are perhaps thirty poets recognized to be of worth, a number of younger poets aspiring to that title and probably several hundred who have published volumes of poetry in English.

More significant than the achievements of individual poets is the rapidity with which Indian English poetry has become a self-sustaining tradition with recognizable models, periods and influences. Where the early Ezekiel and P. Lal offered two contrast- ing models, since then Ramanujan, Parthasarathy, Daruwalla, Mahapatra, Kamala Das, Vikram Seth and de Souza are among those who have moved poetry into new dimensions, as Ezekiel continues to do. Poets have a wider variety of Indian poems, voices, perspectives, forms and subject-matter for models. How a national tradition is being formed can be seen in the way Ram- anujan's poetry is an example for Parthasarathy's *Rough Passage*, while Parthasarathy influenced Santan Rodrigues's poems about his own Goan heritage.

There are identifiable periods when Indian poetry took new directions, such as the focusing on the actuality of personal and family life by Kamala Das and Ezekiel in the early '60s, or the experimental poetry of Mehrotra, Kolatkar, Nandy, Chitre and Mahapatra which began to appear in the later '60s and early '70s. A renewed, more detailed, satirical and yet compassionate focus on communal and family heritage has become evident more recently.

With each decade an increasing immediacy and heightened awareness of actual Indian experience is noticeable. While this might be a matter of kinds of technique and expression, it reflects a narrowing of the distance of the poet's perception of her or himself as poet from the actualities of the community life. I do not mean that the poet is less conscious of being isolated or alienated, but rather that poetry reveals more of the environment, of other lives, and of the specifics of daily life, including relations with others. While this is clear in the verse of Eunice de Souza, Saleem Peeradina and Manohar Shetty, even the older poets write more directly from a context than previously. The increased perception of details and memories of Indian social reality, found in the work of Ezekiel, Kamala Das, and Ramanujan during the '60s, and taken up by Daruwalla, has now been internalized, with recent poetry being richer in its sense of location and range of subject matter.

If at first modern Indian English verse appeared to be indebted to British and a few European models, it now reveals an awareness of most of world literature, including contemporary American, recent South American, and older Indian devotional verse in the regional languages. In this Indian English-language poetry is no different from that of the regional languages, which also during the colonial period followed British examples and conventions of verse. Around the time of national independence it started to reform itself as a modern literature by incorporating the techniques and themes of such major twentieth-century modernists as T. S. Eliot and Ezra Pound, by discovering the great body of French experimental poetry from the nineteenth-century Rimbaud and Lautréamont to the twentieth-century dadaists and surrealists, while learning from the political poetry of Neruda and others. Several of the English-language poets, such as Kolatkar, Ramanujan and Chitre, are also involved with changes in the regional literatures.

The poet's decision to use English is influenced by education, but also by the state of regional-language poetry. Kamala Das says that when she began writing in English there was no modern poetry in Malayalam. Manohar Shetty says that in Tulu, the language of his family, there is no creative literature. The many Parsi poets writing in English may be explained by the fact that Parsi Gujarati is a dialect without a tradition of serious creative literature. The varied interplay of English-language poetry with that in the regional languages is a subject that needs further study.

Besides the role played by Kolatkar and Chitre in developing regional-language poetry in a new direction, the poets have been particularly active in translating from regional languages. There are translations by Ramanujan from classical and medieval Tamil and modern Kannada, by Mahapatra from modern Oriya, by Kolatkar from Marathi, by Chitre from modern and medieval Marathi, by Patel from Gujarati, by Mehrotra from Hindi, by P. Lal from Sanskrit, by Nandy from Bengali, Urdu and other languages. P. Lal and Nandy have been especially active as promoters and publishers of translations from classical and regional languages. Ezekiel and G. S. Sharat Chandra have also been involved with translations from Indian languages. Just as English has become the 'link' language for inter-regional communication for such groups as administrators, academics and the professional class, English translation serves as a link cultural language, making available to the middle classes the various regional languages and the classical tradition.

The English-language poets' interest in devotional verse is part of the increasing range of Indian English-language poetry. Whereas the significant poetry of the '50s and early '60s was primarily the personal short lyric, often confessional or argumentative, in the mid '60s poets found new modes of expression. While Ezekiel and Ramanujan were already familiar with American poetry, the American influence on Indian poetry became more significant in the mid '60s, when Daruwalla, Shiv Kumar and others began to aim for a less formal, direct personal voice and diction and to write about ordinary experience in recognizable locations. The man-alone-in-a-hostile-world attitude, with its sense of opposition, cynicism and the ironies of life, found in the poetry of Daruwalla, has its affinities in American literature, as does Daruwalla's trust in the speaking voice. Although he continues to use traditional prosody and formal stanzaic shapes, the voice seems closer to the experience of the senses than in previous Indian poetry where there was often a distance between moral reflection and actuality. There is also an openness, especially noticeable in the middle portions of the poems, as if association were taking over from logic. Narrative becomes experience itself instead of an example in an argument.

This increasing openness and immediacy is also noticeable in Mehrotra's early *bharatmata: a prayer*, and somewhat later in the poetry of Saleem Peeradina. Besides being the start of a highly subjective protest poetry, sometimes written by Nandy, the counter-culture of the '60s strengthened the interest in surreal, dadaist and experimental verse which had already been explored by Kolatkar, Chitre and others in Marathi. While Marathi, Oriya and other regional languages had recent traditions of experimentalist, avant-garde writing, Indian English-language poetry began developing in such directions after 1965. Among the poets of the avant-garde were Mehrotra, Kolatkar, Chitre, Mahapatra, Nandy and Deba Patnaik; while they have gone on to write other kinds of poetry, some of their best-known poems, such as Mehrotra's 'The Sale' and 'Continuities', Kolatkar's 'the boatride' and Chitre's 'The Ambulance Ride', show how liberating and productive was such experimentalism. If recent poets, particularly Silgardo and Shetty, have taken a renewed interest in the more logically developed, more formally organized lyric, they can do so with a sense of having been freed from the necessity of beginning a poem with a statement which is logically developed to a conclusion. Their poetry is more linear and argumentatively constructed than that of Mehrotra and Mahapatra, but it is still more open, more ready to shift to the unexpected in subject matter and images and to offer unconventional emotions, than the poetry written between 1950 and 1965; it is more associational in organization than logically structured.

The open, associational poetry, with its surprising attitudes, prominence of such topics as guilt, sexuality, ambition, memories of past rebellions, conflicts, shames, childhood and love affairs, and the assertion of an articulate but fractured self, was part of the confessional mode that started in America during the early '50s and which was practised internationally during the '60s. There had always been a confessional tradition in modern Indian poetry as Ezekiel's poetry often makes use of allusions to his life and a desire for personal change, but Kamala Das's highly emotive, self-revelatory, moody poems were much more confessional; she wrote openly about varied, often conflicting emotions, values and hopes, without being concerned—as Ezekiel was—with consistency and the will for self-improvement. Whereas the autobiographical elements in Ezekiel's poetry usually appeared distanced, in Das's poetry her private life was brought forward as the subject matter.

Around 1970 Shiv Kumar took the confessional mode further in poetry filled with sexual desire, anger and rebellion, in which the voice and what was said shaped rhythm and form. While it might seem that anything could be said in whatever way it came to the writer provided that its rhythms, cadence, language and imagery felt like poetry, such recent confessional poets as de Souza, Shetty and Silgardo are highly conscious of craft, revising their poems for understatement, economy and visual shape.

Related to but different from the confessional poem is the kind of open, obscure, somewhat surreal lyric practised by Mahapatra, and which younger Orissa poets have learned from him. In these poems, probably influenced by the 'open field' poetry written in America by Robert Bly and James Wright, an opening observation of the natural world is rapidly overtaken by obscure, highly charged personal associations, sometimes expressed in unexplainable imagery, concluding on an unexpected assertion of guilt, failure or, occasionally, hope. Such poetry appears very different from, and much more arbitrary in content as well as less open than, the confessional mode; but it shows such similar charateristics as rapid fluctuations of feeling, associational organization and a tendency towards the use of fantasy and the exploration of normally unarticulated areas of self-awareness. Even more than confessional poetry it appears addressed to the self. The poet ruminates about life and brings up, in striking and unusual images, feelings that others repress or are reluctant to display.

Besides the immediacy, experimentation, openness and self revelation of modern Indian poetry in English, there is an increasing interest in the long poem, as a means of going beyond the fragmented vision and isolation associated with the short lyric. Such long poems are perhaps the closest modern culture can come to the shared national and communal values and experience of the classical epic. The distance between the modern sceptical individual and the traditional beliefs of a community is, however, the subject of this modern equivalent of the epic, as can be seen from such volumes as Parthasarathy's *Rough Passage*, with its record of alienation and desire for reintegration into a cultural tradition, Kolatkar's puzzlement at the discrepancy between legend and actuality in *Jejuri*, or Mahapatra's attempted reconciliation to his environment in *Relationship*. Daruwalla's 'The Waterfront' sequence is another instance of an Indian English poet seeking reconcilement with a tradition from which he feels alienated and of which he is rationally sceptical. A different approach to the problem of reintegration is Jussawalla's 'Missing Person' in which the alienated middle-class intellectual is satirized for lack of commitment to the revolutionary forces of history. While such longer sequences of poems, with their extended range of themes and subject matter, may seem a world away from Ezekiel's early lyrics, it was Ezekiel who in *The Unfinished Man* first showed how a unified vision could be put together in which diverse lyrics were linked by theme, implied narrative, imagery and recurring but developing concerns.

Indian English poetry has since independence already evolved into a literary tradition with a history of major journals, such as *Poetry India* and *Opinion Literary Quarterly*, interesting little magazines such as *damn you* and *Dialogue*, central volumes such as Ezekiel's *The Unfinished Man* and *The Exact Name*, Kamala Das's *Summer in Calcutta* and Ramanujan's *The Striders*, which began a canon and which, belonging to the mid '60s, are now regarded as part of a golden age. It is a still vital, living, evolving tradition, as is shown by the, often precarious, existence of such journals as *Chandrabhaga*, *Kavi-India* and the *Indian Literary Review*, each and all of which may have disappeared by the time you read this, no doubt to be replaced by other torch-bearers of contemporary poetry. And there have been exciting first volumes published more recently, such as Eunice de Souza's *Fix* and Manohar Shetty's *A Guarded Space*.

While Indian English poetry appears firmly established, in contrast to the 1950s when it hardly existed beyond the self-published volumes of Ezekiel and the publication of Dom Moraes in England, it still has major problems. More poetry is being written than before and publishers receive manuscripts every day from new English-language poets hoping to break into print, but few publishers will publish poetry. The only commercial publishing houses to do so are Oxford University Press and Arnold-Heinemann; the others argue that the market is too small to make a profit. While the Oxford series shows that it is possible to make a profit on poetry, their authors are established names and the books have the benefit of Oxford University Press's name and distribution network. Most poetry in India is privately published or subsidized by the author.

Major differences between the Indian and foreign poetry markets are the lack of the usual republication fees from publishers of textbooks and anthologies, and the lack of institutional support. Foreign publishers are willing to take chances on poetry books because whether or not the volumes sell they hope that if the poet becomes well known there will be fees for republication in school and university textbooks and in anthologies of poetry sold to a general public which otherwise seldom buys books of verse. In the case of India this market hardly exists. Because of a desire to produce school books as inexpensively as possible the relevant government agencies will reprint material without offering a republication fee to publishers, or will offer a small fee hardly worth anyone's effort. The university textbook market might seem to offer more promise; but the number of university English departments currently offering courses in Indian literature is small, although growing, and often the course is taught to small groups of Honours or MA students. As for commercial anthologies of poetry, many are published without seeking permission from the poet or the poet's publisher and no fees are paid. The Parthasarathy and Daruwalla anthologies are exceptional in that commercial republication rates were paid.

Indian English poetry has taken root in India, found a small but increasing readership, and is here to stay. Indian English poetry is one of the many new areas of culture which have resulted from national independence. Perhaps the most exciting literary development in recent decades has been the emergence of national literatures in the Third World and in such former cultural colonies as Canada, Australia and New Zealand. The new literatures have taken their place alongside the older national literatures as equals. There are perhaps thirty Indian poets with whose work I am familiar (there are undoubtedly others), who can stand alongside good English-language poets in other countries. This may not seem a large number, but, considering that the history of modern Indian poetry began around 1950, it is remarkable.

CHAPTER TWO

History and Publishing Circles

A survey of the history of modern Indian poetry will show how the emergence of the new poetry depended on the poets themselves who, along with a few editors and promoters, had to be their own publishers, critics and sponsors. Although the new poetry was often closely associated with the development of other post-independence arts such as drama and painting, the poets had to create their own cultural space, start their own journals and edit and publish each other's manuscripts. There was no continuity between the new poetry and that written before independence. Poetry of the pre-independence period was, the writers felt, a mass of sentiments, clichés, outdated language and conventions, the ossified remains of a colonial tradition badly in need of a new start through grafting on a vital body of contemporary verse and contact with contemporary life and speech. Nissim Ezekiel appears to have been the only poet to have been for a period of his youth influenced by an older Indian poet: Armando Menezes was his first model, but he soon turned to a more modern idiom.

The new poets who began to appear at independence were in love with the English language, excited by their discovery of such late-nineteenth-century and twentieth-century poets as Hopkins, Yeats, Eliot, Pound and Auden; their concerns in their writing were individual or expressions of the human condition in general rather than the peasants and the now superseded issue of political independence. The nationalist political need for a usable past, with its emphasis on national classics, mythology and representation of typical characters, no longer seemed relevant. Instead, the younger poets were more likely to write about life in the city and their personal desires and discontents. Their emphasis was more on the aesthetic, ethical or interpersonal than on politics, nationalism and mythology. The new poetry was part of the post-independence modernization of Indian society and emerged first in, and is still often a phenomenon of, the larger urban areas.

In 1947 C. R. Mandy, an Irishman, became editor of the *Illustrated Weekly of India* and began to transform it from a typical colonial family publication to one more appropriate to the newly-independent India. Mandy, who had appeared in Longman's *Miscellany*, an arts journal brought out in New Delhi in the 1940s, had a strong interest in literature and used the *Illustrated Weekly* to encourage local writers. In 1950 it sponsored a short story contest and towards the end of that year began publishing contemporary Indian poetry, some of which was translated from the regional languages. Mandy's column of 28 January 1951 noted that much of the verse submitted was influenced by G. M. Hopkins, T. S. Eliot and Rilke. Among the poets published early in the *Illustrated Weekly* were B. Rajan, Nissim Ezekiel, P. Lal, Srinivas Rayaprol, Kersey Katrak, Dom Moraes, R. Bartholomew and Kamala Das.

Mandy apparently had first noticed B. Rajan (b. 1920) in the special 1948 issue devoted to Indian writing of *Life and Letters* (formerly *London Mercury*); in his *Illustrated Weekly* column Mandy said that Rajan was the only Indian poet to write in a modern manner. Rajan, who later became a well-known literary critic and novelist, was then lecturing in English literature at Cambridge University. Writing in a style influenced by W. H. Auden, Dylan Thomas and William Empson, Rajan appeared in good British and American literary journals of the 1940s and '50s. While at Cambridge he privately printed 200 copies of a twenty-eight-page volume of verse, *Monsoon* (1945). He subsequently published two poems in the *Illustrated Weekly* in which he treated characters from Indian epics in a contemporary fashion, using psychology, compression of statement and complex word-play. Except for a few poems being included in early anthologies, he appears to have had no influence on or further contact with the new poets in India, although he was for a time Head of the English Department at the University of Delhi.

A far more significant role in the emergent poetry was taken by Nissim Ezekiel. Ezekiel (b. 1924) began writing poetry in Wilson College, Bombay. He first published a poem in 1942 in *Social Welfare*, and later published it in the college's *The Wilsonian*. During college and university days he was politically active in M. N. Roy's Radical Democratic Party and in trade unionism, and he edited *The Student World*. In the late 1940s he met Ibrahim Alkazi, who was to play such a prominent role in the development of theatre in India. Alkazi attracted intellectuals and writers to his drama group and over the years many of the Bombay poets were part of a circle with shared interests in the various arts, especially the theatre. When Alkazi decided to study drama in London, he advised Ezekiel also to go abroad to educate himself in contemporary culture. As Ezekiel could not afford to travel, Alkazi gave him a one-way boat ticket to England. In England Ezekiel met Keshav Malik (b. 1928), who was the first literary editor of the New Delhi political journal *Thought*, started in 1948, and who was going to the inaugural meeting of the Congress for Cultural Freedom. Malik was at that time also a democratic socialist, a follower of M. N. Roy's Radical Democratic Movement. After Ezekiel began publishing in British literary journals he was brought to the attention of Mandy, who asked him to send poems to the *Illustrated Weekly*. He also published in *Thought*. When he returned to Bombay in 1952 Mandy hired him as an assistant editor; among his duties was to advise those who submitted poems to the *Illustrated Weekly* how their work could be improved. Among the early contributors who showed their work to Ezekiel were Dom Moraes (b. 1938) and Kersey Katrak (b. 1936). He also met Kamala Das (b. 1936) who had been publishing in *PEN* since 1948.

Moraes's father was a well-known editor and journalist and Dom Moraes had in his teens published a short story in the *Illustrated Weekly*. Ezekiel advised him not to be willing to accept the easy accolades available in Indian literary circles but to compete against British standards. Katrak, who was an actor in Alkazi's drama group, began writing romantic verse at school, but after his interests turned to modern poetry he had, he remembers, no one to discuss it with at the time except Ezekiel. Ezekiel went through his poems carefully, making him justify each word. Many of the poems in the first books he published are in Ezekiel's style and appear written as part of a dialogue about how to live. The initial group of modern English-language poets had few contacts with and no support from the earlier generation of nationalists, many of whom had returned from Europe and were starting their own short-lived political and literary magazines. Katrak remembers leaving his poems with a famous novelist who returned them to him months later without comment.

Others who published in the *Illustrated Weekly* during this period were R. Bartholomew (b. 1926), Srinivas Rayaprol (b. 1925) and P. Lal (b. 1928). Bartholomew was a Ceylonese living in India who became the literary editor of *Thought* after Keshav Malik left to travel abroad. Rayaprol had come into contact with American poets while studying engineering in California and contributed to American literary journals. He was noticed by Mandy when he appeared in the special 1953 Indian issue of the American magazine *Atlantic Monthly*, along with Rajan and P. Lal. Mandy wrote encouragingly to him, asking him to submit to the *Illustrated Weekly*. After his return to Secunderabad, Rayaprol started an international literary journal, *East and West* (1956–60).

P. Lal was initially part of a circle of students at the Jesuit St Xavier's College, Calcutta, interested in the modern arts. They first made their appearance in the *St. Xavier's Magazine* (vol. 9, no. 3, July 1947) when Lal published an essay, 'In Defence of Modern English Poetry' and edited a six-page poetry section. The next issue in December included Lal's verse translation from the Gita, along with poems by Romen Mookerjee and Utpal Dutt. The photographs which accompanied the literary section are captioned 'Hypermodern' for Mookerjee and 'Modern' for Lal. After Lal began reviewing books and publishing poems in the *Illustrated Weekly* and *Thought*, he wrote a regular column for *Thought* between 1954 and 1957 in which he published several new poets. Between 1955 and 1959 Lal co-edited in Calcutta the *Orient Review and Literary Digest*, which also published some poems. While *Thought* continued to print poetry—and some critical articles and interviews with poets—it was felt by some of the poets to lack standards and was less significant than the *Illustrated Weekly*.

One of the books Lal reviewed in *Thought* (28 June 1952) was Ezekiel's *A Time to Change* (1952) which was brought out in England by Fortune Press. Although few copies became available in India, it showed that Indians could write as well as contemporary British poets and it introduced many of Ezekiel's continuing themes, such as the quest for physical, social and spiritual integration of the self. Although not as complex in style as Rajan's poetry, it had a contemporary voice in which personal, intellectual, moral and religious concerns were expressed concisely and clearly without the mystical diffusion and artificial diction that had been common to previous Indian poetry; it was a substantial volume, showing a variety of techniques ranging from free verse to traditional prosody, and had a distinct *persona* and point of view. It might be considered the beginning of the canon of modern Indian English poetry. If Indian poets often saw poetry as the hobby of an amateur who wrote occasional pieces in spare time, Ezekiel viewed poetry as a way of life; a poem was part of an evolving body of work, an expression of a life as a poet. Soon after his return to India he privately published *Sixty Poems* (1953); as there was then no poetry publishing house and no means of distribution he left copies for sale at the Strand Bookshop in Bombay.

Around 1955 Ezekiel joined PEN and became assistant editor of their journal, *PEN*, which had been publishing since 1934; after Sophia Wadia's retirement he became editor. Over the years the poets appeared in *PEN*, as did reviews and some articles on their work. Ezekiel also founded *Quest* (1955), a general intellectual review associated with liberal democratic politics, sponsored by the Congress for Cultural Freedom. Ezekiel was its first editor until mid 1957 and remained a literary advisor over the years until it ceased publication with the Emergency and was superseded by *New Quest*. As a general intellectual review concerned with the problems of modern India, somewhat on the model of *Encounter* in England, *Quest* helped make modern Indian poetry part of contemporary Indian culture. Among its early contributors were Moraes, Lal, Adil Jussawalla (b. 1940), Kamala Das, Katrak, R. Parthasarathy (b. 1934), A. K. Ramanujan (b. 1929), Dilip Chitre (b. 1938) and Arun Kolatkar (b. 1932); the latter published a poem in the first issue. A bilingual poet who experimented with translating his work between the two languages, Kolatkar—a painter and by profession a graphic designer—was part of Bombay Marathi bohemia rather than English-speaking university or professional circles. He thought for many years that he was the only English-language poet in India, as Arvind Mehrotra (b. 1947) and friends were later to do in Allahabad. Dilip Chitre met Kolatkar in 1954 through the Marathi poetry scene in which Kolatkar was a leader of the avant-garde poets; they helped co-edit *Shabda*, a stencilled Marathi literary journal which appeared irregularly between 1955 and 1960. Chitre became a regular contributor to *Quest* and later one of the editors of *New Quest*. Another poet who appeared in *Quest* was Gieve Patel (b. 1940), a medical student who through Alkazi's theatr group met Ezekiel around 1957. Ramanujan, who followed with interest the way Kannada poets were modernizing their verse, began publishing poems in 1955 in the first issue of *Quest, Thought* and the *Illustrated Weekly*. Ezekiel met Ramanujan in 1956 while planning a special Tamil-language issue of *Quest* (which never appeared); Ramanujan visited Bombay to discuss the issue. Molly Daniels, his wife, knew Ezekiel. The early *Quest* poets became the nucleus of those with a serious interest in writing poetry. After Ezekiel turned over the editorship to others in 1957, he remained a reviewer and consultant. Poets sent him their manuscripts for criticism, advice and encouragement; he suggested where they might publish and sent their poems to *Quest* and the *Illustrated Weekly*.

The later 1950s saw several anthologies of Indian poetry, the start of the Writers Workshop in Calcutta, the special Indian issue of *Poetry* (Chicago), Mandy's departure from the *Illustrated Weekly*, and Dom Moraes's award of the Hawthornden Prize in England for his first book of verse, *A Beginning* (1957). Moraes was the youngest poet to be awarded the Hawthornden Prize, and it was the first time the award had been given since the Second World War.

The *Modern Indian Poetry* anthology, edited by A. V. Rajeswara Rau in 1958, was an old-fashioned affair, mostly of poetry in translation, but included Dom Moraes's 'In Meadows' and 'Sailing to England', P. Lal's 'The Parrot's Death' and 'The Irony', a poem by K. Raghavendra Rao (b. 1928) and two poems by Rayaprol. The Indian issue of the American *Poetry* (January 1959) consisted mostly of translated verse, but included poems by Rayaprol, Rajan, Lal, Moraes, K. Raghavendra Rao and Mary Erulkar. The 1959 anthology, *Modern Indo-Anglian Poetry*, edited by the poets P. Lal and K. Raghavendra Rao, was of more significance. It included a 'Credo' or manifesto for the new poets and poems by Dom Moraes ('Sailing to England' again), F. R. Stanley (who later published as F. Stanley Rajiva), K. Rao, Leo F. Fredericks, Mary Erulkar, Monika Varma (b. 1916), Nissim Ezekiel, Noel Buckenham, P. K. Saha (b. 1932), P. Lal ('The Parrot's Death' and 'Because Her Speech is Excellent'), R. L. Bartholomew, Rakshat Puri (b. 1924), Romen Mookerjee, Srinivas Rayaprol and a few others. Many of the writers would later publish under Lal's Writers Workshop imprint. The non-inclusion of such writers as Kamala Das, Katrak, Kolatkar and Ramanujan perhaps signifies that modern indian poetry in English was already falling into two groups, those associated with Ezekiel, centred in Bombay, and those associated with Lal, centred in Calcutta and to a lesser extent Delhi. During the 1950s and early '60s, however, the groups were not obvious; a mutual interest in promoting the new poetry and themselves kept the writers together.

The departure of Mandy from the *Illustrated Weekly* left the increasing number of poets needing a place to publish. Several felt they had manuscripts ready, but none of the commercial publishers were interested. Ezekiel privately printed his *The Third* in 1959 and Keshav Malik, who had returned from his travels, brought out his first book as a Surge publication. To meet the growing needs of the poets the Writers Workshop, which had started in 1958, began in 1959 to publish volumes of poetry. The seven founding members of the Writers Workshop in Calcutta were a small circle of friends—P. Lal, Anita Desai, Lal's former student Deb Kumar Das, David McCutchion, Kewlian Sio, Jai Ratan and David Crane—Indians and foreigners living in Calcutta. There was a weekly meeting at Lal's house on Sunday.

The first Writers Workshop volume of verse was *The Lamp is Low* (1959) by Robert Perlongo, an American then living in Calcutta. It was followed in 1960 by Lal's *The Parrot's Death and Other Poems*, Ezekiel's *The Unfinished Man*, R. de L. Furtado's *The Oleanders*, Deb Kumar Das's (b. 1939) *The Night Before Us* and Pradip Sen's *And Then the Sun*.

A somewhat defensive ingroupness is perhaps shown by the prefaces that the poets wrote for each other. Lal introduced the volumes of Ezekiel, Furtado, Sen and Deb Kumar Das; K. R. Rao wrote a preface to Lal's book. *The World is Split* (1961) by N. K. Sethi (b. 1936), an Indian teaching in New York, had a preface by the American poet William Carlos Williams. *Entrance* (1961) by Lila Ray (an American married to an Indian) was prefaced by David McCutchion, an Englishman teaching in Calcutta. In 1962 the series expanded to include Adil Jussawalla's *Land's End*, Laurence Bantleman's *Graffiti*, Ira De's (b. 1932) *The Hunt*, Lal's second book, *Love's The First* and Monika Varma's *Dragonflies Draw Flame*. Prefaces were written by Ezekiel to Varma's poems, Pradip Sen to Ira De's and Lal to Bantleman's.

In 1960 the Writers Workshop also started *Miscellany*, a bimonthly journal devoted to creative writing. Early contributors included Ezekiel, Anita Desai, R. de L. Furtado, David McCutchion, Lila Ray, Romen Mookerjee, Malik and C. R. Mandy; in the seventh issue R. Parthasarathy published a poem. The eighth issue (1961) is 'A Garland for Shawn Mandy' which included essays and poems by Ezekiel, Ruth Prawer Jhabvala, R. de L. Furtado, K. R. Srinivasa Iyengar, Lal, Desai, Parthasarathy, Varma, G. S. Sharat Chandra and F. R. Stanley. To the tenth issue in 1962 Jussawalla contributed a poem.

By the early '60s Lal's Writers Workshop was a publishing centre for an increasing group of significant writers. Of those now considered major poets, Parthasarathy, Jussawalla and G. S. Sharat Chandra (b. 1938) had appeared on the scene. Others, although now of less significance, were thought of sufficient interest to be discussed as moderns by K. R. S. Iyengar in his *Indian Writing in English* (Furtado, Pradip Sen and Deb Kumar Das). There were a number of foreign visitors to the Workshop, and *Miscellany* published poems of a few, including the New Zealander James Baxter and the English poet D. J. Enright.

The two most significant early volumes the Writers Workshop published, and which have a place in the canon of significant books of poetry, were Ezekiel's *The Unfinished Man* and Jussawalla's *Land's End*. *The Unfinished Man* (1960) was the first volume of poetry produced in India of consistently high quality and with an overall unity of purpose. The attention to craft, consistency of style and perfecting of an intellectualized ironic tone while treating a record of a personal crisis in a distanced, reflective manner, brought together characteristics of Ezekiel's earlier three volumes. While being varied in subject matter and setting, his poems deftly implied a location, a personal story about the disillusionments of marriage, a love affair, moral choices, and a conclusion about the relationship of the poet–artist to India. It included such poems that have been subsequently anthologized as 'Enterprise', 'Marriage' and 'Jamini Roy.' These are the earliest poems that are still widely anthologized. The importance of the volume was soon recognized in David McCutchion's 'Examen de Midi' (*Miscellany*, 29, 1960) and later in Subhas C. Saha's explication of 'Enterprise' (*Miscellany*, 40, 1970). Eunice de Souza's excellent notes were added to the second edition of *The Unfinished Man* (1969), which was meant for use by university students.

Ezekiel, who recommended poets to Lal, knew Jussawalla's family and met Adil Jussawalla during one of his return trips to

India. He read Jussawalla's previously unpublished poems and suggested he send them to the Writers Workshop for publication. *Land's End* (1962) introduced a very promising young poet at a time when there were still few volumes of Indian verse worth sustained attention. Jussawalla was only twenty-two at the time but already spoke the language of modern alienation in rhythms that were his own. Ezekiel called *Land's End* the best book to be published by a new Indian poet since Moraes's *A Beginning*.

1960 also saw the acceptance by the Sahitya Akademi of English as a national language and the appearance of creative writing and articles on Indian English writing in *Indian Literature* edited by Keshav Malik after 1972. A few academic journals of English studies started which gave support to the new poetry through articles, reviews and the publication of a few poems. The *Literary Half-Yearly*, founded in 1960 by H. H. Anniah Gowda, published in early issues poems by Ezekiel, G. S. Sharat Chandra (a frequent contributor), F. R. Stanley, K. R. Rao, Jussawalla and Parthasarathy, and favourably reviewed Ezekiel's *The Unfinished Man* and Jussawalla's *Land's End*. Gowda was very aware of the Writers Workshop and wrote in support of the new poetry. Ezekiel provided further support when he became literary and reviews editor of a new general magazine, *Imprint* (1961), started by A. D. Gorwala, also owner of the independent political journal *Opinion*.

In 1962 the American poets Allen Ginsberg and Peter Orlovsky visited India. After meeting Malay Roy Choudhury and the Bengali 'Hungryalist' poets in Calcutta, whom they publicized in American literary journals, Ginsberg and Orlovsky moved briefly to Bombay where they read their poetry on the terrace of Alkazi's flat; they accused the Bombay poets of still writing old-fashioned British verse and of not having found their own voice. The same year *Penguin Modern Poetry 2* published Dom Moraes, along with the British poet Kingsley Amis, and Peter Porter, an Australian. The next year Margaret O'Donnell's *An Anthology of Commonwealth Verse* (1963), published in London, included Das, Lal, Ezekiel and others; it was the first of several British and American anthologies in which the new poets would appear. At home Gorwala's *Opinion*, with Kersey Katrak as its poetry advisor, started publishing Indian English poetry. In 1964 *The Century*, a New Delhi publication which had started two years earlier, also began publishing poetry.

Laurence Bantleman (b. 1942), the literary editor, had brought out several promising books with the Writers Workshop, *Graffiti* (1962) and *Man's Fall and Woman's Fall-out* (1964). With Bartholomew he started a Writers Workshop circle in New Delhi from 1964 to 1967 which was especially interested in experimental writing. Kamala Das, who was given a poetry award by the Asian *PEN*, Manila, published regularly in *The Century*.

One of the most exciting periods of modern Indian verse began in 1965 with the publication of Dom Moraes's *John Nobody* and books by Kamala Das, A. K. Ramanujan, Nissim Ezekiel, Gieve Patel and the appearance of many interesting but unfortunately short-lived literary journals such as *Poetry India*. This was the first flowering of the older generation which had started in Mandy's *Illustrated Weekly* and *Quest*, and the first assertion of a younger generation which added an often zany experimentalism to modern Indian verse, making it more international in contrast to the formal, logical English poetic tradition that was the departure point of the first generation of modern poets.

Although Kamala Das had been publishing since she was fourteen, *Summer in Calcutta* (1965), her first book, was self-published with a foreword by Sophia Wadia, editor of Indian *PEN* and a friend of Kamala's mother, herself a famous Malayalam poet. The fifty poems in *Summer in Calcutta*, including such now famous pieces as 'The Dance of the Eunuchs', 'The Freaks', 'Words', 'My Grandmother's House', 'An Apology to Goutama' and 'Forest Fire', caught the attention of many for their frank confession of the dissatisfactions of an arranged marriage and the intensity of sexual desire. The tradition of Indian love poetry seemed re-invigorated by a contemporary voice far from the sentimentality which had been inherited from English Victorian verse and which was still characteristic of Lal and many of the Writers Workshop poets.

Rather than finding salvation in art, Kamala Das's poetry spoke of fantasies, many lovers and the continuing disappointments of love. More important than its themes was the use of an Indian English without the concern for correctness and precision which characterized most earlier modern verse. Instead it appeared unpremeditated, a direct expression of feelings as it shifted erratically through unpredictable emotions, creating its own form through its cadences and repetitions of phrases, symbols and refrains. It seemed to collapse the distance between poet and poetry, the aesthetic distancing at which Lal and Ezekiel aimed and which was common to many British and American poets during the first half of this century. Instead, Das seemed to have her own version of the contemporary confessional mode practised since the late 1950s by such American poets as Robert Lowell and Sylvia Plath. In her verse a Hindu woman's longing for Krishna was present along with the guilt at fleshly desires she had learned in her Catholic schools. Her second book, *The Descendants* (1967), showed tendencies towards depression, self-consciousness and flamboyance as despair alternated with self-assertion.

A parallel breakthrough can be seen in *The Exact Name* (1965), Ezekiel's fifth book and the last volume of verse he was to publish with the Writers Workshop. Many of the poems were in a new manner. 'Night of the Scorpion' spoke of his family life and the conflicts between what a modern Indian believed and felt. Moreover it was unrhymed and written for the speaking voice, to be read aloud. The 'In India' poems were satires of local social manners and behaviour. While Ezekiel had in his early books used free verse as well as traditional prosody, in *The Exact Name* there is a greater fluidity of cadence, a closer approximation of the speaking voice than in the past. The poems expressed Indian life without self-conscious or artificial Indianness. Although Ezekiel had always been an urban poet—in contrast to the Indian landscape painting of the pre-independence poets—Bombay had been a symbolic city of modern dissatisfaction whereas now it had become a place where there were actual events, people, dangers and pleasures. *The Exact Name* was reviewed in *The Literary Criterion*, VII, 3 (Winter 1966) and in the *Indian PEN* (May 1966).

A. K. Ramanujan's *The Striders* (1966) was first submitted to Oxford University Press in India which, not having published any local poetry, sent the manuscript to England where it was accepted by Oxford and recommended to its members by the Poetry Book Society. Ramanujan's poems had a highly accomplished, understated preciseness and economy of statement, symbol and narrative. Without an obvious formality of structure they seemed perfectly formed and showed a range of technique beyond that of any previous Indian English poetry. It was a technique Ramanujan had learned from his study of older Kannada and Tamil verse and the modern Kannada poets who blended Indian and European models into new forms. He showed that Indian poets could both be modern and work from within their own literary traditions. The precision of language and image and the conciseness of each line, with their unpredictable changes in direction, were matched by a somewhat flat, unreverberant, sometimes off-hand sometimes irritated voice that suggested a complicated personality which implied more than was said. Ezekiel and Parthasarathy soon praised Ramanujan as the best of the Indian poets. As important as his technique was his use of his southern Indian Brahmin roots as a source, contrasting his life in America (where he had taken up residence first as a research student, then as a teacher at the University of Chicago) with his Tamil upbringing to create images of contemporary alienation set in specific situations. The divided heritage, Indian and Western, of Indian poets had not before been handled so subtly and without self-consciousness.

Another significant volume was Gieve Patel's *Poems* (1966), the first and only book issued by Ezekiel as part of a projected series meant to offer an alternative to the Writers Workshop. A precise, economical, unmetaphoric poet, Patel often shows a mind reflecting upon actual situations he has observed or in which he has participated. A medical doctor, he is conscious of both the body's weakness and its resilience. His verses are dense and oblique in texture and meaning, and seem purposely to avoid poetic graces and sentiments. Even such a poem as 'On Killing a Tree', which could be interpreted as about human life, provides no analogies or metaphoric words to suggest that it is about anything more than what it says. Patel's compressed manner, distrust of sentiments, physical awareness and the way he writes from personal experience, while guarding himself against emotional involvement, was also new to Indian poetry.

After Ezekiel became Professor of English at Mithibhai College, Bombay (1961), Parthasarathy, who had appeared in *Quest* and was then teaching at another Bombay college, joined the department. Ezekiel introduced Jussawalla to Parthasarathy, and through the latter Jussawalla came to know S. V. Pradhan. Jussawalla was at the poetry reading during which the Beats read their work before Ezekiel and Parthasarathy. In the mood of rebellion stirred by the visit of Ginsberg and Orlovsky to Calcutta and Bombay, Parthasarathy, along with Pradhan, who taught at Mithibhai, and Abraham Benjamin of Elphinstone College, started a magazine called *Bombay Duck* (1964). An early issue was banned by college authorities because of an article quoting Henry Miller. Pradhan and Benjamin began *Dionysius* (1965), which included work by Kolatkar, Chitre and the editors. The combined second and third number was confiscated by the police as obscene because of a prose fantasy by the editors called 'The Ritual-The Trial'. Parthasarathy was also involved with *Blunt* (1967–8), which lasted two issues.

One of the unexpected places the new poetry took root was in Allahabad where, after receiving from an uncle in America copies of contemporary literary magazines, Amit and Alok Rai, along with their neighbour Arvind Mehrotra, started stencilling *damn you: a magazine of the arts*, in imitation of the American publication *Fuck You: a magazine of the arts*. They also began exchanging copies of *damn you* for foreign magazines and rapidly became a temporary outpost of the American and European avant-garde. This was not the first introduction of Indian poets to the contemporary avant-garde as publications were available in the urban centres after independence, before exchange controls made it more difficult, and several of the early Writers Workshop poets were certainly familiar with avant-garde literature, as were poets in such regional languages as Marathi and Oriya. But *damn you* began at a time when the new international counter-culture was beginning to be received sympathetically among young Indians. Arvind Mehrotra had unusual energy as a promoter, while soon showing talent as an excellent poet who, after 1970, appeared regularly in leading American literary magazines, once being included among the San Francisco poets.

After doing a BA in English at the University of Allahabad, where he first published poems in the university magazine, Mehrotra went to Bombay to study for an MA. He soon met Kolatkar, Chitre, Patel, Ezekiel, Parthasarathy and Jussawalla, who had briefly returned to India from England. Besides editing *damn you* (1965-8), which first printed Kolatkar's 'the boatride', Mehrotra began two other stencilled journals, *ezra: an imagiste magazine* (1967-71) and *fakir* (1968), which published Chitre's translation of Tukaram in its only issue. He published a number of pamphlets of individual poets, including his own *Concrete poems*, *15 Poems from the Good Surrealist* and *bharatmata: a prayer* (1966). The last, influenced by Ginsberg's *Howl*, was Mehrotra's response to realizing that he was an Indian poet and not part of the American–European counter-culture. The titles of his other two pamphlets with their direct reference to surrealist and concrete poetry are significant of the way younger Indian poets had been attracted to avant-garde experimentalism in the late '60s and early '70s. Mehrotra in 1967 participated in the first international exposition of concrete, spatial and mechanical poetry at the Gallery Denise Davy in Paris, while his typographical poems, *Woodcuts on Paper*, were published by a London art gallery the same year.

Mehrotra was also involved with an obscure journal called *prisoner* (1968), published at the Bhilai Steel Plant and, through Howard McCord, an American poet interested in the new Indian poetry, helped organize the publication of Indian poetry in several American little magazines. Mehrotra's friend Pavan Kumar began his own stencilled magazine, *Tornado*, and was for a time responsible for an English-language poetry section in a Gujarati avant-garde journal. Through contacts Patel, Mehrotra, Kolatkar and Chitre had with the painters of Baroda, they also published in *Vrishchik* (1967-72), a Baroda magazine of the arts and politics. *Vrishchik* republished Kolatkar's 'the boatride' and brought out a special issue of Mehrotra's *pomes/poemes/poemas* (1971).

During the mid and late 1960s Mehrotra, Patel, Kolatkar, Parthasarathy and others regularly gave poetry readings, first at the homes of friends where perhaps twenty people would attend, and later at the Jehangir Art Gallery where the Samovar Restaurant had become a meeting place for writers and artists. Patel first met Chitre in 1965; his future wife worked in the same office as Chitre. Through Chitre he met Kolatkar the next year. All three share an interest in translation and painting. Through Kolatkar and Chitre Patel next met Jussawalla at a poetry reading during the latter's return to Bombay in 1967. In January 1967 Patel, Ezekiel and Chitre gave a poetry reading at Alkazi's National School of Drama in Delhi. Around this time Patel met Mehrotra in the Samovar Restaurant. As he became further involved in the Bombay poetry scene Patel met Parthasarathy. Patel already knew Ramanujan; their wives were friends before their marriages.

A regular circle of publication was being created and expanded as can be seen from the way the poets published in each other's journals and in foreign anthologies. Chitre, Mehrotra and Ezekiel appeared in *Tornado*. The 'Indian Renaissance' number of *Sameeksa* (Madras, 1967) included Chitre and Kolatkar translated by Chitre from Marathi, and poems by Parthasarathy. The American journal *Intrepid* published in spring 1968 a special Indian issue which included Mehrotra's *bharatmata*, Chitre's 'The First Five Breakfasts', an untitled poem of Kolatkar's, along with poems by Pritish Nandy, Kamala Das and several less well-known poets who had been published by Mehrotra. Mehrotra, Chitre, Patel, Kolatkar and Jussawalla also appeared in the Bombay annual *Pushpanjali*, which started in 1965 and which for a time had Chitre as poetry editor.

The six issues of *Poetry India* (1966–7), edited by Ezekiel, were one of the high moments of modern Indian poetry and a link in the line of serious places of publication that started with Mandy's *Illustrated Weekly*. Besides Parthasarathy (who was awarded the Ulka Annual Poetry Prize for the best poem in English by a young Indian poet published in *Poetry India*), Patel, Gauri Pant (b. 1920), Keki Daruwalla (b. 1937), H. O. Nazareth (b. 1944), K. D. Katrak, Kamala Das, Arvind Mehrotra, Saleem Peeradina (b. 1944) and Adil Jussawalla, Ezekiel published translations from Indian languages (by Kolatkar, Ramanujan, Vinay Jha, Patel, Chitre, Lal, Sujit and Meenakshi Mukherjee), along with reviews and articles on English and Indian-language poetry. The quality was extremely high and as many of the articles, reviews and translations concerned modern poetry the magazine provided during its short life an informed comparative view of what had been happening in Indian poetry during recent decades. Its attempt to treat critically poetry in the many Indian languages along with English was notable; while later imitated by other journals *Poetry India* has remained in its seriousness and judgement unique. Reviews were of high standard. The first issue was spectacular, with translations of Vedic hymns by Lal, of Tukaram and Mardheker from Marathi by Kolatkar and Chitre, of Tamil love lyrics by Ramanujan, of Amrita Pritam from Punjabi by the New Zealand poet Charles Brasch, along with English-language poetry by Patel and Parthasarathy. There were also poems by Thomas Blackburn, Howard Sergeant and Roy Fuller from England. For two years India had a poetry magazine of the highest international standards. Also important were the affinities that were found between modern verse in the many Indian languages; the English-language poets

seemed part of a spectrum of post-war modern Indian verse, rather
than isolated and alien. After *Poetry India* stopped publication,
another attempt to cover the national scene was undertaken by
Indian Writing Today (1967–70). The present canon of major
poets was falling into place, assembled around Ezekiel and *Poetry
India*. Eunice de Souza (b. 1940) reviewed for the journal but was
not yet writing poetry. It was essentially the *Poetry India* circle
that was later represented in Saleem Peeradina's *Contemporary
Poetry·in English* (1972).

Along with the growing number of little magazines in which
Indian poets could publish during the late '60s, a new pheno-
menon was the appearance of critical monographs. Although the
difference between the aims of Ezekiel and Lal had widened
(*Poetry India* strongly criticized Lal's 1966 *"Change!" They
Said*), the first monograph on Indian poetry was from the Writers
Workshop on Ezekiel (1966). Subsequent volumes were on Kamala
Das (1968), P. Lal (1968) and Bantleman's *Kanchanjanga*
(1969)—the latter a long poem which the Writers Workshop
published (1967). Meanwhile Karnatak University brought out a
collection of *Critical Essays on Indian Writing* (1968) by M. K.
Naik and others, while Lal published David McCutchion's
Indian Writing in English. Although the Writers Workshop
remained significant as a publisher of new poets, bringing out in
1968 Gauri Deshpande's (b. 1942) *Between Births*, Katrak's *A
Journal of the Way*, Srinivas Rayaprol's *Bones and Distances*, and
G. S. Sharat Chandra's *Bharata Natyam Dancer*, all first books,
its contributions to a tradition of serious criticism are less appa-
rent. Devindra Kohli's monograph on Kamala Das and
McCutchion's essays on Indian poetry are of value; but there was
still little in the way of extended serious criticism of Indian-English
poetry.

Another phenomenon of the late '60s which contributed to the
visibility of the new poetry was the international recognition of
Commonwealth literature in the form of anthologies, conferen-
ces, organizations and university courses. Indian writing in English
took its place alongside literature from Australia, Canada, New
Zealand, Africa and the West Indies. Although most of the early
academic commentary was on the social content of Commonwealth
fiction, the many poetry anthologies of the period both provided
places for publication and contributed to international awareness

of Ezekiel, Parthasarathy, Kamala Das, Jussawalla and others. *Young Commonwealth Poets* (1965) was followed by *Commonwealth Poets of Today* (1967), *New Voices of the Commonwealth* (1968) and in 1970 *Pergamon Poets 9: Poetry from India* (Ramanujan, Parthasarathy, Ezekiel and Deb Kumar Das). Daisy Alden's American anthology of *Poems from India* was published the same year (1969) as the special *Books Abroad* issue on Indian literature.

The experimentation of the second half of the '60s was taken up by Pritish Nandy (b. 1947), an extremely prolific writer and promoter with an eye for discovering others but whose own talent suffers from a lack of self-criticism. Good images occur in the early poems in the midst of a bewildering outpouring of verbiage, often with no discernible content. Exactly what Nandy had in mind in writing such verse is difficult to say, but he appears to have imitated the obscurity, obliqueness and radical juxtapositions of avant-garde poetry without having a clear reason for such experimentation. But if Nandy's early poetry now appears superficially modernistic, it was widely published by obscure foreign journals and the avant-garde River Run Press of New York. Nandy was friendly with his fellow Calcuttan P. Lal who encouraged his early work. The Writers Workshop printed his first volume, *Of Gods and Olives* (1967), with its Mediterranean eclogues and imagery, and *On Either Side of Arrogance* (1968), while Nandy's own Dialogue Publications brought out *I Hand You in Turn My Nebbuk Wreath* (1968); within the next few years Nandy's verse, along with the counter culture, moved into its political, and perhaps best phase, as seen in his two well-known poems 'Near Deshapriya Park they found him at last' and 'Calcutta if you must exile me'. Nandy tried to bring to English-language poetry the social and political involvement which was characteristic of some of the regional-language literatures. Because of Nandy's growing celebrity status his books had started to be distributed and then published by Arnold-Heinemann.

Nandy next moved rapidly from political protest to popular song lyrics. The rapidity of the changes is startling, with the obscure experimental-political *Dhritarashtra Downtown: Zero* (1974) appearing only a year before *Riding the Midnight River* and the pop song lyrics of *Lonesong Street* (1975), which is reported to have sold 20,000 copies as well as being recorded and made into a film. For many, Nandy had stopped having pretensions of being a serious poet and had become an Indian equivalent of Rod McEuen and other versifiers of easily expressed sentiments who had become popular in North America during the '60s and '70s. Nandy himself was aware that he had moved far from the days of involvement in the protests against the war in Vietnam and his Naxalite commitments. His pop poems became increasingly shorter, as if he had nothing more to say. Around 1981 he announced he had stopped regularly writing poetry.

Nandy for a time played a significant role in publishing poetry, especially younger and experimental writers. His *Dialogue* publications existed in three forms. Between 1968 and 1970 there were nineteen issues of *Dialogue—Calcutta*, usually devoted to a single poet or theme. The second issue consisted of translations of Cuban poets, the third of P. Lal's transcreations from Sanskrit, the fourth of Nandy's *I Hand You in Turn My Nebbuk Wreath* volume. Nandy wanted to create a poetry programme for India which would publish local verse along with poetry in translation from the regional languages and from the European languages (he had learned Spanish to read Garcia Lorca). Numbers of *Dialogue— Calcutta* which were not devoted to an individual poet or theme were called anthologies; no. 17 included Nissim Ezekiel, Kamala Das and Keshav Malik, along with translations from Bengali, Urdu and Oriya. *Dialogue—Calcutta 18* published Jayanta Maha-patra, Malik, Nandy and Gauri Deshpande. After *Dialogue— Calcutta* went bankrupt Nandy, in 1971, started to publish book-lets known as *Dialogue Publications*, devoted to the work of new poets; these included Jayanta Mahapatra and Gauri Deshpande and translations of poets from the regional languages. Nandy then restarted his magazine under the name *Dialogue—India*, which published perhaps twenty issues between 1972 and 1975. *Dialogue—India* was more varied and included book reviews. Suresh Kohli (b. 1947) became assistant editor. The first issue was devoted to Bangladesh. Usually a maximum of 1000 copies was published. Nandy was one of the first to publish the new Orissa writers, Jayanta Mahapatra (b. 1928), Deba Patnaik (b. 1936), Bibhu Padhi (b. 1951) and others. Ezekiel had recommended that Mahapatra send his early poems to Nandy and Mahapatra subse-quently suggested that the others contribute to *Dialogue*.

The years 1970–1 were remarkable for the number of good new poets who published their first books. Daruwalla's *Under Orion* and *Apparition in April*, Shiv Kumar's *Articulate Silence*, Mamta Kalia's *Tribute to Papa*, Jayanta Mahapatra's *Close the Sky Ten by Ten* and *Svayamara and Other Poems* appeared along with Ramanujan's second volume, *Relations*, and the *London Magazine* edition of G.S. Sharat Chandra's *April in Nanjangud*. Despite the outcry that greeted P. Lal's massive *Modern Indian Poetry in English: An Anthology and a Credo* (1969), as lacking selectivity and discrimination, the Writers Workshop continued to be the main publisher of the Indian English poets.

K. N. Daruwalla (b. 1937) had published in *Quest* (1964), *Poetry India*, *Dialogue*, many American magazines, and was one of the poets regularly associated with *Opinion* in the late '60s and early '70s. *Under Orion* (1970) and *Apparition in April* (1971), as Ezekiel said in his reviews, revealed a major poet with an unusually broad range of technique and a substantial body of work. His poetry is both immediately Indian in reference and universal in its concern with love, death, domination, self-control, self-betrayal and the corruptions that result from social and political accommodation. There is often a knife-edge to Daruwalla's tone and an angry, satiric perspective of a kind that had not been heard before in modern Indian poetry. His mastery of both traditional prosody and free verse, creation of new stanzaic forms and mixture of controlled narrative with loosely associated events, showed a blending of the methods of contemporary American verse with the late-nineteenth-century and early-twentieth-century tradition of Browning, Hopkins, Frost and Lawrence. If Mehrotra, Mahapatra, Nandy, Kolatkar and Chitre suggested that the closed, formal, logically organized poetry was being replaced by more experimental, radical methods, Daruwalla showed ways in which traditional kinds of poetry could be made contemporary in subject-matter and style. His language and diction are particularly vigorous and immediate. While the poems that appeared in the early volumes are less impressive than 'Night of the Jackals', 'Hawk' and others in the *Crossing of Rivers* and *Keeper of the Dead* volumes, they were a sign that a new significant poet had arrived , with a sharp awareness of the variety of Indian life and a sceptical view of society and its proclaimed values. Here was someone who appeared to know northern Indian life intimately but who rejected fatalism and placed value in physical existence. In its confrontation with death there was a modern metaphysical dimension in Daruwalla's poetry which seemed more like Hemingway or Camus than Aurobindo's mysticism or Lal's romanticism. His subsequent volumes have shown a steady consolidation of his strengths as he has eliminated excessive and digressive narrative, trite similes, coinages of unusual words and other tendencies which sometimes detracted from his realism, economy and precision.

Shiv Kumar (b. 1921), a professor of English with an international reputation as a literary critic and scholar, unexpectedly emerged as a poet of surprising wit, irony and sophistication. Written in the confessional mode that had spread from America, Kumar's verse often treats of such topics as domestic crisis, the break-up of marriage, the relationship between the sexes and other personal matters. He is especially satirical of sexual repression in India. His tone is wildly humorous, at times savagely farcical, yet cosmopolitan as he brings to problems a curiously double perspective, seeing Indian behaviour in a European light while viewing Europe and America through Indian eyes. If the early poems are striking but erratic, the later verse is more disciplined and controlled.

A major poet whose first books appeared in 1971 is Jayanta Mahapatra, whose earliest volumes were published by Nandy and Lal and who, along with Deba Patnaik, was one of the founding editors of the short-lived journal *Gray Book* (1972-3), a sign that Orissa and Cuttack in particular had joined Bombay, Calcutta, New Delhi, Allahabad, Hyderabad and Mysore as a site of the new poetry. Mahapatra, a teacher of physics, began by testing various ideas of what constitutes a modern poem and quickly progressed through organization by sound, image, theme, creating often obscure, difficult lyrics. Puzzling over his own distance—as a rationalist born into a Christian family—from the traditions of rural Hindu India, Mahapatra showed how it is possible to use modern alienation and the methods of experimental poetry while feeling the continuing relevance of the past. Whereas modern Indian poetry in English often used topics from urban life, Mahapatra's poetry mostly made use of the rural landscape and local traditions while avoiding cultural conservatism and nationalist clichés.

By the early '70s Indian poetry in English began to become generally accepted, although controversies keep erupting despite the short but useful comments in H. M. William's *Indo-Anglian Literature* (1970). Evaluation was becoming increasingly impor-

tant as Ezekiel and those associated with him, including Eunice
de Souza and Saleem Peeradina, began to apply more rigorous
critical standards than had been common in the early '60s. A growing
difference in perspective between those still defending the vali-
dity of writing Indian poetry in English and those who felt the
issue had been superseded by the need to make critical discrimi-
nations between the good and the bad accounts for the contro-
versy that erupted over P. Lal's *Modern Indian Poetry in English:
An Anthology and a Credo*. Lal's massive collection of over a
hundred poets was meant to show how widespread the new writing
had become. The lack of selectiveness, unfortunately reflected in
some of Lal's introductory comments on the poets, brought a
final break between those insisting on more rigorous standards
and Lal's open-door policy. Lal felt that it was important to
encourage the writing and publication of poetry if good poets
were to be found; his critics felt that a mass of bad poetry would
pollute standards, making it unlikely that good poetry would be
written or appreciated.

   In the January 1972 issue of *Quest* (74), devoted to *Contempo-
rary Poetry in English: An Assessment and Selection*, edited by
Saleem Peeradina (b. 1944) and co-published as a book by Macmillan,
Lal's anthology was criticized and rigorous standards applied to
the poets Peeradina had chosen. This was the first serious attempt
at distinguishing who were the better Indian English poets, their
characteristics and faults. So that the anthology could be used by
students, it included short critical essays introducing the poets.
The selections reveal how a group of significant poets had deve-
loped around Ezekiel (who in 1972 was appointed Reader at the
University of Bombay) or had been recognized by him soon after
their first appearance in print. Most had been published in *Poetry
India*. Gauri Deshpande and Mamta Kalia (b. 1940) were inclu-
ded besides Ezekiel, Ramanujan, Kolatkar, Parthasarathy, Katrak,
Mehrotra, Daruwalla, Jussawalla, Patel, Kamala Das and Peera-
dina. While Lal is also included, the introduction to his work is
negative and there is an essay by Eunice de Souza criticizing the
lack of selectivity in Lal's anthology and in V. K. Gokak's *The
Golden Treasury of Indo-Anglian Poetry* (1970). Peeradina's intro-
duction describes Nandy's poetry as 'uninteresting', 'Gimmickry'
and, without mentioning names, criticizes Lal and others associa-
ted with him. Peeradina himself had studied at St Xavier's College,
Bombay, and done an MA at the University. He showed his poems

to Ezekiel who suggested improvements and encouraged him to publish in *Quest* and *Poetry India*. Deshpande was on the staff of the *Illustrated Weekly*. De Souza, who had met Ezekiel at an interview for a job, wrote criticism in *Poetry India* and taught at St Xavier's College, Bombay.

The Lal and Peeradina anthologies were signs of an interest in the new poetry beyond the circle of the writers themselves. The republication by Orient Longman of Kamala Das's earlier poems along with newer ones in *The Old Play House and Other Poems* (1973), the Oxford and IBH publication of *The Poetry of Pritish Nandy* (1973) and Tata McGraw Hill's printing of Shiv Kumar's *Cobwebs in the Sun* (1974), showed a few commercial publishers tentatively exploring the poetry market. The next years saw Nandy's two anthologies for commercial publishers of *Indian Poetry in English* (1972) and *Indian Poetry in English Today* (1973) and Gauri Deshpande's *An Anthology of Indo-English Poetry* (1974).

Adil Jussawalla's Penguin *New Writing In India* (1974) was more significant, offering a selective representation of good writers in English and translations from the regional languages. There was a critical intelligence involved in the choice of material and while it was unfortunate that more of the English-language poets were not represented (for reasons of space Jussawalla excluded the better-known Ramanujan and Moraes), the book showed the general reading public in India and abroad that the best Indian writing did not consist of mystical vaporizing, generalized public sentiments, dated romanticism and amateur experimentalism. The inclusion of Kolatkar and Chitre brought out the complex and sometimes close relationship between the new writing in English and in regional languages. *New Writing In India* was essentially a publication of the Bombay poets. They helped Jussawalla familiarize himself with writing in the regional languages and after he returned to England provided translations of texts. When the anthology eventually appeared it included poems by Mehrotra and Patel, along with Kamala Das and Bantleman, whose early work interested Jussawalla.

Another major event of 1974 was the appearance and unfortunately short existence of *Opinion Literary Quarterly*, edited by K. D. Katrak and Gauri Deshpande. After Katrak returned from his travels abroad in 1960 he settled down to a job in advertising and did some cultural journalism. During the early 1960s he tried to interest A. D. Gorwala in modern poetry. Gorwala, who is also a Parsi, was sceptical but told him he could be advisor for the publishing of Indian poetry in *Opinion*, an independent political journal that began in 1959. Katrak became its poetry editor from 1964 to 1973, after which he and Deshpande teamed up as co-editors of *Opinion Literary Quarterly* (1974), a separate publication which was sent free of charge to the 5000 regular subscribers of *Opinion* for a year, after which they would have to place subscriptions for it. Too few of the subscribers of *Opinion* who read it for its political content wanted what was an excellent literary journal, and *Opinion Literary Quarterly* came to an end with the fourth issue, but not before it had published Kolatkar's *Jejuri* and the first version of Daruwalla's 'Crossing of Rivers' and most of 'The Waterfront'. *Opinion* itself was sold by Gorwala in 1982 and ceased publication in 1983, after which its new owners restarted it in 1984 as *Kaiser-e-Hind*, which also publishes some poetry.

During the time Katrak was in charge of poetry for *Opinion* it built up a good reputation among the poets as a place to publish. It paid well, kept high standards and introduced new poets to the literary scene, including Keki Daruwalla, Gauri Deshpande and Eunice de Souza. Other contributors included Katrak, Kamala Das, R. Parthasarathy, Ezekiel, Rakshat Puri and Jayanta Maha-patra. Katrak, who had published early in *Illustrated Weekly* and in *Quest* (1958), included among his friends Ezekiel, Jussawalla, Deshpande and Pritish Nandy. His first four books were printed by Lal's Writers Workshop. (Ezekiel reviewed *A Journal of the Way* (1968) and *Diversions by the Wayside* (1969) in *The Times*.) Around 1967 Daruwalla met Katrak at Ranikhet, the hill station, and regularly sent him poems for *Opinion* until 1974. They discussed poetry and influenced each other's writing. After reading Daruwalla's *Under Orion* (1970) and *Apparition in April* (1971), Katrak was so impressed that he travelled north to spend a month talking to him. Their differences in views towards poetry and how to live were a stimulus for Katrak's *Underworld* (1979), which expresses his Tantric-influenced mysticism, explained in *Five Little Sermons Went to Market* (1971). The style and themes are developed further in *Purgatory* (1984).

The *Opinion* network had contacts with the Calcutta poets

P. Lal and Pritish Nandy and there is some overlap in publication circles. Although Gauri Deshpande (b. 1942) was one of the Bombay poets and is discussed by de Souza in Peeradina's anthology, her main publications had been brought out by P. Lal and Nandy. These include *Between Births* (1968), *Lost Love* (1970) and *Beyond the Slaughterhouse* (1972). Her *Anthology of Indo-English Poetry* (1974) included Nandy, Katrak and Peeradina, while she and Katrak are in Nandy's anthologies.

The early and mid '70s also saw the appearance of the first critical studies of the new poets by a commercial publisher, beginning with books on Ezekiel (1974), Kamala Das (1975) and Nandy (1976) as part of Arnold-Heinemann's series on Indian writing. Although university studies of this poetry developed slowly, an encouraging sign was the start of *The Journal of Indian Writing in English* (1973). Experience in other newly independent countries shows that university courses and critical studies are necessary to create a market for a new literature and to give it broader cultural acceptance.

With Nandy as its attraction Arnold-Heinemann was the first commercial publisher to risk a series devoted to Indian English poetry (1973). Although more selective than the Writers Workshop and willing to print 2000 copies, the Heinemann series has only published a few authors thought worthy of critical attention. Its main publications to date beyond the volumes of Nandy and Katrak have been *Tonight, This Savage Rite* (1979) which republishes some of Kamala Das's work along with poems by Nandy, Man Mohan Singh's *Village Poems* (1982), Meena Alexander's *Stone Roots* (1980), and several books by J. P. Das.

Although many political and intellectual journals in which the poets appeared stopped publishing, in some cases permanently, during the period of Emergency rule beginning in 1975, 1976 was the most significant year for Indian English poetry since the period 1965–6. It saw the appearance of the first four books from Clearing House, the start of the Oxford University Press New Poetry in India series, two new books by Jayanta Mahapatra, the special Nissim Ezekiel issue of the *Journal of South Asian Literature*, and the first signs of a new, younger generation of poets in the shape of Santan Rodrigues's first book and the start of *Kavi*.

The Clearing House series developed out of the circle of writers, led by Mehrotra and later by Jussawalla, who had been associated

with various Bombay little magazines during the mid and late
'60s, and who were involved with the Penguin *New Writing In
India*. Around 1973–4 they talked about forming a publishing
co-operative to publish manuscripts. For Mehrotra, Jussawalla,
Patel and Kolatkar, the four editors, and others who were in-
volved in the discussions, there were obvious advantages in
bringing out their books together with a collective imprint,
responsibility, style of presentation and publicity for the series
rather than individual books. The first four books had good reviews
and Kolatkar's *Jejuri* was awarded the Commonwealth Poetry
Prize for the best book of verse published that year in any of the
former dominions and colonies. It has been twice republished
and translated into German. The volumes also showed how far
the four poets and English-language poetry had progressed
during the decades since the outburst of publications in the mid
'60s. In *Nine Enclosures* it was possible to see that Mehrotra was
a careful craftsman who slowly revised his material. Rather than
the *enfant terrible* experimenter of the early verse, Mehrotra is a
sophisticated, witty poet who while building upon radical
notions of construction has formed a poetic from local material,
parody and the conscious manipulation of chance. The result is
that his work combines clever social satire with surprising con-
trol over experimental technique. Jussawalla's *Missing Person* is
more politically and socially aware than his 1962 book, while
Patel's *How Do You Withstand, Body* shows the author's increas-
ing complexity of outlook and style.

Jejuri, the first book Kolatkar published in English, made use
of the flat, styleless manner he had been trying out in Marathi
after his initial period of surrealistic experimental writing. Whereas
previously good Indian English poets attempted to pack as much
as possible into a line, aiming for texture, cadence, image, Kolatkar
expressed a new kind of poetic personality, taking odd angles of
vision, leaving space, playing, mocking, treating off-hand what
others regarded as sacred. The often purposefully prosaic, col-
loquial characteristics leave interpretation of the speaker's
attitude open and appear to make a poetry of the unpoetic. The
poetry consists of observing precise details and casual puzzlement
about their significance rather than exposition or expression of
emotion. By writing a book on one subject, his visit to Jejuri, he
also put together what was essentially a long poem, with many

parts; with *Jejuri* a major book-length long poem entered the canon of Indian English poetry.

While the quality of the Clearing House publications is high, acceptance requiring the agreement of the four editors, they still are a version of self-publication and lack the distribution, sales and promotion network of an established commercial publisher. Most volumes have sold out, but only 750 copies have usually been printed and, except for *Jejuri*, they have not been republished. After its original burst of activity Clearing House has proceeded more slowly, partly as a result of the energy required to keep the series going and partly because of the editors' unwillingness to publish many manuscripts that were submitted. They have published Dilip Chitre's *Travelling in a Cage* (1980), his first book of English poems since his pamphlet *Ambulance Ride* (1972), Jayanta Mahapatra's *The False Start* (1980), Mehrotra's *Distance in Statute Miles* (1982) and H. O. Nazareth's *Lobo* (1984). The future of Clearing House is, however, questionable.

The Oxford New Poetry in India series has the advantages of the Oxford imprint, national and international promotion, and standard royalty contracts. The series evolved out of the international Oxford University Press Three Crowns books meant to make more widely available new Third World writing, particularly for Africa. The expansion of the series to India at first had to be approved in England and there was considerable groundwork done in contacting authors, collecting information for publicity and copyright, selecting material and editing manuscripts. Some authors, including Daruwalla, revised their previously published poems for the occasion. R. Parthasarathy, one of the first six writers to be published, was then an editor at Oxford and appears to have played a part in the initial choice and approaches to the poets.

Despite some problems the Oxford series appeared in 1976–7 with six books, including individual volumes by Ezekiel, Daruwalla, Shiv Kumar, Parthasarathy, Ramanujan, and Parthasarathy's anthology of *Ten Twentieth Century Indian Poets*, which beyond the five previously mentioned added Kamala Das, Mehrotra, Kolatkar, Patel and Mahapatra to the canon of Oxford approved writers. Subsequently, additional volumes appeared by Mahapatra, Mehrotra, G. S. Sharat Chandra, as well as further books by Ezekiel, Daruwalla and Patrick Fernando (1931–82), a Sri Lankan poet.

Ten Twentieth Century Indian Poets had the effect of giving the Oxford seal of approval to a canon of authors, thus once and for all putting an end to quibbles over the worth, validity and nature of the post-War English-language poetry. For all practical purposes a canon was being established which might be said to represent what many poets and critics felt to be the best post-War poets up to then, and the anthology soon became an established text for university courses in Indian English literature. It supplanted Peeradina's Macmillan anthology, the only previous highly selective collection, and has to date only been challenged by Daruwalla's selection of seventeen poets. It has several times been reprinted.

There were other outstanding features of the first Oxford books. Parthasarathy had for years been revising his poems into a single continuous work, *Rough Passage* (issued 1977, although dated 1976), which includes all that he felt he wanted preserved. Besides the poems having gained by compression and being seen in relationship to each other, there was an autobiographical frame holding them together; their form also had been revised, with each poem now being written in three-line stanzas of roughly similar line lengths. The result was economy, complexity, density, multiplicity of themes and recurrence of imagery, situations and certain phrases, which create a unity of the three parts of the book. Like *Jejuri*, it became a landmark of Indian English poetry.

Ezekiel's *Hymns in Darkness* published poems from the various phases through which he had evolved since his last published volume in 1965, and was a revelation of how far he had travelled beyond his early formalism, generalizing and aesthetic distancing. Besides making available such 'Indian English' poems as 'The Railway Clerk' and 'Goodbye Party for Miss Pushpa T. S.', it also included his more recent sequences of poems with their emphasis on the luminous in ordinary reality. Daruwalla's *Crossing of Rivers* consisted of two long sequences, 'The Waterfront' and 'Crossing of Rivers' and four other poems, including the excellent 'Death of a Bird' and 'Haranag'. Kumar's *Subterfuges* included his autobiographical 'Broken Columns' sequence and such now well-known poems as 'A Letter from New York' and 'Indian Women'. Ramanujan's book consisted of selections from his earlier two volumes and perhaps gave a somewhat misleading impression of his range of subjects as his poems on life in America are not well represented.

Beyond the appearance of the Oxford and Clearing House series, 1976 was a vintage year in other ways. Jayanta Mahapatra published two books of poems, *A Father's House* with United Writers and *A Rain of Rites* with the University of Georgia Press. United Writers was a Calcutta publishing venture, which also brought out Meena Alexander's (b. 1951) *I Root My Name* (1977) and Pritish Nandy's *In Secret Anarchy* (1976) among its books of poetry from various Indian languages. Its editor was Pranab Bandyopadhyay, a Bengali customs official with a strong interest in the arts. He edited the journal *Etc*, and is a bilingual poet and a Bengali film director and actor. (Niranjan Mohanty, an associate of Bandyopadhyay, was also part of this Calcutta circle. He started *Poetry* (1975), which he now edits from Berhampur.) *A Rain of Rites*, which had the prestige of being published by an American university press, showed that Mahapatra's technique and range had matured; he had moved beyond the awkward angularities and sometimes contrived images of his earlier experimental writing and now polished his verse to a new consistency of texture and mood. The volume was unified by recurring images and themes as Mahapatra's introspective preoccupations were treated from varied angles. The effect was of a distinctive personality and a body of work rather than a writer of individual lyrical moments. He introduced to Indian English poetry the new kind of verse that had been written in America during the previous decade, where various unexplained, often contradictory feelings were held together—although spaces were left between—by being parts of an introspective mood brought about from heightened attentiveness. The unexplained associations appeared to come from hidden recesses of the mind, making articulate feelings which were difficult to define. Although many individual poems often seem no more than mood pieces, the volume added up to something more, a puzzling mind creating itself through continual meditation. Reality seems to dissolve and be replaced by a reality of consciousness. Such poetry opened new areas to the imagination, although it showed similarity, as Daruwalla later noted, to eighteenth-century ruminations on some prospective.

Santan Rodrigues's (b. 1948) *I Exist*, published by the Writers Workshop, was a promising first volume by one of Ezekiel's students. Rodrigues was also one of the founders of the new Bombay journal *Kavi* (1976)—which two years later became

Kavi—India—and one of the co-editors of Newground publications. *Kavi* evolved from poetry readings and other happenings in the '70s, when a new circle of poets, mostly born after 1948, began to appear in Bombay at St Xavier's, K. C. and Siddharth Colleges. Most went on to start, if not finish, MAs in English at St Xavier's College or the University of Bombay, where they studied with Ezekiel. Besides being encouraged by Ezekiel, Jussawalla and Patel, some were influenced by their teachers, Eunice de Souza and R. Parthasarathy. This is a sign that modern Indian English poetry had already gone through three generations and had become self-sustaining, in the sense of poets encouraging and influencing each other, in contrast to the years immediately after independence when there were no usable local models and no older community of poets to encourage the young. The main writers to appear among this new generation of Bombay poets are Melanie Silgardo (b. 1956), Manohar Shetty (b. 1953) and Rodrigues, while Dhiren Bhagat (b. 1957), Darius Cooper (b. 1949) and Aroop Mitra (b. 1955) show promise. Two slightly older writers who have published with them are Saleem Peeradina and Eunice de Souza. Their main publication channels to date are *Kavi—India* and the Newground publishing co-operative. There have, however, been offshoots, such as the Hack Writers Cooperative, which published *45 RPM*, a volume of poems by Rajiv Rao (b. 1950) and Rafique Baghdadi (b. 1947), and Aroop Mitra's own Wildhorse Press, through which he published his first book of poems.

Santan Rodrigues first published poetry in the *K. C. College Annual*, Bombay, in 1970. While at K. C. he knew Saleem Peeradina and was a friend of Rajiv Rao and Rafique Baghdadi. Mrs Parthasarathy was one of his teachers. After R. Parthasarathy gave a talk on modern poets to his wife's students, Rodrigues met him, read his poems and through him met other poets. He met Adil Jussawalla through one of his teachers. In 1972 he sent his poems to Nissim Ezekiel who forwarded them to *Quest* and *Illustrated Weekly*, where they were published.

Starting in 1973 there were poetry readings at the various Bombay colleges in which Rodrigues and Aroop Mitra, who was a student at K.C. College, participated. There were also annual poetry contests for the students, judged by such established writers as Ezekiel and Jussawalla. Darius Cooper, Rajiv Rao and Baghdadi were among the poets included in *Poetry from Bombay*, 1973, published by Siddharth College of Arts and Sciences, while Dhiren Bhagat, still in his teens, published in *PEN*. In 1974 Niteen Gupte of Elphinstone College started *Volume*, a single sheet folded into six pages, which published Bhagat and other young experimental poets. The same year there were 'happenings' at the university, informal readings of poetry in English, Marathi and Gujarati, which received attention in the newspapers. From this an informal group got together called the 'University Poets', who gave readings once or twice a month. At a poetry reading at St Xavier's, organized by Jussawalla and de Souza, Gieve Patel liked one of Darius Cooper's poems; he published it in the short-lived general magazine *Fulcrum* (1975–6) of which Patel was poetry editor. Cooper attended the cultural evenings and poetry readings at Kamala Das's house (which were held between 1975 and 1980), where he met Jussawalla and Ezekiel, who helped him publish in journals and invited him to participate in further poetry readings. He had known Peeradina from college days at St Xavier's. For a year there was a Bombay University English Department journal with no name, but titled ' '. The postgraduate students involved with the poetry readings felt it was time for their own journal and consequently *Kavi* was founded.

Kavi was started in 1976 with Rodrigues, Mitra, Ivan Kostka and Rajiv Rao as editors. It initially was a cyclostyled student publication, but after the first issue of 300 sold out it began to be printed in 500 copies. After the fifth issue, devoted to poetry of the Emergency, it stopped publication, as it was unregistered, but it was reborn in 1978 and officially licensed as *Kavi—India*. Although the editorship has changed over the years, Rodrigues and Rao emerged as the editors, while Ezekiel became a consulting editor. In 1978 *Kavi—India* published three unnumbered issues, followed by volume 1, no. 4 in 1979. Volume 2 (1980–1) and volume 3 (1982–3) each consist of four numbers; but volume 3, no. 4 was poorly printed and the cover describes it as volume 2, no. 4. Volume 4 starts with 1984. Under its new editorship *Kavi—India* published a variety of known and younger poets from around India.

Rodrigues's poems written between 1970 and 1972 were printed in a cyclostyled pamphlet, *I Exist*, which was first circulated among his fellow MA students at St Xavier's. When later published by Writers Workshop, no copies became available in Bombay book-shops. As the young poets felt the need for a local publisher, they discussed forming their own co-operative on the model of Clearing House. Of the original ten poets involved in the project, seven left after disagreements and Newground was formed by Rodrigues, Melanie Silgardo and Raul d'Gama Rose. Silgardo, although not one of those involved in the public poetry readings, was a student at St Xavier's. She began writing poems around 1975, showed her work to de Souza who encouraged her to continue to write about her personal experience, and sent some poems to Rodrigues for *Kavi*. The first book Newground published, *Three Poets* (1978), consisted of selections from the poems of the editors. Newground's next volumes were de Souza's *Fix* (1979), Saleem Peeradina's *First Offense* (1980) and Manohar Shetty's *A Guarded Space* (1981). Although de Souza and Peeradina had been writing verse and had been part of the literary scene for some time, these were their first volumes of poetry. The volumes by de Souza and Shetty were particularly highly praised in reviews by established poets. Shetty did a Bachelor of Commerce degree at the University of Bombay and started an MA in English, where he was one of Ezekiel's students, before becoming a journalist and later a writer of manuals for a computer organization. He had worked with Silgardo on *Keynote* (1982), a general magazine which at various times included Bhagat and Jussawalla among its contributors, as well as printing articles on the poetry of Peeradina, Daruwalla, d'Gama Rose and Mahapatra.

Newground books are usually published in 1000 copies and the poets are asked to pay part of the expense of the printing, as the books must cover their costs before a new manuscript can be considered. Although the original three volumes sold out rapidly as a result of poetry readings by the authors, Shetty's *A Guarded Space* has done less well, despite excellent reviews, probably because he will not do public readings.

The new poets are not interested in radical modernist techniques; they seem more interested in depicting and evaluating their family background, personal life, relations with others and local surroundings. Whereas the poets of the late '60s and early '70s were often interested in open structures, abstract patterns, free associations, immediacy of effect and exploration of highly subjective emotions, the new poets are less experimental and at

times, as shown by Shetty and Silgardo, consciously re-explore
the British poetic tradition with its explicit statement, logical
argument, closed form, and use of the external world as symbolic
of inner feelings. While the American and international moder-
nist influences of the '70s have passed, de Souza and Silgardo are
in tune with the feminist movement in contemporary poetry, in
their directness of speech, self-revelation, and non-nostalgic
memories of family life.

Since the mid 1970s there have been an increasing number of
poetry and other literary journals which print or review volumes
of poetry. These include *The Book Review, The Indian Book
Chronicle, Commonwealth Quarterly, Poetry, Spark, Art and
Poetry Today, Lyric, Cygnus, Ekestasis, Orbit* and many journals
which have existed briefly or which have provided places for
publication or comment. A few, such as *Skylark* (1970–), have
had a long existence for magazines specializing in poetry. Such
journals provide places for the increasing number of young or
lesser-known poets to publish. Of the established writers only
Ezekiel and Mahapatra often contribute to them. More impor-
tant places of publication with higher standards include the
short-lived *Tenor* (1979–80), Mahapatra's excellent *Chandra-
bhaga* (1979), *New Quest* (1977—), *The Indian Literary Review*,
which was founded by Suresh Kohli (1978–9, restarted in 1985)
and which was associated with the *Indian Literary Review* editions
of verse and critical books. Except for the high quality *Chandra-
bhaga* and *The Indian Literary Review* established poets, where
possible, prefer to publish in newspapers or in general magazines,
such as *Debonair* and the *Illustrated Weekly*, which pay their
contributors.

Another sign of the growing interest in Indian English poetry,
and the increasing number of writers, is the appearance of new
anthologies. While Pritish Nandy's *Strangertime: An Anthology
of Indian Poetry in English* (1977), K. N. Daruwalla's *Two
Decades of Indian Poetry* (1980) and A. N. Dwivedi's *Indian
Poetry in English* (1980) have been brought out by commer-
cial publishers, many of the other anthologies, such as *Indian
Verse in English: A Contemporary Anthology* (1977), *New Dimen-
sions in Indo-English Poetry* (1980), *19 Poets: An Anthology*
(1981) and *Modern Trends in Indo-Anglian Poetry* (1982) are
heavily weighted towards new or minor authors who presumably

hope to become better known. Indeed the smaller poetry journals form a network of often third-string and younger writers, many of whom appear not to have learned the lessons of the modern Indian English poets and who continue the vague mystical verse common before independence, or who think poetry consists of simple thoughts and sentiments—too often expressed in naive or inflated language. A few of the minor poets reveal an insecure grasp of English, in contrast to the Indianization of English by the better poets.

The growing stature of Mahapatra is shown by *Relationship* (1980), the first volume by an English-language poet to receive a Sahitya Akademi prize. In *Relationship* Mahapatra attempted to go beyond the fragmentary perceptions and recurring obsessions of his earlier verse to create a twelve-part epic dream voyage through the emotional sources of his guilty feelings of estrangement from his environment. It is similar to *Jejuri* and *Rough Passage* in being a long poem having as its theme the relationship of the writer to his past and Indian culture.

In the first four years of the 1980s, besides the four new books published by Clearing House of poems by Chitre, Mehrotra, Nazareth and Mahapatra, Oxford University Press brought out four more books by Indian poets. These include Ezekiel's *Latter Day Psalms* (1982) which received a Sahitya Akademi prize. Besides three poems in Indian English, the 'Nudes' and the 'Latter Day Psalms' sequences, the volume included selections from the out-of-print *The Unfinished Man* and *The Exact Name*. Daruwalla published *Winter Poems* (1980) and *The Keeper of the Dead* (1982) which has some of his best work, previously not available outside magazines and anthologies, including 'Hawk' and the group entitled 'In the Shadow of the Imambara'. It received the 1984 Sahitya Akademi prize. While G. S. Sharat Chandra's *Heirloom* (1982) drew heavily on previously published volumes, it showed why several critics felt he had been wrongly neglected by Parthasarathy's 1976 anthology. Although he had lived abroad for many years he had continued to write about India as well as his life of exile. *Middle Earth* (1984) made widely available selections from Mehrotra's earlier *Nine Enclosures* and *Distance in Statute Miles*, along with some new and previously uncollected poems. In *Life Signs* (1983) Mahapatra is more direct, less guarded, than in his previous volumes. Among other important books of the early 1980s, Kamala Das's *Collected Poems: Volume 1*, which won a Sahitya Akademi award in 1985, contributed to the sense of Indian English poetry already having a history. By contrast Vikram Seth's *Mappings* (1982) and *The Humble Administrator's Garden* (1985) introduced a very different young poet with a sense of humour, parody and a hedonistic enjoyment of life.

Besides the volumes by individual poets, another notable event was K. N. Daruwalla's anthology, *Two Decades of Indian Poetry: 1960–1980*, which provided another view of the canon of major English-language poets. Along with nine of the poets from Parthasarathy's anthology (Parthasarathy was excluded as he failed to reply to letters), it includes some of the writers who had appeared in *Opinion*. Besides finding a place for Katrak and Deshpande, Daruwalla offers selections from Chitre, de Souza, Peeradina, Sharat Chandra, as well as Jussawalla and Deba Patnaik. Until the next major anthology appears (which might include Rodrigues, Seth, Silgardo and Shetty) Daruwalla's is the latest authoritative word on the subject.

The recognition that India has a significant English-language poetry and that it is the result of a limited if increasing number of good writers can be seen in such publications as M. K. Naik's excellent *History of Indian English Literature* (1982), the critical essays in *Contemporary Indian Verse: An Evaluation* (1980), *Indian Poetry in English: A Critical Assessment* (1980), *Perspectives on Indian Poetry in English* (1984), the various book-length studies of individual poets that have started to be published, and some of the special issues of academic journals, such as the *Journal of Literature and Aesthetics* (vol. 2, no. 4, 1982), devoted to Indian poetry in English. Evaluative book-length critical surveys of the field and collections of essays on individual poets, including Parthasarathy, Daruwalla and Mahapatra, are also available. But it is still necessary to record as much information and collect as much material as possible about Indian English poetry before part of the cultural history of modern India is lost. A welcome sign of such awareness is the new series *Bibliography of Indian Writing in English*, of which the general editor is (who else?) Nissim Ezekiel.

Looked at historically there have been four main publishing circles of Indian English poetry. Three can early be seen in relation to Ezekiel (Bombay), Malik (Delhi) and Lal (Calcutta), with Mahapatra (Orissa) later making the fourth. The Bombay circle begins at the *Illustrated Weekly*, moves on to *Quest*, continues through *Imprint, Poetry India* and Peeradina's Macmillan anthology. By the late '60s it includes the Mehrotra-Kolatkar-Chitre-Patel group and the various magazines with which they were associated. This group is later represented by the Penguin *New Writing in India* and Clearing House. A later offshoot is the *Kavi*–Newground circle around Rodrigues. Another branch can also be traced from Parthasarathy's early appearance in *Quest*, his lecturership at Mithibhai College under Ezekiel, his editorship of *Bombay Duck* and *Blunt*, to his role in the early stages of the Oxford New Poetry in India series and the editorship of the Oxford anthology of ten poets.

A second lineage can be traced from P. Lal's St Xavier's College, Calcutta, group, Lal's column in *Thought*, his editing of *Miscellany* and Writers Workshop volumes. A major offshoot was Nandy's Dialogue publications, Nandy's anthologies and his relationship to Arnold-Heinemann. More tangential are the various Calcutta publications, such as the United Writers Series, *Indian Verse* and *Etc.*, associated with Pranab Bandyopadhyay.

Although there appears a coming together of the Bombay and Calcutta groups around Katrak and Deshpande in *Opinion, Opinion Literary Quarterly* and Deshpande's anthology, as Katrak and Deshpande were published by Lal and Nandy this is perhaps misleading. As shown by Daruwalla's anthology, the *Opinion* group remained Bombay-oriented but accommodated some writers— such as Daruwalla, Mahapatra and Deshpande—who were first published by the Calcutta circle.

The main Delhi publishing circle began with Malik's literary editorship of *Thought* and continued through his editorship of *Indian Literature*, the editing of poetry for *Youth Forum, Art and Poetry*, his advisory role in the Samkaleen Prakashan poetry series, to his present position with the Poetry Society of India. An interesting period of New Delhi poetry was in the mid 1960s when Bantleman and Bartholomew started an experimental writers' group and Bantleman was literary editor of *The Century*.

The Orissa circle begins as an offshoot of Calcutta, where its poets were often first published by Lal and Nandy, and might be understood in relation to Mahapatra and others trying to find a place on the national scene. Eventually an Orissa literary scene developed; their main local channels have been *Gray Book* and *Chandrabhaga*, along with a number of lesser-known journals such as *Vortex* and *Poetry*.

While such poets as Kamala Das, Keki Daruwalla, Jayanta Mahapatra, Shiv Kumar and Nissim Ezekiel had by the late 1980s been recognized as nationally significant by Sahitya Academi awards and now have an established place in Indian culture, others are beginning to attract attention. Ashok Mahajan's third book, *Goan Vignettes*, was published by Oxford University Press, as was Imtiaz Dharkar's *Purdah*. Bibhu Padhi (b. 1951) has published his first volume of verse, *Going to the Temple* (1988). Some remarkably good poetry is being written by Indians living abroad. A. K. Ramanujan, whose *Second Sight* (1986) has been published by Oxford University Press, Agha Shahid Ali (b. 1949), whose recent publications are *The Half-Inch Himalayas* (1987) and *A Walk Through the Yellow Pages* (1987), Meena Alexander (b. 1951), G. S. Sharat Chandra, Deba Patnaik (b. 1936) and Vikram Seth (b. 1952) until his recent return to India, might collectively be regarded as an overseas colony of Indian literature, evolving in its own way in response to American conditions. Seth has rapidly risen to prominence with *Mappings* (1982), *The Humble Administrator's Garden* (1985) and *The Golden Gate* (1986), the latter a witty novel in verse. Sujata Bhatt (b. 1956), who lives in Germany, has published *Brunizem* (1988) in England. That many of the new poets were born after 1947 means that Indian English poetry is likely to develop in unexpected ways, as can be seen from Seth's tongue-in-cheek sense of humour and his use of traditional poetics as a defence against what he sees as the self-destructive introspection of romanticism and modernism.

Further evidence that Indian English poetry has a recognized and expanding role in contemporary Indian culture includes: the Padma Shri Award by the President of India to Ezekiel for his contribution to literature in English; the establishment of *Kavya Bharati: A Review of Indian Poetry* (Madurai, 1988); the founding of Praxis Press in Bombay, which has already published second volumes of poetry by Eunice de Souza and Manohar Shetty; the appearance of a major new anthology of *Indian English Poetry since 1950*, edited by Vilas Sarang; and the unexpected and powerful return to the Indian poetry scene by Dom Moraes with his *Collected Poems: 1957–1987*.

CHAPTER THREE

The Poet's, their Readers and the Market

I. SOCIAL BACKGROUND AND CAREERS

Who are the Indian English poets? The percentage of poets from Hindu family backgrounds (Shetty, Kamala Das, Rayaprol, Bibhu Padhi, Shiv Kumar, Honnalgere, Mehrotra, P. Lal, Seth, Kolatkar) is about equal to that of all the other communal groups combined. Ramanujan and Parthasarathy were raised in Hindu Srivaisnava families. Several come from either reformist or modernizing Hindu groups. Sharat Chandra's family is Lingayat. Chitre's family are agnostics of Hindu descent, while Malik's parents are Arya Samajist. Only two established poets are from Islamic families— Agha Shahid Ali and Peeradina. An unusually large percentage are of the Parsi Zoroastrian community—Katrak, Daruwalla, Patel, Jussawalla, Cooper and Jimmy Avissa. Roman Catholics of Goan descent include Moraes, de Souza, Silgardo, Rodrigues, Nazareth, and Raul d'Gama Rose. Meena Alexander's parents are from the ancient Syrian Christian community; the families of Mahapatra and Patnaik were Christian converts in recent generations. Randhir Khare comes from a Christian family of European and Indian stock. Ezekiel's parents were Jews. Of those from non-Hindu backgrounds, Parsis and Goan Roman Catholics are highly prominent. If a representative group of thirty to forty poets is listed in order of birth or according to when they began publishing , there is no clear pattern of a changing communal or social origin. It may, however, be significant that the younger writers born since 1944 include only two poets from Islamic families. While half the Indian English poets come from communities marginal to the Hindu majority, among those of orthodox Hindu descent Shetty and Shiv Kumar appear rebels against

Hinduism, as in his own way is Mehrotra. Sharat Chandra's father married intercaste. Honnalgere, although from a Hindu family, is a follower of Zen Buddhism. In general the poets are mostly from the westernized, modern elements of society and were brought up in areas of diverse cultural interaction such as Bombay and Lahore or moved as children and never formed close regional ties.

Whereas the poets in P. Lal's massive anthology are about equally from Bombay, Calcutta and Delhi, my more selective list of writers (see Chart 1) produces somewhat different results. About half live in Bombay, about a third live elsewhere in India, and the remainder live abroad. Statistics will, of course, vary according to the poets chosen, but the general impression will not vary. There are good poets in Calcutta and New Delhi and in other cities, but not in the same concentration as in Bombay. Few of the poets come from the Hindi heartland of the north. Lahore, where Shiv Kumar, Daruwalla and Mehrotra were born, is now part of Pakistan. The family of P. Lal was Punjabi but had moved to Calcutta. The largest group of poets was born in Bombay (Shetty, Jussawalla, Nazareth, Ezekiel, Katrak, Moraes). Ramanujan and Sharat Chandra were born in Mysore, Chitre in Baroda, Rodrigues in Goa, Mahapatra, Patnaik and Bibhu Padhi in Cuttack, de Souza in Poona. Often there is some dislocation of cultural context involved, such as Ramanujan being from a Tamil family in Kannada-speaking Mysore, or Meena Alexander being a Keralite born in Allahabad. Kamala Das was born in Kerala but sent to a Catholic boarding school and raised in Calcutta. Parthasarathy was born in Tamil Nadu but educated in Bombay. Malik and Daruwalla appear to have continually changed schools in their youth. It is this social dislocation which may partly explain the urge to write. They are the creative outsiders.

All of the writers had an English-language education, although a few were educated bilingually. Most of the poets, perhaps two-thirds, have a university degree in English (Alexander, Cooper, Patnaik, Ezekiel, Peeradina, Moraes, Shiv Kumar, Aroop Mitra, de Souza, Jussawalla). Those who do not have a university degree in English usually have some university education. Perhaps a third to a half of the poets have either received part of their education abroad or travelled abroad for long periods while young. Certain institutions, such as St Xavier's College, Bombay, the

University of Bombay and St Xavier's College, Calcutta, figure prominently. Many poets went to schools or colleges founded by missionaries. With a few exceptions the poets come from families in which English was used at home, usually along with another Indian language. While Moraes, Katrak, Daruwalla, Seth and Cooper report that English was the family language, only a very few poets—Shetty, Chitre, Honnalgere—come from families who did not use English at home. Shetty was educated at an English-language boarding school. The poets say that they are most competent in English; some could not write creatively in any other language, although many do translate from one or more regional languages. Chitre, Kolatkar and Ramanujan write poetry creatively in other languages besides English. Significantly, Chitre and Kolatkar had bilingual educations.

The family background of the poets is middle class. Often the father or mother was a teacher. Ezekiel's father was a professor of botany, Ramanujan's father was a famous professor of mathematics, Daruwalla's father was a professor of English, Rayaprol's father was a professor of Telugu, and Agha Shahid Ali's father is a professor of education. Mahapatra and Kumar had teachers for fathers; the mothers of Ezekiel and de Souza were teachers. While Nazareth, Katrak and Kamala Das had businessmen for fathers, the fathers of Moraes and Chitre were editors. The fathers of Sharat Chandra, Malik and Padhi were lawyers. Honnalgere's father is an engineer. The fathers of Jussawalla, Patel, Peeradina and P. Lal are homeopathic physicians, Mehrotra's father was a dentist. Although the poets are divided about equally between those who considered their parents highly cultured and those who felt there was no culture at home, even those from supposedly non-cultured families often either inherited many books from a parent, had cultured relatives, or were brought up with sufficient wealth to allow for a good education and travel abroad. Several poets had parents who were writers in regional languages. Rayaprol's father was a famous Telugu poet, Chitre's parents aspired to be writers, Padhi's father wrote plays in Oriya. Kamala Das's mother is a famous Malayalam poet and Malik's mother was a Russian translator. My impression is that at least two-thirds of the poets were raised around books, music, ideas or money.

While the parents of many of the first modern poets were financially secure and from the most westernized sections of the nation

(university teachers, school inspectors, advocates, wealthy business-
men) the younger poets, those born since 1944, are more
products of the spread of westernized, English-language educa-
tion than of an Anglicized upper-middle class. Their fathers
include salesmen, small businessmen and tailors, some of whom
do not speak English. As the use of English has increased in India
from perhaps three million speakers at independence to twenty
million at present, it has spread somewhat downward in society,
from the élite to a broader middle class and with it the social basis
of Indian English poetry has slightly broadened. It is still, how-
ever, a product of those educated in English to a high standard.

Although the careers of the poets are varied, most are part of
the new, urban, English-speaking élite of the universities, communi-
cations and professions. Among teachers or professors of English,
Ezekiel was until recently Professor of American Literature at the
University of Bombay. P. Lal was Professor at the University of
Calcutta. Shiv Kumar was Professor of English at Osmania Univer-
sity. Other English professors and lecturers include Patnaik, Ali,
Parthasarathy, Alexander, Sharat Chandra, de Souza and Padhi.
Peeradina and Jussawalla have also taught English literature. Rama-
nujan was a teacher of English before becoming Professor of Dravi-
dian Linguistics at the University of Chicago. Parthasarathy was
first a lecturer in English and later an editor at Oxford University
Press. Journalists and free-lance writers include Malik, Jussa-
walla, Shetty, Moraes, Kamala Das and Dhiren Bhagat. Public
relations, advertising and other areas of communication are or at
some time were the source of income for Katrak, Chitre, Peera-
dina and Rodrigues. Nandy, after a career in advertising, is editor
of the *Illustrated Weekly*. Seth was until recently an editor with
Stanford University Press. Other careers include college physics
teacher (Mahapatra), former police officer now in government
(Daruwalla), medical doctor (Patel) and engineer (Rayaprol). It
appears that one-third of the poets are or have been school or
university teachers of English, that almost half are school or
university teachers of some subject, and that most of the other
half are in some other form of communications (journalism, adver-
tising, public relations, graphic design, editing). Ten per cent are
in professions other than teaching or an area of communications.

Many of the marriages of the poets are illustrative of their élite,
western yet marginal social status. Although he is a Brahmin,

Ramanujan's wife is Syrian Christian. A Parsi, Katrak is married to a Hindu (raised in Europe). Jussawalla, although Parsi, is married to a French woman. Meena Alexander, Syrian Christian, is married to an American Jew. Mehrotra, a Hindu, is married to a Jain. P. Lal, Hindu, is married to a Brahmo. Kolatkar's first marriage was to a Punjabi, his second to a Parsi. Love rather than arranged marriages are the norm, often involving partners from other religions, castes or regions of India. Several of the poets have divorced and re-married, including Moraes, Pritish Nandy, Shiv Kumar and Kolatkar.

Mobility and foreign travel are also a mark of the poets. Shiv Kumar did his doctorate at Cambridge and often teaches in England and the USA. Ezekiel's two and a half years in England were formative. Rayaprol studied at Stanford University, California. Malik travelled widely in Europe and America, as did Katrak. Ramanujan did his postgraduate work in America, where he now lives. Moraes, Jussawalla, Seth and Bhagat took their university degrees in England. Alexander studied in Africa and did her doctorate at a British university. De Souza, Peeradina, Cooper and Silgardo have studied abroad. Parthasarathy, Kamala Das and Daruwalla appear, by choice, careers or circumstances, to be always on the move in India or abroad. Several of the poets now teach in America.

Before becoming a professor, Ezekiel held numerous jobs ranging from newspaper editor to corporation manager. Many of the poets have a similar tendency towards restlessness and mobility. Chitre has taught at a school in Ethiopia, travelled widely, worked in advertising and made films before becoming a poetry librarian in Bhopal. Shetty did a B.Sc. in commerce, started an MA in English, has worked as a journalist and restaurant manager, and wrote computer manuals before moving to Goa. Peeradina has been a teacher and is now in advertising.

Many of the poets have a wide interest in the arts. Patel, besides being a medical doctor, is also a well-known painter, dramatist and actor. Katrak is an actor. Ezekiel writes plays, and film, art and music criticism. Cooper's Ph.D. thesis is about Indian films. Chitre is a printer and film maker. Malik is an art critic.

While my comments are weighted heavily towards the Bombay and Bombay-connected writers, a glance at the notes to the poets in P. Lal's anthology would suggest a similar pattern. The largest group of Lal's poets are English teachers, followed by journalists,

writers and teachers in fields other than English. Those in com-
munications (journalism, advertising and publishing) are about
equal in number to the teachers. Many of Lal's writers lived or had
lived abroad.

Although poetry in English is now being written outside metro-
politan circles and by those further down the social scale than
previously, the majority of the significant poets are still from or live
in the large cities, especially Bombay, have English-speaking parents,
were educated in good English-language schools and received
their education at well-known colleges and major English univer-
sities or abroad. The writers and their readers represent an
English-speaking cultural élite. The authenticity of the poetry is
its relation to the modernizing, westernizing, educated, intellec-
tual classes who have generally taken a broad interest in modern
Indian culture, society and politics.

The poets might be considered part of the cultural opposition
to the state culture with its Sanskritic and idealized folk tenden-
cies handed down from the pre-independence national move-
ment. As in other nations which became independent after the
Second World War, a split occurred between the nationalists
demanding a traditional culture (a useful weapon in the indepen-
dence struggle), and the avant-garde intellectuals who are more
sensitive to the implications of rapid social change and the new
consciousness and opportunities which followed independence.
The intellectuals and artists are likely to be more modern, less
self-consciously Indian and to sense their own version of tradi-
tion in what feels relevant to them—as is shown by the way Eng-
lish-language poets have been attracted to saints' poetry in the
regional languages rather than the Sanskrit classics. It is true,
however, that as in many cultures the writers are often 'marginal'
men and women who feel outside conventional society; psycho-
logists claim it is as a result of the conflicts caused by their posi-
tion that such people are creative. Creativity is, in a sense, a
resolution of conflict.

II. THE MARKET

Book Publication

Although poetry book publication averages around 1000 copies,
there are large variations. The Writers Workshop usually prints
500 copies. Lal's current policy is that the author buys or sells 100

copies and receives another 50 in royalties. Lal expects to sell another 100 copies in India and 25 in the United States; at about 250 copies (including the author's 100) he starts to make a profit. The author's cost can be recovered through sales. Clearing House is a co-operative that also requires the author's investment; about 750 copies are printed. The decision to accept a manuscript must be unanimously agreed by the four editors. The Newground co-operative has a similar structure but prints 1000 copies. Most Clearing House and Newground publications have been sold out, leaving the writer and publisher with a small profit. The Hacks Co-operative *45 RPM* sold out at 400 copies. Commercial publishers vary. One in Delhi said it printed 1000 copies of poetry, paid the authors no royalties, but did provide some free copies.

Arnold-Heinemann started its poetry series with some extra money it had at the time, and found, mostly because of Pritish Nandy, that it makes a small profit. It usually prints three poetry books a year in 2000 copies and sells 1000 in three or four years; it expects to sell the majority of copies through the post, often among the author's friends or other poets. Royalties are paid but only after a large number of copies have been sold. Arnold-Heinemann receives twenty to thirty requests a week by poets seeking publication but will not read manuscripts unless recommended to the publisher by a well-known writer on a personal basis, as it would be unprofitable to set up a large poetry service. Another publisher explained to me that there is little profit that can be made whether by the publisher or bookseller of a slim volume selling for thirty rupees in 1000 copies. One exception is Pritish Nandy who, Arnold-Heinemann claim, sells from 5000 to 10,000 copies because of his celebrity status and his use of 'visuals' in such books as *Lonesong Street* (of which there was an EMI recording and a film).

Oxford University Press offers a standard commercial contract with royalties and normally prints 1500 copies of a book of poems, but prints upto 3000 copies a time of the *Ten Twentieth Century Indian Poets*. Both home and foreign sales have been steady. Each of the first six books was sold out by 1979 and reprinted. By 1986 *Ten Twentieth Century Indian Poets* was in its seventh printing and Ramanujan's *Selected Poems* and Ezekiel's *Hymns* were in their third printing. While a few books have been let quietly go out of the catalogue after their second impression, as sales did not warrant further reprinting, the series is expanding. Overseas sales in the Commonwealth countries where Ezekiel or Indian poetry is included on an English syllabus may not be large, but they are steady and help to keep the series alive.

Distribution has been a major problem for Indian poets and journals. Oxford has good distribution and Lal has built up his own channels. Clearing House and Newground depend on mailing lists, publicity through friends in Bombay journalism and public readings by the poets. Nandy is good at advertising himself. A very few poets, such as Khare, have produced their own books and done well. He sold 3000 copies of his second book through the mail and at public readings.

Although Indian writers complain that there is no readership for poetry in English the sales compare favourably with poetry published in the regional languages and also with poetry in other English-speaking countries. The readership for modern verse in most Indian languages as shown by journal and book sales appears less than in English. It is useful to contrast the 750 to 1000 copies sold by Clearing House and Newground with the 300 copies which a first book of poems might sell in the United States, or the 1000 to 2000 copies of an established poet. In New Zealand, which is thought to have an unusual number of serious book purchasers and readers of poetry, average printings are 300 to 1000 for volumes of verse. By world standards the sale of poetry books in India is good. The main difference from other countries is that no one is likely to achieve very large sales and there are no well paying literary journals; so far there are at best small fees for republication in anthologies and textbooks. The university market is also still small for poets.

University Courses

University courses in Indian English writing apparently began at Andhra University as part of the MA curriculum when K. R. Srinivasa Iyengar was Professor and Head of the Post-graduate Department of English. By 1955 the University of Mysore, under Professor C. D. Narasimhaiah, offered an MA paper. Since 1958, when it first opened, the Central Institute of English in Hyderabad has been teaching poetry in its courses. Karnatak University (Dharwad) began teaching Indian writing in 1964. Osmania University offered in 1970 two MA courses in Indian literature; since 1976, like several other universities, it offers one Indian and one Commonwealth literature course. The Parthasarathy and Daruwalla anthologies are used at most universities and Ezekiel, Kamala Das, Ramanujan, Kolatkar and Daruwalla appear to be the most studied authors. The University of Bombay started teaching Indian literature in 1975 and has one optional paper in Indian literature at the MA level, using Daruwalla's anthology, and one at the BA level, using Parthasarathy's book. The University of Poona began teaching Indian literature in 1978 and now has a total of six semester courses in Indian and Commonwealth writing at the MA level.

Only a fifth to a quarter of Indian universities offer courses in Indian English writing; novels are set texts far more often than poetry. A more detailed examination of the set texts would reveal a surprising conservatism; Aurobindo, Toru Dutt, Sarojini Naidu and even Tagore are often the main poets studied. My impression is that the more vigorous, productive, better-qualified departments teach Indian and Commonwealth literature. Several professors of English told me that they would like to introduce the teaching of Indian literature in their department but they lacked trained staff. A course may depend on one lecturer and will not be given when that lecturer is on leave. This situation will change as more dissertations are written on Indian literature.

While it is pleasing to see that a growing number of English departments teach modern Indian poetry, until more give courses at both the BA and the MA levels a profitable market for Indian English poetry is unlikely to develop. Such a university market is needed if Indian poetry is to be self-sustaining and no longer dependent on a few enterprising publishers and sympathetic journals.

Journals

Poetry is published in poetry, literary, academic, intellectual and commercial general magazines. While the circulation of Indian literary and cultural magazines varies, it will be found about the same as that of many foreign literary journals. With a few exceptions, 500 is a usual print run. Figures I have for older and recent journals that print poetry include *East and West* (500 copies printed), *Miscellany* (500 copies printed, 200 sold), and *Dialogue* (500 to 1000). *Gray Book* printed 300 to 500 copies, as does *Chandrabhaga*. The obscure stencilled *Tornado* in the late '60s ran from 50 to 1000 copies, usually 500. The stencilled *damn you* was issued in 50 to 100 copies, while *ezra* stencilled 100 to 200 copies. The three stencilled magazines requested donations. *Contra* aimed at 500 select subscribers. *Skylark* has about 300 subscribers and *Vagartha* started with 1000 copies but before it folded up was down to 300. By contrast *Indian Verse* started with 700 copies, went up to 1100 and was printing 2200 by the time it ended, of which only 300 were complimentary. *Volume* printed 500 copies. *Kavi—India* prints 500 copies, has 300 subscribers and 100 bookshop sales, but, like most of the poetry journals, has had problems finding any regular distributor and appears irregularly. The *Commonwealth Quarterly* sells about 300 copies. The *Indian Literary Review* began with 1100 copies but later went down to 750. *Poetry* (Berhampur) prints 1000 copies and sells half; the other half goes to contributors. Among the intellectual-political journals, *Quest* had a circulation of two to three thousand and *Opinion* four to five thousand.

Among the general commercial journals which print poetry, *Debonair* has a circulation of about 130,000. During its short existence *Fulcrum* printed 3000 copies and sold 1000 to 2000. The short-lived *Etc.* printed 1100 copies. *Keynote* printed 20,000 but only sold six to seven thousand. *Illustrated Weekly* has varied from 100,000 to 400,000. Publication in the *Illustrated Weekly*, *Debonair* or similar commercial journals and newspapers brings both money and prestige. Kamala Das told me that when she was poetry editor she received perhaps 3000 poems a month. Poets prefer to publish in journals that pay or in high-quality poetry magazines such as *Chandrabhaga*.

Poetry, academic and literary reviews do not pay contributors. Political-intellectual journals, commercial magazines and newspapers usually do. Kamala Das told me that she would receive twenty-five to thirty rupees when poems were published in *Opinion* or the *Illustrated Weekly*; now she asks ten times that. The usual rate that most poets were paid in 1984 was still twenty-five to fifty rupees for a poem in a magazine. This is in contrast to 350 to 500 rupees for a short story by the same author. Generally fifty to a hundred rupees, sometimes as much as 200, was standard payment for a poem published in a newspaper in 1984; a Sunday weekly magazine might pay 400 to 500 rupees for a spread. Poetry does not pay well. In 1984 a feature article in a commercial magazine might earn up to 3000 rupees, or, supposedly the top rate, a rupee a word.

III. READERS

Assuming that poets read poets the careers of those included in P. Lal's large anthology might be an indication of the readership of Indian English poetry. The contributors are mostly in education, especially English teaching, in the other arts, in various forms of communications (radio script writing, journalism, advertising), with a representation of administrators and businessmen. There is evidence, however, that the normal readership for Indian poetry is neither poets nor English teachers.

Clearing House has a list of its first 350 subscribers and the figures are a further indication of the role of those in media and of other artists as the readers of poetry. Approximately one-fifth of the initial subscribers were other writers, with educators and various artists forming the second and third largest groups. A more detailed breakdown of the subscribers shows the then, and probably continuing, lack of support of the poets by the English studies establishment at universities. Although one of the four editors of Clearing House is a university Reader in English, and while one of the other editors lectures part time in English studies, there were only five English teachers among the identifiable subscribers for the first four Clearing House publications, and only one Indian library placed an order. Ten educators in other fields, such as university professors of Education, Biology and German, and some school teachers were subscribers. Fifteen of the initial subscribers were painters, artists, film-makers and actors. Twelve subscribers were journalists, film critics and people active in the publishing business. There were five medical doctors and psychiatrists, six businessmen and administrators. Of the seventy odd subscribers I can identify, two were university students. It seems that the readership of Indian English poetry consists of those involved in the arts and the media and those with broad cultural interests among the professional and business classes, along with those in various fields of education, including science. Few are professionally involved with English studies. Almost half the initial Clearing House subscribers are directly involved in the creative and performing arts. This general view of the readers of poetry is strengthened by the impression of the Newground editors that the purchasers of their volumes have been from the media, 'street people' and friends.

The composition of the readership can be explained by seeing Indian English poetry as part of contemporary culture. The poets themselves write plays, act, paint, are radio broadcasters and write journalism. Even when they are university teachers, their friends are likely to be other artists, journalists or those in the professional and business classes who follow and support contemporary culture. They are more likely to be appointed to their posts with MA degrees (Ezekiel, Mehrotra, Lal) rather than required to obtain a Ph.D., and it is probable that their appointment and promotion is based rather on their creative and cultural accomplishments than on research.

The role of Ezekiel, Lal and Malik as contributors to general and political magazines appears to have established a relationship between the poets and the editors of such journals. As Indian English poetry gains recognition it seems to be less involved in the political culture and to have found its place alongside the other newly emerging modern arts such as painting, drama, film, and cultural journalism, which appeal to the educated, affluent professional classes of modern urban India. This shift can be seen by contrasting the importance of *Quest, Thought* and *Opinion*, in the earlier years of modern Indian English poetry, to the present, when poets are likely to be contributors to such general magazines as *Debonair, Imprint* or *Femina*. The short-lived *Keynote*, which had an editorial staff mostly composed of poets, was a sign of the change as a new generation of writers, less politically involved than their elders, instinctively sought their readership in a newly emerging social group of cultural consumers.

There is a new English-speaking culture in formation which reflects the interests, tastes, education, travel, mobility and economic standing of the urbanized professional, educational, administrative and creative classes in modern Indian society. The poets belong to these groups, express their vision of reality (including their self-criticisms and alienation from traditional rural Hindu culture) and should be seen as part of the culture of a new postcolonial India rapidly going through changes. An attempt to map this new culture might start by examining the lives of Nissim

Ezekiel, Kersey Katrak, Gieve Patel, Dilip Chitre, and the journals and newspapers with which they have been associated.

It is significant that Ezekiel and Malik, two of the first poets, were actively involved in M. N. Roy's Radical Democratic movement, itself an attempt to find a socialist alternative to the Leninist-Stalinist Communist position sympathized with by many intellectuals, including some of the leading nationalists. Subsequently the poets, including Ezekiel and Lal and later Katrak, Peeradina and Daruwalla, contributed to such journals as *Thought* and *Opinion*, which might be described as part of the independent liberal opposition to the government; while wanting social justice they also wanted individual freedom and were in the cold war closer to the West's and American than to Russian views. The membership of Ezekiel and Malik in the Congress for Cultural Freedom and Ezekiel's founding of *Quest* were significant; later Chitre and Peeradina were involved with *Quest*. P. Lal also for a time had connections with American cultural groups. By contrast to the liberal-left, pro-American leanings of the poets in past decades, the poets at present appear less politically involved. Even poets not long ago active on the left, such as Jussawalla and Nandy, seem disenchanted with politics and movements. The shift in publishing poetry from political-intellectual to more general middle-class magazines may therefore signify more than the presence of a better-paying market. Just as a split occurred between intellectuals and nationalist politicians after India became independent, with the intellectuals moving into opposition as critics of the government, so the poets, while remaining instinctively identified with the intellectual opposition, have become part of a distinct modern Indian culture of the arts and are more likely to give their attention to films, plays, painting and literature than to politics. While this might be criticized as consumerism, it also appears a natural evolution in modern Indian culture which, as it gains strength, demands specialized talents.

CHAPTER FOUR
Towards a Canon

I. AUTHORS

Cultural tastes are usually formed by artists and passed on through the cultural avant-garde to influential critics who in turn persuade the public and students what is valuable. What becomes a canon of recognized authors is originally a reflection of the views of the poets and their aesthetics; but it is modified by the taste of editors and others involved in the publication, promotion and reception of literature who influence taste through control of what is available to critics and the public. This stage in the formation of taste is less important in India than in other new nations as generally the poets themselves have been the publishers and editors of anthologies and journals of poetry.

Poets may know each other's work through the circulation of manuscripts and by appearances in literary journals, but larger recognition comes through book publication either of individual volumes or in anthologies. The situation is always changing as the canon is challenged by each new anthology or publication or by a new group of writers with their own aesthetics. Other factors which have added to reputations, beyond the recognition of the value of individual books, are publication in historically important journals, the republication of individual poems in anthologies, poetry prizes, and critical writings about the poet or particular poems. As poetry criticism in India is still not as specialized an activity as elsewhere, the formation of taste remains mostly in the hands of the poets themselves. For various reasons criticism written by academics has been less significant in India than in other countries; a good review of a new poet by a recognized poet is likely in India to be more influential than an article by a university professor of English.

The main publishers of Indian English poetry have been the

Writers Workshop, Arnold-Heinemann, Oxford University Press, Clearing House and, more recently, Newground. As the Arnold-Heinemann list does not include many volumes that have gained critical attention and as the Writers Workshop, although it has published many significant volumes of verse, including early books by Ezekiel, Jussawalla, Daruwalla and Sharat Chandra, has been unselective, publication by Oxford, Clearing House and, to a lesser extent, Newground has contributed towards a recognized group of significant writers. The superior distribution system of Oxford University Press books, and therefore their availability, also contributes to the establishing of reputations; but distribution is less influential than the prestige of the publisher's judgement. Although Ezekiel published Patel's first volume of poems in a small edition which had poor distribution, the book strongly contributed to Patel's reputation. On the other hand the almost total lack of availability of Ezekiel's first three collections of poems means that they are seldom anthologized or commented upon. Clearing House and Newground both have status because they are co-operatives of recognized poets who must agree among themselves that they are willing to accept a manuscript; they have to date demanded high standards, often rejecting work which has later been published elsewhere. Besides Oxford University Press, Clearing House and Newground there is also the importance of foreign publication. Oxford University Press, England, originally published Ramanujan's two books of poems and Mahapatra's work began to be more visible after the University of Georgia Press brought out his *Rain of Rites*, while the London Magazine edition of G. S. Sharat Chandra's *April in Nanjangud* contributed to a feeling that he was being neglected in Indian anthologies.

Among the many anthologies of modern Indian English poetry, seven have been of interest in showing taste and standards in contrast to the various unselective gatherings of poems by a large number of writers of varying competence. Three anthologies have been particularly influential and are widely used for university courses in English departments. The first was the Macmillan collection edited by Saleem Peeradina, which was originally published as the seventy-fourth issue of *Quest*. It largely reflected the tastes of the Bombay poets and their dissatisfaction with the direction the Writers Workshop had taken and is understood as a direct reply to P. Lal's massive *Modern Indian Poetry in English*. By contrast Peeradina's selection is meant to establish critical standards. Each selection of a poet is prefaced by a short introduction, often of a judgemental nature, in which the praiseworthy is usually balanced, at times over-balanced, with criticism. The anthology is the start of a canon as it is meant to bring standards of evaluation to the study of Indian English poetry. The poets represented are Ramanujan, Ezekiel, Mehrotra, Jussawalla, Katrak, Kolatkar, Patel, Parthasarathy, Daruwalla and Peeradina. Kamala Das shares a section of women writers with Mamta Kalia and Gauri Deshpande. Although P. Lal is represented the introduction to his work is highly critical and there is also a very unfavourable review of Lal's anthology and Gokak's *Golden Treasury of Indo-Anglian Poetry*. Lal was a problem; as one of the original circle of modern Indian English-language poets, and as the publisher of many of the writers, he was regarded as someone who had gone astray. Peeradina's selection appears influenced by Ezekiel, who is included among the critics, along with Peeradina and de Souza.

The Peeradina anthology proposed a list of the poets to be taken seriously at a time when the number of writers had increased beyond the small circle of the early 1950s. The status of Ramanujan had already been confirmed by the publication of his two books of poetry. Ramanujan, Ezekiel and Parthasarathy had appeared along with the odd choice of Deb Kumar Das in Howard Sergeant's *Pergamon Poetry 9: Poetry from India* (1970). Kamala Das's reputation was also well established, as had been Patel's and Jussawalla's by their first books. Daruwalla's first two books, although recent, had been widely praised, receiving favourable reviews by Ezekiel. Significant new names were Mehrotra, Parthasarathy, Peeradina and Kolatkar. The latter two had been active in the little magazine scene both in India and the United States but were not widely known in India outside the circle of Bombay poets, except to readers of the short-lived *Poetry India*. Parthasarathy had published widely in English and in Indian journals. It is noticeable that besides the unfavourable view of Lal the editor found no place for Dom Moraes, who, presumably, was now regarded as a British writer.

While during the next few years there were three other significant anthologies, one edited by Gauri Deshpande and two by Pritish Nandy, they appear not to have had much influence.

Presumably Nandy had insufficient stature among his fellow poets and his tastes were regarded as erratic. Certainly the introductions to his anthologies and the principles of selection showed less seriousness than Peeradina's anthology; Nandy favoured authors he used in his Dialogue publications or poets associated with the Writers Workshop.

Actually Nandy had better taste in selecting poets than he is normally given credit for—only Daruwalla has acknowledged this; but having a flair for publicity he had an unfortunate habit of attacking the still vulnerable English-language poets as apolitical, alienated and inauthentic, while offering his own selection as an example of greater relevance. In practice he published many of the same poets as Peeradina, but his manners certainly did not contribute to the reputation of the anthologies, which is perhaps unfortunate as Calcutta and New Delhi, along with Orissa, were given more of a voice than they have sometimes found. It is in Nandy's favour that he anthologized experimental poetry, but some of the figures he included would appear to be there more for their journalistic influence or visibility in the other arts than for reasons of quality. His first anthology of thirty poets, *Indian Poetry in English: 1947–1972*, beyond the presence of poems by Dom Moraes and Bantleman, confirms that the consensus of the time appeared to be centring on Ezekiel, Kamala Das, Parthasarathy, Daruwalla, Patel, Ramanujan, Mehrotra, Jussawalla, along with Katrak and Deshpande. Nandy included all of Peeradina's poets except Kolatkar, Mamta Kalia and Peeradina. While including himself, P. Lal, Keshav Malik, Suresh Kohli and others, the most significant additions are Jayanta Mahapatra (who had first appeared in a Writers Workshop anthology edited by Shiv Kumar, 1971) and Deba Patnaik. From now on Mahapatra will be in all serious anthologies; Patnaik will only be included by Nandy and Daruwalla. Nandy's second anthology, *Indian Poetry in English Today*, is shorter and more selective but includes the same core of significant poets as before.

Deshpande favoured poets who appeared in *Opinion* and somewhat overlapped with Nandy's taste. She included Ezekiel, Das, Parthasarathy, Daruwalla, Mahapatra, Patel, Jussawalla, along with Peeradina, Katrak, Nandy, herself, Mamta Kalia and a few others. While it is interesting that by now Lal could be ignored, *An Anthology of Indo-English Poetry* lacks stature and representativeness by not including Ramanujan, Mehrotra or Kolatkar. An early poet who appeared in these anthologies but is ignored in the more influential collections is Rakshat Puri, journalist and editor.

Of more importance in establishing reputations than the two Nandy and the Deshpande books was Jussawalla's Penguin *New Writing in India*, which, besides having the reputation of the Penguin imprint, sold 15,000 copies over the years. As Jussawalla's book was meant to cover the main Indian languages he only had space for a few poets and apologized for not including those already known abroad, such as Moraes and Ramanujan. He included Patel, Mehrotra, Kamala Das, Arun Kolatkar and (two poets not in Peeradina's anthology) Dilip Chitre and L. P. Bantleman. Ezekiel is represented by an essay on V. S. Naipaul. Since Jussawalla's selection does not attempt to provide a survey of Indian English poetry, its main significance is not in who is left out, but who is included. Chitre, a bilingual English–Marathi poet, has been closely associated with Kolatkar. Published in *Quest* and *Poetry India* he was also found in the little magazines associated with Mehrotra or in which Mehrotra, Patel and Kolatkar (who with Jussawalla later formed the Clearing House co-operative) also appear. A proponent of a romantic kind of experimental modern poetry, Chitre's work is highly regarded by some poets but disapproved of by others. Of those I consider major poets he is the most uneven in quality and has had the least critical attention. While Bantleman may appear an odd selection, Jussawalla was impressed by his first book. Although he appears someone of passing significance on the literary scene, it is possible that in future critical surveys of Indian English writing Bantleman may be given more attention, although as a minor writer, than he has had to date.

The next major, and still perhaps most influential, anthology was *Ten Twentieth Century Indian Poets*, published by Oxford University Press and edited by R. Parthasarathy. As might be expected Ramanujan, Ezekiel, Patel, Arun Kolatkar, Mehrotra, Daruwalla, Kamala Das and Parthasarathy were included. Also included were Mahapatra and Shiv Kumar. Both surprisingly began writing at a mature age and rapidly produced a substantial body of work published outside the usual places. Kumar quickly moved beyond the Writers Workshop circle to publication by

Tata McGraw Hill (Kumar is the only poet they have published) and Oxford University Press. Mahapatra moved from the Writers Workshop and Nandy's Dialogue publications to regular appearances in major American and British literary journals (he was awarded an annual prize by the prestigious American journal *Poetry*) and to publication of a book by the University of Georgia Press. Regardless of how one ranks individual poets, the ten Parthasarathy chose were unquestionably those who had proved themselves among their peers. The omission of P. Lal confirmed that his place in Indian poetry was likely in future to be that of a publisher and one of the early writers who had first promoted the new poetry after independence. The non-inclusion of Katrak and Deshpande apparently was not controversial and suggested that while regarded as serious by other poets their work was ranked lower than the best. The omission of Jussawalla was more often questioned. Ezekiel, who was consulted, as he had been by Peeradina, is said to have advised including Jussawalla, but Parthasarathy stuck to his own views. Several reviewers objected to the omission of G. S. Sharat Chandra, who had published two books in England since leaving India for a teaching career abroad.

The influence of the Oxford University Press anthology was reinforced by their New Poetry in India series which began with volumes by Ezekiel, Daruwalla, Kumar, Parthasarathy and Ramanujan. Clearing House the same year published their first four volumes by Patel, Mehrotra, Kolatkar and Jussawalla. Some of the Clearing House poets had been asked by Oxford to submit manuscripts, but decided to go ahead with their own project. Oxford would later publish volumes by Mahapatra, Mehrotra and G. S. Sharat Chandra.

Despite the appearance of still another anthology by Pritish Nandy, *Strangertime* (1977), presumably to promote new talents, the recognized major poets appeared to be twelve, the ten in Parthasarathy's Oxford anthology and, some felt, Jussawalla and Sharat Chandra. Moraes was either no longer thought important enough to consider or, more likely, was looked upon as a British poet who had in any case stopped writing poetry. Nandy's third anthology was non-representative; it ignored Parthasarathy, Patel, Mehrotra, but did, unlike his earlier collections, include Kolatkar and Kumar along with Katrak, Deshpande, Patnaik, Chitre and Agha Shadid Ali. Ali is one of those early insights which Nandy often has of promising poets. Although Ali published two books with the Writers Workshop, his early work shows someone with the gift of poetry but who has not assimilated his varied influences, which range from traditional Urdu verse to T. S. Eliot. Later, in poems published in American journals, Ali has started to develop into an interesting writer who might well be considered among the better Indian English poets.

Later, Daruwalla brought out *Two Decades of Indian Poetry: 1960–1980*, which is the only anthology to date to challenge Parthasarathy's selection. It includes seventeen poets and would have included eighteen if Parthasarathy had replied to the editor. Besides the poets Parthasarathy selected—Ramanujan, Ezekiel, Kamala Das, Shiv Kumar, Jayanta Mahapatra, Daruwalla, Patel, Kolatkar, Mehrotra—there are also Jussawalla, Sharat Chandra and six others: Kersey Katrak, Gauri Deshpande and Peeradina (all three were in Peeradina's anthology), Eunice de Souza, Dilip Chitre and Deba Patnaik. Among the poets Daruwalla included, Katrak, Deshpande and Patnaik are perhaps the most debatable as the first has only been published by the Writers Workshop and Arnold-Heinemann, the second has been published only by the Writers Workshop and Dialogue publications, while the third has not to date published a volume of verse. Katrak's best work may be his early books; Deshpande has not published a volume recently. Katrak and Deshpande have, however, appeared in most anthologies except for Parthasarathy's, while Patnaik has only been anthologized by Nandy.

Daruwalla's is the latest significant anthology, but it is not the last word on the canon of major authors. While Clearing House's publication of H. O. Nazareth's *Lobo* produced little excitement, the appearance of Manohar Shetty's *A Guarded Space* was followed by excellent reviews from several poets, including Mahapatra and Daruwalla. Future anthologies may include Shetty. That de Souza, Shetty and Peeradina are now recognized as significant poets suggest that Newground books have taken their place alongside the Oxford and Clearing House publications in the creation of a canon. Several poets have told me that among their contemporaries they particularly like the work of Rodrigues and Silgardo.

A canon is more an average of varied opinions, judgements and tastes than a strict consensus. If Mahapatra, Mehrotra, Patel or de Souza had published anthologies, their choices might be different. In *Only Connect* (edited by Guy Amirthanayagam and

S. C. Harrex, Centre for Research in the New Literatures in English and East-West Center, Adelaide and Honolulu, 1981), Mehrotra selects work by ten poets; while they are not meant as his considered judgement of the ten best writers, they are a rather different list from that found, say, in Parthasarathy's anthology. The writers are Chitre, Daruwalla, de Souza, Jussawalla, Patel, Ramanujan, Kolatkar, Amit Rai and himself. Rai is the promising young poet who co-edited *damn you* with Mehrotra and died young; presumably he is included for memory's sake. The other choices, however, appear to reflect Mehrotra's opinions as expressed in the few critical essays and reviews he has published; he has favourably reviewed de Souza, unfavourably criticized Pathasarathy, and praised Kolatkar.

A canon of Indian English poetry has been forming, although like most canons it is subject to change. While publication by Oxford University Press and in R. Parthasarathy's Oxford University Press anthology has normally been most influential in the creation of this canon, publication by Clearing House or Newground, or appearance in the Peeradina and Daruwalla anthologies, has been of importance. Publication of a book by reputable publishing houses abroad or by commercial houses (in contrast to self publication) in India also strengthens a poet's reputation. Appearance in such publications as *Poetry India* or the Penguin *New Writing in India* helps. Essentially, poets judge other poets. The way something like a consensus has formed and what I regard as influential publications is expressed visually in Chart 2.

As Pritish Nandy is not included in the Peeradina, Parthasarathy and Daruwalla collections, it is questionable whether his appearance in Deshpande and his own three volumes is sufficient to consider him part of the canon. If popularity and sales were in themselves guides, his *Lonesong Street* would deserve top place; but, regardless of one's view of Nandy's other poems, I do not think anyone would consider that volume of literary interest. There are, however, a few of Nandy's poems which, besides being popular, have often appeared in anthologies and school texts, and deserve more attention than the kind of dismissal that is usually given his verse in most critical circles.

While taste and a canon are usually handed down from poets to critics to teachers of literature, there have not yet been major Indian literary critics who have had a role in influencing opinion.

Perhaps it is just as well that so far there has been no Indian equivalent of F. R. Leavis to hand on a great tradition of modern Indian English poetry. At present academic taste is a bit behind that of the poets and anthologizers. There are several books on Ezekiel and Das, a book on Nandy and collections of essays on Parthasarathy and Mahapatra. Several books on Ramanujan have been promised. The three major collections of essays edited by established critics are *Indian Poetry in English* (ed. V. A. Shahane and M. Sivaramkrishna, Macmillan, 1980), *Contemporary Indian English Verse* (ed. Chirantan Kulshrestha, Arnold-Heinemann, 1980) and *Perspectives on Indian Poetry in English* (ed. M. K. Naik, Abhinav, 1984). Each is different in aim and the poets discussed. Four poets, however, are given individual chapters in the three books: Ezekiel, Ramanujan, Daruwalla and Kamala Das. Kolatkar, Mahapatra and Shiv Kumar are the subject of essays in two of the books. The other essays are on Jussawalla, Mehrotra, Patel, Lal and Nandy. In journals there are articles on Shiv Kumar, Kolatkar, Jussawalla, Patel, Mehrotra and a few others. Comment on the work of Sharat Chandra, de Souza and Shetty is more likely to be found in newspaper reviews or in such poetry journals as *Chandrabhaga* or *Kavi—India*. The situation, however, is slowly changing and, as more Indian poetry is taught at universities, academic journals will devote more space to articles on Indian English poets.

II. POEMS

By now there are a number of poems which are well known and part of modern Indian culture, and which are becoming part of world English-language culture. Is there anyone who reads Indian poetry who is not familiar with some of Ezekiel's poems in Indian English, Patel's 'The Ambiguous Fate' or some of the often anthologized work of Kamala Das and Ramanujan? Through their quality or some particular ability to catch attention, such as having a representativeness or defining an essential human situation, these poems have stood out from others and are often republished in anthologies, textbooks or the author's selected poems, or are cited by critics. This process of selection, judgement and popular taste is a canon in formation. These are the poems which, for whatever reason, might provisionally be regarded as the modern classics of

Indian English poetry; while the canon will change as more good poems are written and as tastes change, they are likely to have a place, or be considered, for some future Golden Treasury or Oxford anthology of Indian English verse.

While it should be possible to demonstrate which poems have become canonical, there are problems which prevent a critic or historian from simply counting the number of times a poem has been republished. In some anthologies minor writers are merely puffing their own work and that of friends. Many poems are republished in textbooks. For example *A Pageant of Poems* (ed. C. A. Sheppard, Orient Longman, 1977) includes one poem each by Ezekiel, Ramanujan and Das. *A Book of Verse for Children 8* (OUP, Calcutta, 1975) includes Parthasarathy, Kamala Das, Patel, Nandy and Ezekiel. *New Horizons* (ed. S. K. Prasad, Orient Longman, New Delhi, 1976, '79) only includes Ezekiel and Lal among the well-known modern poets. It is difficult to obtain a sufficient number of school texts to be representative and publishers do not keep figures of which poems have been republished. Recent poems are also less likely to be anthologized than work published earlier. Poems published in the 1960s and early 1970s were available for the many anthologies published in the 1970s, whereas there have been fewer significant anthologies since 1977. Indeed there is a need for an anthology of the poets who published their first books since the mid '70s. Poems often cited favourably by critics and reviewers or which had had an influence on other writers are not necessarily those presently included in anthologies, although they are likely to be in future anthologies.

While no purely statistical approach can be an accurate indication of the canon of a still evolving body of contemporary literature, there is enough readily available evidence of what might be regarded as the canon at present. In the chart I have prepared (see Chart 3) I have used widely available anthologies: P. Lal's *Modern Indian Poetry in English* (second revised and enlarged edition, 1971), Saleem Peeradina's *Contemporary Indian Poetry in English* (1972, reprinted 1977), Pritish Nandy's *Indian Poetry in English: 1947–1972* (1972), Pritish Nandy's *Indian Poetry in English Today* (1973), Gauri Deshpande's *An Anthology of Indo-English Poetry* (1974), R. Parthasarathy's *Ten Twentieth Century Indian Poets* (1976), Pritish Nandy's *Strangertime: An Anthology of Indian Poetry in English* (1977), A. N. Dwivedi's *Indian*

Poetry in English (1980), K. N. Daruwalla's *Two Decades of Indian Poetry: 1960–1980* (1980). I have also taken note of republication in such books as V. K. Gokak's *The Golden Treasury of Indo-Anglian Poetry* (1970), *Ten Years of Quest* (1966), Mary Ann Dasgupta's *Hers* (1978), Jussawalla's Penguin *New Writing from India* and a few texts which I thought relevant. I have listed book publication by the author and republication in subsequent volumes. Since my purpose is to establish which poems are best known, liked or most highly regarded in India, I have, except for the widely available Penguin *New Writing*, limited my references to Indian books. While this works against such poets as Ramanujan, Ezekiel, Daruwalla, Mehrotra and Mahapatra, who have published widely abroad, it was necessary to do this as otherwise the perspective would become international rather than Indian.

My chart works against such poets as Parthasarathy, Kolatkar, Mahapatra and Jussawalla, who have written long poems. Although many anthologists include selections from *Rough Passage, Jejuri* and *Missing Person*, the selections differ. Parthasarathy has revised many previously published poems for *Rough Passage*, in which some lyrics are made from bits and pieces of previous works.

Although it would be possible to raise still further objections to my chart, it will do as a start. It shows that Ezekiel, Kamala Das, Ramanujan, Jussawalla, Daruwalla, Patel and Mehrotra, along with Kolatkar, have written poems which are often republished. A few poems of Pritish Nandy and P. Lal must also be included in a list of the best-known Indian English poems, although Nandy has often been the editor who has republished them. Shiv Kumar and Gauri Deshpande have also had poems republished enough to be noticed.

It is of interest that only five poems have been included in all three major anthologies. Three are by Ezekiel, 'Enterprise', 'Night of the Scorpion', 'Poet, Lover, Birdwatcher'; the others are Kamala Das's 'The Freaks' and Daruwalla's 'The Epileptics'. Poems published in two of the three major anthologies and republished in other collections include Patel's 'On Killing a Tree' and 'Nargol'; Ezekiel's 'Background, Casually'; Jussawalla's 'Sea Breeze, Bombay' and 'Approaching Santa Cruz'; Ramanujan's 'Another View of Grace', 'The Gnomes', 'The Last of the Princes' and 'Breaded Fish'; Mehrotra's 'The Sale' and 'Continuities'; Kolatkar's 'The Bus'; and Parthasarathy's 'Exile 8' ('A Grey Sky').

Poems which have been republished widely include Kamala

Das's 'The Dance of the Eunuchs,' 'An Introduction', 'Summer in Calcutta', 'My Son's Teacher'; Ramanujan's 'Love Poem for a Wife—I' and 'Obituary'; Patel's 'The Ambiguous Fate' and 'University'; Ezekiel's 'Marriage' and 'Philosophy'; Jussawalla's 'Nine Poems on Arrival'; Parthasarathy's 'Trial 7' ('It is night alone helps').

A few other works which have appeared in print often enough to be noticed are Patel's 'Servants' and 'Dilwadi'; Gauri Deshpande's 'Migraine' and 'Female of the Species'; Shiv Kumar's 'Indian Women'; Mehrotra's 'Remarks of an Early Biographer' and 'Between Bricks, Madness'; Parthasarathy's 'Trial 9' ('Over the family album'), 'Homecoming 8' ('With paper boots'), 'Homecoming 10' ('The street in the evening') and 'It doesn't make any sense'; Kolatkar's 'the boatride'; Lal's 'Because Her Speech is Excellent'; Nandy's 'Near Deshapriya Park', 'Calcutta If You Must Exile Me', 'Wildhorses rage in your tresses' and 'What shall we do with these memories'; and various poems of Kamala Das. Most of Nandy's appearances are in his own publications.

A variety of critical tastes, and even ideological positions, are involved in the anthologies. Where Parthasarathy differs from Peeradina and Daruwalla he usually has chosen poems by Das and Ramanujan with themes of nostalgia, or poems set in specific Indian locations. It is also noticeable that some poems which seem well known, such as Ezekiel's 'Very Indian Poem in Indian English' and 'Goodbye Party for Miss Pushpa T.S.', are not well represented in my charts.

Of the recognized major poets Mahapatra is an exception in that, though the anthologists and critics consider him one of India's foremost writers, there is no evidence from anthologies that any particular poems are considered essential or superior enough to be selected for republication or comment. While this may be due to the number of books he has published, it is more likely a result of the difficulty of his poetry. No doubt when more critics have written on him, specific poems will emerge as superior or favourites. It is also possible that Mehrotra's longer, more difficult poems will benefit when they are better understood. Similarly the book-length sequences of Parthasarathy and Kolatkar, which are now judged as a whole, will no doubt provide individual poems more often republished in anthologies than others. Curiously, 'Between Jejuri and the Railway Station' has never been republished, although many critics consider it the most interesting poem in *Jejuri*.

While there is no fixed canon, or permanent Golden Treasury of great poems, as tastes always change and new writing challenges the status of the old, the present mixed opinion about what is or is not essential Indian English poetry reflects the newness of the poetry. In 1950 modern Indian English poetry hardly existed and as late as 1960, when the Writers Workshop started, was still fighting to survive. In general those poems which have become established as classics have used Indian subject-matter, have been explicit in meaning and not difficult in form. The best-known poems of Ezekiel, Ramanujan, Das and the early Patel are examples. The more difficult poetry of Mahapatra and Mehrotra, the poems published abroad by Sharat Chandra, the recent poetry of Daruwalla, along with the book-length verse sequences of Kolatkar and Parthasarathy, will need more time before favourites emerge. By then other poets and poems will also be seen as demanding attention. De Souza's 'Miss Louise' appears to be such a poem.

CHAPTER FIVE

Poetics and Criticism

The creation of a canon of major authors implies accepted standards, values and preferences on the part of the poets and critics who establish taste and influence the judgement of others. Their comments, reviews and selection of who is to be published carry inferences about what is desirable and often reflect the nature of their own work or assumptions which are passed on to others. The elite which judges and sets standards is not monolithic, not a closed circle, not a clique, and may be unconscious of its influence. Often they initially feel outsiders trying to counteract the bad influences of others; they may significantly disagree among themselves upon specific writers, poems or issues and will be found divisible into as many different groups as there are individuals. But as such poets establish the taste by which they are judged, it is useful to examine their various concepts of poetry and the way their views have influenced or been modified by others.

It is best to begin by contrasting P. Lal to Ezekiel as critics. Whereas Lal's views are still often cited outside India as representative of the new poetry, he is now more likely in India to be viewed as insignificant except as a publisher. This perhaps denies Lal full justice. Lal's reviews, columns and publications had a role in bringing the new poetry to attention, until he was overtaken by the rise in standards as Indian English poetry developed. When his *Modern Indian Poetry in English: An Anthology and a Credo* was first published in 1969, the need to defend the existence of Indian English poetry was becoming irrelevant, as was shown by the books of Ramanujan, Ezekiel, Das, Patel and the many new talented poets who had appeared in journals. Lal's indiscriminate publication of writers came into conflict with the need to establish standards; his critical vocabulary, which may have been suitable for an earlier generation of middle-class intellectuals raised in a genteel British colonial culture, was also becoming old-fashioned.

Lal's review of *A Time To Change*, in *Thought* (28 June 1952) was in its time welcome praise, but now seems totally inappropriate to Ezekiel's scepticism, urban attitudes and modern consciousness:

These poems revolve like noons around a bright hard flame. The flame takes many shapes, but its essence constitutes a simple and harmonious [*sic*] way of life, where the mind is free from vexation as far as possible, and the body contented with elementary satisfactions.... Mr Ezekiel flicks like a hummingbird, giving in each poem an aspect of what he believes to be the limpid style of life.

Lal's review shows no awareness of poetic technique, except for 'bright glittering vowels' and its description of the poems is inaccurate. While his review bears testimony to his own version of late romantic aestheticism—even echoing Pater—and his preference for poetry which is metaphoric, melodious, moral (see his 'Preface' to *The Collected Poems of P. Lal*, 1977, p. 9) and unironic, most readers will feel Daruwalla's 'Introduction' to *Two Decades of Indian Poetry* is more accurate where it is claimed that *A Time to Change* inaugurated a new era of Indian poetry by writing of the demands of the present-day world, bringing into play a modern sensibility confronting the confusion, bewilderment and disillusion of the time, while using a modern idiom without the archaisms and jangling rhyme schemes of the earlier poets. While Daruwalla's description of Ezekiel reflects his own work, it shows how far off the mark Lal was. The very title, *A Time to Change*, belies Lal's middle-brow, genteel hedonism. As Daruwalla says, the title poem shows a 'life of loose untied ends'. Where Lal had seen a flitting hummingbird (a phrase perhaps better applied to his own kind of deft, light, romantic lyric poetry), Daruwalla speaks of Ezekiel's realism, 'wrinkles, warts and all'.

It is unfortunate that Lal's anthology of 132 poets appeared when it did. A decade earlier, before the appearance of books by Kamala Das and Ramanujan and Ezekiel's *Exact Name*, it would have been useful; but then, of course, it would have been impossible, as the Writers Workshop and *Miscellany* had only begun publishing in 1960; 1969 was no longer the time, however, to praise R. L. Bartholomew's 'authentic voice of feeling', P. K. Saha for 'the civilized seriousness of an eager beaver' or to defend Dom Moraes by saying 'but does meaning matter in poetry?' More embarrassing was 'F. R. Stanley's precious birdsong' and 'the heaven-knows-what of my own verse'. Eunice de Souza, reviewing the anthology in Peeradina's *Contemporary Indian Poetry in English*, called the introduction 'incompetent, incoherent, and pretentious' and after quoting Lal on Stanley's 'birdsong' added '(tweet, tweet?)'. De Souza argues 'There is a need for a representative anthology, but indiscriminate selection does not fill this gap and, worse still, it swamps the significant work included.' Elizabeth Reuben's introduction to Lal's poetry in Peeradina's anthology begins by saying that with 'absolute unconcern he fills his poems with roses, bees and 'bathos'. The poems 'lack concreteness in their imagery.' 'The roses, birds, and bees are like mere counters; nothing is done to make them real, or to convey their fascination.... It all adds up to something both over-rich and indefinite.'

While the views of Daruwalla, de Souza and Reuben are part of an aesthetic developed in India by Ezekiel, I do not necessarily mean they were directly influenced. I suggest that the moral seriousness, rational, modern, intellectual consciousness, technical competence, concern for high standards and precision of language they demand were introduced into Indian critical thought by Ezekiel and through him spread to and developed by others.

Part of Ezekiel's influence can been seen in the kind of advice he gave others early in the 1950s when he was a sub-editor on the *Illustrated Weekly*. He warned Dom Moraes that the danger to a poet in India was the ease with which a reputation could be gained; he read Katrak's manuscripts, querying every word; Lal has commented on the time when Ezekiel, then editor of *Quest*, returned a poem. 'He twitted me for using an exclamation mark, chided obvious poeticism and sentimental reiteration.' 'A precise observation at the close,' he suggested, 'would strengthen the poem' ('A Few Words', Lal's preface to *The Unfinished Man*). Dedication to being a poet and the art of poetry, international standards, precision in the use of every word, rejection of poeticism and sentimentality, and the need for logic, coherence and moral intelligence are among the qualities which Ezekiel required from the formerly amateur local world of Indian poetry.

Ezekiel's review of Daruwalla's first published book, *Under Orion* (1970), appeared in the *Times Weekly* and is reprinted in Peeradina's anthology. It begins by contrasting the 'remarkably substantial bulk' of *Under Orion* to the slimness of most Indian volumes of poetry in English and claims as a first collection it compares favourably with the first books of Dom Moraes and A. K. Ramanujan. The significance of the size of the collection is 'evidence not only of mature poetic talent but of literary stamina, intellectual strength and social awareness.' After comparing Daruwalla to his contemporaries (Mehrotra and Peeradina resemble him in 'their sharp perception of environment and forthright statement'), Ezekiel praises his 'depth of feeling, economy of language and originality of insight', his irony, his 'bitter, scornful, satiric tone' and 'energetic argument in verse' which is 'the end-product of a rigorous process in which attitudes have been explored and choices made.' Daruwalla's attitude towards India is 'unsentimental'. Ezekiel further comments on Daruwalla's descriptive skill, creation of characters and situations, use of poetic dialogue and the dramatic as well as the 'blend of freedom and discipline, metrical rhythms and the word order of prose, compact and harsh alliterative phrasing.' Throughout the review he contrasts Daruwalla's verse with that of 'poetasters' whose craftsmanship is limited to 'the simple expression of emotion with a sprinkling of imagery.'

This is a remarkable review, remarkable for its quality, perceptiveness and conviction that the first book of a previously obscure poet is among the best achievements of Indian English poetry to that time. It is also remarkable how the initial, somewhat surprising observation of the 'bulk' of the volume evolves into evidence of the way Daruwalla's achievement surpasses that of most of his contemporaries. Key concepts are maturity, stamina, intellectual strength, social awareness, perception of environment, forthright statement, economy of language, irony, tone, blend of freedom and discipline, word order, 'reflection on experience', and the variety of creation. These are expansions of Ezekiel's earlier requirement that a poet be committed to being a poet, that the craft of poetry be mastered at the highest standard, and that poetry should be the result of moral, intellectual and social intelligence expressed in new ways with economy and precision. Much of what Ezekiel says of Daruwalla will be said by others about his own verse. The concern with exactness of language, economy, craftsmanship, 'perception of environment', forthrightness, intelligence and the evaluative comparison of poets will be characteristic of many writers and critics who have been associated with Ezekiel.

Peeradina, for example, introduces his anthology by criticizing those who indiscriminately promote Indian poets, encouraging 'trash'. By contrast Ezekiel is praised for his craftsmanship, and Parthasarathy for his 'polish and precision and exact images'. Peeradina criticizes Ezekiel's recent work as lacking content despite a new, freer flowing style. Mehrotra is criticized for aiming at a purity of language without content; Daruwalla's sensibility is 'acutely aware of and committed to present-day socio-political-cultural reality.' Literature must show an awareness of the physical and human landscape of India and be involved in the local life. While Peeradina's concern with local realities is reflected in his own verse, especially 'Banda', it is an extension of Ezekiel's praise for poets aware of their environment. He also shares Ezekiel's concern with the need to discriminate and to judge who has or has not worked diligently for precision and exactness.

Not a systematic or original critic, Ezekiel has a distinctive view of poetry. Although the concepts and even phrases sound similar to what has often been said, the emphasis and implications add up to a personal position. In his talk on 'Ideas and Modern Poerty' (*Indian Writers in Conference*, ed. N. Ezekiel, *PEN* All-India Centre, Bombay, 1964, pp. 45–84) Ezekiel argues that modern poetry is not used to do what prose can do; the propagation of ideas is not the job of verse. Modern poets try 'to find a language which will match the actual speech habits, rhythms, and typical attitudes' of the twentieth century. While using forms from the past they have used them in new ways, avoiding 'conventional forms used in conventional ways'; they have 'rejected standard images and phrases, the whole tone of the age preceding theirs.' The essay continues with a discussion of how modern poets have needed to construct a framework of ideas through which to unify and express their sensibility; it is necessary to find a language, form and attitudes which express contemporary life.

A lecture on 'Poetry as Knowledge' published in *Quest* (76, May 1972, pp. 45–8) is significant for the tension between the concentration and concreteness of pure poetry and Ezekiel's belief that poetry contributes 'to man's knowledge of himself'. While a poem must 'strive to fuse thought and emotion in images that have moral and philosophical implications', and which therefore make poetry a 'precise and exact' form of discourse, a poem lacks weight without truth, meaning and, especially, knowledge.

Such views echo much of what has been said about poetry in this century, and certainly make no major new advance on theorizing about the nature of the art; but they do set up specific goals which are unlike those, say, of the American New Critics, who emphasized form and purity to the exclusion of knowledge, meaning or truth. Ezekiel requires that poetry be grounded in reality, reflection, experience and have a logical, discursive form. Poetry is seen as a different, more concentrated, economical, precise kind of communication about a person's felt and considered experience of life. Poetry is not just formalized, ornamented, rhetorical self-expression; it results from a fusion of thought and feeling into precise images which give expression to the contemporary mind as experienced and reflected upon by the poet. This requires the discipline to create new forms of precise articulation and as far as possible the modern poet should have an intellectual framework which integrates his or her work.

There are various tensions in Ezekiel's discussion of poetry in these and other essays. He wants the economy and precision, aesthetic distance and unified vision of the major early-twentieth-century poets. But he also wants poetry invested with moral awareness, truth, self-knowledge and mature experience. The former kind of poetry has been the major accomplishment of the modernist movement; in theory and tendency it has aimed at purifying itself of claims to knowledge and truth. Ezekiel's view of poetry would seem to, and does, put more emphasis on poetry as the communication of insight and experience, expressed in concentrated, precise forms. While representative of the modern mind it will be centred on the self's engagement with its environment. To speak of truth, meaning and knowledge in poetry does not return it to versified feeling and ideas, but does mean that it will be more immediately, concretely related to society and situations, and more moral and spiritual in its tendency than art which aims at purity or meta-poetic statements about itself and the nature of the imagination: thus Peeradina's insistence that Indian poetry should both have precision of language and social awareness. These concepts were also in Ezekiel's review of Daruwalla and his comments on Jussawalla and Mehrotra. Although Ezekiel's view of poetry is influenced by his own spiritual yearning and intellectual awareness, it was extended by other poets to further areas of social, political and cultural concern. Attempts to bring

together purity and concentration of image with political aware-
ness can be seen in Jussawalla's poetry, while Parthasarathy is
concerned with overcoming the cultural effects of colonization.
In the mature work of both poets, there is a pressure of argument,
the saying of something, and an attempt to reach a conclusion,
although the mode is imagistic rather than versified talk.

Parthasarathy in particular seems to extend the range of Ezekiel's
criticism into other areas. Parthasarathy's poetry has an unusually
dense compression, economy and reliance on imagery drawn from
his environment which is used symbolically. The poetry reflects
personal self-knowledge, emotion reflected upon, and aims at
maturity of vision; experience is placed within a dominant intellec-
tual framework in which the main concern is to overcome his alie-
nation from Tamil culture caused by colonialism and a westernized
English-language education.

In his Introduction to *Ten Twentieth Century Indian Poets*
Parthasarathy begins by citing Ezekiel's editorship of *Quest* and
mentions that the Contemporary Poetry issue of *Quest* offered its
pages to an 'assessment' of the recent poetic scene. His own selection
includes a sample of what he considers 'significant' in twentieth
century Indian English verse. After a brief survey of pre-in-
dependence writing in which Toru Dutt is singled out for her
'concretization' of her nostalgia for India in the poem 'Our
Casuarina Tree', Parthasarathy says that Indian verse in English
did not seriously exist before independence. The Indian poet in
English feels alienated by his language from the environment and
from a living idiom. There is no tradition from which to 'evaluate'
his work. Therefore he is conscious of his Indianness, which reflects
a crisis of identity. The tension of using a foreign language with its
lack of roots in the local environment becomes a main theme of the
Introduction as Parthasarathy discusses those who use English to
examine critically their own culture, those who are bilingual poets,
and those who have been conscious of the incongruities of writing
in English in a still largely traditional India. Whereas early poets
were interested in Indian legend, the contemporary poet is con-
cerned with finding a personal language; those who are successful
have, like Ramanujan, turned 'language into an artifact' and, like
Kolatkar, Mehrotra and Kumar, used images as 'the kernel' of the
poem. In our time poetry is becoming increasingly concise; it is
moving towards metaphor. Parthasarathy's prefaces to the indi-

vidual writers are revealing of his own interests. Daruwalla is said to pare language to the bone; 'images are concrete and exact'. Ezekiel's poems show a 'keen, analytical mind trying to explore and communicate on a personal level feelings of loss and deprivation.' In Kolatkar's 'the boatride' imagination and reality are 'fused'. Kumar is praised for 'ironic humour' and his imagery and nostalgia are mentioned. In Mahapatra's poems 'the economy of phrasing and startling images' recall classical Sanskrit. Mehrotra piles images 'one on top of another'. Of his own *Rough Passage* Parthasarathy comments it is the start of 'a dialogue between the poet and his Tamil past. The strength of the poem derives from his sense of responsibility towards crucial personal events in his life.'

As in Ezekiel's criticism, Parthasarathy sees poetry arising from personal experience which is reflected upon; thought and feeling are fused into concise, precise images which are used to communicate knowledge. Irony is valued, as are deep emotions maturely considered. A poet has responsibilities as a human being and as a poet. Although Parthasarathy seems to allow more freedom for purely structural experiments (Mehrotra) and the imaginative (Kolatkar) than Ezekiel, while giving even more importance to image, his main contribution to what had been previously said by Indian critics is a new approach to the national concern about recovering a traditional culture. Whereas Ezekiel dismisses this problem as not relevant to himself (although in recent remarks he has acknowledged a possible role of his Jewish past in his poetry), Parthasarathy sees it as essential if the English-language writer is to overcome a sense of alienation from his environment, past and language. Ramanujan is cited as evidence that it is possible to overcome such problems by recovering an apparently lost tradition through hard work. Rather than the social, political and intellectual awareness of Ezekiel, Parthasarathy is concerned with a cultural crisis as represented by his writing in English, a language without geographical roots in India. *Rough Passage* fuses personal crisis and cultural crisis into a series of linked, precise, compressed images which, to use Ezekiel's terminology, offer truth, meaning and knowledge.

In his essay 'Whoring After English Gods' (*Writers in East-West Encounter*, ed. Guy Amirthanayagam, London: Macmillan, 1980, pp. 64–84), Parthasarathy claims that Ramanujan and Ezekiel, by expressing in an 'unobtrusive personal voice' their vision of 'everyday Indian reality', indicated the direction Indian English poetry would take. 'Although a poem is an object made up of words', the poet by dedication to words arrives at a truth; understanding poetry is related to the problem of being a human being, of growing up emotionally and intellectually. 'Ramanujan's repossession, through his poetry, of the past of his family, and of his sense of himself as a distillation of the past' is a possible model for how to use one's own voice. His poems are products of a specific culture which he has translated into the terms of another culture. (These views are further developed in 'How it Strikes a Contemporary: The Poetry of A. K. Ramanujan', *The Literary Criterion,* vol. 12, nos. 2 & 3, 1976). Again there is the claim that a poem is an object, a series of images, though related to everyday reality, and to the problem of 'being a human being'. But the emphasis is different from that in Ezekiel. The poem seems more an object in itself than a kind of transmission of knowledge to others. As English is not a regional language in India and therefore as used by the Indian poet will not have the social and cultural nuances it would in England and America, there is a need to forge an unobtrusive voice, to use language as artifice. While this may account for Parthasarathy's greater acceptance than Ezekiel of a poem as object and a structure of images, it is also related to this attempt to root himself in a Tamil tradition. This takes the form of a kind of reverse translation, in which an English poem is written as if it were Tamil. Parthasarathy claims that since 1971 his poems are close in style, content and irony to Tamil verse.

Whereas an Ezekiel poem is a negotiation with the modern world, Parthasarathy's concern with the present is in its relationship to the past. T. S. Eliot sought in tradition an answer to the fragmentation of modern liberal individualism; Parthasarathy seeks in tradition a means of overcoming the effects of a western education which disrupted his roots in a tradition. This is a sophisticated, nuanced, complex version of regional nationalism in which the individual attempts to find his or her identity in terms of a specific culture. The simplicities of nationalist demands for folk and historical themes have been replaced by an argument which is recognizably in one of the main streams of modernist poetic theory.

The theoretical assumptions of Ezekiel are shared by many of the better Indian critics and poets. There are, however, other Indian poets who do not write in precise, economical language, use sharply defined images, develop their poems rationally or speak from knowledge developed from mature reflection and involvement with

social situations. There are, for example, poets who are experi-
mentalists and those who write obscure, difficult, hermetically-
sealed verse. Mehrotra's experimentalism might seem to fall outside
Ezekiel's middle path between pure image and versified rhetoric,
but because of his excellent craftsmanship, and perhaps because of
the social awareness of his *bharatmata: a prayer*, and the use of local
details in his later poetry, Mehrotra is accepted by most of the
poet-critics influenced by Ezekiel.

While Mehrotra's methods of making a poem are unique among
Indian poets, they have some resemblances to the use of the surreal
in the early work of Kolatkar and Chitre, to the free-associational,
experimental early writing of Pritish Nandy, to some of Deba
Patnaik's poems and to the poetry of Jayanta Mahapatra. Starting
with Kolatkar and Chitre, a number of Indian writers began experi-
menting with a variety of avant-garde techniques ranging from
surrealist free association to concretism and visual poetry. Although
there was no one particular objective or set of assumptions involved,
different kinds of poetry were being written which could not easily
be fitted into an aesthetic of preciseness, economy, the distillation of
thought and feeling into images and mature reflections on personal
experience and the modern world. Little magazines in Bombay,
often associated with Mehrotra, and later Pritish Nandy's *Dialogue*
in Calcutta, often published this experimental poetry.

The new poetry had no theoreticians or influential practising
poet-critics like Ezekiel or Parthasarathy. There were certain, often
opposing directions that the new poetry took, sometimes by the
same poet. Either there were surrealist free-association techniques,
often combined with an immediacy of a colloquial speaking voice
(as in Beat-influenced poetry) or there was a tendency towards
abstract constructions. Either poetry tended towards the loose
rhythms of prose or the poems might be made up of contrasting
juxtapositions of material or employ visual typographical effects. It
was 'open' rather than 'closed' in form, and its methods of construc-
tion were more likely to be private associations than sustained logic.
It was either extremely subjective or extremely public, either hermeti-
cally sealed against interpretation or openly addressed to a wider
readership than is usual for poetry. The shared assumption
among such diverse poets as Chitre, Nandy and Mehrotra was
that something had happened, some cultural shift that required
expression through a radically different kind of verse than in the

immediate past; they, however, recognized that such poetry had its own tradition in earlier revolutionary and avant-garde writers.

An early statement of this aesthetic is Chitre's Introduction to his *Anthology of Marathi Poetry* (1967). Starting with the uprootedness of the modern mind and the disintegration of traditional culture, Chitre asserts that at present poetry 'begins either with a total denial of moral values or in the spirit of unflinching moral commitment.' Mysticism, anarchy and cries for order are the only kinds of poetic expression. Chitre praises the Marathi poet Mardheker for his obscurity: 'the obscurity arising out of a specific communication-technique based on his private poetics'. It is the defiant obscurity of modern poetry in the face of hackneyed techniques of communication; to understand the poetry we must 'grasp the grammar of the poet's individual consciousness.' Mardheker used musical organization of imagery and counterpoint. Chitre offers his own aesthetic of the avant-garde. He claims that 'anything creative challenges, nullifies all previous moulds of consciousness'. New speech rhythms, new syntax or vocabulary or imagery, result from a 'revolutionary structural upheaval deep within the creative poet's personality'. Such changes show a change in society itself during a generation. A major poet breaks away from previous modes of consciousness and thus will always be obscure to most readers. He or she will, like Mardheker or Kolatkar in Marathi, 'hit upon the new' and crash 'into the unknown', annihilating in the process the habitual poetics of past generations. Chitre concludes his introduction by claiming that all kinds of knowledge and experience are now part of what goes into poetry. Allen Ginsberg and LeRoi Jones are published in Marathi, Indians read Pablo Neruda, Rilke, Rimbaud, Kafka, 'a fantastic conglomeration of clashing realities ... visions ... a living confusion'.

Some of the key concepts here are: new formal structures; new speech patterns reflecting a shift in consciousness which destroys the old; a shift in consciousness caused by the conglomeration of cultural influences and new and increased communication since the Second World War, which has shocked traditional societies and while making life absurd created new kinds of meaningfulness. In other words great poetry expresses a new consciousness, and there has been a new consciousness in recent decades; therefore there is a need for a new poetry which will either express the anarchy of the time or impose order on it by some alignment of what would other-

wise seem incongruous. Its form is likely to be a musical orga-
nization in space rather than logical exposition of ideas, thoughts
and feelings.

In 'The Emperor Has No Clothes' (*Chandrabhaga* 3, 1980 and 7,
1982) Mehrotra, another of the experimentalists, complains about
the absence of excitement and despair on the Indian English poetry
scene, the kind of extreme emotions that come when a major new
work of art appears, such as Eliot's 'The Love Song of J. Alfred
Prufrock', which radically changes the direction of literature while
at the same time being a reflection of a new state of contemporary
consciousness. Such a work challenges literature still written in
older modes. For Mehrotra, Kolatkar's *Jejuri* has such a significance
in its idiomatic, concise precision. Mehrotra sees in the modern
period a rift between language and experience; while poetry reflects
this disintegration, being what George Steiner calls 'structured
debris', it is necessary to forge a personal language to express the
particularities of experience.

'The Emperor Has No Clothes' attacks Parthasarathy's poetics
and reveals Mehrotra's own ideas about the direction Indian poetry
should take. He argues that literature has both near (regional
language) and distant (international) relatives and calls Partha-
sarathy's concern with reintegration into Tamil tradition the
provincialism of a 'Hindu revivalist mind'. An Indian English
poem is a 'construct, housing two or more ways of seeing; four-
eyed'. 'The native idiom ... has to seep through the English
poem ...; how could it not?' Each poet writes in a distinctive
idiolect. 'Ramanujan's consists of English–Kannada–Tamil,
Kolatkar's of English–Marathi–Bombay Hindi, Mahapatra's of
English–Oriya, and so on. Each poet belongs to a tribe of one or
two, seldom more than of six or eight':

Most Indian English poets are bilingual and, though it is too early to say how
or where, the other language is the torsional force in their work in the same
way that Russian presses on 'Nabokese' and non-native French, German and
English glow beneath Borges' Spanish. Indian English literature belongs
with the work of these new 'esperantists'.

Where Parthasarathy sees a specific gap inherited from coloni-
alism between Indian experience and the English language, Mehrotra
sees a general modern crisis. 'The rift, moreover, does not vary from
place to place', the Indian English poet does not suffer from a
specific alienation brought about by colonialism; the poet must

'hammer out' a 'most personal' style from language.

Believing that 'Poetry is perception's flames', Mehrotra accuses Parthasarathy of writing in a language of generalizations, without specificity, concreteness or immediacy. He complains that such poetry does not arise from attentively seeing and listening. Besides demanding that poetry be made of specifics, he challenges Parthasarathy's claim that Indians, not being heirs to a European cultural tradition, should aim at an unreverberant use of English. Where Parthasarathy argues that an Indian poet will not feel the various nuances of English words and expressions, Mehrotra claims that a writer uses words with associations gained through reading. These are two radically different notions of poetic language. Parthasarathy thinks of language as communication within a specific culture; Mehrotra regards language as dead material to which the poet gives life in the making of the poem. Such art builds on art and has its own international tradition(s) in which each poet shares according to his personal situation and history.

While the possible evolution of Mehrotra's aesthetics will need to be looked at more fully when discussing his poetry, it is clear that he began with an interest in surrealist notions of chance and constructivist concepts of art as object. These two views come together in the importance of the image. A poem is a construction of images, finding its inspiration in such varied sources as memory, the trivia of modern life and humorous, unexpected juxtapositions. Later he argues for the superiority of the particular over the general and for 'location—whether cultural, geographical, or fictive'. He wants 'luminous details'. A poem is seen as an artifical and ideal order using particularized materials. While such an aesthetic would seem to imply a musical-spatial, rather than a rational, argumentative structure, the concern with location and specifics allows for poems which treat of the external world rather than solely of the subjective. Where Chitre seems to feel poetry reflects shifts in consciousness expressed in radically new, unpredictable ways, Mehrotra's aesthetic requires that some kind of real or imagined world be ordered and given a particularized existence. While responding to a crisis in the relationship between language and experience, the poem need not be radically open in form.

When Jayanta Mahapatra writes about poetry it is as an expression of his inner world and problems about the relationship between the self and reality. In an essay published in *The Literary*

Criterion (xv, no. 1, 1980, pp. 27–36) Mahapatra speaks of a poet's mental landscape, an 'inner world of his own making—a world spaced by his own life, of secret allusions, of desire and agony, of a constantly changing alignment between dream and reality.' Rather than moral choices, Mahapatra speaks of being 'uncertain' of his 'very existence' and of groping from poem to poem for the key to human understanding. In 'Face to Face with the Contemporary Poem' (*Journal of Literary Studies*, vol. 6, no. 1–2, June 1983, pp. 9–17, Utkal University, Bhubaneswar), he says of poetry 'that a part of the mystery of one's self comes out' but rather than the content being of significance 'the act of making or writing the poem itself becomes a *full* experience.' A 'great poem lets us embark on a sort of journey or voyage through symbols and allusions to encompass the human condition.' Mahapatra speaks of the poem as an experience reflecting the processes of the poet's mind:

When the 'confessional' poetry of the sixties in America (markedly) gave way to a new 'surrealism', it evidenced a new ambiguity—not what the lay or common reader could follow, not something he had come to regard as poetry through the years. Generally speaking, today's poem utilizes a number of images and symbols to form a whole, leaving the reader to extricate himself with the valid meaning or argument from them. Thus the reader is left to find out his own meaning from the poem; this, I admit painfully, is true of much of the poetry I have written. If contemporary life is no longer what it was, say, twenty-five years back, can one expect the same content, the same form, the same substance from contemporary poems?

It is useful to see how these different poetics influence or are reflected in reviews. There are signs of an evolving, but still confused, experimentalist poetic in *Gray Book*, with which Mahapatra and Deba Patnaik were associated. Patnaik's review of Mahapatra's first two volumes of poetry in *Gray Book I* sounds at times like Ezekiel ('the economy of words and clarity of perception'), but there are also new, quite contrary critical concepts: 'In these poems words converge into or hover around a distinct image without using one explicitly.' Rather than mature knowledge, Mahapatra's poetry, Patnaik claims, 'expresses a sense of tentativeness'. Patnaik's review of Pritish Nandy's poetry calls attention to the 'flow of vivifying impressions and images—montages against the poet's sifting and shifting mind' and mentions the beauty in juxtapositions in which 'desire, memory, dream and silence' are counterpointed by a world of reality. Although Patnaik seems to fluctuate between various kinds of poetics, including praise of simple language and sincerity, the kind of comments I have quoted could be the basis for a shared aesthetic by Mahapatra, as well as the early Nandy, Chitre and Kolatkar.

In Mehrotra's review of de Souza's *Fix* (*Times of India*, 10 February 1980), form, personal voice, distance and concern with the local are assumed to be significant. When Mehrotra compliments de Souza on letting her feelings settle down before writing of personal hurts, or when he speaks of the bristling surface of her poetry and its characters, he appears to have in mind something different from Ezekiel's wisdom and mature reflection of experience communicated through images. He appears to have an idea of the poem as object, as a surface covering and distanced from personal experience. At the same time, he feels poems should be made from Indian materials (memories, characters, situations) and be about being Indian. The assumptions are those of his later poetry which is made from a pattern of personal memories and local allusions and often concerns his childhood and local society in Allahabad.

As several poets reviewed Manohar Shetty's first book, *A Guarded Space* (1981), it is possible to offer a few comparative examples of differences in critical assumptions and concerns. Daruwalla's review (*Indian Horizons*, 4 November 1982, pp. 51–3) mentions images, craftsmanship, 'powerful vignettes, which really bring the neighbourhood alive', 'control', and discusses details of rhyme, metaphor and dynamics. The emphasis is on craftsmanship. By contrast Jayanta Mahapatra's review (*The Telegraph*, Calcutta) is more focused on the subliminal private world behind the poem: 'Shetty is certainly adept at using the English language for those indescribable things that all of us have felt inside of us but haven't been somehow able to articulate'; 'its fascinating but dark ending'; 'The process of introspection becomes complete'; 'the unspoken menace of death'; 'We are at the centre of things, and we watch our lives being thrown back at us for us to see our revealed selves': 'The tightness and accuracy of construction; the unforgettable silence that is held in the world of his poems, helps to substantiate that feeling which throbs in our bones.'

There is a different aesthetic in Mahapatra's review of Shetty's poems, which is not similar to the shared assumptions and varied emphases of Ezekiel, Daruwalla, Parthasarathy and Peeradina. The poem is a 'construction' (presumably Mehrotra would agree) which brings to light otherwise unshaped, often inarticulate, deeply introspective feelings. The construction reveals the subliminal, the indescribable, the inarticulate, the world of silence, the unspoken, that which is felt in the bones. Such a view of poetry (which describes Mahapatra's own work) might be said to have similarities to Chitre's claim that major poetry expresses new kinds of consciousness. Although Chitre sees such consciousness as part of a cultural rupture, radical shifts in sensibility, Mahapatra assumes a universality of processes of extreme introspection ('feeling which throbs in our bones', 'Things that all of us have felt inside of us'). Chitre's radical poetics are still wedded to the modernist concern with cultural crisis; Mahapatra's assumptions are part of a new period of sensibility in which art is seen less as object than as a structure of often contradictory, unresolved, deep feelings.

Since Mahapatra's poetry is different from the mainstream of Indian verse, it is of interest how other poets have tried to find a place for him within existing canons of taste. Many critics have been content to remark on his use of Indian landscape. Parthasarathy says that Ezekiel and Daruwalla are 'intensely aware' of their 'environment'. 'Mahapatra observes similar incongruities in the Indian landscape.' In his preface to his selection of Mahapatra's poems Parthasarathy says, 'Mahapatra explores the intricacies of human relationships, especially those of love.' Such observations do not suggest what is different about Mahapatra's writing. Daruwalla's comments come no closer. 'Jayanta Mahapatra writes on the countryside.' 'His metaphors carry the reek of freshly upturned earth.' But Daruwalla does say that the 'landscape is utilized to set him off on his pensive reveries.'

'Pensive reverie' might be a starting point for a discussion of Mahapatra's poetry. Meena Alexander's essay, 'Jayanta Mahapatra: A Poetry of Decreation' (*The Journal of Commonwealth Literature*, vol. 18, 1, 1983, pp. 42–7) begins by describing a moment when she and Mahapatra observed the twilight together in Cuttack. Alexander, a poet of whom Mahapatra has spoken favourably and who has appeared in his *Chandrabhaga*, has written obscure poems in a private symbolism based upon images of the Indian landscape. In her essay she speaks of Mahapatra's 'quality of attention which is the finest refinement of desire', establishing 'a fragile self waiting'. But 'language fails us, even as we struggle to understand'. Alexander writes of Mahapatra's 'withdrawal of the will, the power of a visionary consciousness filling up the place the will had bent to its own purposes.' In India the writer has an 'anguished need to define a self, out of the bottomless flow of time.' Although the world must be 'remade through the visionary instinct' there is no 'real solid self'; the movement out of such darkness, 'the gesture of grace involves an attentive waiting, emptying out of the self, waiting, watching, witnessing.'

This is a rather different kind of criticism from that seen before in India, although perhaps anticipated by Chitre's Introduction. Instead of the poem as the crystallization of images of maturely considered experience, the focus has shifted to the mind's awareness of unwilled feelings arising during moments of silence, perceptions of feelings which are seldom articulated and which are normally suppressed for the sake of daily survival. Instead of the willed self, with its responsibility, the existence of the self is at least temporarily questioned. While only the reality of the external world exists, even its reality is in doubt; a poem is a construction made by allowing such subversive feelings to arise; they may not be resolved within a poem. For the critic the poem itself becomes less important than the attention, the desire, the vision, the 'cosmogony', the kinds of symbols and consciousness exhibited throughout an author's work.

Such a criticism became necessary when Mahapatra in particular, but also such other Indian poets as Alexander, began writing a new, puzzling, obscure kind of poetry, filled with private symbols, concerned with other kinds of feelings than those usually felt in social situations. In this poetry landscape often figures prominently as the poet is concerned with the problematic or fragile nature of the self and its relationship to external reality.

I have suggested that new poetry at first is promoted by the poets themselves as are the specific values by which it is judged. In India Ezekiel's concern with craftsmanship, intellectualized observations of life, moral realism and integration of personality ousted the amateurism, late romanticism, aestheticism, nationalist subject matter and vague spiritualism which were characteristic of Indian English poetry before and at independence. The standards of Ezekiel created the main critical discourse which others, notably Parthasarathy, developed in accordance with their own work. Parthasarathy has put more emphasis on the purity of image, problems of tone and association, the need to locate writing within a tradition, and themes reflecting the problems of biculturalism.

In contrast to the criticism of Ezekiel, Daruwalla and Partha-sarathy are the comments on poetry by the experimental writers

according to which a poem is both a constructed object and a record
of the inner life. In the cases of Chitre and Mahapatra the poetry is a
record of an evolving consciousness, with all its desires, guilts,
frustrations, contradictions and false starts. Mehrotra and Maha-
patra put emphasis on memory as a source, and both require poetry
to reflect the specific locale of the writer, although this may be more
implied than given in detail. These three, along with Meena Alexander
(and, apparently, although he does not write criticism, Arun
Kolatkar) regard a poem as a construction which in its open
structure reflects or is part of the act of making poetry.

CHAPTER SIX

Ezekiel and His Influence

Of the group of poets attempting to create a modern English poetry in India, Nissim Ezekiel soon emerged as the leader who advised others, set standards and created places of publication. His main significance is not, however, as a promoter of poetry; it is in his will to be a poet, his continuing involvement in the poetry scene and the ways in which the developing body of his work expresses his personal quest for a satisfactory way of living in the modern world. Whereas previously Indian English verse was a hobby, something done in spare moments, Ezekiel made it central to his life. Others wrote poems, he wrote poetry. The difference is reflected in his craftsmanship and purposefulness; this is as much a matter of will as of talent. Ezekiel brought a sense of discipline, self-criticism and mastery to Indian English poetry. He was the first Indian poet to have such a professional attitude.

He knew very early what he wanted; he wanted precision of diction and imagery and what I would describe as moral purpose, which was structurally embodied in the rounding-off of a poem with an observation. He aimed at a contemporary manner which would voice modern concerns and which in style and theme would avoid the dated provincialism of colonial verse. When styles throughout the English-speaking world changed in the 1960s from formality to openness, Ezekiel's poetry took a parallel direction. He constantly renewed himself in his work and kept up with the times. Colonial, provincial, amateur poetry is old-fashioned; art must reflect the present and be part of its day and age.

Life in the city, sexuality, the problems of marriage, the need to overcome alienation and to create integration among the various aspects of his character are Ezekiel's early and continuing themes.

Such modern characteristics as irony, heightened critical self-con-
sciousness, strong intellectual purpose (in contrast to philosophi-
zing in verse), a multiplicity of tones, the artistic distancing of
emotion through a persona were among his contributions to Indian
poetry. There is a distinct personality expressed in the voice, themes
and style. Life is seen as a quest for wholeness, for intellectual and
spiritual satisfaction, for maturity. While the aim is salvation of the
spirit from distractions and obsessions, it is grounded in the physi-
cal and social. The quest essentially concerns how to live happily,
calmly, ethically as an integrated human being.

Ezekiel showed that it was possible to write about oneself with-
out being self-consciously Indian and that an Indian poetry could
express the experiences of the educated and urbanized and need not
be obsessed with mythology, peasants and nationalist slogans. With
him a post-colonial poetry started which reflects the lives and identities
that an increasing number of educated Indians knew or would
seek. Being a Jew and raised as a secular rationalist by his scientist
father made him an outsider to Hindu-Muslim culture; it is his
very outsiderness, his marginality, which makes him a represen-
tative voice of the urbanized, western-educated Indian.

In his first volume of poetry, *A Time to Change* (Fortune Press,
London, 1952), the title poem is a moral allegory using the journey
and quest motif. There are Old Testament echoes reminiscent of the
Book of Psalms or the prophets; Ezekiel in London could be the
Jews in Babylon corrupted by unlawful desires, strange gods and
defiled by foreign practices: "We who leave the house in April,
Lord, / How shall we return?' The subject is a mind tormented by
awareness of following false gods, disgusted by continuing restless-
ness while desiring stability, quiet, discipline, purpose, order. This
is expressed rather in terms of achieving, building, ownership,
workmanship, planting, than renunciation, withdrawal or purga-
tion. The outlook is Judaic, not Christian. His concerns are man-
hood, loving, family and proper conduct which redeems 'the private
country of the mind / Where the worser part, as Socrates would say, /
Presides'. In these early poems desire and imagination lead the mind
into unquietness; the quest is for a way which will offer wholeness
and bring such restlessness to an end. Although 'A Time to Change'
shifts abruptly, angularly among its multiplicity of themes and
kinds of experience, it is characterized by clarity, precision, logic,
statement, resolution and by concern with moral being as revealed

through social conduct. It is a complex poem, part lament, part prayer.

The writing of poetry is treated as a moral act and a prayer; art is, for Ezekiel, the product of a secular moral conscience, its hopes and desires—

> Redeemed with prayer
> The aspiration
> Found again
> I start again
> With secret faults concealed no more.
>
> For hours and days
> The singing voice
> To utter praise
> A bit of land
> A woman too
> Grapes or figs
> And metaphors
> Insight illumination
> Secret faults concealed no more.

Many of the poems concern conduct, judgement, behaviour or how, as in 'On an African Mask', 'passion of mind or heart / Acquire the equilibrium of art'. Such equilibrium between body and soul, heart and mind is the desired state in contrast to 'The Double Horror', a poem which begins 'I am corrupted by the world' and concludes 'infected I corrupt the world'. 'On meeting a Pedant' begins 'Words, looks, gestures, everything betrays / The unquiet mind, the emptiness within'. 'Robert' begins 'The way to do it, Robert said':

> And then I saw him clearly, the long
> Epic story of his errors shouted
> Deceptively of courage, hope and song,
> But every small endeavour had been routed.

Although the poems in *A Time to Change* range in manner, rhythm and style there is an underlying consistency of preoccupation in Ezekiel's desire for a lucid personal poetic voice in which emotion and reason will be balanced:

> ... let me always feel
> The presence of the golden mean
> Between the elan of desire
> And the rational faculties.

The poem 'Poetry' contrasts a 'poem' which is 'an episode' with 'poetry' which is 'something more'. 'Something to Pursue' argues that 'There is a way' which may be followed 'Through works or poetry' or 'From works to poetry' or 'from poetry to something else'. Ezekiel recommends 'Order and incantation, calm / Earnest, confident creation' in words and action, poetry and prayer. The aim is 'a limpid style of life / Whose texture is poetry'. Often the city is viewed as a place of confusing distractions and waste of spirit. The aim is not stasis but rather renewal, an acceptance of change, to be 'young again' while achieving a wholeness or unity of personality.

Redemption and rebirth of the spirit, as it governs behaviour and as exemplified by poetry, is the central theme of *A Time to Change*. The concern with spiritual wholeness takes various forms including love, religion, poetry and style of life. Often varied themes appear in the same poem as they are part of the quest. 'To a Certain Lady' proclaims that while 'Change is permanent and real' 'the dancing moments of a kiss / Are real too'. Life requires 'contact with the unknown and the strange / A feeling for the mystery'. Love sharpens 'our responses to the colours of creation'.

This is poetry of the moral intelligence attempting to find balance between various needs and desires; the poems are concerned with how to live sanely, fully and morally in the secular world. Characteristics of the poems are intelligence, dedication, seriousness, self-critical awareness, and a voice trying to find an appropriate mode of expression. Ezekiel's problem will be to find an appropriate style for what is rather a poetry of a mind thinking about feelings than the expression of emotion.

Sixty Poems (privately printed, Bombay, 1953) consists of eighteen new poems written since *A Time to Change*, along with unpublished work from 1945 to 1951. As early as the 1945–8 group, Ezekiel's verse had the same moral concerns and plainness of style:

> The problem is to put our acts
> Upon a shelf in clean labelled bottles;

> To move within the depths
> And fill the sources of our daily being.

The newer poems tend towards rhyme, regular rhythm and logical argumentation through metaphor and imagery. Thoughts and syntax are better phrased to fit the lines, which in turn expand into verse paragraphs. In 'A Poem of Dedication' the Ecclesiastes imagery of seasonal change as an expression of the organic is blended with imagery of flowing rivers into a sustained logical exposition:

> There is a landscape certainly, the sea
> Among its broad realities, attracts
> Because it is a symbol of the free
> Demoniac life within,
> Hardly suggested by the surface facts ...

> Both poetry and living illustrate:
> Each season brings its own peculiar fruits,
> A time to act, a time to contemplate.

The poetry expresses a complex modern mind attempting to integrate and order experience through an appropriate style in which imagery and allusion are part of thought.

By the time of *The Third* (privately printed, Bombay, 1959), Ezekiel had developed a personal if still somewhat limited manner, now based on balanced rhythms and rhyme while playing on clichés, idioms and sayings. Despite the modern use of colloquial odds and ends of ready-made speech, Ezekiel's is not a modernist poetry concerned with cultural and political crisis. But then in the 1950s the modernist tradition was at a low ebb and many poets were reasserting the values of the well-made conversational poem. In Ezekiel's case the personal is distanced as the mind observes, generalizes, abstracts and judges; intellectual control is reflected in the regularity of rhyme and metre.

The Third is stylistically more unified than the earlier books. Ezekiel appears to have learned from Yeats how to make poems about the self while standing at a distance; the stance is that of an observer intellectually discussing personal emotions and conduct in abstractions. Yet the generalities are made poetic through such quiet, subdued metaphors as 'heart at play' and 'cold, determined intellect', which both summarize and suggest. The plainness of style has the advantage of unobtrusively revitalizing what have become clichés. In his poems Ezekiel establishes a persona of mature wisdom, although at the time of publication of *The Third* he was only thirty-five years old. In 'Division' he looks back on his marriage:

> With cold, determined intellect
> I watched the heart at play,
> And heard it sing of blessedness
> Upon a nuptial day,
> I warned it of a changing time
> It would not sing that way.

The problems and disappointments of marriage will become a major theme, alongside new temptations of the flesh and an awareness of repressed, deep, wild emotions. 'Midmonsoon Madness' contrasts the desire to 'smash it up and start again' with the recognition that to go away would probably change nothing: 'the future stuff of dreams / repeating what has always been'. 'What Frightens Me' begins: 'Myself examined frightens me' and speaks of the contrast 'Between the self-protective self' masked 'And the self naked'. As the poems speak of the disillusionments of marriage and the temptations of new loves they move towards the confessional.

By the late 1950s Ezekiel's verse reveals a moral intelligence confused by the experience of marriage; while he is critical of his self-deceptions and lack of control over emotions, disillusion is recognized as something that was previously known about and that was expected. Despite this he had hoped love in marriage would bring the unity of self he wanted. A desire to flee is opposed by awareness that outside marriage he would still be himself, carrying the same inner baggage of unsatisfied lust, fantasies, hopes and dissatisfactions. Ezekiel's reflective intelligence remains in control, assessing conflicting feelings in search of a way to live which will be wise, unified and bring emotional renewal. The distance travelled from the certainties of *A Time to Change* and 'A Poem of Dedication' in *Sixty Poems* to *The Unfinished Man* (Writers Workshop, Calcutta, 1960) is striking.

A significance of the poems written in 1959, published in *The Unfinished Man*, is indicated by the title, an explicit recognition of another time of change. Instead of wholeness and equipoise, the poems speak of a time of incompleteness and record a period of personal purgatory concluding with the possibility of redemption. The ten poems are a sequence concerning the discontents of a supposedly settled life; they are related more by theme than by story. The first poem contrasts the city man with his dreams of the natural world. Imagery from nature is used to symbolize the innocence, freedom and depth of vision not found among the distractions of the city. In 'Urban' the subject 'never sees the skies', never feels the 'shadows of the night', 'welcomes neither sun nor rain. / His landscape has no depth or height'. But instead of leaving the city, his mind turns to 'kindred clamour close at hand'. Essentially a poem about bad faith ('The river which he claims he loves') and lack of will, its tone is admonitory. While the abstractness of imagery suggests the subject's lack of depth of perception, the images suggest more than is said. The mind's 'traffic' is a generalized image but perfectly links the urban theme with the man's distractions, while 'kindred clamour' slyly introduces the family as one cause of the problem.

While 'Enterprise' concludes 'Home is where we have to gather grace', in 'A Morning Walk' the 'He' has 'dreamt of being lost / Upon a hill too high for him'. He sees the city and its 'million purgatorial lanes'. He asks whether he is 'among the men of straw' who delude themselves that they are free. He knows that nothing will change, 'his will is like the morning dew'; he belongs to the city, 'an active fool.' In contrast to the discontents of urban life, the scene of 'Love Sonnet' moves to the hill from which the lovers descend to look 'inquiringly at road and sky' while thinking of sexual pleasure ('to die'). The redeeming possibilities of love are taken up by 'Commitment' in which the dangers of passion are superior to the lost men

> Who wanted only quiet lives
> And failed to count the growing cost
> Of cushy jobs or unloved wives.

'Event' distinguishes between what is actually felt and acting according to ideas of what should be felt. The woman, naked, naive, talks of trivia and offers sex, while the speaker (the 'he' has become an 'I'), conscious of how the flow of time has 'become a drift', is aware that they both are living in 'day-dreams ... Reflections of the cheated mind'. The next poem sarcastically traces the progress of

'Marriage' from the paradisial complacency of lovers who assume they will never be separated to their fall from grace. A key passage is the fourth stanza with the puns on 'came':

> However many times we came
> Apart, we came together. The same
> Thing over and over again.
> Then suddenly the mark of Cain.

Rather than a sense of intimacy and unity, the sexual act has resulted in separateness and monotony. The penultimate poem in *The Unfinished Man* is 'Case Study'. After admitting wasting time on politics and 'useless knowledge' and once more complaining of marriage as a hell ('A man is damned in that domestic game'), the speaker realizes the need for some decisive action: 'The pattern will remain, unless you break / It with a sudden jerk'. 'Jamini Roy' concludes the volume by offering that painter as an example of someone who found a solution to 'adult fantasies / Of sex and power-ridden lives'. 'Jamini Roy' appears to resolve the earlier problems by showing how to find renewed joy in life; it is claimed that an art of assent rather than hostility, and rising above one's self to give voice to the 'people', bears fruit.

The Unfinished Man is remarkable in its self-scrutinizing psychology and polished craft. The volume moves from generalization towards the personal, from complaint to decision and ideal. Variety is created by various juxtapositions; there are recurring situations, themes and images. The general regularity of strict traditional metre and rhyme is appropriate to the intellectual concerns and logical pressure, making the changes of stanzaic shapes and rhyme schemes appear more varied than they really are. The poems show the advantages of a formal, reflective manner in which images make their metaphoric point without calling attention to themselves and in which allegories and symbols are used without fuss and then dropped without causing a sense of incompletion. The rounding-off of each poem with a conclusion provides satisfying formal closure to what are unresolved situations. There is terseness, irony, wit, lucidity, depth and seriousness. Ezekiel showed how to avoid the excesses of romanticism when writing about the self and its concerns, when making art based on autobiography.

The Adamic vision desired in 'Jamini Roy' can be seen emerging in *The Exact Name* (1965), twenty poems Ezekiel wrote between 1960 and 1964. 'Philosophy' rejects the kind of intellectual analysis which destroys the reality of experience:

> What cannot be explained, do not explain.

> The mundane language of the senses sings
> Its own interpretations. Common things
> Become, by virtue of their commonness,
> An argument against the nakedness
> That dies of cold to find the truth it brings.

This is followed by 'Night of the Scorpion', in which Ezekiel recalls the behaviour of 'the peasants', his father, his mother and a holy man when his mother was poisoned by a scorpion's sting. Here the aim is to find poetry in ordinary reality as observed, known, felt, experienced rather than as the intellect thinks it should be. While the peasants pray and speak of incarnations, his father, 'sceptic, rationalist', tries 'every curse and blessing, / powder, mixture, herb and hybrid' and a holy man performs a rite. After a day the poison is no longer felt and, in a final irony, his mother, in contrast to the previous feverish activity centred upon her, makes a typical motherly comment:

> My mother only said
> Thank God the scorpion picked on me
> and spared my children.

The 'Thank God' is doubly ironic as it is a commonplace expression of speech in contrast to all the previous religious and superstitious activity. Ezekiel's purpose is not, however, an expression of scepticism but rather the exact notation of what he saw as a child. The aim is not to explain but to make real by naming, by saying 'common things'. The poem is a new direction, a vision of ordinary reality, especially of Indian life, unmediated by cold intellect. The new purpose is seen in the poem's style, unrhymed, with line lengths shaped by natural syntactical units and rhythm created by the cadences of the speaking voice into a long verse paragraph, rather than the stanzaic structure used in earlier poems. While Ezekiel used free verse in many early poems before the purposefully stylized high regularity of *The Unfinished Man*, his poetry increasingly from the mid 1960s onwards is different in being written for oral delivery. It is poetry of the spoken voice as much as or more than for the printed page.

A similar focus on ordinary events of Indian life is found in the satiric sketches in the four 'In India' poems with their various communal groups who regardless of their behaviour ('bullied, stole … bragged … Broke') 'never missed their prayers' and the Indian women who at parties 'do not talk, / of course, they do not kiss'. In 'The Visitor' the poet awaits 'An angel in disguise, perhaps, / Or a temptation in unlikely shape?' but instead is visited by someone who has no other purpose but to 'kill a little time'. The poem shows what should be known, 'The ordinariness of most events'. Several of the other poems, such as 'Progress', 'A Warning', 'Virginal' and 'Beachscene' are also concerned with naming reality in contrast to imagined ideals. 'Virginal' argues 'The Universe is much too small to hold / Your longing for a lover and a child'; 'A Warning' ends 'Better hold to the seawall: / I don't want to hear you scream'.

As after his break with the Writers Workshop Ezekiel did not publish a new volume of verse for eleven years—although selections from manuscripts appeared in the special Ezekiel issue of the American *Journal of South Asian Literature* (XI, no. 3, 4, 1976)—the next phases of his work are represented by the collections *Hymns in Darkness* (1976) and *Latter-Day Psalms* (1982). 'Background, Casually', a poem first published during 1965, is a verse autobiography tracing what Ezekiel saw as the main stages of his life to date. It records his childhood when

> I went to Roman Catholic school,
> A mugging Jew among the wolves.
> They told me I had killed the Christ,
> That year I won the scripture prize.
> A Muslim sportsman boxed my ears.

After going abroad at twenty-two to a life of 'Philosophy, / Poverty and Poetry' in a 'basement room', he learns he 'had failed' and returns to India, ill at ease, marries, and afterwards discovers 'that verse betrays' and his dreams 'were all of words'. He now takes 'a plainer view: / The wise survive':

> I have made my commitments now.
> This is one: to stay where I am,
> As others choose to give themselves
> In some remote and backward place.
> My backward place is where I am.

Ezekiel's focus had shifted from the quest for integration to an acceptance of the actualities and the ordinariness of life. The senses, survival, even worldly prizes became worthy of attention. The task was now to describe the real and this led him to a greater use of Indian subject matter.

The poems in 'Indian English' (1967–72) are part of his commitment to 'stay where I am' and treat of ordinary life. These poems are, I think, often misunderstood as simply satire of the Gujarati-influenced English often used in Bombay. As most educated Indians have aimed at speaking approved British English, there has been no attempt by poets to use local varieties in the way Nigerian and West Indian writers of serious literature mix dialect, patois or various shades of supposedly sub-standard with standard English; of the major Indian poets perhaps only Kamala Das unselfconsciously uses Indianized forms of English. Ezekiel's poems might be seen as a step towards using local speech in serious verse. While some of the Indian English poems do make use of the kind of humour associated with dialect verse, they are not simple satire at the expense of incompetent mastery of a foreign language. Language reveals the speaker's mind and social context; clichés, triteness, unintended puns are among the devices used to imply hypocrisy, pretence, limited opportunities and confusion. 'Goodbye Party for Miss Pushpa T. S.' is a satiric self-revelation of the speaker. He is uncertain whether she is going abroad 'in two three days', does not understand why she smiles when he refers to her 'internal sweetness', speaks of her 'very high family' but cannot remember where they live and drifts off into his own memories of a visit to his family in Surat where the cooking was good. The situation is demeaning to Miss Pushpa who is socially required to listen to such speeches and afterwards will be expected to 'do summing up'. 'The Patriot' is a portrait of a confused mind which has withdrawn into a parody of Gandhiism, mistaking platitudes for thought and action. In a modern India with Pakistan and China as neighbours the patriot's only solution to national problems is to drink milk and talk of brotherly love ('Though some are having funny habits'). 'The Professor' also is an example of mental confusion and superficiality. All his children 'are well settled in life' but 'Every family must have black sheep' (apparently because some of his children do not have cars). The final word of the poem, 'backside', describes him fittingly. 'Irani Restaurant

Instructions' reveals similar confusions: 'Do not write letter ...
Do not comb ... If not satisfied tell us ... God is great'. 'The
Railway Clerk' is a more complex poem which moves from satire
to sympathy. The poor English is a reflection of the half-educated
clerk's social and economic situation. After reading the poem we
are likely to see the opening lines in a new light although resentful-
ness is part of the psychology.

The poems in Indian English can be seen as part of an awareness
that confused thought and speech, slogans, and talk of traditions
contribute to the unchanging poverty of the masses and their ex-
ploitation. The unwillingness of 'The Patriot' and 'The Professor' to
acknowledge reality, the way they think in readymade, comforting,
slipshod ideas, slogans and phrases, might be contrasted with
Ezekiel's own awareness of Indian social reality. 'The Truth
about the Floods', 'Rural Suite', 'Undertrial Prisoners' and
'Poverty Poem' reflect his social and political concerns, which
began with his early involvement in the Royist movement and
union organizing and which were later seen in the founding of
Quest and the editing of *Freedom First*. 'The Truth about the
Floods' is a found poem, a technique of editing prose into verse
by minor revisions and creating lines from syntactical units. Here
the contrast is between the government officials who can only
hand out statistics and complain that nature 'conspired against
them' and the unaided, disaster-stricken villagers who fear the
officials. When a relief party does arrive, it consists of five stu-
dents who distribute some biscuits, take pictures and quietly
leave.

The earlier attempt at self-integration had failed and the many
parts of Ezekiel's life had refused to fuse into a unity. Sexual desire,
love, family, politics, philosophy, poetry, the spiritual had become
separate and would not go back together again. His poems increas-
ingly reflect a number of distinct lives he led which, while often
parallel, sometimes diverge. The concern with the real, the physical,
the practical, for example, contrasts with a new developing interest
in the spiritual which followed experimentation with LSD; there are
poems recording many love affairs alongside poems about Zen and
Tao philosophy. His poetry rapidly goes through phases as he turns
to new techniques and kinds of poems, such as the poster, postcard
and passion poems between 1972 and 1975. What remains constant
is the desire for continual renewal, to remain young at heart, the

attractions of sex, and the awareness that such restlessness, although necessary to avoid the self-satisfied, confused coziness of 'The Professor', does not lead to satisfaction and that something else is needed to calm the mind, to satisfy the spirit. Ezekiel is particularly concerned not to achieve wholeness the way others do as they become older at the cost of abandoning many previous interests and forsaking new paths.

During the early and mid 1970s his poems celebrate the inarticulate and the ordinary, for their mystery, not their simplicities. In the 'Poster Poems' Ezekiel remembers his dying father attempting to speak the truths he had learned as he approached death: 'I felt the breath of his love / but could not hear a word'. Another 'Poster Poem' concludes 'Life is not as simple / as morality'. It is not the commonplace which is of value in itself; rather value comes from commitment, concern, involvement, passion. By contrast, 'The Neutral' is someone who makes 'love to many women / as to the same woman' and who signs manifestos, works on committees and joins political parties; but 'It made no difference. / The common language / hid my absence'.

Out of the new emphasis on sense experience, at the neglect of moral consistency, arose a need for the religious or spiritual to soothe the mind, as previously tranquillity was expected from wholeness of conscience. The discovery of a need for some God, however, is often expressed ironically. These are poems of the modern city man, unattached to any faith, sceptical of ritual and doctrine, but needing some kind of method, technique or belief to calm the self of its disquiet. The ironic, sceptical attitude is conveyed in the poems of 'The Egotist's Prayers':

> O well, if you insist,
> I'll do your will.
> Please try to make it coincide with mine.
>
> The price of wisdom
> is too high,
> but folly is expensive too.
> Strike a bargain with me, Lord.
> I'm not a man of ample means.

The sceptical, ironic attitude towards the divine finds expression in 'Hymns in Darkness' (1974), poems partly derived from the elliptical profundities of the Vedic hymns and, formally, from

the stanzaic shapes of their English translations. That Ezekiel's
'Hymns' are 'in darkness' suggests their deconstructive relation-
ship to the Sanskrit classics. These are not hymns celebrating the
divine unknowable darkness; these are tough, wry, obliquely
epigrammatic songs of the modern spirit unable to know any ulti-
mate reality beyond the life it experiences:

> All you have
> is the sense of reality,
> unfathomable
> as it yields its secrets
> slowly
> one
> by
> one.

Irritable, undeceived, lacking humility, unable to believe or dis-
believe, always conscious of 'breasts, thighs, buttocks', the speaker
knows that the 'darkness' with its dissatisfactions is superior to
routine and conventional behaviour: 'The enemy is God / as the
Unchanging One'. These then are poems which in a different form
and spirit return to the themes of Ezekiel's early books, but instead
of finding a way to redeem the spirit there is only a parody of the
negative way of the mystic, an emptying of the self of the vanity of
expecting redemption, an acceptance of change and the need for
renewal as the supreme truth in contrast to those who

> ... rot in families, in castes,
> in communities, in clubs,
> in political parties.
> They stay stable.

'Nudes 1978', a sequence of fourteen sonnets, uses varied angles
of perception to explore the relationship between reality and ways
of seeing. The poems play on various distinctions between nudeness
and nakedness. In ordinary usage nakedness is associated with
shame, while nude is more neutral yet refined in its associations.
Nakedness, however, is the natural state of being without clothes
whereas nudeness is often shown in cultural products such as art.
'Nudes 1978' might be the title of an artist's group of paintings or
sketches; the relationship of the nude to the naked is analogous to
poetry's relationship to reality. Although the poems themselves

seem 'naked' in being unrhymed, they are 'nude' in their fourteen-line form and such varied techniques as careful repetition and place-ment of key words, including the recurring allusions to nakedness and nudeness. Throughout the poems parallels are suggested between human sexual desire and the reality of its object, between the artist and the reality painted, and between poetry and its source. These are further poems which celebrate, by exploring, the nature of reality.

The sequence portrays such varied relationships between a man and a woman as desire of the other's body as a 'form' which gives pleasure, sensuality without love or enjoyment of the sexual act itself, loss of identity in sexuality, obsessively imagined pleasures, delight in sophisticated betrayals, progressive idealization of a body 'from nakedness to nudity', differing attitudes to 'the art of love', the way sexuality can develop into a 'cosmos' of 'the soul', and such apparent, although often misleading, characteristics as shyness and dominance. While the sequence ends with a return to the reality of nakedness, this too is a product of the 'desire' of the 'Artist of the nude', who, seeking a direct, unmediated route to reality, uses Zen philosophy.

Using a more distanced, cooler version of the confessional mode Ezekiel has made a complex statement about the nature of poetry and his own restlessness of spirit. 'Nudes', like the 'Hymns', concludes by affirming metaphorically a philosophy of the imme-diacy of the real:

> 'Yes, this is me as I am,'
> naked seen, seeing nakedness,
> named, flawed in detail,
> womanly and vulnerable.

But the nakedness of sonnet 14 is another poetic nude, a reality which no matter how detailed, flawed and directly perceived still must be 'named', just as the ordinary in *The Exact Name* had to be created through a conscious act of reflection. Ezekiel appears emotionally unable to leave sensual experience ungrounded in some larger intellectual or spiritual vision. In praising the reality of the actual he keeps moving towards a metareality, a seeing of the divine in the experiential.

His impatience with older forms of belief is expressed again in 'Latter-Day Psalms', which are replies to the Old Testament Psalms:

Give ear to new parables, unlike
the old ones, and to darker
sayings than our fathers passed
on to us.

...

How long are we to rely
on those marvellous things
in ancient Egypt?

Tell me of the
marvellous things in Nazi Germany.
Even with manna in our mouths,
we are not estranged from our lust.

The 'Psalms' show Ezekiel's increasing interest in his having been
born a Jew and in his heritage. Besides the use of Old Testament
material and references to Nazi Germany and the holocaust, Ezekiel
says in the concluding 'Psalm':

The images are beautiful birds
and colourful fish: they fly,
they swim in my Jewish consciousness.
God is a presence here
and his people are real.
I see their sins. I hear
His anger.

Now I am through with
the Psalms; they are
part of my flesh.

The often direct way in which Ezekiel has been a model for or
influence on other Indian poets can be seen in the themes, form,
manner and craft of the early poems of K. D. Katrak. There is a
similar use of confessional material reflected upon and intellec-
tualized from the standpoint of how to live. 'A Poem For My
Wedding Night' in *A Journal of the Way* (1968) sounds like
Ezekiel's early poetry in its stiff, regular rhythms, generalized
diction ('With missile, lust and war'), moral reflections, such
stylistic traits as inverted word order ('love relaxed and true') and
occasional lapses from the formalized colloquial into ready-made
lyric phrases of early-twentieth-century Georgian verse. At
times Katrak even alludes to Ezekiel's poems. The well-known

stanza of Ezekiel's 'A Time to Change' which begins

> To own a singing voice and a talking voice,
> A bit of land, a woman and a child or two,
> Accommodated to their needs and changing moods
> And patiently to build with these;
> Practising a singing and a talking voice
> Is all the creed a man of God requires

is alluded to in 'A Poem For My Wedding Night':

> A house, a piece of land
> A woman, wine and bread,
> Contentment, skill of hand
> Were virtues of the dead
> To live the life alone
> Circumscribed by choice,
> To listen to the bone,
> Practise the singing voice.

For many years Ezekiel was Katrak's 'hero' as well as an influence on his poetry. In 'A Letter to Nissim' Katrak comments:

> If you were with me here you would be muttering
> Your soft and final wisdom 'things could be worse,
> Make over, come to terms; the rest
> Is poetry and prayer.'

While his writing resembles Ezekiel's in its blend of confession, autobiography and prayer, and in using such forms as the verse letter to a friend, Katrak is preoccupied with going beyond the quest to a vision of 'The Way'. *A Journal of the Way* is Katrak's answer to Ezekiel's *The Unfinished Man*. It begins with a time of dissatisfaction and moves from crisis through experiment to hope. The poems are linked by such symbols as bone, sea, hill, journey, snow and open door, and are concerned with the problem of how to live with the knowledge that, as expressed in 'An Elegy For Jacob Epstein', 'even the great / Are subject to mortality'. The answer is found in love and sex: 'And fondling casually her left and smaller breast, / My thoughts slipped back from Epstein into bed'. 'Malabar Hill' is also concerned with death and the inability of art, in contrast to love, to offer a solution to spiritual dissatisfaction. 'On the Birth of My Daughter', the concluding poem of the sequence, is an affirmation and celebration that 'earth itself is flesh' and 'soul is hidden in the body's womb / Till found within the person of a wife':

> So may you find in body, as we found
> Through earthly love, a door to the Most High.

These poems are not merely celebrations of domestic bliss. The journey is spiritual and concerns how to live facing death. Katrak appears to have found the answer in Tantric yoga, with its use of sex as a means of attaining illumination. The joy of sex is a short-cut to spiritual satisfaction. This is the argument of 'The Kitchen Door' (retitled 'Alchemists' in *Underworld*) and of *Five Little Sermons Went to Market* (1971), a prose work on 'The Way', which Katrak co-authored with his wife. *Diversions By the Wayside* (1969), dedicated to Ezekiel, is mostly entertainment about falls from the grace of 'The Way'. These are poems of vanity, mocking spiritual self-satisfaction, and include 'Poet (for Nissim)', a parody of Ezekiel's earlier manner in such poems as 'Advice' and 'Communication' where a poet observes or listens to someone who is an example of how not to live: 'You must write better he said: / A minor poet gone to seed.'

Underworld (1979), written in the mixture of comical banter, satire, mysticism and preaching of the *Five Little Sermons*, shows what happens when ideas and mysticism become more important to a poet than his verse. Instead of the careful precision of the earlier poems comic doggerel is used to express the fun of 'The Way'. *Purgatory: Songs from the Holy Planet* (1984) has a similar blend of pastiche, jokes, parody and chat to assert spiritual joy. Katrak now aims at a visionary poetry which is playful, recognizes the flesh and physical world, and has a surface simplicity, while being an incantation, a chant 'For God alone'.

While his influence on early Katrak is obvious, Ezekiel is also a model for other, often younger, poets who write allegories on moral situations involving choices about how to live and poems in which the speaker meets or addresses someone who represents incorrect choices and failure of will. There are secular prayers and confessional autobiographies, poems of the urban landscape and their Goan equivalents, as well as poems describing episodes of family life during the poet's childhood. Poems in Ezekiel's tradition are argumentative yet conversational and the scene may function as symbol. Speech, diction, imagery are compressed, economical, while the tone will be firm yet ironic.

The characteristics of what I think of as the poetry deriving from Ezekiel are not just those of British as contrasted to more experimental American and European poetry. Dom Moraes works in the British tradition, but his verse is more cluttered by artifice, poetic diction, elaborate syntactical constructions and Christian and European classical symbols. His poetry is not about personal choices, moral relationships and the active self in society; it records sentiment, pity and social ironies. Many poems are about the sensitivity of the poet as artist in contrast to the insensitivity of others. Although his later poetry is somewhat tougher in attitude, he tends to view the craft of poetry as if it were the construction of an aesthetic object around moments of self-pity, hurt, compassion, confusion.

Without trying to trace poetic lineages, the example Ezekiel provided can be seen in subsequent poets, especially those sometimes called the Bombay school, regardless of their actual place of habitation. Such poets as Parthasarathy, Patel, Jussawalla, Peeradina and Rodrigues have a similar intellectualized and moral focus on the problems of living.

Ezekiel's influence on Indian poetry is more than advice to other writers, the editing of journals, the teaching of standards and the creation of types of poems; he provided an example of a poet intellectually and morally concerned with living in the modern world, and making poetry out of the experience. In his poetry there is the truth of acknowledging what is felt and experienced in its complexity, contradictions, pleasures, fears and disillusionments without preconceived ideas of what poetry should say about the poet and life. The opening up of Indian English poetry to reality in its many guises is perhaps Ezekiel's most significant influence.

CHAPTER SEVEN

The Poet's India I

EZEKIEL, RAMANUJAN, PATEL,
DARUWALLA, SHIV KUMAR

Although the process of decolonization of perception has been commented upon in such countries as Australia, New Zealand and Canada, where Europeans settled in an alien environment and had to learn to see the new land in which they lived and the new societies which they built, a similar process has taken place in Indian English poetry as it has evolved from its British roots into a product of an independent nation and its culture. India has existed for thousands of years but the society and culture which produces Indian poetry in English, and modern poetry in other Indian languages, is recent. Significantly the pre-independence verses in V. K. Gokak's *Golden Treasury of Indo-Anglian Poetry* seldom focus on local society and realities. The few poems which are aware of the injustices, problems and tragedies of Indian life have no immediacy; the inflated rhetoric of colonial poetry romanticizes and sentimentalizes. Kasiprasad Ghose's 'To a Young Hindu Widow', despite its subject matter, could have been written about any sad topic, any place:

> Ah, fair one! lone as desert flower,
> > Whose bloom and beauty are in vain;
> How dark was that too fatal hour
> > Which brought thee lasting grief and pain!
> What is the world to thee forlorn!
> > Thine every path is desolate;
> From all enjoyments rudely torn,
> > How drear and comfortless thy fate!

Many of the older poems on Indian subject matter in Gokak's anthology suffer from lack of relationship to an environment. Their language, attitude and perception are distant, vague, unfocused.

But then such colonial poets had the job of trying to introduce Indian themes, subject matter and landscape into what was basically British poetry. Kasiprasad Ghose's 'To a Dead Crow' badly rewrites a Keatsian ode.

This is not the place to trace the slow, often unsuccessful attempts to accommodate a foreign, usually outdated, poetic idiom, with its accompanying attitudes, to an Indian environment. There were a few minor successes, notably by the Goan Joseph Furtado, but in general Indian English poetry at independence was still set in a no-where land of poeticisms or set in an India generalized by the European imagination, represented by mysticism, mythologies or legends of great emperors, typical of a colonial poetry in which writers feel a need to assert a national past. Even the aestheticism of P. Lal's 'Because Her Speech is Excellent' has earlier parallels in West Indian and Australian pre-independence poetry:

> The poignance of her eyes, her words!
> Sun grappling with blue skies,
> Apples, birds,
> Apples and birds, apples and birds.

Many of the early post-colonial writers used local themes but were too involved with the aesthetic tradition for their poetry to have much contact with reality. Mary Erulkar's 'For a Child in Time of Famine' is a reworking of Dylan Thomas's incantatory celebration without his transforming vision of a world of process. Indeed her meaning seems to be the denial of Thomas's vision: 'And no, not all his anguish will find that field / Golden, like a cloak, his thin skeleton to cloth.' While R. de L. Furtado starts with the immediate, the poems shift their interest to the aesthetic and facile word play. 'Buffaloes' become:

> Muddy water
> Corrugated
> With circles
> Concentric.
>
> A thousand O's.

A change was, however, taking place in the ways Indian poetry in the 1950s and 1960s focused on reality. The first major shift of perspective was to the poet himself; this also included an awareness of others, specific situations, and on the edges an awareness of an often urban environment. Whether their mode was immediacy (in the American manner of Srinivas Rayaprol), the autobiographical nostalgia and irony of Dom Moraes or the more distanced, intellectualized moral reflections of Ezekiel, the poets were creating their space (which was no longer a generalized, stereotyped India) from themselves and their experience.

The directness of Rayaprol's 'Married Love' was seldom heard before in Indian poetry:

> Every evening
> I am met at the gate by my wife
> Her hair in disorder and her dress a mess
> from the kitchen.

Although Moraes's diction and many of the preoccupations of the poems in *A Beginning* (1957) were a superior version of the kind of romantic aestheticism represented by Lal's verse, in *Poems* (1960) the focus, if not always the kind of diction, was much more personal:

> I have grown up I think, to live alone,
> To keep my old illusions, sometimes dream
> Glumly that I am unloved and forlorn,
> Run away from strangers, often seem
> Unreal to myself in the pulpy warmth of a sunbeam.
> I have grown up hand on the primal bone,
> Making the poem, taking the word from the stream,
> Fighting the sand for speech, fighting the stone.

While Ezekiel still used a generalized mode, and a sometimes readymade, ironical diction, his poetry expressed a reality of emotions; its generalizations were formed from a close observation of the self in 'Situation':

> The upshot of their meetings was a quiet despair.
>   She never spoke her mind. He looked beyond her eyes.
> The fading light of evening gathered round her hair.
>   She lied to be with him. He had his stock of lies.

> The moment's banal beauty filled him with despair.
>   He saw a vast illusion smoulder in her eyes.
> If he should make a sign, for instance touch her hair,
>   Her 'tenderness' would get a chance eclipsing lies.

In *The Unfinished Man* Ezekiel was still writing in what seemed
a distanced manner, but the subject matter was clearly personal,
having to do with the dissatisfactions of marriage and the dissatis-
factions of approaching middle age, while the poems draw upon
Bombay for their allegorical images:

> Barbaric city sick with slums,
> Deprived of seasons, blessed with rains,
> Its hawkers, beggars, iron-lunged,
> Processions led by frantic drums,
> A million purgatorial lanes,
> And child-like masses, many-tongued,
> Whose wages are in words and crumbs.
>
> ('A Morning Walk')

Despite the abstract manner of *The Unfinished Man*, there is a
strong confessional element in such poems as 'Case Study' ('His
marriage was the worst mistake of all'). In 'Jamini Roy' that artist's
paintings are used as an example of how a fresh perception of local
reality can lead to personal renewal while providing society with
new images of itself.

A breakthrough to poetry about everyday Indian life written in a
more colloquial-seeming voice occurred in the volumes published
by Ramanujan, Ezekiel, Gieve Patel and Kamala Das in the mid
1960s. Das wrote in a colloquial and open manner about herself, her
moods, her love, her marriage, her grandmother, and the cities in
which she lived. There was an intimacy with the reader, a sponta-
neous acceptance of her life and its happenings in a way not seen
before in Indian verse:

> Our house crouches in dust in the
> Evenings, when the buffaloes tramp
> Up the road, the weary herdsmen
> Singing soft Punjabi songs, and
> Girls from free municipal schools
> Pause shyly at our gate and smile.
>
> ('The Snobs')

> I don't know politics but I know the names
> Of those in power, and can repeat them like
> Days of the week, or names of months, beginning with
> Nehru. I am Indian, very brown, born in

Malabar, I speak three languages, write in
Two, dream in one.
('An Introduction')

The shift from the legendary and sentimentalized India of the
pre-independence poets to a more socially conscious, contempo-
rary, localized, personal India can be seen in the title of her first
book, *Summer in Calcutta* (1965), and in the titles of such poems as
'The Dance of the Eunuchs', 'My Grandmother's House', 'Visitors
to the City', 'The Child in the Factory', 'The Sea Shore', 'To a Big
Brother', 'Punishment in Kindergarten', 'Farewell to Bombay' and
'A Hot Noon in Malabar'.

In some of the poems in *The Exact Name* Ezekiel made a similar
breakthrough to the use of a speaking voice, a less formalized
diction and the significant use of Indian life and details. Memories
are not sentimentalized:

> I remember the night my mother
> was stung by a scorpion. Ten hours
> of steady rain had driven him
> to crawl beneath a sack of rice.
> Parting with his poison—flash
> of diabolic tail in the dark room—
> he risked the rain again.
> The peasants came like swarms of flies
> and buzzed the Name of God a hundred times
> to paralyse the Evil One.
>
> ('Night of the Scorpion')

The difference between this and earlier Indian poetry is the
acceptance that India is a worthwhile subject for poetry without
having to be inflated to the sublime by an artificial diction, noble
sentiments or aestheticizing its scenes. The ironic, satiric, unself-
consciously personal are not just new notes; they are parts of a
different kind of song than previously:

> The men are quite at home
> among the foreign styles
> (what fun the flirting is!),
> I myself, decorously,
> press a thigh or two in sly innocence.
> The party is a great success.

Then someone says: we can't
enjoy it, somehow, don't you think?
The atmosphere corrupt,
and look at our wooden wives ...
I take him out to get some air.

('In India')

In Ramanujan's *The Striders* (1966) and *Relations* (1971)
poetry seemed to grow out of Indian experience and sensibility
with all its memories of family, local places, images, beliefs and
history, while having a modern stance with its scepticism, ironies
and sense of living from moment to moment in a changing world
in which older values and attitudes often are seen as unrealistic.
While Ramanujan can evoke the warmth of traditional Indian
family life and the closeness of long remembered relationships,
more often he shows conflict, arguments, surprises; he also
shows that the supposed glory of the Tamil cultural heritage is a
fiction which ignores the reality of the past.

Ramanujan's memories are located in the specific society of the
Tamil Brahmins. The poems avoid vague generalizations about
India and are set in particular situations or scenes or develop from
reflections on specific topics. Nor is there a fixed attitude or
stance which the poems set out to communicate; rather they
change direction and seem unpredictable as they develop, with
the ending often different from the values implied at the begin-
ning of a poem.

the day my great-aunt died
I was there by one of those
chances children never miss,
looking for a green ball
I never lost ...

...

they didn't know she wore
her napkins on
to the great disgust
of the orthodox widows
who washed her body
at the end,

and the dark
stone face of my little aunt
acquired some expression
at last.

The sophistication with which Ramanujan recreates and treats
South Indian culture is also reflected in his techniques, which,
like his translations, often seem a modern recreation of the spirit
and methods of Tamil and Kannada verse. The word play, puns,
inner rhymes, rhetorical devices, ironies, distanced neutrality of
tone, understatement, compression and elliptical progression of
the poems have similarities to his translations. This does not
mean that Ramanujan is unaffected by his reading of Yeats, Eliot
and other moderns (who have influenced him), but he is highly
aware of the conventions, techniques and structures of Indian
verse and these have been used and transformed in his English
poetry.

The complexity, instability and irony of Ramanujan's poems
seem very modern, as is the way they appear to offer themselves
as imagistic statements to be appreciated and interpreted as the
reader wishes. But acquaintance with the various introductions,
prefaces and afterwords to Ramanujan's translations of medieval
Kannada and Tamil verse reveals that what seems original and
modern is partly based on older Indian poetic conventions. The
understated, neutral standing at a distance from description can
be found in the Tamil classics he translated. The use of the self as
a centre for a poem filled with ironies, which unpredictably chan-
ges direction and attitudes and which resists conclusion, is within
the tradition of medieval saints' poetry.

Gieve Patel's *Poems* (1966) also made honest use of local
subjects. His own interest in the peasantry is ironically contras-
ted to that of his 'Grandfather', a landowner, who asks:

But for what, tell me, do you look in them,
They've quite exhausted my wonder—

Difficult, ungrateful,
Double-faced, unreliable;
I have dealt with the peasantry
Over three quarters of a century
And I fail to follow your thinking.

In 'Naryal Purnima' seasonal change and direct observation of the scene lead to reflections on himself and the ambiguous place of well-off, westernized Parsis in India:

> Our interiors never could remain
> Quite English. The local gods hidden in
> Cupboards from rational Parsi eyes
> Would suddenly turn up on the walls
> Garlanded alongside the King and the Queen ...
> Today it is simpler to admit with relief:
> The men are too greasy, their speech
> Is too nasal, their wives either plain
> Or overdone; they choose for their dresses
> A shattering blue and choke their flowers
> In tinsel; Their mind is provincial,
> Their children are dull.

There is a different relation to the scene in writers from Hindu backgrounds (Kamala Das, Parthasarathy, Shiv Kumar, Ramanujan) and those raised in Jewish (Ezekiel) and Parsi (Patel, Jussawalla, Daruwalla) environments. Although this difference is apparent in the way those raised as Hindus refer more often to their family, rituals and temples, it is also a matter of emotional involvement. No matter how distinctively an Ezekiel, Patel or Daruwalla observes his environment, there is a space between himself and how he perceives others. Patel's excellent poems derive much of their strength from the way he is both strongly aware of local conditions of life yet defends himself from involvement.

A few poems such as 'Nargol' in his first book reflect the social tensions and feelings of guilt for being 'a rich man's son'. In 'Evening' the Indian guests are unable to be at ease with their English host as 'The servants / were watching'. Peasants and servants are felt by Patel as an otherness, despite his knowledge that people are similar under the skin. His instinct is, however, towards self-preservation. In 'Seasons' he begins by saying he would like 'To be able to believe in / Universal love' and the oneness of all creation, but the difficulty of enduring and overcoming 'The blisters of touch, / The shyness of the soul' shows that such universal love is false. We remain imprisoned in ourselves. The trees 'cannot care / Whether I live or die'.

'On Killing a Tree' implies that all forms of life are essentially

similar in their desire to live, expand, reproduce, and their simi-
larity in suffering, pain and ageing. Uprooting the diseased tree is
similar to performing a surgical operation in requiring a lack of
compassion:

> So hack and chop
> But this alone won't do it.
> Not so much pain will do it.
> The bleeding bark will heal
> And from close to the ground
> Will rise curled green twigs,
> Miniature boughs
> Which if unchecked will expand again
> To former size.

Such images as 'simple jab of the knife', 'its leperous hide', 'sensi-
tive, hidden', 'choking' sustain the surgical analogy, while con-
veying sympathetic awareness:

> And the strength of the tree exposed,
> The source, white and wet,
> The most sensitive, hidden
> For years inside the earth.

Patel's perception is influenced by his medical career. The thirty
poems in his first book include such titles as ' Cord-Cutting', 'Post-
Mortem Report', 'Post-Mortem', 'The Difference In The Morgue',
'Old Man's Death' and 'Catholic Mother (Your child at hospital)'.
Many of these poems, including 'For Kennedy', reveal the physi-
cian's awareness that 'inside— / The always red muscle and
blood', people are the same, 'one', and that the doctor's compas-
sion is useless in the face of the body's destruction through
illness, accident or assassination. Yet always there is the doctor's
responsibility, which requires self-control and the avoidance of
the kind of emotional involvement that might lead to divided
attention and mistakes. That moment of alertness at the delivery
of a child in 'Cord-Cutting' is also symbolized in 'Spider' where
the spider, though stationary, is still 'A central spring / of
thought and feeling'. 'Pavement' treats ironically of emotional
and moral involvement. After seeing a man collapse on a pave-
ment the speaker comes to the rescue, but the man rises and
rushes off 'Mocking and embarrassed'.

Such poems develop out of the tensions that result when ideas about conduct conflict with the realities of experience. Patel's elliptical, compressed style reflects the struggle of an intelligence aware that compassion is often useless when tested by the world. He has said (*Illustrated Weekly*, 1 September 1974) 'It's more practical today to teach our children survival rather than an ethical code.'

The poems in *How Do You Withstand, Body* (1976) are often even more compressed, oblique, elliptical and unillusioned than those of the earlier volume. Patel appears to be aiming at a thickly textured, economical, rough, vigorous, colloquial style which expresses a mind thinking through its emotions and conflicts towards some logical resolution. The title poem is, like 'To Kill A Tree', a celebration of the physical will to life continuing despite the pains suffered in living. Again the perspective is that of a doctor, aware that the body is 'Dumb, discoloured / Battered patches', which the medical man with his instruments and needles injures while performing a kind of love. The will to life, power, self-asser-tion is affirmed in 'The Arrogant Meditation'; whereas contempla-tion of nature in poetry or spiritual study usually lead to humility, Patel shows the naturalness of aggression by the physical world where 'Trees / Push their way upward' and even 'Grovelling under-ground / Tubers acquire volume'. The sexual analogy is obvious.

There is no reality beyond the physical. 'To Make a Contract' mocks those who 'pick upon / A tree or a rock' as an image of God. Better to choose

> A thing in the lowest scale
> Of credibility ... dirt, or faeces,
> And run to it for sanctuary.

Patel's scepticism of ideas and ideals is reflected in social atti-tudes. 'The Ambiguous Fate of Gieve Patel, He Being Neither Muslim Nor Hindu in India' ironically refers to the horrors of communal rioting, 'To be no part of this hate is deprivation'. 'The Multitude Comes to a Man' mocks the way the masses accumu-late power by giving it to the powerful. The purpose of their res-pect is to create their own power. They exchange 'power / For power'. Taken as a whole, Patel's poems suggest someone with a sensitivity to social injustice and suffering who to survive has found it necessary to harden himself.

By the later 1960s poets had learned to write freely and natu-
rally about India. They might write from the inside of Hindu
society, like Kamala Das, Ramanujan or Shiv Kumar or from the
outside, like Patel and Daruwalla, but there was a sense of fami-
liarity, although the result was less often ease than tension and
feelings of alienation from what was known. The English language
had also become used less formally, with more unconscious
Indianization of idioms and Hindi-like coinages of compound
words. This may be partly the influence of the colloquial manner
of American poetry, which was widely read by the writers; the
immediacy of response to scenes and the use of sense impressions
may also be an American influence.

The increasing awareness of recent American poetry is noti-
ceable in Shiv Kumar's use of the confessional mode and his
directnesss. In Kumar's 'Before the Beginning' the pun on 'eye-
catching', used to suggest attracting and flirting, is an Indian
coinage (like 'colleging' and 'gifting') not common elsewhere:

> It's now time to roll up the picnic basket,
> put away the crumbs of bread,
> for she is already eye-catching a stranger
> on the other side of the beach.

Social satire, pioneered by Ezekiel, has been established and its
range extended as well as become more weighted with allusions
and specific in reference, as in Kumar's 'Epitaph on an Indian
Politician':

> All his life he shambled around
> in homespun yarn,
> socializing his soul,
>   while his sons flourished
>   in the private sectors of big business.
>   Here he lies, silenced by tongue
> cancer, during the stormy budget session.

In Kumar's poetry historical monuments, landscape and en-
vironment are often viewed with a savage irony as part of his own
sexual desires, anger at incongruities and sense of the grotesque
and macabre. In a poem set at the 'Crematorium in Adikmet,
Hyderabad', his 'father's head / awaits' his hand while 'The
priest chants louder for a generous tip'. Instead of the dreary

palm-trees-and-lagoon poetry written in the past about the beaches of western India, Kumar describes 'Kovalam Beach' in a series of sexual analogies ('the sea foreplays with the shore') and the passing of time is represented by sea-shells and lobsters 'clasping abortive dreams'. Kumar's India is seen in the perspective of his own strong sexual desires which are projected on nature mockingly and sarcastically, in opposition to Indian modesty, piety, respect, tradition. 'The Taj' in moonlight reveals a pair 'of shaggy dogs caught / in a hot clasp behind the rear minaret'. After noting the 'Fissures' in the rear of the Taj (its rectum'), he asks 'How long can it withstand / the riverbed's lethal teeth? A 'Mango Grove' is imaged as 'clusters of virgin breasts'. At 'Lord Venkateswara's Temple' he recalls a legend about a woman who had a vision of the Lord's arm rising in benediction. In Kumar's version of the legend as the woman lay on the shrine's threshold the high priest surveys 'the woman's flanks— / the length of a cushioned bed'.

In 'Broken Columns', a sequence of twelve poems, the poet's sexuality is counterpointed against the teachings of his parents, school and Indian wisdom. While he chants from the Gita 'Feed not thy desire / on objects of sense' he is aware of 'a girl's skirt / and two tender legs'. Throughout the sequence the focus is on representative particularities of Indian Hindu life. Although the ironies reflect Kumar's rebellion, the presentation has a cold, ruthless detachment. A teacher preaches that Indian 'degeneracy' not 'British might' brought about colonialism. But the teacher's vision of regeneration is undercut by the buttermilk on his moustache. Kumar's father, suspecting him of libidinous interests in women, sends him to a high priest who beckons him into a dark chamber of the Shiva temple and begins sensually caressing his neck.

The freedom with which Shiv Kumar satirizes India as repressive of his desires and the ways in which he sexualizes the landscape, beaches and monuments are a further stage in the Indianization of English-language poetry. In Ezekiel's early poems India is out there, an environment of which he is aware as a setting and a source of symbols. Increasingly the environment comes into his poetry and soon there are some representative characters ('The Patriot', 'The Professor'), situations ('Goodbye Party for Miss Pushpa T. S.', 'Irani Restaurant Instructions'), poems on places ('Island', 'On Bellasis Road'), scenes from family life ('Night of the Scorpion',

'Jewish Wedding in Bombay') and various kinds of social comment and satire ('How the English Lesson Ended', 'The Truth about the Floods', 'In India'); but Ezekiel always appears to be on the outside, watching, observing, commenting, impersonating, rather than someone directly engaged in the experience. Partly this is a matter of technique and partly it reflects his tendency to intellectualize, order and judge experience—whether social, moral or sexual. But it might be explained in terms of Ezekiel's formative years as a rationalist Jew in a Hindu-Muslim society.

By contrast Kumar's poetry seems immediate, as if written at nerve end, and in the heat of or with still vivid memories of conflict. Again, this is partly a matter of a kind of technique, partly a matter of how Kumar channels emotions and experience into poetry; and it might be explained historically in terms of a further stage in using Indian life for poetry, especially after American confessional verse had become a model. It is tempting to see Kumar as someone very much within Hindu society rebelling to get out while still retaining emotional and personal ties to it. Like Ramanujan he has in recent decades lived abroad and his work reflects his experience as an expatriate, someone with a foot in two cultures. But whereas Ramanujan's memories of India are mixed between nostalgia for the warmth of the past and relief at being freed from ties, deceptions and absurdities, Kumar's poems, for all their wit and humour, are angry, satiric responses to an India of passivity, sexual repression, political hypocrisy and an over-glorified, crumbling past.

Whereas Ezekiel's 'In India' includes social satire on the unsatisfactoriness of relations between the sexes in India, Kumar's portrayal in 'Indian Women' is closer to sarcasm: 'Patiently they sit / like empty pitchers ... pleating hope in each braid ... they guard their tattooed thighs'

> till even the shadows
> roll up their contours
> and are gone
> beyond the hills.

Although he often uses such formalizing, distancing methods as narrative, dramatic monologues, rhyme, traditional prosody, projective symbolism (in which the external reflects the subjective) and closure, Daruwalla's poetry also has an immediacy and anger. It contrasts the naturalness of violence, aggression and sexual desires with repression, hypocrisy and deceit. Usually the

speaker and sympathetic characters appear alone, isolated, alie-
nated from their society. There is anger at incompetence, passivity,
official lies, romantic illusions and the repressiveness of communal
solidarity; but there is also a strong interest in Indian history and
traditions.

A characteristic of Daruwalla's verse is the often uneasy mixture
of freedom and control. This is not only reflected in the way he
moves from metre to free verse, from rhyme to unrhymed verse, but
more significantly in the way a poem will begin in a controlled man-
ner, then become more immediate and less clearly related to what
preceded it, before being brought back under control with some
final observation or technique of closure. This presumably reflects
the tensions found in the themes of the poet's writings—between
freedom and responsibility. Control represses desire but is neces-
sary for survival in an India which is dangerous and in which
the individual's life is threatened by society and by nature. In
such poems as 'Death of a Bird' and 'Routine' such themes are
explicit; in 'The Hawk' the world is predatory, violent and sur-
vival is all. Daruwalla's vision in his early poems is strongly but
only partly expressed in 'Towards Reality', where after mocking
definitions of Metaphysics, Ethics, Morality and Religion, he
concludes:

> Pathology only knows, for he's no fool
> he deals with faeces, droppings, stools
> > He knows his bit
> > We have a lot of names
> > > for the same
> > > > shit.

This explains his emphasis on the physical, the concrete, the imme-
diate, on survival and being tough. 'Collage II' says 'corruption is
the chemistry of flesh / no wonder the senses suppurate, passions
putrefy'. Angrily addressing India as Mother, who will 'crawl
towards Benares to die', Daruwalla mocks:

> Then why should I tread the Kafka beat
> or the Waste Land
> when Mother you are near at hand
> one vast, sprawling defeat?

While Daruwalla might seem to reduce reality to the purely
physical and detest those who accept fate and do not fight to

survive, the actuality of his poems is more complex. There is not only anger at the incompetent, but also a strong ethical and moral consciousness often expressed in savagely satirical comments. This apparent contradiction between a physical realism and moral awareness is a theme of 'Poetry Talk', the fifth of the 'Dialogues with a Third Voice':

> —I think of sin
> as a curio, not an archetype
> Hence guilt wears thin
> There's nothing much to choose between
> a ghostly presence and a ghostly absence
> yet at night sometimes
> the ghost-beard haunts me
> burning through my chin.

The conflict between conscience and a view of life as power and physical reality is also a conflict between two poetic modes, one reflective, the other immediate:

> 'You have escaped your deserts
> by the skin of your teeth
> but guilt, that inner nemesis
> you can't avoid.' I face up squarely
> and kick him in the teeth
> guilt is a moral delicacy
> I cannot stand
> Crudeness is power, power claw and teeth
> ...
> 'Concreteness is only stone
> Do you favour the half-truth or the half-lie?'
>
> I take an air-gun
> and blow out half his eye.

Although Daruwalla's poems are striking, concrete, physical, immediate, they often shift perspective from the physical to commentary and conclusions. The poems may seem like a kind of American writing in their concentration on the physical, but the descriptions themselves have neither the transcendence nor the denial of transcendence (and affirmation of the physical as all) which are often the kinds of consciousness expressed in American poetry. Daruwalla is ironically aware of contradictions in his own attitudes:

'In a curved universe, a straight metric line
is floundering in a rut
you must give it multiple meanings
A work of art must hit you in the gut.'
I strike an attitude and knife a pig
and tough-guy that I am, I bring out his guts
'Three dimensions of space, one of time
dreams, memories, senses,—your meagre tools
—and a tradition that is portly
Can you fashion reality with these tools?'
I agree. I will be starting
a sausage-factory shortly.

If the world is simply physical existence, a place of time, dreams, memories, senses, then there can be no tragedy, only disappointment, accidents, ageing and failure. 'Tragedy Talk', the sixth of the 'Dialogues', denies the possibility of older views of tragedy in the modern world:

but we all agree
that you and i
are unfit subjects for a tragedy
our tragic-wheel gets stuck
in every rut
our passions slick
get lost within our guts
destiny, stars, fate
we don't measure up to such words
if fate were to squeeze me hard
all that would remain of me
would be a bit of turd.

While mocking our 'little lives' as subject for tragedy, the poem concludes by strongly implying that there is tragedy of a kind neglected by art of the past with its grand myths, legends, fate and other schemes which see man within a spiritual dimension. Instead modern tragedy will reflect our personal feelings of 'angst' and physical and social evils:

so let me hold tight to the angst, the fear
it's all i have, my dear
the things i panic from
could never excite a lyre
—parents drunk in the basement
while children roast in a fifth-floor fire.

The redefinition of tragedy is also the theme of 'The Professor Condoles', where, adopting an ironic mask, Daruwalla has the speaker claim there can be no modern tragedy in an absurd world of accidents. An awareness of the need to celebrate death then is part of Daruwalla's aesthetics and follows from his concentration on memories, dreams and the senses. The physical and emotional world is, however, not all, as there is also 'conscience', wit, an awareness of the need to face death. In 'The Parsi Hell' he says that while 'Our hell and heaven have no locus, the scriptures forego / all reference to the damned', he carries his hell within him. This is a similar anguish to Protestant guilt: 'Anxieties congregate / and claw at your dreams as they prospect for hell'.

While Daruwalla's poems give expression to desire, memory and senses, they are grounded in concrete images, characters and situations. The poems record a modern India during a 'Curfew in a Riot-Torn City' and 'Pestilence'; of 'The Epileptic', 'The Beggar', 'The People' and 'Fellow-Indian Poets'; of 'Love in Meerut', 'Love among the Pines' and 'Indian Adolescence'. It is a well-populated world of politicians, writers, lovers, family, fakes, the corrupt, the tragic, set in many places and with many events. It is a larger, fuller, often more tragic (although not necessarily deeper or poetically superior) world than that found in the poetry of Ezekiel, Kamala Das or Ramanujan. Yet for all its involvement with Indian life it seems to be written from the outside rather than, like Shiv Kumar's, from the inside. Daruwalla's poetry seems private, personal; people, even lovers, are out there, to be observed, rather than part of shared experience felt at the finger tips.

The withholding of the self is part of his poetry's strength as it communicates an intelligence poised between anger and reflection, a knowingness towards what is seen and experienced. He has a fascination for passionate commitment which involves dedication, violence such as he finds, and would appear to identify with, in Muslim culture. Some of his best poems are the 'In the Shadow of the Imambara' group in *The Keeper of the Dead* (1982) where there is highly realized description, characterization, speech and emotions:

> Before passion such as this
> you can only offer humility!
> They have awaited Moharram
> like a tree aching for leaf!
> They long for him to walk

the firebed of their dreams!
And even as the body shrivels like a fig
they wet their lips with your name, Husain!

Daruwalla seldom appears at ease among the passivity, fatalism and rituals of Hindu culture. His attempt to merge his own concern with dying into a collective Indian psyche in 'The Waterfront' sequence strikes me as unconvincing despite the high competence of the verse. A thirteen-poem sequence, 'The Waterfront' begins in puzzlement at observing the apparent grotesqueness of Varanasi in which sewage emptying into the river is overlooked by those who regard its water as holy:

What plane of destiny have I arrived at
where corpse-fires and cooking-fires
burn side by side?

At night Varanasi seems 'a city of the dead / brooding over a ghost-scape'. At dawn some worshippers appear like bizarre illusions who have 'crawled out / from the sediments of time'. 'Vignette I' observes 'Lepers', a 'dwarf', 'Beggars' and concludes that the Ganga exists 'not to lighten the misery / but to show it'. But in the ninth poem, 'The Dip', Daruwalla surprisingly claims that for those immersed in the water 'the ship of doubt is wrecked':

I who came to feel her frozen paws
find myself in her warm, dark heart.

In 'River-Silt', the concluding poem, Daruwalla now claims that the 'collective layers of my psyche sleep here' and that the skulls will speak to the future of the Indians:

a syllable-seeding
coated against death
like mummy-wheat.

The bravura display at the conclusion of the poem does not disguise Daruwalla's theme of Hindu India as a land of despair, illustrated by those who come to Varanasi. His more usual attitude to the Hindu tradition as represented by Varanasi is shown by the remark in 'Crossing of Rivers' that 'begging for food' is 'the old slave-route of the Hindu psyche'. What comes across mostly strongly in Daru-walla's poetry is rather the self-control and repressed anger of the alienated, as in 'Routine' and 'The Hawk'.

The range, variety, themes, attitudes and voices of Indian English poetry have increased greatly in recent decades. Instead of India being ignored by the poet's imagination or reduced to stereotyped sentiments, India has become a reality. It is seen, felt, experienced; the poet responds to its various details, events, happenings, politics, values, peoples, behaviour and legends. Rather than on the periphery of his consciousness it has become a focus of it, a place where the imagination works and creates. The charge once made by Pritish Nandy that the English-language poets do not have as close a relationship to local culture as do the regional-language poets is no longer accurate, although it is true that there has been little of the politically committed verse and sustained attention to injustice sometimes found in regional writing. Rather, the English-language poets have been more concerned with exploring their relationship to the past, to their families, to local society and their immediate relationships with others. Although Indian English poetry has emerged as a national literature, the imaginative world of the poets is still mostly centred on themselves and their emotions, rather than on society or some larger community. This is neither bad nor good, neither to be desired nor rejected; rather it is a fact about most of the significant poets who had appeared by the early 1970s.

Indian poetry in the later 1970s and '80s, however, began to take on some more representative, larger ambitions and go beyond the individual self to a greater concern with its environment, with the poet's communal identity and its place within the national culture. There were more poems about specific locales, poems about the community in which one was raised, poems which consciously took positions on matters of cultural heritage or were criticisms of the concern with the self and its way of perceiving reality. The poets earlier had to avoid facile nationalism to write of the world as they perceived it; they Indianized their poetry by making it an expression of Indian life as experienced rather than preconceived ideas about reality. As the poetry naturalized itself and took in larger and more varied areas of experience it expressed greater variety and range of subjects, as represented by the writings of Kumar and Daruwalla; it subsequently both moved more into the inner world of the consciousness as well as into other kinds of observation and awareness of the society in which it is created.

CHAPTER EIGHT

The Poet's India II

PEERADINA, RODRIGUES, DE SOUZA,
SHETTY, SILGARDO

In 1978 Newground, a Bombay co-operative modelled after
Clearing House, published its first book, *Three Poets*, which re-
presented work by its founders, Melanie Silgardo, Raul d'Gama
Rose and Santan Rodrigues. A new generation had appeared on
the scene. Subsequent Newground publications were Eunice de
Souza's *Fix* (1979), Saleem Peeradina's *First Offense* (1980) and
Manohar Shetty's *A Guarded Space* (1981). Each of the poets is or
has been resident in Bombay and each except Peeradina and Shetty
is from a Goan family. While the poets have been associated with or
students of Ezekiel and build upon the kind of moral realism he
initiated in Indian English poetry, they tend to focus more closely
on society.

The only one of the younger poets previously to publish a
volume was Santan Rodrigues, whose first book, *I Exist* (1976), was
originally circulated in typescript to members of Ezekiel's MA class
at the University of Bombay. Written between 1970 and 1972 when
Rodrigues was in his early twenties, they are poems of someone
spontaneously responding to friends, youthful love affairs, sports
and other occurrences in one's life, including writing poetry, with-
out any formulated stance, attitude or position. Their lack of intel-
lectual, social, moral, psychological or political dimensions was new
to serious Indian English poetry and cleared the decks for other
kinds of subject matter, such as the celebration of athletics, and the
confusions and changing views of youth. There are poems, such as
'To Bed' which express simple delight in being oneself:

> hurrying to bed, then strip
> off the airs, manners, society yelps
> that i wear all day. i leap

into the bed naked to myself.

It is possible to object to some of the unnecessary or fanciful comparisons ('the rain's lathi charge') and the striking of poses ('so without a farewell / must i part ... if you are happy now, i'm glad!'); but Rodrigues is impressive when writing about physical sensations. In 'The Hang', about an athletic technique for doing the triple jump and the long jump, the lines and verse have the movement of the sensations experienced:

> and the wind moved piercing your side.
> till your weight
> laid you to rest in a sepulchre
> of sand.

The way the verse realizes such focus on immediate sensation, although anticipated in the immediacy of poems by Kumar and Daruwalla, is appropriate to the experience with which Rodrigues is concerned. The poems seem spontaneous impressions, thoughts and expressions proclaiming the existence of small realities.

This Far, the selection from Rodrigues's verse written in 1973–6 in *Three Poets*, has a similar immediacy and spontaneity to the earlier book but is modified by reflection on his Goan heritage. A different locale is being put on the map of Indian English poetry as Rodrigues writes of aspects of Goan culture. 'Nightfall in a Goan Village' does not so much criticize as record a small, enclosed society in which the bragging among the drinkers in the tavern contrasts to the lonely church, deserted roads and fear-ridden homes. Rodrigues's 'Grandfather' is celebrated for having broken the centuries of feudal labour to create a new, freer world in Goa for future generations. 'The Homecoming' contrasts the poet's nostalgic memories of his youth in Goa, when the grass was green and he rode in carreiras, with the present where

> ... the roads
> all asphalt now has bid
> the carreiras farewell.

These poems establish a reality in poetry for Goa beyond its often celebrated beaches. Part of its history, culture and present is recreated within the space of a few poems which Rodrigues's imagination fills with various people, landscapes and Goan habits of mind. In 'Nightfall in Goan Village' the characters include a farmer, 'small families', a 'white frocked priest', 'grandma', a 'baffled child' and a dog. There are such details as feni, the angelus, the priest's hemline, a rocking-chair, the dog's leash, various local fears, including a ghost and imaginings that the Marathas are 'on a looting spree'.

Enlarged, detailed consciousness of local realities and writing of one's roots are characteristics of the new poets. The way such writers as Rodrigues, Silgardo and de Souza make use of memories of their local cultural background (rather than a generalized pan-Indian Hinduism) was pioneered by Ramanujan, followed by Parthasarathy; but Tamil society and culture for the two older poets does not seem immediately present the way Goa, Poona and Bombay are for the new poets.

In contrast to Rodrigues's nostalgia for a Goan childhood among the sound of church bells, the greenery of the landscape and the places of his ancestors, Eunice de Souza's memories of Catholic Goan life in Poona are of its repressions, prejudices, ignorance, social injustices and the place of women. The anger and bitterness is not directly expressed; the experience has settled and been fixed into representative scenes and details with the descriptions, conversation and events offered as in the present. Putting past memories into the present, making them seem immediate and unreflected, is a technique also used by Rodrigues and shows the ways Indian English poetry has moved increasingly nearer to its environment and the cultures in which the poets live or were raised. While it is tempting to generalize that Indian English poetry has come closer to expressing the experience of life or that it has been liberated from an inhibiting formalism, such statements would not be true. The experiences found in the poems of Kamala Das or Ramanujan are just as real, and sometimes more significant, while their verse appears an expression of their speaking voice. The new poets have, however, learned how to build upon Ramanujan's poems of family life, Ezekiel's urban landscapes and Kamala Das's confessional verse in writing of local society. Their imaginations are more engaged in detail, more focused on places; people are named, distinctions are noted, and the society of their poems is more textured, denser, richer, and present. The poet's speech and that of the characters is more colloquial, direct, contemporary. The collapsing of the distance between the self and the external world, between present and past, between reflection and event creates an immediacy, vitality and drama as if the subject matter were being witnessed and experienced. With the collapse of distance between poet and subject, and the use of detail and contemporary voice, the poet, rather than being conscious of the environment, appears part of the environment.

Fix is partly an album of snapshots of de Souza's Goan family in Poona. 'Here', smiling is 'Francis X. D'Souza / father of the year', who has had seven children in seven years, complaining 'these Hindu buggers got no ethics'. The poet describes and dramatizes, but says nothing herself about the portrait; the satiric perspective comes from the juxtaposition of the father's views and the reality which surrounds him. While he claims 'We're One Big Happy Family' and India will 'Suffer', there is his silent, suffering, always pregnant wife. The clichés ('Father of the year', 'By the Grace of God', 'God Always Provides', 'Pillar of the Church') contrast to the reality represented by the wife. The phrases fit economically into the lines, their control contributing to the satiric perspective on the falsity of what the Father, Priest and Mother Superior say.

Other poems report on Goan marriages, 'Feeding the Poor at Christmas', the sexual prudery which leads to misinformation about menstruation and impregnation, a Christmas party and a Portuguese-bred aunt who mistakes a small Shivalingam for an ashtray. De Souza's satire is seldom sarcastic; rather the satire comes from ironic juxtapositions and details. In 'Marriages Are Made' (with its ironic allusion to 'marriages are made in Heaven'), Cousin Elena is examined for her family history, the solvency of her father, her height, health and colour before the other family decides she will do 'justice' to their 'good son of Mother Church'. The feeding of the poor at Christmas is a display of small snobberies and meanness: 'Don't try turning up for more'. The society portrayed is densely textured but petty in its attitudes; it is a society of romantic illusions and lives wasted through ignorance and conformity. Miss Louise 'dreamt of descending / curving staircases' and of children:

> till the dream rotted her innards
> but no one knew:
> innards weren't permitted
> in her time.

Still dreaming of love and conquests, she is humiliated by the way the community dismisses her as an ageing eccentric. Religion holds the Catholic community together rather in rigid social conformity than in love and justice. An attempt by the Archbishop in 'Varca, 1942' to make the landlords and peasants worship together fails. After the Archbishop is shot at, he refuses for many months to perform the Mass; eventually the status quo is restored: 'the land-lords were landlords / and the peasants peasants / ever after'.

Melanie Silgardo, one of the *Three Poets* and a former student of de Souza's, also writes about Goan society, but her portrayal is more compassionate and there is a close identification with her dead father. The confessional, compassionate, familial and social often blend; the personal is set within a context of others. Silgardo uses more imagery than de Souza, especially for psychological expression. In 'Family Photograph'.

> The room descends
> in awkward places. There's
> a cramp stampede for my brain.
> A release, and
>
> my four-legged mind
> is romping home.

Memories of family life become Silgardo's way of understanding herself. The poems speak directly while moving rapidly through sentiments, anger, sympathy, tensions, understanding; by recover-ing the past there is self-definition. Many of the poems, like 'For Father on the Shelf', concern her dead father or are addressed to him as confessions.

> The days you drank too much
> I cowered from your smell.
> You never knew it hurt
> to see your clear eyes go blurred,
> to see your fingers fumble for a match
> that never lit the dangling cigarette.
> ...
> And now I'm writing with my life.
> The price of an inherited crutch.

In such poetry the subject matter has largely shifted from the external world to the psychology of the self. It is the poetry of memory, dreams and anxieties, fears and self-revelations. Whereas

Ezekiel's revelations were offered in formalized, highly controlled verses, and seen through a reflective consciousness, Silgardo's emotions appear to come direct in highly charged imagery. Daruwalla's poetry, with its emphasis on the experience of the senses and its narrative organization, asserts and celebrates the self's journey through a messy, painful, dangerous world. Shiv Kumar's poetry, like Silgardo's, presents self-revealing emotions through expressionistic images, but his emphasis is on the sexual, on events from his marriage and its failure, and the tone is often humorous, comical, even farcical. There are elements, whether formal, narrative distance or tonal, of self-protectiveness in the male poets. By contrast, the women poets—Kamala Das, de Souza and Silgardo—increasingly strip away such self-protection and create a world of what appear direct self-revelations. The feeling of unmediated, freely associated expression is, of course, deceiving. The poems of the women writers are in their own ways as well constructed as those of the male writers; but the constructions are different, since the women map a psychology of contradictions, humiliations and defeats rather than self-assertions and triumph. Their assertion is of the self in its more characteristic female roles in relationship to father, mother, social restrictions, love, marriage, underdogs, the poor and defeat. Silgardo's 'The Earthworm's Story' is a metaphor for feminine survival through self-humiliation:

> I lost this last bit of shine
> scraping along the way.
> The crow pecked,
> the ant bit,
> and the gravel sneered underbelly.
>
> …
>
> It does not matter
> if that's your foot over me.

In Silgardo's poems on the family there is a merging of the confessional with the social. Her concerns, like those of de Souza, reside in the tensions between herself and her family and the Goan Catholic community. The psychological emphasis is rather on conflict, love and hate, competence and maladjustment, wounds, rejection and understanding, than the inner world of fantasy, isolation, the sources of poetic inspiration and questioning selfhood—themes more likely to be found in such poets as Chitre and Mahapatra.

Silgardo and de Souza have enlarged the kinds of Indian reality found in Ezekiel's poems; and, as in the poetry of Rodrigues, the new territory comes from the acceptance of ordinary life and relationships as worthy subject matter for poetry. By writing on such topics as athletics, the enjoyment of being young and alive, the sexual ignorance of a sixteen-year-old girl, the restricting conventions of Goan society and the unwillingness of Indian students to accept that poetry written by Indians is good, Rodrigues, de Souza and Silgardo have mapped large, previously neglected, areas of Indian reality in their poetry.

The larger social awareness that Saleem Peeradina thought desirable in his introduction to his Macmillan anthology can be found in his *First Offense*, the first part of which consists of fragments of modern Indian urban life in the form of a panoramic survey of the Bombay suburb ('Bandra'), a collection of attitudes towards a mother ('There Is No God'), an urban mock-pastoral ('Morning Glory'), ironic juxtapositions of Muslim, Hindu and Christian religious services ('Time: The Same'), a wedding procession ('Marriage Poem'), movie-going ('The Real Thing') and snippets from marriage advertisements and other trivia found in popular magazines and newspapers ('The Only Man'). While such poems may, at a casual glance, appear like some of the unstructured experimental verse published in the late 1960s, they are organized to progress through various stages towards a firm conclusion. The construction is, however, less by way of argument, logic or narrative than by large areas of related fragments through which the poem moves. Such a technique seems appropriate to the immense amount of information, misinformation, sentiments, contradictory attitudes, advertisements, slogans and other similar characteristics of the confusion of modern Indian urban life in which people of various religions live side by side, attend movies, read magazines with cover girls, read newspapers with quizzes, listen to politicians on the radio and are bombarded with more impressions than can be reduced into a consistent vision. Spatial organization and juxtaposition are means of giving an over-all structure to such an otherwise incoherent, unhomogeneous mixture. It also allows the bringing into poetry of aspects of modern reality which because of their fragmentary or trivial, but representative, nature would be otherwise neglected in more closed, formalized, internally consistent kinds of writing.

Peeradina's poetry, to refer to his introduction to *Contemporary Indian Poetry in English*, reveals 'an awareness .... of the physical and human landscape that is India' and involvement 'in the life around it'. It shows the lesson that Indian poets have learned from their knowledge of American writing, and particularly of the poetry of William Carlos Williams and Wallace Stevens, how to let the poem arise out of the place where the poet lives, so the poem, a created artifice, is made from local materials and has an immediacy and local relevance.

'Bandra', which has been republished in *First Offense* with a few minor changes from Peeradina's anthology, uses the metaphor of the Bombay suburb as a whorish woman to survey its history and characteristic features, the mixture of cultures and sub-cultures which forms its identity. The technique here is less immediate than in some later poems since the narrator's voice and the controlling metaphor distances what is observed rather than offering an unmediated presentation of sights and sounds. The poem moves from an initial reference to the growth of Bandra from 'a sea-front town' to a 'settlement / of shops, cafes, cinemas, churches, / hospitals, schools, parks'. The focus shifts to the mosque with its flower-seller, policeman controlling heavy traffic, smells of street stalls, and slaughter house. The third section concerns Bandra as a slum ('dirtheaped', 'guttersmell', 'shitimmemorial lane') and its living conditions ('attic-study facing the gallery kitchen facing / the terrace bedroom'). The scene then moves to Bandstand, a place where local lovers meet among the clothes and fish, crab hunting and public defecation. Next the poem has the refrain 'Give everyone' in which Bandra is whoregoddess offering a variety of goods, sights and cultures—supermarkets, small provisions stores, roadside stands, large villas, wealthy Parsis, westernized Christians, Mercedes cars, toughs, whores and an annual Christian religious ceremony (balancing the Muslim scene in section two). An ironic prayer in which traditional superstition remains in a modern setting concludes the portrait:

> Preserve us
> Take all
>   evil spirits
>   driven into an offering
> and dropped
>   from a train window

into creek water
to the sea.

The narrator's metaphor of Bandra as a whorish woman unifies
'Bandra' as a poem, but introduces a soft, romantic cliché to the
reality of the place. By interposing such obviously external control
on the varied urbanscape, immediacy is lessened and turned into
sentiment. Peeradina's other poems are closer to the reality of the
urban experience with its immense variety of trivial stimuli which
makes modern life both exciting and fatiguing and which is nor-
mally taken for granted and ignored as somehow natural to city living
today.

'Morning Glory' is an ironic urban mock-pastoral, a traditional
sub-genre of poetry used by Swift among other eighteenth-cen-
tury writers in which the reality of urban life is implicitly contras-
ted to idyllized rural pastoral landscape and behaviour. The poem
begins, as have previous urban mock-pastorals, with images of a
city morning (in implicit contrast to waking to a sun rising in the
countryside). 'The public wakes' recurs three times, ironically
recalling the Cynthias and other beautiful mistresses who awake
to the rising sun in older poems; but instead of country delights
there are 'the beggar's early morning wail', 'mill-sirens',
'phlegm-bursts', 'broomdust' and 'newsprint'. Even 'The cocks
have turned neurotic / crowing at odd hours of the night'. The
reference to the morning newspaper leads into a different, more
contemporary kind of poem in which in place of considered,
sophisticated ironies of the mock-pastoral, the conflicting, dis-
organized information of modern communications is offered
directly and allowed to parody itself through the resulting
incongruities of government statements, political slogans, adver-
tisements for marriages, jobs and commercial products, editor-
ials, weather bulletins, sports reports and various readymade
figures of speech ('By no means. Evidently, it is doubtful. There-
fore / In Fact. It is high time …'). As the contrasts become absurd,
Peeradina introduces references to typical newspaper photographs
and the way their captions often belie the actuality shown. In keep-
ing with the urban scene, and the bombardment of information,
sounds, notices, the poem includes ironic notices: 'NO SPITTING',
'INCONVENIENCE REGRETTED'.

Characteristic of contemporary reality is the massive amount
of trivial news, signs, advertisements, photographs and other

auditory and visual information which constitutes a large area of
the environment. Such communications, and the ways of living
they represent, are a challenge to the poet whose domains have
traditionally been the celebration of the communal and the assertion
of subjective emotions. The quantity of modern communications
challenges, distracts attention from and dulls receptivity to the lite-
rature of high culture and especially has resulted in the diminishing
of the readership for poetry, the most complex, stylized and highly
organized form of language. Along with the inattention to the art of
the written word there has been an accompanying loss in the art of
the spoken word, as the formalized rhetorics of the past have been
replaced with clichés, readymade phrases, incomplete sentences,
and similar expressions of fragmented, hurried, dulled perceptions
of reality. A poem such as 'Morning Glory' assimilates such incon-
sequentiality and inattentiveness, and by compressing, juxtaposing
and structuring it, heightens it, giving it a representative signifi-
cance, challenging the diffuseness and anesthetizing effect of an
overdose of signs and communication by making an ironic artifice
of such materials. The result is both immediate and focuses atten-
tion on the environment.

Peeradina carries such techniques further in 'The Only Man',
which begins directly with newspaper and popular magazine clichés
without, as in 'Morning Glory', having a traditional framework
against which its materials can be seen in ironic juxtaposition. Here
the materials themselves create the ironies as trivia and clichés
accumulate without intervening commentary:

> *Wanted*   personality. colour. family.
>   salary. irrespective of
>   caste community province.
>   doctor. engineer officer.   *Male*
>
> *Wanted*   suitable. beautiful. highly.
>   convent-educated. family
>   well-to-do. extremely
>   decent extremely respectable.   *Female*
>
> How do you tell a gentleman from a wolf?
>
> Mr. & Mrs. A and their son
> cordially invite
> Mr. & Mrs. B and their daughter
> to a mutual friendly inspection.

While it might seem that such poems as 'Bandra', 'Morning Glory', 'The Real Thing' and 'The Only Man' could have been written in any modern city, this is only partly true. Although urban landscapes and an excess of signs and communications are typical of the modern world, the subject matter, forms of English and specific situations in Peeradina's poems are often uniquely Indian or a distinctive Indianization of western forms of culture. Peeradina incorporates an enormous amount of Indian reality in his verse: marriage advertisements, negotiations for marriage, the cinema booking-office, wedding processions, the mixture of religious communities and their services, Hindi-ized English compounds ('phlegm-bursts', 'Shock-Distress-Messages', 'freedomposter') and such words as 'paan' and 'crore'—which are unfamiliar to someone in England or America. In these poems the noise, traffic and confusion of the city mentioned in Ezekiel's poetry are seen close up and felt as specific stimuli and a chaos of conflicting messages and values.

One poem in the opening section of *First Offense* is different as it treats of an individual in depth and with careful attention. 'Poet Running' derives as a kind from Ezekiel's urban character sketches; but whereas the people Ezekiel meets are representative warnings of what he might become unless he asserts his will to change his ways and break from the temptations of the city, Peeradina records the dedication, isolation, dissatisfactions and uprootedness of a modern Indian English poet. The poem does not satirize, judge or sentimentalize; its strength results from an unusual compassion which develops in spite of a failure of communication and understanding, as among the noise and bustle of the city Peeradina comes into contact with a more profound, purposeful, mature experience which stands out from the failed executive, bored teachers and greasy garagehands who populate his other poems:

> 'You must exercise more control
> over words', he said.
> It was disconcerting
> I couldn't answer then to his advanced
> state of loneliness
> shifting from city to city to village to
> scorned city.
> 'The land I want to inhabit
> remains undiscovered.'

The second section of *First Offense* consists of memories of rural
life in contrast to the previous urban poems. This is the world the
city has forgotten. Sentimentality is avoided by careful, exact
descriptions which turn the scenes into images. In these poems
Peeradina is aware of William Carlos Williams's technique in which
line breaks are used to convey the act of perceiving an object or
scene and which by conveying an immediacy of perception make
reality seem charged, a work of imagination. In 'Vanishing Species'
he alludes to Williams's famous poem 'The Red Wheelbarrow';
here the presence of the 'one / common / bird, animal, or passing /
human form' on 'an air-field / of grass' which is 'so essential' to an
aesthetic vision contributes to an affirmation of the natural world in
contrast to the abstract:

> And a neighbourhood
> of sounds
> of insect-life
> constantly
> creating
> silence.

If I read these rural poems correctly they show the natural, as
contrasted to the urban, world necessary for the imagination and
the renewal of attention. At 'Aksa Beach'

> Stopping travel, I turn
> and the sea finds me.
>
> Obeying the sea-air's quiet goading
> towards water heel, eye, ear stand
> at the ocean's feet. A wave breaks
>
> ...
>
> The mind is a hollow shell
> conscious only of the ocean's single statement.

A Guarded Space, the title of Manohar Shetty's first book,
suggests a careful, defensive concern with the self and its feelings.
The short titles of Shetty's poems are an indication that he will
project his sensitivities and introspection on the external world:
'Fireflies', 'Spider', 'Pigeon', 'Mannequin', 'Pedestals', 'Cocoon',
'Fog' and 'Mirror'. Careful control is shown in the physical shape
of Shetty's poems, which consist mostly of stanzas and lines of

regular lengths, so that the printed page offers a feeling of en-
closure.

Childhood memories of trapping and caging 'fireflies', which
consequently become dim, lose their flashing light, wilt and die,
are the subject of the first poem. This introduces several of
Shetty's main themes, including the problems of growing up and
the contrast between the attractiveness of the outside world and
its reality when seen closely, and the way the routines of adult life
kill their spontaneity. Memories of past experience are brought
into the present to become the subject for reflection. The child's
cruelty towards the firefly is innocent as the child is only aware of
a desired attractiveness; by contrast the adult, knowing what it is
like to be caged into a routine made necessary by the economics
of survival, no longer is innocent and sees himself in the trapped
insects:

> I felt nothing then,
> Only a small pang for the loss
> Of a schoolboy's ornament. But now,
> Travelling my daily groove
> In the hunt for food and habitat
> I remember their trapped blank lights.

'Fireflies' is impressive in its art. The contrast between 'Out-
side' and being caged is conveyed in the language. The fireflies are
'flashing streamers', 'wavering lanterns', 'burning crystals', but
trapped 'Soon dimming', the glass walls 'baffling' them. In con-
trast to the vitality, movement and bright images of the opening
stanza, with its active -ing words, the final stanza, representing
the present life of the speaker, is purposefully abstract, dull,
clichéd ('hunt for food and habitat') and the -ing words appro-
priately dull ('nothing', 'Travelling'). The diminishing of the quality
of experience between innocent youth and adult routine is reflected
in the adjectives and similes: the world of youth is filled with bright
descriptive words ('like luminous dials', 'like wavering lanterns');
the adult's perception consists of fewer, duller adjectives ('daily
groove', 'blank lights') while the implied metaphor of adult life as a
jungle in which one fights to survive is purposefully made flat,
energyless and without any excitement ('groove', 'hunt', 'habitat').

Shetty's fireflies are the nightingales of disillusioned expe-
rience; observed closely they are found disappointing insects that

soon die. But they represent the active, attractive, free ('stray-ing'), natural world of childhood. With the shift from child to adulthood the hunt changes from youthful illusions of 'emerald embers' to learning the reality that attracted is merely an insect, and life will now consist of a deadening routine. 'Fireflies' is unusual in that the child, though innocent, is a hunter, and the child's hunt unnecessarily kills what is attractive. Youth in Shetty's poems is not joyful or edenic.

'Growing Pains' uses a similar stratagem to 'Fireflies' in first recounting a situation in youth, and then commenting upon it again as seen from an adult perspective:

> It began with dark stairs
> Invaded by white shapes
> With oval gaps for eyes
> And a creak amplified
> To startling sounds.

In contrast to such fears, there was 'the solid door' behind which there were 'many lights', 'warmth', 'disarming laughter' of family and friends. Such protection is no longer available: 'Now the same faces grow strange / And the nights are cold'. The adult's present isolation and lack of warmth seem a further development of the fears of being alone in the dark experienced while young.

An awareness of life as competition ('hunt') is also expressed in 'Bread and Fishes', where the speaker notices the 'Glum-faced fish' entering 'the fray' for the bread he throws into the water. It is, however, only the middle-sized ones who compete. The ana-logy to adulthood becomes explicit in the last stanza:

> The younger ones revel
> In a little school by themselves.
> The fat old fish slumber at the side
> Like elderly men in armchairs or satisfied
> Businessmen.

Many of the poems recall or report on the comforts of guarded spaces, the doors of childhood, the spider's web, in contrast to outside terrors and the competition to survive. But there is also a sense of vacancy within the self, of being unable to go beyond the limits of the guarded space. Such feelings provide the subject matter of 'Mannequin', in which the poet enters into the supposed vision and thoughts of a clothes dummy in a shop window. It is significant of Shetty's preoccupation with the routines of adulthood that the first face the mannequin singles out from the 'scudding hordes' is a man with

> Worried brow, the perpetual brief-case
> Weary with age, as he vanishes past
> Too pressed for time to appreciate
> My groomed slender frame, my glass blue eyes
> Gleaming all day from my elevated place.

While the mannequin could be seen as symbolic of the poet or poetry, like the fireflies it also offers a deceiving, transitory attractiveness. Art, the poet, the sensitive, the attractive, the ornamental seem unable to 'erase' the longings they create as the pleasures they offer are outside forms of an inner darkness:

> I would like to erase that longing
> In her eyes—ornaments can be replaced;
> But a vacant darkness swarms
> Within me too, and I cannot go beyond
> This fixed fond smile.

In these poems set in recognizable social situations, Shetty creates a space for private feelings having to do with the relationship of self to the external world. While reality is harsh, the self is not necessarily superior; there is no romanticization or sentimentalization of the poet. The poet's art might be considered the 'Cocoon' of the poem with that title:

> i weave myself
> a cocoon breathe
> the air in the inky
> gloom entranced by
> this inky den i
> bare my teeth like
> other men.

There is a pattern to Shetty's imagination. The images are of enclosure, caging, weaving, spinning, hunting, shaping, building, preening, gloom and light. The dilemmas of isolation are a recurring theme; 'The Recluse' is undisturbed but remains tense as he listens for the train's whistle 'Fading into sun-stroked hills, / Immense in their lonely will'.

Many poems treat of emotions masked by social adjustment. The excellent poem 'Fog' is of interest in the way the movement of the syntax through the lines imitates the movement of the bus and in the increasing focus on the emotions of the poet and companion:

> The bus snorts, hesitates
>   in dense white space as
> glazed headlights stain
>   the serpentine road.
> Nudged awake, you watch
>   the writhing veil slither
> and roll over the gaping
>   void below. Afraid, you
> hold my arm, stare down
>
>   . . .
>
> . . . your face
>   suddenly sheds years
> of accumulated age, till the
>   bus coughs and stops out
> of reach and you return
>   to the old masquerade,
> forgetting again that
>   innocent terror sinking
> away in your brain.

Other poems reveal the masks, as in 'The Strangeness', which sees in an adult's fears a 'deeper' problem, 'but you / Do not want to face it'. Similarly, 'The Malaise' concerns 'an eternal erosion of the soul', which grows slowly, deeply and 'Unfurls in defeated nerves, Warm white wings of a death-wish'.

Shetty maps the mind's pains, fears, wounds, disillusions and moments of insanity. The poems define areas of the inner self, its defences and relation to reality. The poems in the first part of *A Guarded Space* (the second part, titled *Legacy*, is a sequence of lyrics about a doomed love affair) are in clusters with related themes; they are structured to proceed through images of childhood, images of selfhood, images of enclosure, poems about illness and depression, to poems which grope towards some resolution of private fears:

> Both method and end uncertain

I step now into the jarring air;
Though the protective veil always
Falls in place
Distorts images, cancels communication
Leaves me groping still,
Drinking and talking
Fitfully, mid-air.

('Personality')

In *The Indian Literary Review* (vol. 1, no. 10, February 1979),
M. Sivaramkrishna, reviewing *Three Poets*, noted the way the
poets aimed at clarity. He objected to what he felt was a banality
of diction, a lack of individual idiom, while realizing that the flat-
ness was often meant as a reflection of what was being described.
A characteristic of the Newground poets is that the dead, ready-
made expressions common to speech are used, unlike in Auden or
Ezekiel, without tonal ironies and implied quotation marks.
Rather than using such language within an otherwise stylized
diction and manner, they create a directness of speech in which
common expressions seem natural to the voice and attitudes
expressed. Such flatness is a necessary part of coming even closer
to reality, directness and confessional immediacy than previous
poetry. It is a less elevated equivalent of the conversational manner of
someone such as Dryden, who often made poetry from common-
place metaphors and ready-made expressions. It is less elevated
because contemporary urban society aims at a style or appearance
of naturalness and spontaneity in contrast to the elevated, formal
and premeditated. Poetic language always needs to be renewed
and one way to renew it is by eliminating whatever at the time
feels poetic and distant from contemporary sensibility. This does
not mean that Rodrigues, de Souza, Silgardo and Shetty write as
they speak. Their poetry is much more economical in expression,
more imagistic, metaphoric and structured in development than
speech. Such ready-made phrases as 'sheds years', 'void below',
'Do not want to face it', 'observed clearly', 'haunting mist',
'Brought into the open' and 'Falls in place' are, as used by these
writers, a form of poetic diction, a contemporary style of realism
appropriate to communicate supposed unpremeditated self-reve-
lation.

The Newground poets have expanded and redefined the areas
of reality first mapped by Ezekiel in Indian English poetry. There

is increased attention to and analysis of life in Bombay and its suburbs, of the effects of public signs, advertising, newspapers, the radio and motion pictures; more concern with family, personal history and the past as part of character and the sources of emotional problems; more psychology, especially the revelation of weaknesses, fears and moments of loss of control. In terms of space the new poetry has moved further into the streets and lives of Bombay and the suburbs, as well as making a start towards charting Goan and Poona Christian society. The poetry has also begun to make fuller use of memories and dreams to recreate the past and to explore normally masked feelings within the mind. The territory of Indian English poetry is much larger, more varied than a few decades ago. The new poets have found appropriate techniques for their perception of reality; these range from the spatial organization and ironic juxtaposition of 'found' materials (advertisements, signs) in Peeradina's poetry, the selected snap-shot album memories of de Souza with their seemingly objective presentation, to the impressive craftsmanship by which Shetty knits together a guarded space from rhyme, stanzaic shapes, repeated parts of speech, recurring sounds and other devices of closure.

CHAPTER NINE

Women's Voices

KAMALA DAS, DE SOUZA AND SILGARDO

Kamala Das's *Summer in Calcutta* (1965) appeared at a time when English poetry by Indian women had moved on from such colonial and nationalist themes as the rewriting of legends, praise of peasants, and from general ethical statements to writing about personal experiences. While outmoded diction and sentiments were at last overtaken in favour of a more contemporary and less artificial manner, the subject matter of the women poets was often limited to well-meaning platitudes about romantic love, which were treated without depth, complexity, interest or even the projection of much emotion. By contrast the poems of Kamala Das when focused on love treat it within a broader ranges of themes, more realized settings and with deeper feeling, bringing to it an intensity of emotion and speech and a rich, full complexity of life. Das's themes go beyond stereotyped longings and complaints. Even her feelings of loneliness and disappointment are part of a larger-than-life personality, obsessive in its awareness of its self, yet creating a drama of selfhood.

Having started writing verse in school and having early published in *Indian PEN* (1948), Kamala Das evolved from a rudimentary poet using traditional verse methods to someone with a highly personal voice but without strong awareness of technique or theory. She is a natural poet with an excellent feeling for sound, rhythm, phrasing, image, symbol, word play and drama. The prosody of her early poems is mostly a matter of counting syllables in a regular rhythm. Later, as her versification and sense of form became freer and looser, her style changed but did not necessarily improve. Always a hit-or-miss poet, who wrote regularly but trusted the muse more than revision, she began to miss more often.

Her early poems are primarily concerned with her marriage, love life, desire for intimacy and the various results—including guilt—and her fame as a writer. There is a basic story which Kamala Das tells about herself in her poetry and autobiography, *My Story*. Raised in the warmth of a tight-knit Kerala matrilineal society, she was uprooted when her father moved to Calcutta. For a time she attended a Catholic boarding school and was suddenly at a young age married to a cousin for whom she apparently had little affection, while he was too preoccupied with his career to expect more from his young wife than a cook and sexual partner. Left by herself as she and her husband moved home in accordance with his job, rebellious, angry and confused, Das turned to others for affection. Her husband's willingness to let her have her sexual experiences was a further blow to her ego. What he saw as freedom for a writer she saw as a lack of caring.

Significantly many of her poems are about the warmth of her childhood and the family home in Kerala. Similar to other South Indians, such as Ramanujan, Parthasarathy, Meena Alexander and Sharat Chandra, she writes of memories of childhood, family relations and the family's great house. In her poetry there is an idealized time of childhood at 'My Grandmother's House' when she felt the security of love within familiar surroundings innocent of sexual fears and frustrations. It was a period of love, roots and freedom, in contrast to her present insecurity:

> ... you cannot believe, darling,
> Can you, that I lived in such a house and
> Was proud, and loved ... I who have lost
> My way and beg now at strangers' doors to
> Receive love, at least in small change?

The contrast between a familiar, secure, loving home and the world she now experiences since leaving her family for marriage, its dissatisfactions and her love affairs is the theme of 'The Corridors':

> Why do I so often dream
> Of a house where each silent
> Corridor leads me to warm
> Yellow rooms—and, loud voices
> Welcome me, and rich, friendly
> Laughter, and upturned faces.

> ... once awake, I
> See the bed from which my love
> Has fled, the empty room, the
> Naked walls, count on fingers
> My very few friends.

Despite the mercurial changes of mood, attitude and self-regard in her poetry there is an inner core of identity to which she refers— her name and aristocratic blood, her mother's family, life in the South and her youth in contrast to her marriage.

'Composition' contrasts Das's present life to 'lying beside my grandmother':

> That was long ago.
> Before the skin,
> intent on survival,
> learnt lessons of self-betrayal.
> Before the red house that had stood for innocence
> crumbled
> and the old woman died
>
> ...
>
> The tragedy of life
> is not death but growth,
> the child growing into adult.

After reviewing her marriage when her husband offered her 'freedom' to do as she wanted and the uncertainties and the self-doubts such freedom brought, often including lack of sexual satisfaction, she says that while she offers 'autobiography' to excite desire

> The only secrets I always
> withhold
> are that I am so alone
> and that I miss my grandmother.

In 'Composition' Das claims that by 'confessing / by peeling off my layers', she will come nearer her 'soul' and 'the bone's / supreme indifference'.

There is a dualism in her writing, in which soul is contrasted to body. She seems to imagine overcoming this dualism only through death; her poems are filled with longings to die, especially to drown in the sea, water being associated in her mind with an all-encompassing, universal calm, a formlessness in contrast to the conscious mind and body of the anxious individual. The dualism results from the fall from childhood innocence into the adult world of sexuality, marriage and life among strangers, especially an uncaring husband. 'The Suicide' makes explicit the contrast between the happy security of childhood at her grandmother's and the search for love as an adult:

> I had a house in Malabar
> and a pale-green pond.
> I did all my growing there
> In the bright summer months.
> I swam about and floated,
> I lay speckled green and gold
> In all the hours of the sun,
> Until
> My grandmother cried,
> Darling, you must stop this bathing now.
> You are much too big to play
> Naked in the pond.

Rather than a poet of free love, she expresses the disappointments of sexuality. She describes a void to be filled with others or with alternative passions. In 'The Freaks' she laments a lack of deep sexual passions of the kind that go with love; there is mere appetite without feelings of intimacy.

Alongside Das's unfilled need for love, another prominent subject of her poems is the need to assert, to conquer, to dominate. There is, for example, her obsession with an older man who 'hurt' her in her teens and whom she obsessively feels she must capture as her lover. In her poetry love and hate are often neighbours, just as an assertion of sexual freedom sits near feelings of self-disgust expressed through depression. The theatre of Das's poetry includes the revelations, the confessions, the various contradictory bits and pieces. While the poems describe a longing for a man to fill her dreams with love, she is also proud of her conquests and ability to make men love her. Having taken a lover she will mock him. Rather than the seduced, she often appears the seducer, the collector, especially of those men known as lady killers. Driven by a need for an all-encompassing love to fill her days, she is also someone involved in the game of sexual triumph with its trophies.

Often her poetry offers its versions of the *carpe diem* theme, a seizing the day both in awareness of the passing of time and youth and in a need to live intensely. To a person who objects that her sexual adventures are spoiling her name she replies: 'I know I have a life / To be lived, and each nameless / Corpuscle in me, has its life':

> … Why should I remember or bear
> That sweet-sounding name, pinned to
> Me, a medal, undeservingly
> Gained, at moments when, all of
> Me is ablaze with life?

If many poems speak of unhappiness and the desire for an all-absorbing love, others are filled with Das's discovery of the life around her on the streets and in bedrooms. While marriage has hurt her ego, leaving her unfulfilled, her poems also record a woman enjoying the newness of the world as she wanders the streets and pursues her own interests. The poems in *Summer in Calcutta* and even the later, sometimes more sombre, depressed verses, written after serious illness, reveal someone younger, more questing, more sexually driven than the author of *My Story* with its claim that being treated brutally led to adultery and its self-apologetics and spiritualist conclusion. The poems show that through her sexual confessions her writing has made her a selfconscious celebrity; and she plays up to it, often bragging and celebrating.

The interest of Das's poetry is not the story of sex outside of marriage but the instablility of her feelings, the way they rapidly shift and assume new postures, new attitudes of defence, attack, explanation or celebration. Her poems are situated neither in the act of sex nor in feelings of love; they are instead involved with the self and its varied, often conflicting emotions, ranging from the desire for security and intimacy to the assertion of the ego, self-dramatization and feelings of shame and depression.

There is another, more interesting story behind the tale of a bored woman seeking refuge from an uncaring husband. In 'An Apology to Goutama' it is her husband who must comfort her from the rejection by another man. 'I Shall Some Day' recognizes her own fear of the attraction to domestic comforts and her fear of freedom:

> I shall some day leave, leave the cocoon

You built around me with morning tea,
Love-words flung from doorways and of course
Your tired lust. . .
. . . and I shall someday see
My world, de-fleshed, de-veined, de-blooded,
Just a skeletal thing, then shut my
Eyes and take refuge, if nowhere else,
Here in your nest of familiar scorn....

Which returns us to the theme of freedom in 'Composition':

When I got married
my husband said,
you may have freedom,
as much as you want.
My soul balked at this diet of ash.
Freedom became my dancing shoe,
how well I danced,
and danced without rest,
until the shoes turned grimy on my feet
and I began to have doubts.

In 'Substitute', even with her first and only great love:

End it, I cried, end it, and let us be free.

This freedom was our last strange toy.
Like the hangman's robe, even while new
It could give no pride. Nor even joy.
We kissed and we loved, all in a fury.
For another short hour or two
We went all warm and wild and lovely.

>   After that love became a swivel-door,
>   When one went out, another came in.

Writing is a means of creating a place in the world; the use of the
personal voice and self-revelation are means of self-assertion. Das
opened areas in which previously forbidden or ignored emotions
could be expressed in ways which reflect the true · voice
of feeling; she showed how an Indian woman poet could create a
space for herself in the public world. She brings a sense of locality to
her poems. There are the rooms in which she lives, the homes she
has left, the bedrooms, restaurants and streets in which she meets

her lovers, the rides in cars, the people she visits or notices, the people she addresses in personal terms. Whereas Ezekiel consciously refers to his environment, Das's poems assume their location, create their space by being set in situations rather than by observing or alluding to their environment.

Kamala Das's most remarkable achievement, however, is writing in an Indian English. Often her vocabulary, idioms, choice of verbs and some syntactical constructions are part of what has been termed the Indianization of English. This is an accomplishment. It is important in the development of a national literature that writers free themselves from the linguistic standards of their colonizers and create a literature based on local speech; and this is especially important for women writers. Such a development is not a matter of national pride or a linguistic equivalent of 'local colour'; rather it is a matter of voice, tone, idiom and rhythm, creating a style that accurately reflects what the writer feels or is trying to say instead of it being filtered through speech meant to reflect the assumptions and nuances of another society.

As this may seem a large claim for Das's poetry, a few examples may be useful for comparison. Monika Varma, one of the better women poets of an older generation, who often appeared under the Writers Workshop imprint, has criticized Das for falling into flat, adolescent and old-fashioned expressions. But here is the opening stanza of Varma's first poem, 'In the Domino Dusk', of her *Dragonflies Draw Flames* (1962, 1966) volume:

> Read Rimbaud in the domino dusk of the stalagtite
> > evening
> > when little bats go wheeling
> > blackly into shadows asprawl upon the ground.

While 'domino dusk', 'stalagtite evenings' and 'shadows asprawl' show a poet's love of words, they are part of a self-conscious poetic diction with no roots in common speech. Gauri Deshpande, one of the younger, university-educated women poets, often writes of love and motherhood without intensity of feeling. In the concluding stanza of Deshpande's 'December' the language is abstract and pretentious and far from spoken speech:

> When I feel the sun warm on my back
> And tend to forget
> It's winter

And you about to depart
Then the other times clearly felt
Futility of my life assumes import
As a vast preparation
For our confrontation
And its brief but vicious anger that set
Your hands hard about my face
Before you went.

Contrast such artificiality with the natural, direct speech rhythms of Das's 'Words':

... Words are a nuisance, but
They grow on me like leaves on a tree,
They never seem to stop their coming
From a silence, somewhere deep within ...

In 'An Apology to Goutama' the naturalness of expression and rhythm is powerful and the scene rapidly created. Even 'woman-form' seems an Indian compound word coinage:

... and yet Goutama,
The other owns me; while your arms hold
My woman-form, his hurting arms
Hold my very soul.

The detail, the naturalness of speech, the Indian use of 'gift' as a verb and the cadence of the lines are noticeable in Das's 'The Looking Glass':

... Notice the perfection
Of his limbs, his eyes reddening under
Shower, the shy walk across the bathroom floor,
Dropping towels, and the jerky way he
Urinates. All the fond details that make
Him male and your only man, Gift him all,
Gift him what makes you woman, the scent of
Long hair, the musk of sweat between the breasts,
The warm shock of menstrual blood, and all your
Endless female hungers. Oh yes, getting
A man to love is easy, but living
Without him afterward may have to be
Faced....

In the poetry of Kamala Das and such younger women poets as
de Souza and Silgardo the directness of speech rhythms and collo-
quial language is an expression of emotional involvement. Their
language reveals feelings in all their quirkiness and unpredictability,
whereas with previous women poets language stands in the way of
emotion, poeticizing and generalizing rather than reflecting it. Das,
de Souza and Silgardo offer a range of highly volatile emotions with
poems unexpectedly, changing direction and gaining effect from
their inner contrasts, conflicts, ironies and extremes.

While Das can be said to have created a climate for a more honest,
revelatory, confessional poetry by Indian women, her abundance of
manner, with its repetition of words, phrases and symbols, its
curious blend of Indian English usage and the introspection of an
Elizabethan sonneteer, seems at present overblown, even theatrical
in the grand nineteenth-century romantic fashion, in contrast to the
stripped-down style, street language and forcefulness of some con-
temporary women poets. The present contemporary manner
appears to have been initiated by Mamta Kalia who explored the
themes, attitudes, voices and registers of speech which have been
taken further by de Souza and Silgardo. Instead of Deshpande's
love poem about awaiting the return of her man, Kalia complains
of the effect of being a housewife on her individuality:

> I no longer feel I'm Mamta Kalia
> I'm Kamla
> or Vimla
> or Kanta or Shanta.
> I cook, I wash,
> I bear, I rear,
> I nag, I wag,
> I sulk, I sag.

('Anonymous')

In 'Tribute to Papa' she rebels against patriarchy and the inhibit-
ing world of middle-class respectability, with its 'clean thoughts,
clean words, clean teeth'. As in some feminist writing the poems
are haunted by her father:

> You suspect I am having a love-affair these days,
> But you're too shy to have it confirmed.
> What if my tummy starts showing gradually

> And I refuse to have it curetted?
> But I'll be careful, Pap,
> Or I know you'll at once think of suicide.

Eunice de Souza's *Fix* is also a thinner, less rich world than Kamala Das's; sounds, images, language, phrasing, cadences and line lengths have been stripped down to little more than bare statements. There is little here of the complaints or attacks, demands for freedom and sexual enjoyment found in Das's poetry. Instead of Das's excess of emotion and self-dramatization, there is economy and control. Many of the poems are satires or are in a confessional mode similar to Sylvia Plath's miming of deep fears and resentments which are expressed through self-ironic wit. Where Das's grandmother's house seems an Eden, a paradise lost, de Souza's childhood among the Goan community of Poona appears to have been a hell. The subjects of her satires are the church, marriage, Catholic motherhood, Indian colour prejudice, sexual prudery and hypocrisy, Goan vulgarity and the alienation felt by many Goan Catholics towards Hindu India. In 'Conversation Piece':

> My Portuguese-bred aunt
> picked up a clay shivalingam
> one day and said:
> Is this an ashtray?
> No, said the salesman,
> This is our god.

In such poems de Souza has mapped a society in which she grew up and which she feels made her what she is now. The poem 'De Souza Prabhu' rejects her past and alien mixture of names and language, but claims that she belongs with 'the lame ducks' ever since she heard her parents 'wanted a boy'. Often de Souza suggests herself through satire; in these poems the implied personality appears off-hand, cold, controlled, self-distancing, ironic.

Poems record what her elders said and are satiric in intent, although without commentary or a satiric manner. Rather they report and use juxtaposition for ironic contrasts. Her manner in the Goan poems is more that of a novelist who concentrates effects through using scene, dialogue and irony. Poems grow out of situations, as when her aunt discusses the physical features of a bride, or from the way Goans arranging a marriage will examine

the girl and her family and will look for any signs of insanity in
the girl's family history, as they know that some Goans will
attempt to marry off a woman who is insane in the hope that it
will cure her. Although there is an obvious anger at the social and
moral attitudes of the women in the Goan Catholic community,
there is also compassion and sympathy for how they have been
victimized by their conformity, passivity, illusions and accep-
tance of the behaviour expected of women.

The Goan satires were among her early poems in which she
appears a nationalist; she rebelled against a stifling, crude reli-
gious and family upbringing by, in reaction, identifying with the
poor, the Hindus and India. This stage was followed by a larger
awareness in which Hindu India, as well as the Goan community,
is repressive towards women. The poem 'My Students' satirizes
those who think poetry can only be written by foreigners and
that only men can write about their sexual life:

> My students think it funny
> that Daruwallas and de Souzas
> should write poetry.
> Poetry is faery lands forlorn.
> Women writers Miss Austen.
> Only foreign men air their crotches.

Some of de Souza's most interesting poems are psychological
and have mainly to do with the results of conflicts with parents.
Her poem 'Forgive Me, Mother' is explicit:

> It was kill or die
> and you got me anyway:
> The blood congeals at lover's touch
> The guts dissolve in shit.

Her poems are stripped down to their bare bones. Some seem
settled, fixed in point of view; others appear immediate responses
to conversations with friends. Aiming at an apparent naturalness
and to avoid glib conclusions and rounding-off of poems with
observations, she uses abrupt endings. She avoids making poems
literary artifacts and uses normal diction. The poems, reflecting
de Souza's Catholic childhood, are a means to gain control over
private fears, anxieties, angers. Such poems are in the confessional
manner, where instead of consistency of character there is a
mosaic of guilts, desires and revelations, especially about how

one's emotional life has been formed by the past. 'Forgive Me Mother' concludes 'In dreams / I hack you'. 'For My Father, Dead Young' has as its refrain 'I'm you'. 'Autobiographical' begins by confessing feelings of guilt for her father's early death, for several disastrous love affairs and for learning nothing from experience:

> Right now here it comes.
> I killed my father when I was three.
> I have muddled through several affairs
> and always come out badly.
> I've learned almost nothing from experience.
> I head for the abyss with
> monotonous regularity.

She then shifts to what others think of her, admits a suicide attempt and claims that everyone is trying to 'cut me down go through me / with a razor blade', before she realizes that's what she 'wanted / to do to the world'. Self-exposure is a defence.

Although de Souza's poems arise out of alienation and the feeling that life is a mess, they are also highly conscious of the situations and problems faced by women. This consciousness is expressed through understated irony rather than articulated comment. De Souza's persona is, however, that of someone negative about herself as well as others. This is not a poetry of heroics, nor does it seek pity. While it has no affiliation in politics, community, humanistic ideals, religion, it is feminist in its kind of awareness, female vision, and affinities to the mode of other women poets—rather than in a proclaimed commitment.

Melanie Silgardo's *The Earthworm's Story* is dedicated to her teacher. From de Souza she learned how to write about herself and her past in a direct, colloquial style, and to use her Goan childhood and relation to her parents as a basis for self-analysis:

> You never knew I wet my pillow
> oftener than I had ever wet my bed.
>
> Forgive me for the things I said.
> Grown fifteen and above I thought
> that wisdom lay in startling words.
> In saying *cad* and *bastard*
> fifty times inside, and finding

> substitutes in my pair of eyes,
> I lied.

Silgardo tends to project her anxieties onto disturbing emotional images. As in the work of many women writers, the making up of a face in front of a mirror is a symbol for the unauthentic self, the smiling, cheerful, passive, unambitious woman expected by society:

> Daily faces crumple,
> die in front of mirrors.
> Scraping to uncover
> ratted faces,
> to uncover endless faces.
>
> Bleak as the sun snuffed out.
> Darkness and shadow
> leap and hit the face.
> A tear shocked inside an eye.
> A mouth a gaping cave.

This is a further uncovering of the kind of panic suggested in Kamala Das's poem 'Substitute':

> It will be all right if I join clubs
> And flirt a little over telephone.
> It will be all right, it will be all right
> I am the type that endures.
>
> It will be all right, it will be all right
> It will be all right between the world and me.

An earlier generation of women seemed to feel that the problems of life could be solved through a man's love. There are no love poems in de Souza's first book, rather there are cool, ironic, satiric pieces on the relationships between men and women and on male predatoriness and feelings of dominance. Silgardo's one love poem, 'A Memory', rejects her earlier image of the man standing 'at the waiting end, / big and brave like a brother' and asserts 'If I must meet you / it must be 'half-way'. Instead of the oneness and intimacy wanted by a previous generation of women poets, Silgardo says 'No there is no togetherness for us / I cannot merge …'.

In de Souza and Silgardo the women seem to be on their own: if they make a mess of their lives it is their mess and not the fault of a husband or lover. But this must be qualified. Like many contempo-

rary feminist writers both de Souza and Silgardo are preoccupied
with their relationship to their father. In 'For Father on the Shelf'
Silgardo's seemingly rebellious claim 'The year you died / I inhe-
rited a mind' is quickly explained by 'the letters you wrote ... be-
came my manifesto'. The poem develops around two conflicting
emotions, her love for and shame of her father, 'both villain and
hero of the piece'.

Both de Souza and Silgardo seem to contrast their father's assu-
rance and crude ease in the world with their own insecurities and
fears. Where the fathers belonged to settled societies which were
deadening for women, the poets' own more liberated world is filled
with anxieties, often influenced by their family, education and
cultural inheritance. Silgardo's strongest poems, along with those
on her father's death, reveal a psychology of horrifying fears, dep-
ression, self-hates, insecurities, self-humiliations and failed emo-
tions. '1956–1976', the first poem in the selection, begins:

> Twenty years ago
> they laid a snare.
>
> I emerged headlong
> embarrassed, wet.
> They slapped me on my bottom
> I screamed.
> That was my first experience.

'A Finale', the concluding poem, uses the metaphor of a failed dare-
devil circus performer to catch her sense of panic and insecurity; she
is not really free as she has inherited her family attitudes, ambitions,
angers and models of gender roles:

> I sit amid the clutter.
> Dead animal.
> Bowels loosened all around.
> Night is heavy on my back
> and I, towering
> on my mother's stilts,
>
> the new act
> on the painted bill.

While the liberation of Indian poetry from a conscious, forma-
lized British speech and diction occurs about the same time in the

mid 1960s for both male and female poets, a directness of expression
and natural, idiomatic, colloquial vigour is more often found in the
verse of Das, Kalia, de Souza and Silgardo than in the male Indian
English poets. In their rebellion against the traditional role of Indian
women the women poets, led by Das, had to fight against the kind
of diction used by such poets as Varma and Deshpande, in which
refined, lady-like language was associated with a conformity of
behaviour and attitudes. Just as in rejecting the spiritualism of Auro-
bindo the male poets insisted on precision and economy, the
women in expressing new attitudes required a new, more appro-
priate way of writing about their emotions, experiences and conscious-
ness of themselves as women. As is often the case with poetry,
language is a index of content.

CHAPTER TEN

Two Bilingual Experimentalists

KOLATKAR AND CHITRE

That most Indian English poetry should be realistic, use ordinary syntax and present arguments or narrative in sequence is not surprising as its early model was the British poetic tradition. With this it shares a similar moral utilitarianism, ethical awareness, and valuation of the tangible, actual, practical world as the object of attention and use. There are, however, excellent Indian English poets who have written in such non-realistic poetic modes as surrealism and constructivism, in which the poetry is different from a superior kind of logical and emotional communication; such poetry may be concerned with the irrational, with chance, or with structures of art. Because experimental poetry fore- grounds technique, new concepts, or explores uncommon expe- rience it usually neglects the common world and environment or treats it in strange, unconventional ways. Few artists remain pure experimentalists for long; the fascination with techniques, fanta- sies, games and the subconscious is a product of a period of an artist's life which will eventually give way or be assimilated to a sense of reality—if only in a preoccupation with one's difference or alienation from communal or cultural perceptions of reality.

The major Indian poets who have been experimentalists both in form and view of reality are Arun Kolatkar, Dilip Chitre, Arvind Mehrotra, and Jayanta Mahapatra. There was, however, a period during the late 1960s and early 1970s when experimentalism was championed by the young Pritish Nandy. In most cases the poets were at first unconcerned with empirical reality; in each case this mode changed and the poet became more concerned with local life or his relation to India. But, while no longer pure experimentalists, the poets still approach local life in ways that are distinctive from those of the realists; their relationship is more oblique, more ironic, more in doubt, or secondary to the attention given either to processes of imagination or to the poem as construction, art object or work in progress.

Experimentalism began in Indian regional-language poetries during the 1940s, usually as the writers became familiar with such English-language modernists as Eliot and Pound, and through English translations of the French romantic-modernist tradition of Lautréamont, Rimbaud, Baudelaire and the Surrealists. While each modern Indian-language literature has a slightly different history, the general pattern is similar. Sometimes there is a distinct relationship between modernism in the Indian regional languages and in English, as is shown by the influence of M. G. Adiga on A. K. Ramanujan in Kannada and the way B. S. Mardheker precedes Kolatkar and Chitre in Marathi. In the case of Oriya, Jayanta Mahapatra was aware of the modernism of his contemporaries, some of whom he has translated, but it is less likely that there was a direct influence rather than a parallel evolution.

B. S. Mardheker (1909–56) had made his own blend of the modernism of Eliot, Pound and the Surrealists with the Marathi saints' poetry of Tukaram at a time when Kolatkar began his own rapid progress through various kinds of experimental verse, sometimes in Marathi, sometimes in English, often translating from one language to the other. Kolatkar's early Marathi poems are what he calls 'cluster bombs', densely packed with sounds and metaphors. His early verse in both English and Marathi often seems surreal; it is obscure and difficult to interpret, but consists of projections of sexual desires and anxieties into sinister, extraordinary, irrational images. Such poetry channels the subconscious into images, shortcutting any engagement of emotions with the outside world. His early poems in Chitre's *Anthology of Marathi Poetry* appear to have as their scenes beds, hotel rooms and sexual unions, or exist in a nowhere world of words and images ('The goat of glass in the corner / Takes a metaphysical leap'). Besides extraordinary expressions of emotional anxieties and incongruous juxtapositions of images Kolatkar appears to have aimed at purposeful opaqueness. In poems such as 'The Renunciation of the Dog' the surreal combines with the spiritual:

> Tell me why the black dog died
>   Intriguingly between
> God and our heads.

As no detailed bibliography of his publications exists the chrono-
logy of Kolatkar's work is obscure; but during the 1960s his style
changed from highly imagistic, uninterpretable private poetry to an
anti-poetic as represented by the well-known 'Three Cups of Tea',
originally written in Bombay-Hindi and translated by the poet into
parody tough-guy American speech:

> i want my pay i said
> > to the manager
> you'll get paid said
> > the manager
> but not before the first
> > don't you know the rules?

In reaction to his earlier hyper-modernism Kolatkar was evolving
towards a conscious styleless poetry using (like Tukaram and the
saint poets) colloquial, common speech. Chitre has suggested that
such poems might be regarded as an Indian equivalent to the neo-
Dada, humorous pop poetry of the 1960s. Like such poetry it resists
depth; without embarrassment and with some humour it uses
stereotypes and refers to reality by way of popular culture. In
other poems, such as 'the boatride', Kolatkar went even further
towards removing the 'poetic' from his verse. Here and in *Jejuri*
he charges trivialities with significance by viewing them with
attention while at the same time using a flat, toneless voice which
denies importance to its subject.

By profession a visual artist and designer, Kolatkar , in works
from the mid '60s onwards, looks at aspects of ordinary Indian
reality as capable of being made interesting by an unusual pers-
pective or by the addition of some imagined details. The surreal
which once seemed to prevent entrance to the meaning of the
poem now becomes a way of investing ordinary reality with possi-
bilities for the artist's mind. Two characteristics of Kolatkar's
poems since the mid '60s are a tendency to play with vision or a
scene for its abstract qualities, as a painter or designer might, and a
tendency towards a cool, non-committal attitude in what is said.
The poem 'Temperature Normal' (in *Kavi—India*, January 1978)
illustrates both the conscious manipulation of sight lines, like an
artist or cameraman, and the throw-away I-could-not-care-less
manner towards the subject matter:

> i lean back in the armchair

and bombay sinks

    the level of the balcony parapet rises
and the city is submerged
...
i hear a cheeping sound
i see a sparrow

is there a connection
i am afraid i do not know.

In 'the boatride' an ordinary trip around Bombay harbour is trea-ted by Kolatkar as both incredibly boring and as a source of wonder while the poet observes and sometimes fantasizes upon the trivial and stereotypical. The trivial is viewed with a coolness which curiously creates a complexity of tone, while the poet as observer will suddenly imagine other possibilities for the scene, especially of a surreal or incongruous manner. Kolatkar is aware as a visual artist that a slight manipulation of sight lines, of angle of vision, can defamiliarize and turn into art what is normally regarded as dull, commonplace reality. By taking an odd, non-committal tone and by bringing in unusual perspectives Kolatkar turns the common-place into an aesthetic experience, using the ordinary as the basis of art. Like his 'Three Cups of Tea', 'the boatride' is non-poetic in subject matter and style.

Consisting of eleven sections concerning a tourist trip, 'the boatride' ranges from satire on the absurdities of social behaviour to surrealist fantasies:

       because a sailor waved
           back

to a boy
    another boy
waves to another sailor

in the clarity of air
the gesture withers for want
of correspondence and
the hand that returns to him
the hand his knee accepts
as his own
     is the hand
of an aged person
     a hand

> that must remain patient
> and give the boy it's a part of time
>   to catch up.

The flat but highly self-conscious narration is significant; Kolatkar reveals that art is made by the artist and not by reality. How the scene is broken into compositional parts can be seen from the sailors waving and the way the 'hand' becomes independent from reality. This is self-reflective post-modernist poetry which simultaneously seems to say 'I am recording reality and that reality is what the poem says it is as a result of how I choose to perceive and describe it.' The mind plays with unlikely possibilities and wryly views behaviour; as the boat returns

> we are prepared to welcome
> a more realistic sense
> of proportion.

But the poet never lets reality become familiar; he turns the familiar into art. 'The boatride' ends:

> an expanse of
> unswerving stone
> encrusted coarsely
> with shells
> admonishes our sight.

Radicalness here is less in technique than tonal, which in turn influences our reading. The meaning of the poem, in so far as its varied elements are reducible, is the aesthetic possibilities of ordering reality, an aestheticism made possible by a refusal to accept the visual as stable; instead what is seen is always a possible source for the astonishing, the miraculous, the satiric—for a range of attitudes and imaginings. Delight in free association and visual design are among the qualities of the poem.

After 'A Low Temple' from *Jejuri* was published in *Dionysius* (vol. I, combined nos. 2 & 3, p. 95), a little magazine of the mid '60s, the editor lost the whole manuscript; Kolatkar eventually rewrote *Jejuri*, which first appeared in the *Opinion Literary Quarterly* (1974) and later as a Clearing House publication (1976, 1978, 1982). As Kolatkar does not use the surreal and astonishing in *Jejuri* it might be asked whether his style had changed much during the next decade. The only change in the text between the

Dionysisus version of 'A Low Temple' and the later version in *Jejuri* is minor; where line six reads 'revives and dies' he originally wrote 'revives like invisible ink', which is more surreal but conveys the same scepticism.

The thirty-six sections of *Jejuri* consist, like 'the boatride', of varied, difficult-to-analyse perceptions and attitudes of someone on a journey. Here it is an apparently sceptical tourist who arrives in the ancient place of pilgrimage; at the end he is waiting with irritation for a train so he can depart. The opening poem establishes themes of perception and alienation:

> Your own divided face in a pair of glasses
> on an old man's nose
> is all the countryside you get to see.
>
> ...
>
> At the end of the bumpy ride
> with your own face on either side
> when you get off the bus
>
> you don't step inside the old man's head.

'The Priest', the second poem in the sequence, sceptically views a priest calculating what he will get from the tourist's offerings. The tour bus stands

> purring softly in front of the priest.
>
> A catgrin on its face
> and a live, ready to eat pilgrim
> held between its teeth.

The discrepancy between appearance and possible reality, between the commercialization of the ruined places of worship and what in the speaker's view is divine, is shown in the next poem, 'Heart of Ruin', about a mongrel bitch and her puppies in a ruined temple: 'No more a place of worship this place / is nothing less than the house of god'. The difficulty in knowing what has been seen and the way reality can be revisualized, re-perceived, is shown by 'The Doorstep':

> That's no doorstep.
> It's a pillar on its side.
>
> Yes.
> That's what it is.

Passing through the temple complex the speaker notes the water-supply pipe, a pair of undershorts left to dry on a temple door, eighteen arms on an 'eight arm goddess' and a calf in what may either be a cowshed or another temple. The commercialization of Jejuri and the razor's edge between legend and falsification is suggested by 'A Scratch':

> what is god
> and what is stone
> the dividing line
> if it exists
> is very thin
> at jejuri
>
> ...
>
> there is no crop
> other than god
> and god is harvested here
> around the year.

One context is supplied by an old woman wanting fifty paise to take the tourist to a shrine. When he attempts to get rid of her she says: 'What else can an old woman do / on hills as wretched as these?'

Contrasted to such scepticism and realism are the three Chaitanya poems. The word means a life force or dynamism and refers to the Bengali saint who came to Jejuri intent on reform. The first Chaitanya poem ('come off it') contrasts the red painted stone to simple adoration with flowers. The second Chaitanya poem offers an ironic contrast between the decayed, commercialized for-tourists temple complex and the astonishing, living faith of the saints and devotional poets (whose paradoxical manner seems imitated here):

> he popped a stone
> in his mouth
> and spat out gods.

The third Chaitanya poem makes explicit the contrast between the placid, cow-like faith of most religious activity and the dynamism of the saints:

> when he disappeared from view
> and the herd of legends
> returned to its grazing.

Jejuri juxtaposes the ability to astonish, to give life interest and value, with what is conventional and dead. The artist is like the saint in being unconventional, in seeing life differently, in having a direct or renewed appreciation of living. In contrast to the priest's son who is uncomfortable when asked if he believes in the legends he retells to tourists there is the butterfly, life itself, with no future, no past:

> Just a pinch of yellow,
> it opens before it closes
> and closes before it o
>
> where is it.

A similar divine dynamism is represented by the scene of the cocks and hens dancing 'Between Jejuri and the Railway Station'. In contrast to the petrification of the spirit in the temple town with each of its priests, houses, pillars, steps and arches numbered by guides and guide-books, the fowls do an astonishing dance. The typography which represents the dancing puts the themes of dynamism and perception into visual terms. The dancing chickens, like the butterfly and mongrel puppies, stand for a divine quality in life which the legends of Jejuri represent but which has been lost among its ruins and commercialization.

A failure to perceive the miraculous, divine and surreal in the ordinary world is similar to a deadening incompetence found at the railway station. Just as the ruined temples and their commercialization represent a lack of spirit, a lack of vitality, so the railway station from which the tourist attempts to leave Jejuri is another kind of ritual of modern India:

> the spirit of the place
> lives inside the mangy body
> of the station dog.

The station indicator and clock do not work. No one knows when the next train is due. No one answers questions. The speaker vows to

> slaughter a goat before the clock
> smash a coconut on the railway track
> smear the indicator with the blood of a cock

if only someone would tell you
when the next train is due.

Jejuri is, I think, less a poem of scepticism and a poem about a
modern wasteland's loss of faith than a poem which contrasts dead-
ness of perception with the ability to see the divine in the natural
vitality of life. If the crazy hens and cocks dancing are like the
simplicity of vision of the saints, then presumably the artist
shares, if only ironically, some of this freedom of spirit. In Kolat-
kar's hands the tradition of saints' poetry takes the form, in our
age of self-conscious disbelief, of an ironic parody of a pilgrimage
which while mocking institutionalized religion affirms the free
imagination and the dynamism of life. The long poem about
Jejuri is a way of making the kinds of affirmations which in the
early dog poem are shrouded in surrealistic obscurities and para-
doxes.

Kolatkar's flat, colloquial, sceptical tone complements his
focus on particulars. The doorstep is a pillar on its side. A pair of
shorts dries on a temple door. The goddess has too many arms.
While paying attention to the real, and trying to see it as it is
rather than what it is supposed to be, Kolatkar's poem disturbs,
since we tend to make some analogy, to draw some parallel,
between the secular view of Jejuri and the traditional religious
meaning of a pilgrimage. We might see the emotional withdrawal,
scepticism and humour as a kind of modern equivalent of the
medieval Bhakti saint who could ignore rituals and address his
God directly, conversationally, even sceptically. Kolatkar replied,
when asked by an interviewer (*The Indian Literary Review*,
vol. I, no. 4, August 1978, pp. 6–10) whether he believed in God—
'I leave the question alone. I don't think I have to take a position
about God one way or the other'. The sequence of poems seems
to affirm both an undisturbed equilibrium in the viewer and the
divine in the vitality of the real. It shows reality as it is, both in its
deadening normality and in the divine life with which nature is
charged when perceived by a playful and imaginative vision.

A prolific poet in Marathi, Dilip Chitre has published less in
English. Although he privately published two hundred copies of
Ambulance Ride (1972), his first volume of English poems—
Travelling in a Cage—did not appear until 1980. His poems are

mostly autobiographical and, while in a variety of moods ranging from the lyrical and meditative to the incantatory, reflect what seems a continuing crisis of his inner life. Influenced by the great Marathi Bhakti poet Tukaram, but himself a rationalist with mystical leanings, Chitre creates a large, intense world from his emotions, especially his obsessions with sex, madness and death. There is in his work, as is shown by the poem 'Prayer to Shakti', a Blakean romanticism which celebrates living intensely, excessively, and being open to experience, as a desire to be one with the universe. Not surprisingly, often such poems develop from free associations, use incantations and invocations which bring the sub- or unconscious into view. Chitre writes in cycles of lyrics which often have their significance in the sequence rather than in any individual poem.

The early 'Private Poem in a Public Garden' (translated from Marathi) begins with a surreal image ('Listening to the explosions / Of roses in the garden') but is a somewhat oblique, argumentative meditation on the ways the materials of reality are used, especially by the contrasting private and public imaginations:

> A superior gardener uses
> The season itself to cut
> And carve out his intended garden.
> He never touches trees in reality.
> Sitting upon newspapers spread out.
> Beneath his bottom mutely in bold type
> Atomic Bombs explode
> While he listens to the roses'
> Monologues

In section six a correspondence is implied between God's creativity, writing and the subconscious:

> Written by a vast, invisible
> Private instrument
> Earth that's dug open
> Bears the exact mark
> Of that instrument.

The natural world itself is private and unconscious, but given significance and public meanings by human imagination and the need to find meaning:

The garden, mutely burning
In various colours, passes
A flame to the eye—
Souls are lighted
On the rose's matchstick.
When in the gradual
And burning night
The trees stand like innocent clowns.
The newspapermen arrive on the lawn
And, slapped hard,
Roses in a poem are shocked into awareness.

In another of his Marathi poems, which Chitre in his anthology
has translated into English—the autobiographical 'In Ethiopia'—
contrasts are made between the artist's life, his creativity and the
work of art. Paradoxically the remoulding of the intensities of ex-
perience 'into a dumb vase', with its accompanying repression of the
essential self so that the superego can have its will, creates a world of
metaphysical significance and anxieties. Words create symbols
while the raw experience of the self becomes transformed by the
work of art into a permanent metaphor for varied, changing, larger
significances far different from what was intended or felt at the time
of the original experience:

It's the death of all earlier motives, a transformation
Of all apparent purpose into the terrifying
Ambiguity of the word: I become my own symbol,
My own other and author: a durable doorframe.
In nothingness: an entrance and an exit
For less permanent meanings, a formal metaphor.

The reality created by Chitre's poems is that of the romantic self
becoming its 'own symbol', 'own other and author', a metaphor of
nothingness and meaning. His poems express a broad range of
heightened, intense consciousness often in opposition and conflict.
In the 'Travelling in a Cage' sequence of eighteen lyrics such con-
trasting emotions and perceptions exist simultaneously, usually in
counterpoint to each other.

Travelling in a Cage consists of three parts: first the 'Travelling in
a Cage' sequence, written during 1975–7 when Chitre taught in
America; then a group of poems entitled 'From Bombay', many of
which are set in specific places; and, part three, *Ambulance Ride*, a

surrealistic funeral elegy written earlier on the death of a friend.

In his *Poetry India* (vol. 1, no. 1, January 1966) introduction to Mardheker, Chitre says that the Marathi poet revived the old tradition of saint poetry and combined it with modern European trends. 'Like the surrealists', Mardheker 'plumbed images out of a Freudian underworld, and strung them together'; but he did not use free-association or surrealist automatic writing. Despite the seeming obscurity images are strung together with a purpose; often there is a counterpoint making 'two processes of consciousness sound simultaneously'. Throughout Mardheker's poems 'one gets the feeling that one is trapped and enclosed in a death chamber from which there is no escape.... The trap is absolute and eternal'. The concern which Mardheker feels is therefore religious, not socio-moral, nor socio-cultural.

Chitre's sequence of poems entitled 'Travelling in a Cage' may seem unintelligible to those brought up on what by world standards is a rather conservative English-language tradition of poetry, but like many modern poems which appear obscure the themes and images are concerned with the inner self. Rather like Chitre's description of Mardheker, the first poem uses counterpoint with the longing for transcendence beyond the caged self contrasted to death and defeat. Madness is the pivotal concept, with the first poem schizophrenically implying both insanity and saintly ecstasy. The poetic structure is musical, organized by repetition of phrases, images, sounds, and by contrast rather than by argument or formal patterns. The first poem consists of four verse paragraphs unpunctuated except for the refrain, 'Has my time come', which occurs five times as the opening line of the first stanza and the closing line of each stanza. Among the techniques of poetical organization are syntactical parallels and patterns of sound:

> There is no watch here
> There is no calendar
> But I know

The way parallelism can create poetic coherence while being used for the irrational or surreal is shown by:

> Mirrors are walls
> Walls are coffins
> Coffins are capsules

Floating in space
(lines 7–10)

The images of mirrors, walls and coffins recur later in the poem, as
do images of 'madness' and 'blind':

The quiet point of madness (line 6)
I am going wild (line 12)
Dancing in blind bliss (line 16)
I dance wild (line 39)
The catatonic smiles (line 42)
Has corridors of bliss (line 51)

The poem represents a range of consciousness with its various
contrapuntal, paradoxical emotions:

I am going wild
Seething with serenity
Like a saint
Gouging out my own eyes
Dancing in blind bliss
Measuring the raging distances
Between me and me
Performing
My own autopsy
The contents of skull and guts
The joints and the seams
Of my being
The leather pouch in which
I kept the universe safe
Has my time come?

The self-awareness of the polyphony of voices, ranging from the
blissful to the dead, from the serene to the mad, is implied by
'Between me and me / Performing'. Unity is provided among the
paradoxes and contrasting images through a pattern of recurring
sounds (I, wild, my, eyes, blind, my, my), some end rhyme (sere-
nity, me, autopsy, seams, being) and such devices as alliteration,
repetition, recurring particles (seething, gouging, dancing, etc.) and
recurring doublets (me and me, skull and guts, the joints and the
seams). The poem would bear up to endless stylistic analysis and
builds on the techniques of the early Eliot for rather different
purposes.

Here the consciousness of extreme emotion, isolation, madness, bliss, alienation from the self, is expressed in terms of separation of spirit and body, words and feeling, appearances and reality. But these are not contrasts. The various extremes are simultaneously present so that in the final stanza insanity may well be saintliness, the hospital may well be heaven. The lack of punctuation contributes to the technique of ambiguity with lines being capable of various meanings according to how the stanzas are mentally divided into sentences. The poem is a representation of a state of awareness, a compression of the thoughts, emotions and self-consciousness within a personality. Two of its most significant themes are the sense of fullness of possibility trapped within the body and the difficulty of putting the fullness of experience into words. The subsequent poems in the series develop these themes of life being 'travelling in a cage' of the self and of words.

The second poem with its echoes of Dante's *Inferno* and ironic twists or clichés is about a middle-aged, greying writer in a 'Furnished apartment' facing his typewriter while being aware that 'A poem hardly / Upsets the balance of nature', and , 'In the middle of my life / I have come to a white page in which I must live'. The third poem makes explicit the poet's presence in Iowa ('North Dubuque Street') and feeling of estrangement from Indian culture. Is exile in Iowa a time of suicide or a time to find oneself?

In reviewing the contempoary Marathi poet Purushottam Shivram Rege (*Poetry India*, vol. 2, no. 2, April 1967), Chitre claims that the search for identity by Marathi poets 'is of a schizophrenic origin'; feelings of disinheritedness, alienation and unrelatedness result from the conflict between 'two cultures, two sensibilities, two conceptual structures'. Chitre, who lived in Ethiopia for four years and in America for three, uses the 'schizophrenic' search for identity as a source of his poetry. In these poems written while in exile the poet's relationship to the new country becomes a metaphor for his relationship to himself, its possibilities and defeats. Allusions to and echoes of American poetry interweave through the narrative, which in several poems involves sex with a local woman, symbolic of America and freedom. Other poems return to the themes of agony, 'questioning mirrors', the relationship of walls to space in contrast to the cage of oneself, and the need to feel a vital reality.

While some of the poems are extremely oblique there are points of return to recognizable reality to avoid total obscurity. The vision

oscillates between what appear to be actualities and extreme emo-
tional states. Images of sex, death, suicide, cages, light, pleasure,
God and poetry recur and build towards a thematic statement of the
suppressed psychological source of the poems:

> I have no country no continent to wear
> Travelling without legs or language
> Exposed and caged by my own condition
> What doors can I open in this fear
> What windows look out
> And will I ever find my own face out there.

Writing is itself a cage, in contrast to silence. Desire is a cage. Words,
feelings, self, are all cages:

> These bars of music are my last prison
> The quietness of an emptied vein
> Lies beyond manifestos and stars
> ...
> Spinning a deeper silence I vanish
> At the edge of my own voice a world is ending.

Those last words fittingly conclude the sequence and suggest that
consciousness is itself the cause of our intensities and dissatisfaction;
consciousness, like words, creates space and walls which close in the
space. We are our own world, our own cage.

Despite the apparent obliqueness and impenetrability of Chitre's
poems, they are not surrealist poems; rather they are poems in
which surreal effects, especially of disjunctive imagery, are used as a
projection of consciousness. The tradition of Chitre's method is the
dramatic monologue as it developed out of Browning through
Pound and Eliot. Chitre has taken the method a stage further by
carrying the imagery of emotion to radical extremes, by further
reducing the suggestion of narration to a bare minimum.

There is a surprisingly talkative, almost American characteristic
about some of Chitre's poems written in Iowa, published in the first
part of *Travelling in a Cage*. Some seem to aim at the directness
and immediacy which has marked the American tradition from
Whitman to William Carlos Williams 'Dick Bakken came here
driving his old van'. There is a poem entitled 'Pinball Concerto' and
even one on 'Pushing a Cart' in a supermarket! But even when

Chitre is direct and talkative his mind rapidly moves through associations and levels of experience, playing off clichés, idioms and registers of speech to reveal a complexity of sensitivity. 'Poem in Self-Exile' begins with a series of seemingly random impressions:

> The season's first dead butterfly
> Has freshly frayed wings. Meanings are transferred
> Like the wet on the grass
> To shoes. America is incredibly erotic.
> Too many legs makes all these streets sexy.

The middle of the poem is slack talk:

> I am homesick, which is stupid of course.
> I was never a famous chauvinist back home,
> Nor is America not beautiful. But I am terrified.

And concludes ironically: 'America, here I come, too / Late'.

A poem called 'The Translator' is concerned with problems of language and culture. Language is a lie distorting the true meaning of things:

> Who crafted the first words out of wild corn
> And the bones of animals?
> Who told the first lies
> Upon which our profession is based?

The discrepancy between words and thoughts, between signs and what they supposedly represent, is especially a concern at present when theorists have claimed that language is a trap which expresses only what a culture permits and not what is felt and perceived. For a translator, who is living in a different country, the discrepancies between languages are acute; the problem is multiplied by being a poet, someone who is now expected to translate the meaning of silence into words. The poem says that awake the translator can soothe himself by activity, 'asking difficult questions':

> But once he goes to sleep,
> His own ambivalence disturbs him,
> Producing nightmares
> Out of the savage silence of four different languages.

Chitre's Bombay poems reveal a similar alienation and attempt to use poetry as a means of holding together an otherwise fragmented reality. 'Mumbai' claims:

                        like a poem
                this city the garbled relic
                of someone's empire
                        the remaining
                voice now peopled
                        by estranged millions.

Bombay is a symbol of the modern Indian chaos resulting from
contact with the West and of 'Man's estrangement from a manmade
world'. 'Father Returning Home' offers a dreary vision of a com-
muter returning to stale food and a sullen family; he goes to sleep:

> Listening to the static on the radio, dreaming
> Of his ancestors and grandchildren, thinking
> Of nomads entering a subcontinent through a narrow pass.

But these are not poems nostalgic for tradition, organic com-
munities and other romantic nationalist ideas of an innocence lost
with colonialism, industrialism, materialism or some other for-
bidden fruit which resulted in the problems of modern life.
Chitre's poems imply that there is no Eden, no state of innocence
that can be recovered. Reflecting in 'Sanctuary' on the darkness
which surrounds the god, he says 'Nothingness must be con-
cealed from human eyes' as 'It is the clearest of mirrors'. Although
proclaiming scepticism, there is an implicit mysticism; the poems
contain often conflicting significances.

The long poem *Ambulance Ride* is a surrealistic funeral elegy in
which Chitre addresses his dead friend as if he were both dead and
still alive. The incongruities of tone and the self-consciousness of
style could at first appear comic; but, rather than being humorous,
Ambulance Ride uses wit as it does the grotesque, repetition and
other techniques of poetry to raise the level of emotion to an apo-
calyptical intensity. The method, with its foregrounding of the
artificial and the absurd, avoids the sentimentality which mars most
funeral elegies written in our time.

Ambulance Ride is dedicated to Bhola Shreshtha, Chitre's friend,
'who believed it was possible to create a whole symphony out of
discordant elements'. *Ambulance Ride* is a funeral elegy made from
discordant elements. It begins with the speaker addressing the dead:
'Remember the ride? / The one on which you died?', moves on to

details of the journey to the hospital with the friend who they did not know had already died:

> You were very still
> Only your head shook a little
> With subtle sarcasm.

The 'remember' motif continues in allusions to the hospital and the funeral. It is typical of Chitre that the elegiac themes of sorrow and memory should be expressed as paradoxical extremes and as distortions:

> Sorrow may grow
> Like a cancer
> Sorrow may ripen
> Like a wine
>
> ...
>
> Memory may trap
> A single event
> In a cage of mirrors.

From this point the poem passes on to other movements and associations, including the desire to be freed by deep mourning, to become part of death, to be analytical, before returning to variations on the theme of remembering. The question 'Do you remember the drunken conversation' develops into a cosmic vision in which order is dissolved into a unity of contraries:

> From the slums of my mind
> To the galaxies I open my arms to,
> From this blind hemorrhage of feelings
> To the massacre of all art-forms
> From the pus in my festering wound
> To the clarity of the water
> In which all language dissolves
> And silence begins to ripple.

But these are 'only words', 'nothing'. From such 'nothing', however, the poet will 'chisel out' a permanent memorial of the 'sunday in april' when his friend died. As in many other modern poems the poet making the poem is revealed as the underlying theme:

> I will be at the centre

Of the ride
On which you died.

Chitre's poetry expresses an intensely subjective, inner world which ignores the physical and social world except as a stimulus of the eye and imagination. In Chitre and the early Kolatkar the great tradition of romantic exploration, expression and liberation of the self is brought up to date, made Indian, made psychological, as the poetry expresses intense emotions of desire, frustration, self-consciousness and the longings of transcendence and unity.

In the early period of their poetry Kolatkar and Chitre found, in the extreme romantic rebellion of such writers as Rimbaud and the Surrealists, a way to avoid the burdens of intellectual responsibility and ethical self-laceration usually found in English-language writing. The intellectual and ethical places the poet in society, frames her or him in a repressive context of otherness, of necessary and accepted limitations; Kolatkar and Chitre are, instead, amoral, more concerned with the reality of what is desired, felt, imagined, without questioning its validity. This different consciousness finds another kind of expression in Kolatkar's later poems, such as 'boatride' and *Jejuri*, where a flatness of tone and distanced attitude, along with a concern to be very exact about what one sees, defamiliarizes the familiar, shifting it from normal contexts to the perception and emotions of the viewer. In his 'From Bombay' poems, the second part of *Travelling in a Cage*, the city and places are a setting for Chitre's imagination, self-assertion, fantasies, moods, reactions. The local world is a setting for his psyche:

> I plot seductions and rapes, plan masterpieces
> Of evasion. The loudspeakers blare at me.
> Bedbugs bite me. Cockroaches hover about my soul.
> Mice scurry about my metaphysics, mosquitoes sing
>   among my lyrics.
> Lizards crawl over my religion, spiders infest my politics.
> I itch. I become horny. I booze. I want to get smashed.
> And I do. It comes easy at Chinchpokli,
> Where, like a minor Hindu god, I am stoned
> By the misery of my worshippers and by my own
> Triumphant impotence.

The relaxed tolerance of Kolatkar's *Jejuri*, represented by

'Ajamil and the Tigers' ('well fed tigers and fat sheep drink from the same pond') incorporates the external world as a distanced object within the consciousness of the poet. After impatience, humorous scepticism, and announced refusal to enter 'inside the old man's head' when leaving 'The Bus', Kolatkar recreates Jejuri in terms of his own personality. 'Ajamil ', 'Yeshwant Rao', the 'dozen cocks and hens' 'in a kind of harvest dance', the parody holiness of the railway station and the final image of the setting sun as both the longed-for locomotive and as a spiritual event— all these subvert the conventional significance of Jejuri as a place of pilgrimage and recreate it in terms of the self's perceptions and sensibility.

Although the cool, wry and humorous distance of *Jejuri* is far from Chitre's impassioned absorption in himself, the way Kolatkar's English poems seem to be written—from the perspective of someone who has disengaged from society—is related to and a development of the romantic concern with the ultimate reality of the self, its imaginings, perceptions, interests and assertion of its own being. The assertion now takes the tone of a refusal to assert or respond. The coolness of Kolatkar's English poetry furthers a tendency Chitre had earlier commented upon in his Marathi anthology: 'He suppresses feeling through a symbol or an image'. The inner violence is anaesthetized into an enigmatic blandness and comedy. There is a quiet mysticism in such writing, a guarded nostalgia for the divine which has shifted from its oblique articulation in the early 'The Renunciation of the Dog' to an investing of the simple with traces of the spiritual as perceived by the self. The old deities and legends will not come to life in the modern Indian world of bored priests and inefficient railway stations; but Kolatkar retains sentiments which personally invest the unlikely with an ironic spiritual approval. The quiet tensions between the incongruities debunk while guardedly suggesting there might be other possibilities. The puzzling attraction of Kolatkar's English poetry is this unresolved tension between a concern for precision and the investing of the simple with provisional imagined wonder. It is a contemporary instance of the breakdown of older certainties; the spaces between connections and the provisionality of all statements themselves become reality.

Chitre's poetry belongs to the modernist movement of the first half of this century in such formal characteristics as its open-ended musical forms, its reliance on recurring symbols or motifs for formal coherence, its lack of interest in the material world and its location in the estranged artist's subjectivity. For all its play and surreal elements it is consciously high art in its rejection of the contemporary and technology. Its roots go back to Blake and the Romantics.

By contrast Kolatkar's later work is post-modernist, although a different version of post-modernism from Mehrotra's. Kolatkar appears to be aiming at an anti-art in which the artist's memories and personality are of no importance and in which the art work has no depth. Its art is in a purposeful transparency or apparent superficiality, in contrast to the formal and elaborated texture of high art. 'The boatride' and *Jejuri* are similar in that there is no existence beyond the snapshot-like reality of what is seen; Jejuri is like the events of the boatride, without significance except as a subject for the creation of a text. There is no sense of meaningful relationships. Reality appears fragmented, bits and pieces to be accepted on their own or played with for amusement. Rather than waiting for Godot, it is better to enjoy the sight of chickens dancing. Kolatkar's seriousness is his conscious lack of depth, his own quiet fun-house nihilism in which a mongrel bitch is a goddess.

The styles and attitudes reflect religious assumptions. Chitre's romanticism is that of an agnostic with spiritual cravings, while Kolatkar, after an early period of intense personal feelings, now seems to treat them in an off-hand, sceptical manner, as no longer of pressing concern.

CHAPTER ELEVEN

Experimentalists II

MEHROTRA AND MAHAPATRA

The main, often conflicting concerns of modern experimental poetry with investing the personal and the immediate with significance, with the relationship of the self to the external world, with the introspective sources of imagination and with the poem as unstable assemblage open to varied interpretations reflect a collapse of older notions of what is real. The fracturing of reality has been one of India's cultural inheritances from colonialism and from its rapid modernization since independence. If Ezekiel and Daruwalla attempt to steer a steady course through the resulting intellectual and ethical confusions, Chitre and Kolatkar adjust by accepting, even welcoming contradiction. The different kinds of experimental poetry of Arvind Krishna Mehrotra and Jayanta Mahapatra are further attempts to link poetry to kinds of Indian reality.

Mehrotra and Mahapatra, early in their careers, appear to have viewed the poem as object, a structure of images, but in differing ways have increasingly been concerned with the need to bring to the poem's surface the obsessions, memories, doubts and other personal experiences which are the source material of the imagination. The approaches, concerns and products of the two poets are, however, as divergent from each other as they are from Chitre's plunge into the whirlpool of his psyche, Kolatkar's neutralization of chaos and Ezekiel's wish to find intellectual and spiritual order in the fragmented instability of the modern world. Although both Mehrotra and Mahapatra make poems from disorder, their means of control are different. Mehrotra revises continually a small body of work, polishing, crafting, aiming at elegance, wit, precision and an impersonality which will fix the poem and the personal memories that are its source. Mahapatra's large and rapidly growing body of poems continually worries his perceptions, his relationship to his feelings and his environment, often going over the same themes from different angles while calling into doubt the various links between reality, self, statement, poem and reader. A Mehrotra poem is a construction, a Mahapatra poem often deconstructs itself and what it expresses.

Mehrotra's poetry largely falls into three groups. His earliest work is an immediate reaction to his discovery of various modern, post-modernist and earlier avant-garde styles and poetics. These range from French surrealism of the 1920s to the contemporary Beat and constructivist poetry being written in the 1960s. Other influences include the collage-Cubist methods of Apollinaire and Ezra Pound. *Bharatmata* (1966) and *Woodcuts on Paper* (1967) belong to this varied period of his work, as do the early versions of some poems belonging to his second period when surrealist games of chance are assimilated into a constructivist poetic, with poems now being conscious assemblages. Such assemblages are meant to enclose the reader within the poem itself, without the poem having a visible subject. This poetry is one contemporary kind of post-modernism in which the imitation of reality is replaced by the dominance of the art object; but unlike earlier forms of experimental literature the work is an open structure and is not given an appearance of coherence through an implied narrative, mythic substructure or musical organization with recurring motifs.

Mehrotra's third and present phase is different as it involves a precise recording of external reality, a making of art from specifics and details, the notating of what he calls 'location'. Often the subject matter comes from memories of childhood or from reading history. While poems such as 'Genealogy' imagine a mysterious past which cannot be recovered, others such as 'Continuities' and 'The Roys' are autobiographical. 'Company Period' and 'On the Death of a Sunday Painter' appear to be historical reconstructions. Mehrotra is especially fascinated by childhood, places associated with his family and the culture of the colonial era.

While it is perhaps ingenious to trace Mehrotra's later development from the exuberant welcoming of various kinds of avant-gardism in his early poems and comments, some of the contradictions of his work can be seen in his first poems and enthusiasms. The cyclostyled journal *damn you*, which he co-edited, represented a youthful, uncritical but significant attempt to be part of the international avant-garde of the 1960s, especially as represented by the San Franscisco scene with its Beat poetry, counter culture and rebellion against bourgeois, conventional and traditional values. The 'statement' signed by Mehrotra which prefaces the sixth and last issue of *damn you* is representative of the rebellious, romantic, adolescent, stick-your-tongue-out attitudes which made the magazine, and other journals of the period, attractive:

we are illiterates. unaware of ists/isms. if we find a liberated soul on a creative adventure we might join him. we might let him go his way ... creation is done when a pair of red hands tap an insane brain. when a crow in flight scratches its paws over a desert its a canvas we try to get hold of, before wind and sand pile in.

The youthful rebelliousness, anarchy and surrealist acceptance of chance is one side of Mehrotra; but the title of *Ezra, an imagiste magazine* that he also started in the late '60s shows another side rooted more in Pound and his American followers. For Mehrotra, like Chitre and the early Kolatkar, a poem consists of images presented in juxtapostion without connecting links; the result is often an incongruous assemblage. Mehrotra also self-published a pamphlet of 'concrete poetry', typewriter-designed shapes made from words and sounds. The typographical, visual, concrete poetry aspects are continued in *Woodcuts on Paper*, published by an avant-garde art gallery in London, part of which was reproduced in a London Institute of Contemporary Art bulletin (August 1967), along with experimental work by others. In the Baroda avant-garde magazine *Vrishchik* (July 1970) Mehrotra published 'Song of the Rolling Earth', prefaced by a quotation from the French poet Apollinaire: 'I believe that I have found a source of inspiration in prospectuses ... catalogues, posters, advertisements'. His *Pomes/Poemes/Poemas* (published by *Vrishchik* in 1971) includes the visual, typographical poem 'culture and society' in a shape which may be a bomb, skyscraper or phallic symbol; there is a page also of 'epilogues', quotations from Ezra Pound, Dylan Thomas, the surrealist André Breton, William Blake and others. The attitudes range from nineteenth-century romantic assertions of infinite human possibility and Breton's definition of surrealism as 'pure psychic automatism'—which expresses 'the real process of thought'—to Octavio Paz's up-to-date claim that modern poetry has no exterior object of reference: meaning is not what the words say but 'what is said between them' .

With hindsight what might seem a jumble of contradictions and affinities has a pattern. While Mehrotra asserts the importance of the artist as a romantic, superior free spirit, artists are cited for their attention to art and for their curiosity. Poems are constructions and the space between the words, like surrealist chance, is the area in which to seek their meaning. Despite the emphasis on spontaneity, romantic claims to reveal the depths of the hidden real self are ignored; good writing is seen as a construction which develops from curiosity, originality and chance—which are part of a protest against conventional, commonplace bourgeois attitudes. This is a different aesthetic from the impassioned, autobiographical, soul-searching, self-revelatory, crisis-ridden consciousness of Chitre's modern romanticism.

In *bharatmata: a prayer* Mehrotra claims to look at modern India with anger while attempting, like Walt Whitman, to make himself the voice of national multiplicity. There is, however, much humour in the anger and visionary incantations. The poem is filled with parody, even comic literary echoes and references. What starts as a Ginsbergian howl of protest and a Whitmanesque cosmos soon becomes a display of youthful free association and humorous self-display, less concerned with social injustice than with cultural play and adolescent sexual rebellion:

> i'm everywhere because i feel everything
> > because i feel god's pulse
> in the slut's womb
> > because my heart has the shape of a
> linga
> > because the Travellers Companions
> bind me into a unity
> > better than the Ramayana
> because when i masturbate
> > the universe throbs and continents clap

Despite the references to beggars, washerwomen and pot-bellied children *bharatmata* is less an angry howl than a mixture of literary jokes and social satire on the Indian urban middle class and their culture:

> each house complete
> with
> refrigerator

transistor
telephone
car
record player
a newly married sofa set

The uses Mehrotra makes of incongruity, choice and free asso-
ciation and the ways his methods differ from the surrealists' can be
seen by comparing two published versions of his 'The Exquisite
Corpse', a party game which the surrealists used to tap the uncons-
cious to produce art by chance. Exquisite Corpse is usually played
by a person writing a line of verse, then folding the page over and
passing the sheet to the next person, who will write another line
without seeing the preceding one. Mehrotra's 'The Exquisite
Corpse' first appeared in the American magazine *The Nation*
(16 October 1972, p. 342) as a twelve-line poem:

Smoke makes faces, grey hair burns
Children who don't play with me
Are taken away by jackals

Each vowel is wrapped in dead skin

Once a year I open my cellar
The old woman comes out of her shoe
Instead of Hickory I find a young genital

The goat's bleat has turned pink

Clouds of black stubble roughen the sky
Out of my father's cupboard
Rush clusters of tiny walking sticks

The smell is of good manure.

The juxtaposed material is mostly literary, being largely from child-
ren's stories, tales and play, scenic descriptions and two lines which
parody ready-made phrases ('Each ... is wrapped in', 'The ... has
turned pink'), but which also seem like the kind of extreme meta-
phoric statements found in French romantic and surrealist poetry.
    Mehrotra published a nine-line, radically revised version of the
same poem in *Middle Earth*:

Smoke makes faces, ladders burn
Children who don't love me

Are lifted by hyenas

Once a year I inventory my cellar
The old woman's alone in her shoe
Georgie Porgie's a pimply beau

A cluster of bamboo walking-sticks
Force open my father's chest
The goat is dead, long live the baa

Here there are many of the motifs from the early version (smoke, faces, the threat, the cellar, the old woman, walking sticks, the goat), but they are more carefully structured to focus upon typical memories of childhood. The goat's bleat of the earlier version has become a parody of 'the king is dead, long live the king' which in this context would be applicable to memories of the father. The revised version is open to interpretation as an opening of the cellars of memory and finding (possibly invented?) reminders of childhood threats, games, stories, rhymes and articles connected with the father. There is also more internal rhyme and other combinations of similar sounds which link the material (me, hyenas, inventory, Porgie's, pimply, cellar, cluster). Surrealist techniques have been used by Mehrotra in 'Exquisite Corpse" as a method to create an open, amusing, sophisticated poem based on nostalgia of childhood.

He likes to juxtapose bits and pieces of sensibility as represented by clichéd language, sentiments and situations. Parthasarathy quotes Mehrotra as explaining that a poem may consist of 'games, riddles and accidents ... and the poet creates as many accidents as he can'. While Mehrotra begins by using the well-known surrealist technique of automatic writing in which free association is supposed to liberate the subconscious, he edits, shapes and revises the results into a carefully constructed poem. He is too elegant and clever a craftsman for formless sprawling.

Many of Mehrotra's better-known poems, such as 'The Sale', 'The Book of Common Places' and 'Index of First Lines', are developed from similar illogical but cleverly humorous juxtapositions. Despite the use of chance and play there is a distinctive sensibility in these poems. Witty, sophisticated, mocking clichés and stuffiness, the poems parody middle-brow attitudes, middle-class social conventions, the wooden phrases and descriptions in bad writing, well-known quotations and other bits and pieces of literate bourgeois culture. Mehrotra's poetry offers a cool, clever, ironic catalogue of received ideas and ready-made speech. Surrealist techniques are used for social comedy.

In 'The Sale' the situation varies but provides a framing context for speeches in which surrealist juxtapositions create humorous parodies of salesmanship and similar social contexts. The clichés— 'It's yours for the price', 'they may not be available', 'I can't press you', 'were I not leaving', 'I would never have thought of selling', 'Had you come yesterday'—are followed by the use of incongruity to turn social situations into absurdities:

> Would you mind if I showed you
> a few more things now yours?
> Be careful, one river is still wet
> I wish you had asked me earlier
> The paintings have been bought
> by a broken mirror
> but I think I can lead you
> to a crack in the wall.

The implied situations and objects mentioned are from a comfortable, upper-middle-class way of living which seems dated and is representative of the established bourgeois colonial culture of the late-nineteenth and early-twentieth centuries with its travellers, explorations, trophies, anatomical specimens and various other collections. There are such collectables as a tiger-skin, antelope bones, carved wheels, a skeleton, butterflies. The salesperson at times resembles a Victorian collector or lecturer pointing out the exotica of the world.

The poem is in three sections. The topics of the first part are geographical: 'This is Europe, / that America, this scarebug Asia'. In the second section the geographical materials evolve into bric-a-brac connected with explorations and anthropology: 'Must also show you a tiger-skin / that once hid a palace'. The third section alludes to the kind of paraphernalia found in a Victorian attic, reminders of recently past culture. Many of the objects here appear to allude to Mehrotra's own family history: 'I've also a wheelchair to show you; / it belonged to my uncle'. Mehrotra's uncle, Kewal Krishna Mehrotra, Professor of English at the University of Allahabad (1959–68), was probably the possessor of the two books, Ruskin's *Lectures on Art* and *A Short History of English Lite-*

rature by Legouis'. Autobiographical allusions, nostalgia, memories of the past and references to Allahabad, where he lives, become increasingly frequent in Mehrotra's poems as he attempts to invest the local with personal significance.

One explanation for Mehrotra's nostalgia and increasing use of Allahabad in his poems is offered by his long two-part essay in *Chandrabhaga* (3, 1980; 7, 1982), where he claims that 'To a poem the location— whether cultural, geographical, or fictive—is everything'. This is related to his insistence on 'specificity'. Having early accepted the tenets of Pound and imagism, he criticizes Parthasarathy's use of generalizations and universals; he wants particulars: 'Pound hears words ('Yurra Jurrmun!') not ideas; and sees luminous details'. Further he cites Rilke's insistence on 'Things' and quotes: 'If you can manage it, return with a portion of your weaned and grown-up feeling to any one of the things of your childhood with which you were much occupied'.

Mehrotra's poems insist on particulars (especially the things of childhood), are made from images and have over the years become increasingly set in locations—although the location in a poem such as 'The Sale' is rather different from the scenery of realistic description. This does not explain, however, the spaces between the images, the extreme use of discontinuity.

An explanation might be found in Mehrotra's essay where he refers to 'the modernist crisis: the inward collapse of words, the fragments of speech' and cites Valéry's claim that the poet's language 'constitutes ... *an effort by one man* to create an artificial and ideal order by means of a material of vulgar origin'. Mehrotra's essay, with its many quotations, is an example of his poetic method of constructing an order from images, allusions, particulars. Since language fails to embody the quality of individual experience—the rift between language and experience—it is necessary to disestablish the dead commonplaces of expression and from the resulting debris create a poetry based on particulars and personal experience.

Without trying to compress Mehrotra's complex argument, which often works by juxtaposition of quotations, into a simplified statement, it is still possible to see the basis of a poetic which explains his art. It has similarities to Chitre's claims that the significant poet turns away from the debased babble of modern communications and constructs a private language to express his unique sensibility; such a language at first seems obscure until the reader becomes familiar with the poet's consciousness as expressed through his forms of speech. Whereas Chitre implies that images arise from the subconscious, Mehrotra refers to particulars, observation, memories and experience; thus Mehrotra tends towards social satire, parody, nostalgia and autobiographical reference.

The relationship of the later autobiographical and localized poetry to the earlier mixed constructions of parody, the surreal, memories and fantasy can be seen by comparing 'The Book of Common Places' with 'Genealogy' and 'Continuities'. The impossibility of separating witty parody from the personal in 'The Book of Common Places' (I quote from the *Middle Earth* version, which revises the version in *Nine Enclosures*) may suggest some of the difficulty in trying to interpret other poems. 'The Book of Common Places' is largely parody of ready-made literary phrases and situations, and probably should be read as such. Its purpose is to construct a space for the reader; it consists of fifteen sections, each of which is made of fifteen lines, divided into stanzas of ten and five lines. Such an arbitrary construction is typical of postmodernism with its insistence that literature is artificial, a construction of language and not an imitation of reality. But throughout the poem there are memories of childhood, references to the neighbourhood and thoughts about family history:

> I brought home the first pigeon
> I shot
> And hid it
> Under a flowerpot.

Towards the end of 'The Book of Common Places' there is a radically epitomized history of Mehrotra's India from the Aryan invaders to the coming of the Europeans:

> My childhood
> Wanders off into the family tree,
> And the tree gets lost
> In the North.
> I'm told we followed the tracks
> Left by none in particular,
> The horse
> Was our animal,
> And once in the plains
> We settled among rivers.

> The shadowless tribesmen
> Easily picked out the gaps
> In the procession
> Of mountains;
> Then a few ships
> Filled with white traders
> Swung around the Cape
> And sighted the west coast.
> They redid the land
> From sea to sea.

Perhaps it is the context of a lost past, and with it the lost ability of language to express reality, that we should understand:

> Yesterday
> All the rare lines
> In the book
> Were traded
> For common ones.

The poem 'Genealogy' follows on from the racial and ancestral fantasies of 'Common Places'. The speaker describes himself as 'the last survivor of what was a family'. The poem is both a parody narrative implied by fragmented allusions to journeys and creates an impression of a lost world where 'Fowl and dragons play near the shores / My sea-wrecked ancestors left'. It concludes: 'But you who live in fables, branches, / And, somehow, icebergs, tell me, whose seed I carry'.

The autobiographical poem 'Continuities' tells of an upper-middle-class Indian childhood: 'At eight I'm a Boy Scout and make a tent', 'I wear Khaki drill shorts', 'My first watch is a fat and silver Omega / Grandfather won in a race fifty-nine years ago'. After memories of his cousins' history books, postcards Mehrotra's grandfather sent from Germany, his father and mother playing cards, and other impressions from childhood, the poem concludes with a short lament at the rupture from continuity: 'The dance of the torn skin / Is for much later'. The poem is constructed by assemblage; the method is in the accumulation of precise, understated images and memories as building blocks which are placed together to make sections or enclosures while suggesting a vague narrative. Rearrange the details of 'Continuities' so the autobiographical links are lost and the result would be a surreal assemblage.

Mehrotra's increasing preoccupation with personal and local realities derives from his imagism and his demand that poetry be made of specifics and express its 'location'. 'The Roys', a poem about a family he knows in Allahabad, is filled with reminiscence, detail, specifics, social observation:

> We've rented a flat in Ghosh Buildings, Albert Road,
> And the Roys live across the street. Mr. Roy,
> General Merchant, dresses in white
> Drill trousers, long-sleeved cotton shirts,
> And looks like a friendly barn-owl.
> His sons are in school with me. Ganesh,
> The eldest, has a gleaming forehead,
> A shelled-egg complexion, a small
> Equilateral mouth; he belongs to a mystical
> Group of philatelists.

The relationship between these autobiographical poems and the earlier apparently surreal poems might be seen from the various allusions in 'The Roys' to stamp albums, autograph books and the auctioneering of 'dead advocates' libraries' (which bring to mind details from 'The Sale').

There is not so much a tension as opposing poles in Mehrotra's work. One tendency found in the early work is constructing poems by assembling and parodying bits of older social and literary habits which by juxtaposition are revivified and open to interpretation by the imagination. The other tendency is to seek the permanent in the local landscape, the past, childhood legend and myth. 'Engraving of a Bison on Stone' celebrates such permanence:

> ... The land is of one
> Piece and hasn't forgotten
> Old miracles: the engraving of a bison
> On stone, for instance ....
> ... The land
> Cannot sign its name, it cannot die
> Because it cannot be buried,
> It understands the language.

The two polarities between which his poems oscillate might be thought of as the deadening flux of the present, 'the dance of the torn skin' and the lost continuities of the past. Such poems as

'Company Period' and 'On the Death of a Sunday Painter' enclose bits of local history, turning what would otherwise be lost memories into records, a recovery, assertion and re-creation of local realities. In his own way Mehrotra is constructing the kind of local map of Indian realities which has been undertaken by de Souza, Silgardo, Peeradina and Rodrigues. In his review of *Fix* (*Times of India*, 10 February 1980) Mehrotra says: 'Ms. de Souza is among the few Indian poets to have paid any attention to the truth of Wallace Stevens' remark 'The gods of China are always Chinese'.' By focusing on local realities Mehrotra is creating continuities and connections between language and experience. The poems are increasingly less like delightful games as the realities which were the sources of the puzzles are brought to the surfacce and fixed into place.

Mehrotra's early poetry has several of the characteristics of what is known as a post-modernism. The form is highly fragmented and relies on collage and montage, with no mythic, formal or symbolic structure to create coherence. As in much post-modernist literature, it seems to enclose itself with the focus on the text rather than society or history. There is no apparent author or narrator to guide the reader through the text. Mehrotra's early stencilled publications and typographical and concrete poems could be cited as evidence of a post-modernist acceptance of technology. While Mehrotra's poetry shows little of the feeling of exhaustion and hopelessness noticeable in some post-modernist writers, such as Samuel Beckett, there is a strong sense of loss; his essays show that he sees the modern world as fragmented, with language estranged from reality. His early poetry also reveals post-modernist anti-art attitudes in its use of slogans, clichés and mockery of high culture, although this may be more youthful high jinks than a serious position.

By contrast to Mehrotra's verse constructions, Jayanta Mahapatra seems closer to the modernist movement of the first half of this century with its open-ended literary forms and reliance on recurring symbols to provide coherence to non-linear, fragmented structures. Mahapatra's persona is an estranged, distanced, sensitive artist rather than an invisible or playfully prominent post-modernist author. As in modernist writers there is less importance on the material world and more emphasis on subjective memory and the inner self, the psychological, in contrast to the post-modernist's emphasis on almost totally self-enclosed art forms. Mahapatra's is an élite art, aimed at a small, discriminating readership—whereas the early Mehrotra's humour was iconoclastic and his anti-art position had populist tendencies, common to some post-modernists who have turned to popular culture or contentless writing in reaction to high culture. But while Mehrotra's style is post-modern he has none of the sense of life as an endless repetition, an unchangeable chain found in some of the present-day avant garde; Mahapatra's vision and obsessive writing of poetry as a hopeless search for meaning in the human condition is, however, a characteristic of post-modernism as found in Beckett's later work.

The basic problem haunting Mahapatra's poetry is the relationship of the self to the other, the distance felt by the consciousness between being aware and what one is aware of. This is a central problem of modern poetry, reflected in Mehrotra's claim that language in the modern world fails to embody experience and has become a cage from which it is necessary to escape by creating a personal language. Mahapatra expresses similar themes to Chitre's feeling of the self being a cage for its potential. In Mahapatra's poetry these feelings are intensified as he questions the existence of the self; the other often takes the form of local society, and especially Hindu culture, ritual and spirituality, symbols and the past from which he has been alienated by his grandfather's conversion to Christianity and his own English-language education. In this poetry everything is problematic, put into doubt, as Mahapatra observes his environment and listens quietly, sensitively to his inner feelings, the sources of his poetry, bringing momentary perceptions of relationships and fleeting images of contrast. It is a difficult, often obscure poetry of meditation, recording reality as an unknowable flux; it more often deconstructs what is perceived and itself than affirms or celebrates. It is a poetry of inner spaces, of psychology, of contradiction and renewed feelings of depression, guilt, desire, lust and attention. Many poems seem sealed against interpretation. Others begin with meditation and make sudden leaps into unexpected areas of feeling and hopes. While the process of the poem seems more significant than what is finally said, and the narrative often fragmentary if not oblique, the poems are carefully crafted in their tight dovetailing of sounds and images to create, often, an incantatory mood.

Mahapatra seems to have evolved his poetic largely on his own as an intellectual act. Many of the poems in his first book, *Close the Sky, Ten by Ten*, are curious experiments and read more as if willed by the intellect than produced by emotion. The poems treat of loneliness, the impossibility of expressing the meaningful, the difficulty of people understanding each other, moments of sexual desire, the pregnancy of silence, the mind's imaginings, the contrast between the private and public world, Indian myth and ritual, dreams and identity. Poems about love and sexuality treat desire and relations obscurely as if they were metaphysical abstractions. Sexual attraction for some woman or women is often the disguised subject; others have as their subject poetry, writing, and the problems of using words. Certain words and images recur throughout the book and become motifs. Many of Mahapatra's later symbols are present—the sky, crows, flames, trees, the seasons, the sky, walls, distance. Some of the links are subtle: 'Loneliness', the title and subject of the first poem, is picked up by 'leave thought alone' in 'Love', the second poem. 'Love' ends on the word 'sun'; the third poem is 'To My Father', which includes the line 'The tree's tight nearness, which has not moved'. The next poem is 'The Movement'. The penultimate line of 'To My Father' is 'as you fall to air; we would not know how those'; the first line of 'The Movement' is 'As if to avoid a fall, leaning'.

The use of recurring motifs and images is a means of giving unity to a volume of poems and bringing the individual lyrics into closer relation, so that they seem continuous meditation on such themes as loneliness and personal relationships. The technique in *Close the Sky, Ten by Ten* is significant of the nature of Mahapatra's early work in which experiment with form, language, image, sound prevails over emotion. The meaning of 'Sanctuary' is that one withdraws into the self and writes poetry about the potentialities of full experience of the outside world from which the poet has withdrawn; there is a suggestion that a love affair, or some desired woman, is the hidden source of the reflections on the relationship of the poem to experience and to the poet's inner space:

> now i close the sky
> with a square ten by ten
>
> the roof essential
> hides the apocalyptic ideal

> the space sings
> where i live
>
> at home
> to hyperbola of sky-tasted love
>
> for the blessing of absence
> is its essence.

The poem is a construction in which the larger themes are stated obliquely through unusual images and odd, highly stylized verbal constructions while the original experience is alluded to by the symbolism.

Many of the lyrics treat of poetry and the subjective imagination, of the gap between what is felt and what can be expressed. The poem 'Loneliness' is a sequence of similes, each of which attempts to express isolation through unusual images. Loneliness is both deadly silence in which the world disintegrates and moments of intense self-realization. 'Love', one of Mahapatra's more explicit early poems, makes an analogy between the experience of love and the experience of poetry. It warns:

> leave thought alone
> to find the meaning ...
>
> it will not turn
> to
> a sentence.

Poetry is created from love of poetry and is untranslatable into common discourse.

Svayamvara and other poems, published the same year as *Close the Sky*, shows that Mahapatra had already developed a recurring vocabulary in which words become concepts and symbols. A recurring theme often associated with sexual love is how the making of poetry distances the writer from the reality which is its source. In 'Morning' the coming of day leads to the poet's withdrawal into poetry:

> The morning seems distant
> as I climb into words
> shrinking from the lotus.

Many of the early poems are obscure and the images often seem artificially contrived or arise from unusual private associations. The argument or narrative proceeds angularly, disjointedly, and both sentence constructions and the phrasing seem unnatural, as if the poet were going out of his way to disrupt continuity and expectations while the focus shifts between different levels of thought and emotion.

By the mid '70s, however, Mahapatra's poetry began to lose its appearance of being contrived. Although it retained the same obliqueness, surprising imagery and rapidly shifting levels of experience, it became more co-ordinated, less choppy, rhythmically much better cadenced, its phrases and sentences closer to normal syntax, less a product of a mind constructing obscure, tortuous arguments. While its concerns and themes remained private moments of illumination, despair, guilt, desire and other momentary fluctuations of feeling and insight arising within the mind, they were presented as the result of speculation on external stimuli, particularly the landscape and environment of Cuttack, where Mahapatra was raised and lives. Although there are some imagistic poems on scenes among his earlier work, this attention to the outside world, the other in contrast to the self, was new.

Mahapatra, along with Chitre in some poems, appears to have learned from Robert Bly and other American poets of the late '60s and early '70s a new means of using the external world to present subjective feelings. Although poetry often uses the other as symbol, projection, or image of the self, or as a start for reflection on the self (as in the Romantic ode where the nightingale or Grecian urn is the start of rumination and reflection), the American poets had given such methods a new twist. They spoke of organizing by 'field', itself a poetic derived from William Carlos Williams and Pound, in which the logic of the poem was its inner relations rather than narrative or argument. A poem was an image of what one saw, felt, thought, and sensed at a particular moment. There was an immediacy, but unlike the immediacy of imagism and the poetry of Williams, the emphasis was not on describing the precise appearance of what is seen but on subjective feelings which brought to the surface otherwise unchannelled, repressed, deep anxieties, fears, desires, hopes.

In *A Rain of Rites* (1976) Mahapatra uses symbols from his environment to articulate an inner space of feelings. The titles of the poems are indicative of how the external world, especially the Indian landscape and seasons, becomes the starting place of the imagination: 'Dawn', 'Village', 'Old Palaces', 'A Rain of Rites', 'A

Rain', 'Listening', 'Summer', 'Main Temple Street, Puri', 'A Twi-light Poem', 'Appearance', 'Silence', Dawn at Puri', 'Indian Summer Poem', 'Evening'. These are poems of solitude, expressions of the nuances of feelings which arise during isolation, loneliness, silence. The world is seen and then decreated to allow emotions at the edge of awareness to come forward. Such poetry suggests more than is said as it reveals areas of the mind unstructured by rational concepts and logic. There are contradictions, oppositions, con-trasts and unexpected revelations. The poem creates a space sepa-rating the poet from the external world. There are consequently two realities, that which is the external source of the poem and those immediate personal feelings which are revealed or discov-ered.

'Dawn' begins with one of Mahapatra's striking openings which tend to disorient the reader, thus allowing the rapid move-ment into the unknown:

> Out of the dark it whirls back
> into a darkly mysterious house.
>
> Is it the earth within?
> Does it keep us waking, give brief respite?
>
> Like a hard crossword puzzle
> it sets riddles crowding against one another.

Then follows a description of an Indian early morning in which the scene seems distant to the poet yet charged with detail which suggests undefined possible significances. The dawn is next dis-missed as rather the start of activity than the silence in which associations are found and discovered. In contrast to the activities of morning, however, there is the quietness, passivity, of waiting, of accepting:

> Is the dawn only a way through such strange terrain?
> The frenzy of noise, which a silence recalls
>
> through companions lost, things suddenly found?
> There is a dawn which travels alone,
>
> without the effort of creation, without puzzle.
> It stands simply, framed in the door, white in the air:
>
> an Indian woman, piled up to her silences,
> waiting for what the world will only let her do.

'Dawn' is representative of Mahapatra's poems which begin
with an observation, puzzle it, create their own space, and
conclude with their own subjective reality. It is also typical in the
importance given to 'silences', 'waiting'; the use of 'temple bell',
'crow', 'sun', 'door', 'waking', 'air' and 'dark'. Similar themes
and symbols recur throughout the volume, as Mahapatra returns
to the same materials, going over them from different angles or in
new ways, so that a book becomes more than a selection of poems
and his work takes on a consistency of vision and personality.
Mannerisms of style include the repetition of key words ('silent
night', 'silence recalls', 'her silences'; 'dark', 'darkly'; 'without
the effort', 'without puzzle'), similar words ('mysterious',
'puzzle', 'riddles') oppositions and contrasts (noise / silence;
dark / sun; lost / found; companions / things; whirls / waiting;
and the two dawns). The striking use of adjectives ('hatchet-faced
banana leaves', 'acid sounds') charges the scene with nuance suitable
for an art of reflection, brooding, listening and waiting. The Indian
woman in the doorway is a symbol both for unknowable, passive,
traditional India and for the poet, passively waiting for the poem
brought to him by the dawn of the awakening world.

Few poems affirm. Most question, ending in uncertainty or
defeat. They are lyrics of a troubled soul, of a weary, undefined
unhappiness. The monsoon season, which provides symbols for *A
Rain of Rites*, is both a time of grey skies, disasters and depressions
and also a period of renewal, birth, vegetation, after the dry, stifling
Indian summer. But the rains bring no renewal to the poet. In 'A
Rain of Rites' a contrast is made between the surprising moments
when the sun shines through the clouds of the grey rain and the
poet's lack of illumination and renewal:

> Sometimes a rain comes
> slowly across the sky, that turns
> upon its grey cloud, breaking away into light
> before it reaches its objective.
>
> ...
>
> Numbly I climb to the mountain-tops of ours
> where my own soul quivers on the edge of answers.
>
> Which still, stale air sits on an angel's wings?
> What holds my rain so it's hard to overcome?

The listening, waiting, questioning solitude is a reflection of

Mahapatra's being unable to be part of the traditional Hindu culture around him. In 'An Orissa Journal: July to November 1972' (*Queens Quarterly*, vol. LXXX, no. 1, 1973, pp. 65–73) he has written of such traditional life: 'Each time I am here I feel the soft flutter of the earth, the sensation like the physical touch of a feminine hand in mine. More like the beginning of some mystical rite.' But he cannot be part of the mysteries and rites. In the Great Temple at Puri at the inner sanctum there are 'Ten feet away, three gods, dark, dark and strange, limbless, grotesque—and I am here. Stark eyes, white, unblinking, gazing into my abyss'. He leaves feeling he has 'missed something', an 'infinity' he has 'not been able to fathom'; leaving the temple he looks back on the crowd and thinks 'Perhaps I would like to be with *them*. Within and without'.

Mahapatra's poems often record a distance between himself and the customs of his surroundings. There are the sounds of temple bells, the prayers of priests, the funeral pyres, the uncomplaining acceptance of the past, representing a possible reality, or a mentality, of which he is not part. The listening and waiting are, however, a result of consciousness, the rational mind which is aware of its individualization and difference. The poems keep returning to the desire to overcome such alienation through passive attention, in the hope that some renewal will occur. 'Listening' concludes 'You merely wait, listening, pinned to the stone'. 'The Sentence' ends:

> Behind
> the locked door you're waiting for things,
>   those reasons:
> something that lives in the brittle reeds of your veins
> something that urges the relentless trees
>   to whisper of their years.

While a sentence is a term in prison it is also part of the prison of language which distances experience from its expression. 'Ruins' contrasts reality with the attempt to bring past memory into poetry; it paradoxically asserts that the wholeness he seeks is just as impossible as an art made from it.

A Rain of Rites balances inner with outer world; in *Waiting* the tension collapses in poems of description and transparent statements. 'Song of the River' announces the futility of expecting songs of living India as its 'words' are in its stones and 'in a trance'. Instead of the dead symbols of the past 'A sacred river grows silently in my mind', but 'The rhythm of dark waters only comes and goes'. In attempting to create a plain poetry of statement, the complex, fragmented, exciting inner space of the earlier volumes is lost. There are fewer images; such symbols as stone have lost their metaphoric value. The sense of isolation, which before created a rich world of feelings and possibilities, is reduced to assertion. By contrast, 'Strike Your Secret Earth', one of the more interesting poems, has the hermeticism of *Close the Sky, Ten by Ten*, while looking forward in its sustained argumentative method to some of the later poems; it also shares with the early and later poems the guilt, self-laceration and concern with the nature of the poetry. It criticizes the easy fall into self-doubt and weak affirmations which are characteristic of many poems in *Waiting*:

> You are only used to seeing your own hands rise
> against the throats of your words.
> Don't let your timidity, your suspicious response
> turn you into awkward parrots, furtive crabs,
> or into windows, always shut, rumps to the sky.

Instead of such writing:

> For some time you must begin,
> you must exhaust all your memories and solitudes,
> hear the foaming water
> thunder into the dark pool,
> the leaden mind,
>
> hear the embryo of pain grow
> its keen fingers, and walk water in the river,
> as it draws those sunsets from time's outer rim:
> raw vision, a flash of consciousness,
> waters slowing over to melt the bone.

It is natural, since the world of Mahapatra's poetry is based on uncertainty, self-doubt, guilt and brooding, that *Waiting* should be followed by *The False Start*. These are more interesting, complex poems in their imagery and tense conflicts between what 'The Retreat' terms 'my sudden need for life' and 'the desert of dead bone and dust'. Time, immortality, desire, passion, the mutability of life, the fear of death and ageing are among the themes of the volume. There is a renewed sense of energy and desire, especially against the ravages of time, and a heightened sense of the inner life and its dominance over external reality. 'The Moon Moments' complains:

> How can I stop the life I lead within myself—
> The startled, pleading question in my hands lying in my
>   lap
> while the gods go by, triumphant, in the sacked city at
>   midnight?

Basically these are poems of the shapes of solitude, the life within the self in its variety, recurrences, obsessions, anxieties, desires, imaginings, dreams, speculations, memories, betrayals, bursts of illumination and vitality, and moments of poetic creation from its own inner realities. An explanation of what Mahapatra is doing can be found in his essay 'The Inaudible Resonance in English Poetry in India' (*The Literary Criterion*, 15, no. 1, 1980, pp. 27–36) where he says that the 'experiences at various times in the writer's life have clothed the essentiality of his being, which the writer exploits in symbols of his own making'. As a writer proceeds from book to book 'he begins to be drawn into an inner world of his own making—a world spaced by his own life, of secret allusions, of desire and agony, of a constantly changing alignment between dream and reality'.

In the same essay Mahapatra complains that there has been no change in his poetry, 'simply a renewed flight of birds'; instead he now wants to 'celebrate' his own 'Humanity' through 'feeling and language which pass on the mythic forces of life'. *Relationship* is an attempt to go beyond the repetition of small lyrics treating of fragments of experience, to go beyond the self, to write a long poem, a modern epic which will embody the myths of his culture, particularly the history, legends and mythology of the area of Orissa where Mahapatra lives, which was once part of the ancient empire of Kalinga.

Although *Relationships* has many epic-like characteristics, including a raised or 'sublime' manner of speech, expressed through heightened diction and long, winding sentences, an introductory announcement of its theme, an invocation of the muse, and is divided, like most epics, into twelve books, it is a modern long poem concerned with the self's relationship to the kinds of historical materials which have in the past been the basis and culture of the epic, rather than, like the epic, a narrative of a great legendary event of national history. The epic traditionally is objective in the sense that the artist is at a distance from his material, unlike the lyric poem, which is a form of self-expression. In *Relationship* such distinctions collapse as the narrative is the poet's attempt to regain the materials of an epic culture through a dream-like pilgrimage. The aim is to relieve the self of its guilt of alienation, of its feeling of distance from the other by recreating the other and confronting it within the mind. It is a poem of crisis, a psychic reliving of one's imagined origins. It is also work descended from the autobiographical, confessional long poem of the Romantics, through the Symbolists, with their insistence on poetic purity, so that there are few linking narrative connections. Images are given musical organization, related to each other spatially rather as recurring motifs than by story.

Relationship begins with a poet attempting to understand the myths, rituals, legends and history which are his past from which he is alienated. The vision comes as 'dreams' found in the carving of the Konarak temple. Recalling ancient history but baffled by it ('time has no mouth'), aware that 'my existence lies in the stones', the poet wants to find the 'mouth' of the earth (probably an allusion to Krishna creating the world), he wants to feed on 'the stones' like a child on its mother. Memories come and vanish, and their origins are questioned. Are they 'just voices / of another world, / pretending from the throat'?

While it is possible to imagine a narrative for *Relationship*, the poem is not constructed on such linear lines and resists translation. There is, however, a detectable process which moves from listening to the words of the shivalinga, looking through the window of consciousness on buried Mother India, the awareness that one is situated in the flux of time while attempting to understand time past, the dialogue with the Father, and the continuing theme of solitude, to an awareness that such alienation and its resulting depression can be overcome and new sources of energy tapped by a participation in the past: 'I know I can never come alive / if I refuse to consecrate at the altar of my origins'. Section Four ends with the poet feeling that 'now' is the time to satisfy his solitude in a prayer-poem which reflects 'the earth's lost amplitudes'. Section Five begins with a vision of the myths of India contained in the temple stones, but questions whether it is possible to find renewal ('blood throbs') in 'the pallor of dreams'. Yet something is there, which speaks through the 'wall' that encloses such realities from the self. The more Mahapatra worries about the problem the more he creates the world he seeks: 'This sleep is a song / that is heard from all sides continually'.

The problem is in the self; it is separate from the object by its isolation and solitude, its desires, hungers and guilts, its making of song. Section Eight is a moment of breaking through the wall to fusion, of going beyond the self, to an orgasmic relationship: 'So through this door, through the gleaming skin of the three kingdoms'. The meaning sought and experienced is not in one thing itself, not in a single realm or satisfaction. The many symbols on the temple are imitations of what is desired and not experienced. The ultimate understanding of the human condition is the participation in the totality of creation, the world once again made sexual as in the oldest Aryan Hindu belief:

> This is the real body: raging pachyderm
> with the crazy testicles, red and wild,
> the lusting god of the blackest Siva night;
>
> ...
>
> For now I touch your secret order
> embarrassed *yoni*;
> before me lie the sulking years of dreams,
> the stricken purposes of the muscles,
> the violent splashes of sunsets
> in the fibres of the being.

By Section Nine the moment of orgasmic, primeval unity and happiness has passed and now is referred to as 'the hope of soothing myself'. But what was it? The reality of the spiritual pilgrimage is questioned as the poet returns to the present of 'the burning sun' and newspapers. While in the past he felt alienated from the people around him, now 'We are delivered by the myth'. 'Fear of my guilt, I bid you farewell'. The poem ends by affirming the life force and the harmonious energies of continuing creation as represented by the temple dancers, the 'dark daughters': 'In *your* dance is my elusive birth'.

Mahapatra's poetry forms a continuous work revealed by his titles. After writing *The False Start* and having established *Relationship*, it is appropriate that *Life Signs* should follow. Such poems as 'Grandfather' and 'The Lost Children of America' are much more accessible, focused beyond the self on others; other poems—'Morning

Signs', 'A Monsoon Day Fable', 'Again, One Day, Walking by the River'—use more details from the external world and seem more directly addressed to the reader. But the poems in *Life Signs* mostly ask the same questions about reality and develop in the same way, by a dialectic of questions which generate categories, from the same kinds of feelings and problems as the earlier volumes: 'the song that reaches our ears is just our own'; 'It is the silence which says the world is not ours'; 'So we drag the meanings / from what we see'; 'Yet how real is it?'; 'Or is it only desire, hoping to resume its inner light'.

Although there are distinct periods of his poetry and differences in manner, Mahapatra's work has no clear demarcations of contrasting opinions, new kinds of material or radical departures in organization. The poems appear a continuous relation of aspects of the isolation, loneliness, solitude and alienation of the self from external realities in a world without apparent purpose. This is the existential dilemma of most modern literature. While Mahapatra's world is filled with personal pain, guilt, remorse, hunger, desire and moments of renewal, his environment is filled with symbols of belief by the ordinary lives of the people of Cuttack, the temples, the Hindu festivals, the ancient monuments. The poems are varied attempts to bridge an epistemological, phenomenological gap—to know, be part of, enclose, experience—with the world and the other, whether it be a woman, temple stones, a Hindu priest. The skies, the wind, time and waves are symbols of the world of change and flux which raise questions of the nature and purpose of life as represented by the unchanging, fixed, rooted (stones, trees, the past); but these questions can never be answered by the mind, its perceptions and emotions. Thus nothing can satisfy longings, provide the answer to being human. Guilt is bid 'farewell' at the end of *Relationship*, but the final words of the poem refer to the poet as 'a spiritless soul of memory'.

In *Life Signs* there is a continuing air of sadness, defeat, spiritlessness and consciousness of death ('the sleepless line I walk on leads nowhere'; 'defeated as I am by my own tactics'):

> If I had that girl with the tender touch
> beside me now, would it have merely prepared myself
> for a world of illusion without my poems.

It would be easy to focus on 'world of illusion' and claim that Mahapatra makes a distinction familiar to Hindu metaphysics between the illusions of the world of appearance and spiritual reality. While Indian philosophy may have coloured and shaped his inwardness, and certainly is reflected in the desire to find some unity, some being at peace with the tradition around him, it would be too facile to see that as the meaning or central concern, or even the philosophical framework of his poems. The quoted lines are from 'Will a Poem of Mine be the Only Answer?', in which he contrasts the animal, sexual excitement of his past with his present sense of futility as he ages and knows he must face death. The poetry speaks of 'needs', the need to feel alive, the need to impregnate the world with significance, love it, wed it:

> No man points to the sky
> without being aware of the desire to live
> in his belly where the earth-snake lies.

These are the 'life signs'. He is himself like 'The Lost Children of America':

> here on earth
>   when history does not reverberate any more
> with the pulse of the drum
> or with the chant of the tide on a sacred Puri shore—
>
> . . .
>
> as the burden of ununderstood things billows upward
>   like smoke.

There is much that could be said of Mahapatra's poetry, the way he plays on and revivifies clichés, the habitual romantic sadness, the significance of beginning to write poetry in middle age and the obsession to create an impressive body of work almost as a defiance against solitude and death, the way that creation of poems becomes god-like—the creation of a meaningful world from reflections on a world which cannot be 'understood'.

Mahapatra has attempted to construct a body of poetry which has the kind of relationship with his environment and the problem of finding significance in 'this time of darkness and lost ones' that is similar to the major poets of our age. One thinks of Wallace Stevens's desire to create a 'supreme poetry', a metapoem which by explaining how belief grows from perception of local realities will replace belief with an epistemology. His imaginative world might even be described as post-Samuel Beckett—the mind grinds on as memories, desires and hungers present themselves as material for writing.

There is, however, an awareness of other people, the landscapes, the changing skies, desirable women, a world desired from which the perceiving self by being distinct is distanced. If we think of the imagination as desire isolated from the other, from the totality of experience (as symbolized in the eighth section of *Relationship* by 'raging pachyderm', 'the lusting god', the '*yoni*', the ultimate fusion of desire with the sky and earth in ancient Hindu symbolism), then we have another explanatory metaphor of Mahapatra's poetry. It is another version of the modern desire to live fully, physically, spiritually, socially and creatively.

CHAPTER TWELVE

Exile

RAMANUJAN, SHARAT CHANDRA, KUMAR, NAZARETH,
SETH

Many Indian poets now live, or have lived for long periods, abroad, mainly in the United States, and a number hold university posts teaching English literature or creative writing in English departments—A. K. Ramanujan is Professor of Dravidian Linguistics, Shiv Kumar was and Meena Alexander is a university English teacher, Agha Shahid Ali and G. S. Sharat Chandra teach courses in poetry writing. While Darius Cooper appears to be starting his teaching career in America, H.O. Nazareth lives in London and makes films. B. Rajan, one of the first modern Indian poets, was before his retirement a Professor of English in Canada. Vikram Seth was until recently an editor with Stanford University Press. The literature of exile is not peculiar to modern India; former colonies and new nations—with their limited home literary market for professional writers—have tended to have expatriate writers. Usually expatriate writers are novelists; this is partly because the market for poetry is small even in metropolitan centres and there are fewer opportunities for a career as a professional poet. Another reason poets stay at home is the need to be close to the culture of their own speaking voice. Indian poets, however, are an exception; no doubt the greater opportunities (especially at universities) outside India have contributed to their exile.

Indian expatriate poets do not write from the position of a distinct foreign community, such as the exiled black or West Indian novelists, but their writing reflects the perspective of someone between two cultures. They may look back on India with nostalgia, satirically celebrating their liberation or asserting their biculturalism, but they also look sceptically and wryly on their new homeland as outsiders, with a feeling of something having been lost in the process of growth. The ability to tolerate, accommodate and absorb other cultures without losing the consciousness of being Indian marks the expatriate poets.

A. K. Ramanujan makes use of his South Indian Brahmin background in complex ways, seeing in the tight-knitness of Indian family life both the security of closeness and bonds from which he is now thankfully liberated. We can ignore critics who assume that the interest of Ramanujan's poetry consists of nostalgic memories of South Indian life, that his poetry is limited by an inability or unwillingness to embrace some larger assertion of an Indian ideal or tradition, or is limited by a failure to express a fuller or a more comprehensive vision of Indian society. Such demands on literature belong more to the world of politics, sentiments and rhetoric than to actual experience, the realities with which literature is usually concerned. The truth of literature is in its awareness of such falsities and in its refusal to proclaim simple traditions where there are in fact discontinuities or complexities.

Ramanujan's 'A River' is about truth, the reality of the river and kinds of relations between the present and the past. In Madurai the poets of the past sang of the city, its temples, and of the river as full. While 'every summer' the river 'dries to a trickle' the 'poets sang only of the floods'. When there are floods, they are in fact destructive, causing deaths and damaging property; but present-day Tamil poets still echo the old poets and ignore reality. No one writes 'of the pregnant woman / drowned, with perhaps twins in her'. Ramanujan's poem is in part an answer to such poetic myth-making. 'The river has water enough / to be poetic / about only once a year'. While the poem shows a realistic debunking of the romanticization of traditional Tamil culture, the irony of the conclusion distances the speaker and shows alienation rather than involvement. This is the kind of irony found in Jules Laforgue or the early T. S. Eliot, in which the poet's self is defended by an anaesthetizing of possible emotional response into a non-committal, witty disdain:

> it carries away
> in the first half-hour
> three village houses
> a couple of cows
> named Gopi and Brinda
> and one pregnant woman

> expecting identical twins
> with no moles on their bodies
> with different-coloured diapers
>
> to tell them apart.

Such wit is unstable; the satiric comment could as easily be seen as
focusing on the speaker's emotional non-involvement as on the
dreariness of the continuing reality which is depicted in contrast
to the romanticized Madurai of the poets.

The attitude in ' A River' is a more witty, complex, distanced
version of the satire found in 'Epitaph on a Street Dog' with its
similar insistence on sordid reality: 'She spawned in a hurry a
score of pups, / all bald, blind, and growing old at her paps'.
Again there is purposeful deflation of romantic India, this time
through references to 'the low melon moons' and 'Peacocks'
which contrast to the reality:

> But She had in a row four pairs of breasts,
> where blind mouths plucked and swilled their fill
> till mouths had eyes, and She was full of flies.

Although I have described the irony of 'A River' as Laforguean,
there is no need to seek specific sources. Ramanujan is widely read
in Indian, western and western-influenced modern Indian poetry in
Indian languages. This unpredictable fusion of varied roots in
Ramanujan's poetry is true of the attitudes it expresses. The
apparently derisive view of India in 'A River', 'Smalltown, South
India' and 'Epitaph on a Street Dog' might be contrasted to 'Love
Poem for a Wife I', with its memories of shared family relation-
ships and a common heritage:

> Really what keeps us apart
> at the end of years is unshared
> childhood ...
> Or we should do as well-meaning
> hindus did,
>
> betroth us before birth,
> forestalling separate horoscopes
> and mothers' first periods,
> and wed us in the oral cradle
> and carry marriage back into
> the namelessness of childhoods.

This is one of several of Ramanujan's poems about the problems of marriage and should not be regarded as simple nostalgia for the closeness of Hindu family relations. The details within the poem of a shared heritage are a bit absurd:

> Only two weeks ago, in Chicago,
> you and brother James started
> one of your old drag-out fights
> about where the bathroom was
> in the backyard.

The conclusion of the poem builds up to humorous exaggeration:

> ... Probably
> only the Egyptians had it right:
> their kings had sisters for queens
> to continue the incests
> of childhood into marriage.

The 'namelessness of childhoods' refers to a time before the development of personal identity and ego; while it does symbolize a time of unity without the strife that arises from separate wills, it can hardly be considered an answer to the problems of marriage. It is rather used here tongue-in-cheek as an unrealizable ideal. Within the poem there is enough family conflict mentioned ('one of your old drag-out fights', 'you wagered heirlooms') to show that a common family past does not prevent disagreements.

Ramanujan's concern is with memory and the way it establishes or falsifies relationships in a changing world. The poems of disdain towards India could be matched by poems which offer a less attractive portrait of Chicago, where Ramanujan lives and teaches. Ramanujan is neither a nostalgic traditionalist nor an advocate of modernization and westernization. He is a product of both and his poems reflect a personality conscious of change, enjoying its vitality, freedom and contradictions, but also aware of memories which form his inner self, memories of an unconscious 'namelessness', which are still alive, at the foundations of the self.

The memories are seldom as pleasant as the shared past of family relations in 'Love Poem for a Wife 1'. In 'Breaded Fish' memories recall a half-naked woman dead on a beach. While the memory is not explained, there is a symbolic relationship between the affectionate gesture of a woman (perhaps his wife) specially preparing the fish for him and the dead woman 'breaded / by the grained indifference of sand'. The association of death and an indifferent universe is brought to mind by the dead fish. In the poem 'Still Life' the half-eaten sandwich carries 'the shape / of her bite'.

'Snakes' recalls the snakes of his South Indian childhood. They not only terrified him but are associated with family. They are 'like some terrible aunt'. His mother uses them in rituals for which his father pays money, 'But I scream'. As his sister braids her hair he imagines snakes. Fear haunts him until he actually steps on and kills a snake:

> Now
> frogs can hop upon this sausage rope,
> flies in the sun will mob the look in his eyes,
>
> and I can walk through the woods.

As in other poems there is little offered beyond memories, events and description. The poem presents an image, a complex of feelings, distilled memories and events which are not elaborated or commented upon. But as it begins in the present 'now' of museums and bookstacks which contrast with rural India and family life, the poem celebrates a liberation from the fears of the past, 'ghosts' from which Ramanujan now feels safe.

He is not really liberated from his memories; if he were he would not be recalling snakes in foreign libraries. The past keeps intruding. In 'Still Another for Mother' he is an observer of a scene in London between an aged man and woman. Although he does not know exactly what took place between them:

> something opened
> in the past and I heard something shut
> in the future, quietly,
>   like the heavy door
> of my mother's black-pillared, nineteenth-century
> silent house, given on her marriage day
> to my father, for a dowry.

The image of the conflict between the man and woman, he angry, she pathetically hoping he will forgive her, is projected on his family's past and perhaps on his own future. The 'heavy door' of the 'black-pillared' 'silent house' contributes to the sense of marriage as a shutting in of deadly private quarrels, with the implication that this too will be his fate.

The importance of memory to Ramanujan comes up in Rama Jha's 'A Conversation with A.K. Ramanujan' (*The Humanities Review*, vol. 3, no. 1, January-June 1981, pp. 5–13), where the poet says that his writing obtains its 'nourishment' from his Indian culture: 'those are the roots. That is what binds us back to our childhood and all the early years.'

AKR: Because, you cannot entirely live in the past, neither can you entirely live in the present, because we are not like that. We are both these things. The past never passes. Either the individual past or historical past or cultural past. It is *with* us, it is what gives us the richness of— what you call it—the richness of understanding. And the richness of expression. We bring that to whatever is present and some of this understanding might be simply ironic, that is, so much of it cannot be truly supplied, or related to the present.

RJ : You mean the points of departure?

AKR: Yes, the disconnection is as much an understanding of the past as making the connection. And people living in the present have to see both, because to assert continuity where there is none, where we cannot see any, is to be a revivalist.

An expatriate, he lives 'in two different worlds—the one within, the one without'. But with modern mobility older notions of exile have taken on a new significance. Ramanujan is not different from other Indians living abroad:

Creativity comes out of sustained attention to one's own experience, one's own locality, one's own landscape, you know. And the circumstances which one can understand and feel and experience deeply without any schemes, without learning this, that and the other.

He distinguishes 'one's own experience' from self-conscious, willed cosmopolitanism or pan-Indianism or an unaware provincialism:

I did not mean by regionalism, provincialism, nor did I mean by it just the devotion to a particular region. What I was saying was the particularity of the experience. Even when you are cosmopolitan, you ultimately have to know something quite deeply.

The particularity of personal life treated in depth, the attending to 'experience', is significant. Being representative or contemporary is the possible result and not the aim of poetry, which should enclose a world:

Whatever world it may be. It may be a personal world, it may be a social world but a world which is fully embodied in poetry. We need enough of that, some parts of our experience—to explore it as best we can.

The use of private experience, and especially the inner world of memories and the continuities and discontinuities with the past, can be seen as the basis of many of Ramanujan's poems. They are not attempts to intellectualize and make moral choices like Ezekiel's early work, nor do they have Daruwalla's sense of a violent world in which fulfilment is doomed to tragic failure, nor are they Maha-patra's metaphysical meditations on the relationship between the creative impulse and the world outside the perceiving self. They are memories of a past which shifts while the self and others change. In 'Self-Portrait' he is, although a product of his past ('my father'), a stranger to himself. As there is no fixed, essential being, rooted in an unchanging 'namelessness of childhoods', so there is no pure existential product of personal choice. The core of the essential self remains as an inner world, but this is modified by changed circumstances and decisions. The essential self develops, evolves, changes; it grows from seeds in the past towards a future which while unknowable is already being formed. The vision is in 'Carpe Diem', an early Ramanujan poem published in P. Lal's *Modern Indian Poetry in English*:

Pluck the moment,
said Epicurus.

But when we pluck,
does the fruit forget
the tree's inverted image
moping in the root,
and the slow certainty
of the earth-shouldering volcano
waiting in the green hereafter?

The body of criticism which has grown up around Ramanu-jan's poetry has been slightly misleading in emphasizing either a revivalist search for roots, some ossification of the past, or in positing a contrasting modern existentialist outsider. An organic world in process, changing, growing, but continuous, is closer to the vision of Ramanujan's poetry. 'Looking for a Cousin on a Swing' shows how the 'innocent' physical context of childhood becomes adult sexuality, sexual awareness and hypocrisy:

> Now she looks for the swing
> in cities with fifteen suburbs
> and tries to be innocent
> about it
>
> not only on the crotch of a tree
> that looked as if it would burst
> under every leaf
> into a brood of scarlet figs.

The sexuality was there all the time, and was felt, but its adult significance could not have been known. The poem, however, is not just a psychological insight into evolving sexuality; it is like 'Love Song to a Wife 1' a statement about the desire, and its comic absurdity, of wanting the unselfconscious feeling of wholeness, of unreflecting being, of unthinking self-identities supposedly found in childhood.

'Small-scale Reflections on a Great House' might be read as symbolic of the mind in which all new experience and information becomes part of the past and is changed, just as the past is changed, by experience of the modern world:

> Sometimes I think that nothing
> that ever comes into this house
> goes out. Things come in every day
>
> to lose themselves among other things
> lost long ago among
> other things lost long ago;
> ...
> And also, anything that goes out
> will come back, processed and often
> with long bills attached,
>
> like the hooped bales of cotton
> shipped off to invisible Manchesters
> and brought back milled and folded.

The house, representative of the Indian Hindu tradition in its accommodation to disparate myths, ideas, philosophies, gods, its

tolerance of eccentricities and failures, its assimilation of the new
without producing the transformations which conflict brings to
the European mind, is both unchanging and continually changing
as the foreign is domesticated:

> And ideas behave like rumours,
> once casually mentioned somewhere
> they come back to the door as prodigies
>
> born to prodigal fathers, with eyes
> that vaguely look like our own,
> like what Uncle said the other day.

Ramanujan's attitude here may be thought nostalgic of a great
tradition, but the comic absurdities throughout the poem and the
ironic distancing at its conclusion (when a wounded nephew
appears unexpectedly, having been brought by airplane, train and
'military truck', 'On a perfectly good / chatty afternoon', before
the telegram announcing his return) imply the complacency of
such a comforting view of tradition and continuity which ignores
the harsh actualities of experience.

The inner world consists of fears and desires as well as memories;
the fear of snakes, sexual desire, the desire for unreflecting identity
and harmony and, as several poems record, anxiety. 'Anxiety' has
'naked roots and secret twigs'. Anxiety also is a continuing process;
'anxiety / can find no metaphor to end it.' 'Entries for a Catalogue
of Fears' also uses images of growing from the past but they are of
an unwanted future imprisoned by an unhealthy sense of tradition:

> I'll love my children
>   without end,
> and do them infinite harm
>   staying on the roof,
>   a peeping-tom ghost
> looking for all sorts of proof
>   for the presence of the past:
>
> they'll serve a sentence
>   without any term
> and know it only dimly
>   long afterwards
> through borrowed words
>   and wrong analyses.

The tension between inner world of the past and the need to be freed from its fears and traditions is a major concern of the poems. 'Some Indian Uses of History on a Rainy Day' offers three contrasts between reality and the nostalgic imagination. 'Fulbright Indians' visiting Egypt only see a past of mummies 'swathed in millennia / of Calicut muslin'. An English-speaking Indian Professor of Sanskrit in Germany in 1935 is lost and does not understand the language, but suddenly feels he is at home seeing a Nazi swastika. 'Prayers to Lord Murugan' are, like Ezekiel's *Latter Day Psalms* and *Hymns in Darkness*, modern, sceptical secular equivalents of traditional Indian religious literature. Lord Murugan, the ancient Dravidian god who was later usurped by Hindu mythology, is an attractive god from whom the poet asks deliverance from both the weight of history and the abstractions of the modern world:

> Deliver us O presence
> from proxies
> and absences
>
> from sanskrit and the mythologies
> of night and the surreal
> roundtable mornings
>
> of London and return
> the future to what
> it was.

The prayer is for the concrete results ('a litter / of six new pigs') of living experience and for freedom from the anxieties which turn people to worship:

> Lord of answers,
> cure us at once
> of prayers.

Ramanujan's imagination resembles the water bugs in his poem 'The Striders'. They seem to be perched weightless on a continually changing stream on a 'landslide of lights' while being eye-deep in the waters:

> and drowns eye-
> deep
> into its tiny strip
> of sky.

The oblique significance of the water bugs as 'prophets', or poets, is clearer in the original version (*Poetry*, Chicago, 98, July 1961, p. 228) from which the first line, 'Put away, put away this dream' has been deleted. (Noted by G. N. Devi, 'The Two Faces of Aliena-tion: The Poetry of A. K. Ramanujan and R. Parthasarathy', Mas-ter's thesis, University of Leeds, England, 1979, pp. 23 & 101.) Put away dreams and deeply search (drown) one's own small spot of reality in a changing world.

'The Striders', weightlessly posed on dry legs, might also be an image of Ramanujan's style, light, tight, distanced, but enclosed in its own world so that the poem seems self-contained, without wider resonances of the kind most poets hope to establish through allu-sion, reference or symbolism. In 'The Striders' the only explicit broadening of association to make correspondences with the image is 'prophets' (since 'dream' has been deleted in the final version). Although in free verse, shaped visually to suggest the water bug perching, 'The Striders' is a wonderfully concentrated poem held together by sound patterns (search, certain, perch; stemmed, them; bubble, bugs; eyed, dry, eye, sky), lightly rhymed line endings (of fifteen words eleven in rhyme positon have 's' sounds: bugs, legs, weightless, skin, stream, prophets, sits) and the positioning of linking words (for, on, of, into) at the beginning of lines to form a rhetorical structure.

Each of Ramanujan's poems has its unique shape. There is the formal organization of 'Small-scale Reflections on a Great House' into seven parts, each of the thirteen lines consisting of four three-line stanzas followed by a single line. There are the eight-line stan-zas of 'Love Poem for a Wife 2', each of which has a short sixth line. The irregular right-hand margin of 'Still Life' visually seems like the half-eaten sandwich in the poem. In such poems each word is used carefully, precisely, economically; spacing and line breaks are important, to produce a self-contained artifice in contrast to the changing stream of time and memories of the past which are their subject. The poem itself becomes the stability, the fixed point in contrast to the self, its anxieties, other persons, India or the past.

While G. S. Sharat Chandra, like Ramanujan, has memories of the closeness of South Indian family life, a satiric perspective on modern India and a sense of being uprooted in his new country, the United States, his poetry shows the self as insecure, except among family. Being at home neither in India nor in the New

World, he often fantasizes a third nation where he will be at ease. The similarities of theme between Ramanujan and Sharat Chandra might be explained by both being South Indians from well-established families from Mysore, and by both having emigrated to America. But Sharat Chandra's poems are thinner in texture and treatment of theme, and more colloquial in voice and manner. In the poetry his memories are of the close-knit warmth of family rather than, as with Ramanujan, childhood as a time before the fall from unselfconscious unity into a fragmented identity.

Sharat Chandra's themes have remained constant, although over the years his style has changed. He writes of India, in contrast to his family, as a place of financial, moral and cultural corruption, a land of social injustice and poverty except for those in power or positions of influence. The brief biography on the cover of *April in Nanjangud* says he left India because of its social and political oppression. This is reflected in his poems. 'Bharata Natyam Dancer', the title poem of his first book, describes an artist who, although as heavy-footed as an elephant, is acclaimed by her audience of government ministers and politicians; she is the daughter of a famous dancer 'who was a great social hostess / who had many friends and relatives in the government'; 'i knew her mother... said the chief minister'.

Poems which examine social conditions include 'Matrudesh', which describes the hungry and poor; they search garbage cans for rotten food, are forced by poverty to live like animals and will sell their children for a meal: 'I know a nation where death / Is a blessing to the dead and living'. 'Abdul and Fatima' is about the small, unrecognized lives of the poor and their religious superstitions; they trust prayer rather than hospitals to cure the ill and when they die are forgotten with no reminder that they ever existed. Other poems concern the new sights discovered while living abroad: the men's room in an American petrol station with its clean lavatories; Bermuda, the 'white man's resort' with its black waiters, caddies and shoe boys who do the menial labour; the American met at a bar who talks knowingly of Zen Buddhism but has never been 'as far east as detroit'.

Heirloom offers a representative selection of Sharat Chandra's work. There are poems concerned with Indian sexual prudery ('Indian Miniatures I'), the way Indian poverty is made to seem holy

('Beggar'), social injustices masked by religion ('Death of the Second-Division Clerk'), contrasts between Indian government pronouncements and the actual condition of the country ('Letters from My Father'), the cynical greed of Brahmin priests ('At the Burning-Ghats') and the superstitions connected with idols and Hindu holy places ('Black Ganesh, Halebid', 'Tirumalai', 'The Black Deity').

While having in disgust washed his hands of India, Sharat Chandra appears rootless and undefined in his American surroundings. Apparently this is the kind of freedom he prefers. 'In the Third Country' he contrasts his probable funeral in India, America and 'the third country'; in the latter:

> No one wants your whereabouts
> no one worries your mail
>
> If you changed your mind
> and returned there
> no one wonders if it was appropriate
> whether you acted hasty
> or with taste.

The effacing of himself, a willed lack of identity is the subject of 'Self-Portrait', where he appears to have chosen nonentity instead of the anxieties of a strongly defined place:

> There are scars instead
> of lines on my palm
> I've no biography
> only remembrance ...
>
> ...
>
> I'm not their man
> I assure them
> walking away
> my hands squirm
> in my pockets like fish
> gasping for air...

The results of being in exile, rather than having an emotional commitment to the land of his birth or the country to which he has emigrated, can be seen in 'Once or Twice' where, after claiming

No country would have me

Where I was born slips my mind
Uncontrollably

he is surprised by someone being interested in him: 'For the first
time / You notice me'.

Apparently such an insecure sense of belonging and identity start-
ed early in his life. 'Consistently Ignored' concerns his feeling of
neglect in a family of ten when he wondered whether he was really
his mother's son and thought that he might be sold to some trader.
In 'Reasons for Staying' the justification for living abroad is his
sense of having created his own world from his labours and wishes:

> There are roses because I say so,
> the vase is mine
> so is the kitchen
> I like them red
> I pay for the water.

Although Sharat Chandra's later poems are more colloquial,
lighter in touch, more focused on himself and his condition of
exile, isolation and freedom, they record deepening reflections on
his experience or the creation of a personal world. Either he prefers
such a condition or he has responded to his isolation by writing
poetry which speaks directly, sceptically from a position of exile,
rented rooms and an apparently small life. It may be significant that
in the two poems he has written on his thirty-third and thirty-fifth
birthdays, the first mocks poetic inflation of reality ('It's none of
these but myself / Turning thirty-three on a grey morning') while
the other consists of angry memories of his childhood in India.
Taking realistic attitudes and using a direct speaking voice in his
poetry, he continues to mock social and religious pieties. In 'The
Funeral of My Procession' he imagines what it would be like after
death, the sound of friends with smoker's cough at his funeral, the
waiting to be reborn:

> These are my ancestors
> Shouting, 'Surprise! Surprise!'
> Zooming their archaic faces
> In and out the coffin
> Laughing their silly heads off!

> I should've known
> Of the line in waiting
> Six feet under a previous life....

It is perhaps significant of the reasons why some Indian poets
have emigrated and of the resulting social disorientation they feel
that Shiv Kumar's poetry reveals a similar anger towards India to
that of Sharat Chandra and a similar sense of not really belonging
anywhere. While Kumar's 'Broken Columns' sequence shows the
contrast between his awakening youthful sexuality and the repres-
sions of Indian life, especially as represented by Hindu religious
teachings, his 'A Letter from New York' speaks disparagingly of his
living conditions, broken American families, and the lack of social
relations. There are no beggars, lepers or cripples on wheelbarrows.
There are 'Only eyes, eyes, eyes / staring at lamp-posts'; the only
conversation reported is with a stranger 'In the Gents' who asks him
'Are you a Puerto Rican? / A Jamaican? A Red Indian?'

Kumar, however, seldom writes about his experience of exile
except as a background to his main concern with his sexuality,
desires, broken marriage and the constructions of life in India.
In 'Walking Down the Avenue of the Americas' he sees the
skyscrapers in contrast to a man collapsed on the sidewalk and
the rats in a garbage can but thinks 'Every passerby in polaroids /
is my wife's seducer', which leads him to reflect on his 'ashen
middle-age'. Many of Kumar's poems have no identifiable natu-
ral location; they are concerned with his sexual desires and fears
of ageing. In what country are 'At the Customs Counter' or
'Autumn' or 'Midnight Musings' situated?

> Any woman can get me now.
> The moment of despair
> has no age
> no discretion.

While Kumar's best-known poems, such as 'Kali' and 'Indian
Women' are about Indian life, he writes surprisingly little about
his experiences abroad. Although he claims to look at both Indian
and western culture from the perspective of an alien, he writes
mostly about India with an anger which takes the form of comic
satire.

H. O. Nazareth, from a Bombay Goan family, has for many
years lived in London, although his only book, *Lobo* (1984), was

published by Clearing House. Nazareth is one of the many Indian poets now residing and often settled abroad whose work continues to make use of their early years and Indian experience; but Nazareth is also concerned with the Indian in England whom he sees as part of an often unaccepted black racial presence. His poetry therefore has similarities in diction, attitude, manner and commitment to West Indian writing; socially, economically, culturally and politically the Indian and black West Indian English communities share a similar experience of displacement, prejudice and lack of assimilation. Influences on Nazareth's verse include the two major contemporary West Indian poets, Edward K. Braithwaite and Derek Walcott, who have used West Indian speech, rhythms and personae in naturalizing the English poetic tradition to their own society.

Nazareth's persona, Lobo, who links the series of poems, is a distant spiritual descendant of Byron's Don Juan with his romantic aspiration and contrasting sarcastic, ironic awareness; he is aloof, disdainful, both hero and anti-hero, a confusing mixture of undiscriminated thoughts, feelings, and experiences which usually end unsatisfactorily. The poems provide a loosely knit biography of Lobo. In creating such a representative, if probably distanced, autobiographical persona, Nazareth is following on a method developed in America by John Berryman and used with social and political awareness in Jussawalla's 'Missing Person'. *Lobo* is a portrait of the continuing effects of the colonialism which has resulted in fragmented, rootless, westernized individuals from the Third World. Lobo, wolf in Portuguese, is a common Goan Catholic family name and is representative of the colonial heritage of the former colony. Beyond the effects of colonialism the poems also contrast the inflated ideals of rulers, politicians and revolutions with the realities of life as felt by an ordinary person.

The early poems in the sequence contrast Lobo's childhood of sports, dances, friends, girls, desires and family with the larger, public, adult world. Lobo's youthful dominion is a 'make-believe world' of toy soldiers and flags made of rags, which in its falseness and self-centredness is symbolic of independent India:

> thorough Indian patriots usually rest
> on the laurels of a glorious past
> while other nationalities wield power
> or expect grandchildren to tower
> over the rest.

The abrupt, staccato, brusque manner, and use of cliches and ready-made figures of speech reinforce the ironies and help create a satiric perspective. While using such techniques as distanced irony, compression and rapid shift of focus, Nazareth is also explicit, relying on statement and rhyme:

> A people that once sculptured
> deities in erotic tangles,
> frowns on celluloid kisses now.
> The technological revolution
> jogs beside the wooden plough.

In the first section of *Lobo* Nazareth looks mostly back on the past of his persona; the contrasts between foolish innocence and experience have a political purpose:

> Not so innocent now,
> he can't assign
> to some no-man's land of the mind
> the Goan countryside that miners have moled
> for iron and manganese ore.
> And the red road, roasted to a turn,
> is to be tarred and feathered with stones.

The second section of *Lobo* concerns the young hero's travels and expatriation. He is a mock-Columbus discovering the 'new world' of Europe, but London is uninterested in his arrival and suddenly 'F. X. Lobo's boy' has become 'You black bastard'. There are references to living in London bedsitters, the crowded suburbs and the way the British retreat into their houses, leaving the puzzled outsider wondering what life there is behind the drawn blinds. Poems describe brief affairs with widows picked up at parties, the local pub, futile late-night political talks with like-minded friends, a trip to the west of England, the break-up of a love affair and other common experiences.

The third section of the book includes poems of travel set in Jamaica, Spain and America before Lobo returns to London where he has an intense brief affair before settling into mediocrity, the romantic revolutionary adventurer tamed, falling into routine and beginning to feel old and nostalgic at thirty-two. Although he remains politically aware and is conscious of such social evils as the destruction of neighbourhoods for property redevelopment, he is helpless. In the concluding poem 'he feels old / and something of a failure'. Life seems 'barren'. 'He knows he's stuck in London.'

Nazareth shares Jussawalla's political consciousness, alienation and awareness that colonialism left scars on much of the Third World. His vision is shaped by a knowledge that people are not free without power to shape their own destinies. The young wolf of the Bombay schoolyard and the seemingly disillusioned mature wolf in London are the same in lacking the sense of reality, power, character and circumstances to do more than posture, have an affair, comment on others, accumulate minor experiences. Lobo is Ezekiel's Unfinished Man, with more political and racial consciousness but without the depths of moral seriousness and the acceptance that salvation is personal and depends on will and character. He is Jussawalla's Missing Person, the uprooted, helpless product of colonialism and bourgeois romantic individualism.

It is perhaps unfair to compare Ramanujan's poetry with the work of other Indian writers in exile as their aims are different. It would appear, however, that each of the poets has memories of their Indian past, especially their childhood. Ramanujan's engagement with the past, the unsentimental acknowledgement of the poet's inner world and his consciousness that time has changed the significance of his memories and that freedom of exile requires some fixing of identity—even if it is only the self aware of being caught in a process of change—provides the more complex, rich, significant material for poetry.

There is, however, another approach, exemplified by Vikram Seth, who only came to prominence when his *The Humble Administrator's Garden* (1985) won the Commonwealth Poetry Prize for Asia and when Random House, New York, brought out *The Golden Gate* (1986), a long novel in verse. Seth's *Mappings* (1982) records his dual feelings of nostalgia for India after studying abroad for many years and his continuing attraction to the 'notes of other birds, / The nightingale, the wren'. Many of the poems in this first volume are of youthful restlessness or concern rebellion and ambivalent feelings towards family, especially his father, with whom he appears to have strong disagreements. 'I had few memories of your love / Or kindness, even speech.' In 'Departure Lounge' he attempts to understand what there was about his father's past which drove them apart:

> Orphaned at two, you ran away
> From Baoji at fifteen.
> The tin shack, the Mussourie store,
> Hunger, the freezing rain,
> Nothing could split the shell of hurt and pride.
> You would have rather died
>
> Than faced that uneasy ease again.
> Unsure of tenderness
> Where you most craved it, did it grow
> Too anguished to express?
> You screened your love: though Mama says you cried
> The day Baoji died.

Many of the poems are very anti-romantic, proceeding from a rational, hedonist philosophy that as this life is all there is you might as well enjoy what you can, whether sex, experience, travel or games of Scrabble. Comic rhymes, used to keep feelings under control and ideas in perspective, contribute to a poetry of surfaces, of conscious superficialities, of youthful playfulness. How rhyme, form and a low or mixed rather than an elevated or aesthetic diction are used to deflect deep feelings into tongue-in-cheek humour can be seen here in the third of 'Six Octets':

> You don't love me at all? O God. O shit.
> You still 'respect me.' Thanks. I value it.
> About as much as one who's asked to use
> A second hat when he's in need of shoes.
> Since, I discover, my own self-respect
> Is quite enough to keep my spine erect
> Why is it true my ample self-affection
> Will not suffice to buoy me in rejection?

Some poems are pastiches or parodies. Such self-conscious, self-mocking, self-deflating art rejects the high cultural seriousness and élitism of Modernist literature. It shares in the post-1960 collapse of distinct cultural registers, with the result that poetry is viewed as similar to a pop song or fashionable clothes; art is a commodity to be enjoyed.

Seth's aesthetic is as distinctive as those of Ezekiel, Chitre, Mehrotra or Mahapatra. Many poems in *The Humble Adminis-*

trator's Garden are metaphorically about the nature of art. Seth's
'The Humble Administrator's Garden', the title poem, offers a
real pleasure garden of Chinese art built from the practical ex-
perience of life in implied contrast to the ideal imagined worlds of
a Keats or Yeats:

> He eyes the Rainbow Bridge. He may have got
> The means by somewhat dubious means, but now
> This is the loveliest of all gardens. What
> Do scruples know of beauty anyhow?

Other poems refer to Seth's loneliness, sense of being conti-
nually on the move and the various fears and anxieties which are
close to the surface, awaiting an uncontrolled occasion to erupt:
'They have left me the quiet gift of fearing. / I am consumed by
fear, chilling and searing'. 'Homeless' begins: 'I envy those /
Who have a house of their own's. Significantly, each of the three
sections of *The Humble Administrator's Garden* is represented
by a tree whose name is symbolic of a different country in which
Seth has lived: Wutong (China), Neem (India), and Live-Oak
(America). The California poems are of interest for their mixture
of amused enjoyment, witty defensiveness, sense of danger,
comic incongruities and feelings of loneliness among easy acquain-
tances, adventures and comforts. In 'Abalone Soup':

> They tug their wetsuits on. Jim strips a plant:
> 'It smells like liquorice.' The oval moon,
> Squeezed by a fog-bank, loses shape. I can't
> —No wetsuit—go with them. 'We'll be back soon.'
> Custodian of their spectacles and keys,
> I sit upon the least moist rock and freeze,
>
> Watching them bob and strain to the far rock,
> Four buoyant blots against a lightening blue.
> Eight thirty. Where are they? At nine o'clock
> I'll call up next of kin. 'How do you do—
> Mrs Gebhart? Your son was lost at sea,
> A martyr to cuisine.' Ah, abalone,
>
> The gourmet's edelweiss, of the four A's
> Of California—asparagus,
> Ab, avocado, artichoke—you raise
> Our palates to the most vertiginous

Conception of sublimity.... But here
Four heads, four snorkels, once again appear.

The poetic upon which Seth's highly original poetry is based can
be found in 'Ceasing Upon the Midnight' and 'Unclaimed'. In the
former, instead of the great nineteenth century romantic ode

He stacks the dishes on the table.
He wants to die, but is unable
    To decide when and how.
    Why not, he wonders, now?

A piece of gristle catches his eye.
The phone rings; he turns to reply.
    A smell of burning comes
    From somewhere. Something hums.

His 'meandering' memories, like those of the poets in the great odes,
range to foreign lands and the exotic; but instead of wishing to die
like a romantic poet in ecstasy from some rich experience while
drinking wine, he is shielded by sleep, common sense and the tradi-
tional rules of poetry from self-destructive introspection:

The alcohol, his molecules,
The clear and intimate air, the rules
    of metre, shield him from
    Himself. To cease upon

The midnight under the live-oak
Seems too derisory a joke.
    The bottle lies on the ground.
    He sleeps. His sleep is sound.

'Unclaimed' proclaims the value of living on the surface of life, of
enjoying what the moment has to offer while avoiding depths of
emotions and entangling complexities:

To make love with a stranger is the best.
There is no riddle and there is no test.

Seth's acceptance of and delight in exile combined with a highly
self-conscious traditional poetic form and prosody result in surpris-
ingly original poetry. Like most good art, it is very much of its time.
Timothy Steele, an American poet whom Seth admires, also uses
form as a defence against self-destructiveness. Such neo-formalism
is one kind of post-modernism, as is the tongue-in-cheek, low-

pressure, pop-art plot and style of Seth's narrative in verse about young love in San Francisco. While *The Golden Gate* is similar to the playful cartoon quality of some recent American popular songs and films, it is also part of a literary tradition which includes Byron's comic satires, and the self-conscious artifice of Ariosto's great narrative poem *Orlando Furioso*.

Seth's celebration of San Francisco, travel, cosmopolitan pleasures, and American comforts has a dual function. It wards off the loneliness, the continuing consciousness of having left home, and it creates an exciting, sophisticated world to replace what has been lost. Seth's poems offer a strong sense of being uprooted, lonely and of needing to enjoy the moment (not just because this is all there is but) because there are no lasting deeper relationships available, and life is an adventure abroad. While his feeling of marginality is furthered by his declared bisexuality, it is also the typical perspective of the alien in a foreign society in which for many years you are the observer of natives and their strange, often humorous customs. Life abroad is exciting, cosmopolitan, a bit absurd and often lonely.

CHAPTER THIRTEEN

And Return

PARTHASARATHY AND JUSSAWALLA

R. Parthasarathy and Adil Jussawalla have expressed their feeling of alienation and disappointment in England as reasons for their return to India and attempt to find a vital relationship to its culture. Both began and remain critics of existing Indian society while seeking its renewal and transformation. The routes they have chosen are, however, different. Parthasarathy claims he is engaged in a dialogue with the Tamil culture of his origins, while Jussawalla desires a political revolution which will result in new forms of consciousness unlike the colonial mentality which he sees as characteristic of the Indian middle-class intellectual. Despite their feelings of marginality within India both writers have significant, energetic and continuing roles in modern Indian culture. Both have written long poems based on their lives and the need for a commitment which will overcome their continuing sense of alienation; both attempt to understand its sources and try to forge new mentalities from their awareness. While Jussawalla traces his marginality to being part of the Indian middle classes, with their colonial and capitalist alienation from the masses, Parthasarathy gives more emphasis to the loss of rootedness through his English-language education and poetry which place a wall between himself and the traditions of Tamil culture.

Parthasarathy's poems began to be published in such journals as *Quest*, *Miscellany* and *The Literary Half-Yearly* between 1956 and 1963. They were often slender romantic lyrics: 'Late Lovers', 'Epitaph', 'Let's be Strangers, Always', and 'Lovers'. Delicacy of perception, lightness of touch, striking images and a romantic view of love might summarize Parthasarathy's early work. In *Quest* Parthasarathy published a poem, 'False Teeth', which implied that as love poetry, the English language and traditional verse forms had proved false he might not write any more poetry:

> For many years now he has had his teeth
>   in the English language—false teeth.
> His earliest poems were rhymed.
> Now rhymes are more fashionable in toothpaste ads.
> . . .
> And he had not found the rubies in lips, the Niagara
>   in her hair.
> His heart that had travelled to this day blew up like a tyre.
>
> It is easier to leave words alone than to like them.
> And so at twenty-five he retired from the field
>   without having written a poem.
>
> > (*Ten Years of Quest*, p. 356)

The significance of romantic love, writing poetry and using the English language were to remain the themes of Parthasarathy's later work along with indications that he might 'leave words alone'.

After lecturing in Ezekiel's department at Mithibhai College, Bombay, Parthasarathy was a British Council Scholar at Leeds University, England, during 1963–4, where he obtained a post-graduate diploma in English Studies before returning to India. The year in England was traumatic, a classical case of cultural shock. He found that his English was not idiomatic; moreover, contemporary England was a dirty place, unlike his previous ideal of it. Many of the British had racial prejudices and retained imperialistic attitudes towards India and Indians. Lonely and dissatisfied he learned what other colonials and students have often learned by going abroad: a love of English literature does not make an Englishman. In a sequence of four poems, titled 'Under Another Sky', published in *Poetry India* (vol. 1, no. 1, 1966), Parthasarathy wrote:

> He had spent his youth whoring
> After the English gods.
>
> There is something to be said for exile:
> You learn, roots are deep. That language
> Is a tree, loses colour
> Under another sky. The bark

Disappears with the first snow
And branches become hoarse.

Apparently after his return from Leeds Parthasarathy decided
to move beyond writing occasional lyrics to a longer work con-
sisting of a sequence of short poems linked by recurring themes,
images and autobiographical details. At first the sequence
covered the period from when he was twenty-nine and went to
England to his return to India, and was written between 1963 and
1967. Later he expanded a sequence of love lyrics which now con-
sists of poems written between 1961 and 1974. A third section,
'Homecoming', consists of poems written since 1971—although
lines can be found in them from poems of the 1960s—which are
mostly about the eight years he spent in Madras as a regional editor
of Oxford Universtity Press.

The poems in the 'Homecoming' section of *Rough Passage* reveal
Parthasarathy's study of and admiration for the poetry of Ramanu-
jan; from Ramanujan he learned how to use the poet's past ex-
perience, especially memories of the complex South Indian network
of family relations, as a way of evoking Tamil culture in English.
Besides poems on family and the ancestral house ('Small-scale
Reflections on a Great House'), Ramanujan showed in 'A River'
a way to make use of Tamil cultural traditions, writing of them
from a contemporary perspective while using his own equivalent
of the understatement, irony and distancing found in classical
Tamil verse.

When Parthasarathy describes some of his poems in 'Home-
coming' as Tamil he has in mind such stylistic traits as the dis-
tanced, rather anonymous voice, noticeable in Ramanujan's
translations of classical Tamil verse. Parthasarathy is also referring
to characteristics of Dravidian language and poetry which he has
taken over into his later English verse; these include the use of
object-verb syntactical order (in contrast to the usual English
subject–verb–object order), intimate colloquial terms, prominent
alliteration, especially initial alliterations, and the foregrounding
of metaphor. Although his verse is poetic in its metaphors, sound
and stanzaic form, it also aims at a prosaic, pedestrian anonymity.
While the revision of his style to squeeze out the 'literary' qualities
seems to Parthasarathy in keeping with characteristics of classical
Tamil verse, a major tendency of modern poetry has been towards
the incorporation of the quotidian and the formerly unpoetic. In

moving from the romantic lyric towards 'unliterary' characteristics
Parthasarathy is similar to other poets, such as Kolatkar, who began
with a highly poetic manner and later consciously aimed at a more
colloquial, flat or prose-like manner.

Two of Parthasarathy's concerns have been what he feels to be
the lack of an Indian English and the lack of a tradition in which to
write. Whereas most writers depend on tone and the various social
and cultural associations of words, Indian English poets may feel
they are working in a foreign language cut off from such roots. This
handicap, Parthasarathy claims, Ramanujan turns into a virtue.
Parthasarathy praises Ramanujan for using 'ordinary and incons-
picuous' words, 'rarely, if ever, reverberant'. Their strength is in
their 'cold, glass-like quality. It is an attempt to turn language
into an artifact'. Parthasarathy's concern with writing within a
tradition is shown from his interest in such an otherwise insignificant
nineteenth-century writer as Madhusudan Dutt, who abandoned
English verse for Bengali; Parthasarathy himself for a time turned
from English to Tamil. Ramanujan offers an example of how to
handle biculturalism; writing from the vantage of exile permits
him to draw from his past, from his memories, from the study of
South Indian literature, to write poetry in English which, to Partha-
sarathy, continues the Tamil literary tradition. A poem such as
Ramanujan's 'A River' builds on and answers previous Tamil
poetry and situates itself within a literary and cultural history.
'Homecoming', the third part of *Rough Passage*, is a similar
attempt to use the past, family memories, Tamil landmarks and
characteristics of Tamil literature as part of Parthasarathy's attempt
to re-root himself within the tradition, or, as he explains, initiate
a dialogue between himself and the Tamil past. In its specific
regionalism Parthasarathy's poetry might be said to express Tamil
rather than Indian nationalism.

Parthasarathy's views show the influence of T. S. Eliot, whose
opinions on culture and literature he has applied to the problems of
an Indian and, specifically, a Tamil. In contrast to romantic praise of
individual originality, genius and spontaneity, Eliot sees the writer
as a product of a culture which he expresses. The poem should be
impersonal; instead of a revelation of feelings it should reflect the
culture of the time. The poet edits and revises the material provided
by emotions and experience into an impersonal work of art. The
best poetry draws upon accepted cultural myths and uses language

which reverberates with cultural associations from the past. Tradition is not a chronology of past events but a living experience of the past for which the writer must work by selecting and emphasizing what is useful in his or her situation. Culture is not the international élite culture of the cities but is found in small, rooted, organic communities which share similar beliefs, manners, habits, symbolism, blood stock.

Parthasarathy has been in his own way working through these problems in relation to his own uprooting from Tamil culture. But as he feels an Indian poet writing in English cannot make use of the cultural associations of words available to a British writer, he claims to treat English as a foreign language, without reverberations. He attempts to create a tradition of Indian English poets troubled by biculturalism who abandoned English for their first language; and he sees Ramanujan as a start of a new relationship between the English-language Tamil poet and Tamil-language poetry, thus establishing both a continuing tradition and a tradition selected by modern personal need. In contrast to the fragmented, westernized, liberal culture of the large cities, he emphasizes the close-knit family relationships of a specific region, similar to the way those other followers of Eliot, the Agrarians, sought their roots in the small towns and history of the American South. Although Parthasarathy's poetry is more openly autobiographical than Eliot's, he edits and revises it to achieve an impersonal distance, through coolness of tone, regularity of form, economy of language, and by the juxtapositions of images which situate his own life in the context of the effects of colonialism, the decay of the grandeur of the Indian past and the ossification of Tamil culture along with its accompanying modern vulgarity. Although the resulting poem is unlike anything of Eliot's, Parthasarathy uses many similar techniques, such as grubby concrete details as images of the modern world and a decayed tradition, and, surprisingly, echoes of and allusions to other English-language poetry. The Delhi poems, which have been published in the American magazine *New Letters*, reflect Parthasarathy's acquaintance with the Eliot of the *Four Quartets*: 'The ochre air irritates / the tongue'; 'The squalid city groans / under the loo'; 'they stick to its face / like turds'; 'The present is troubled / to distraction'; 'scrap of paper blown about me'.

I mention Eliot not to show influence but because the emphasis of Parthasarathy's various comments on *Rough Passage* might be misleading. While it would be useful to know modern and classical Tamil poetry to see how he makes use of it in the 'Homecoming' section of *Rough Passage*, another context is provided by *The Waste Land*, *Four Quartets* and Eliot's criticism and cultural writings. Parthasarathy is after bigger game than the neo-nationalist reassertion of a cultural identity. He is concerned with the problems of the poet in modern, specifically Indian, culture, and with such tools of the writer as language, symbol, allusion and reference to a body of already existing writing. And this is part of a larger, almost universal problem of the twentieth-century writer faced by rapid modernization, the loss of cultural traditions, the influence of mass media on language, the alienation which results from mobility and education, and the relativity and fragmentation of values and standards caused by the expansion of our sense of the world due to increased communication, travel and the internationalization of culture.

Central to Parthasarathy's themes is a concern with personal responsibility for his life and how the poet lives as a human being. Many of his lines sound like Ezekiel, in their precise, economical but generalized examination of the moral condition of the poet's life. The autobiographical, confessional thread in *Rough Passage* is similar to Ezekiel's *Unfinished Man* in making a linked sequence of poems from an analysis and record of the author's life along with resolutions to improve it. The cultural concerns are part of the intellectual, moral awareness; although they take on a different significance, being specifically associated with his Tamil background, Parthasarathy has Ezekiel's dual concern with the coherence of the individual life and with the nature of modern culture. A difference is that Parthasarathy is concerned with problems caused by the use of English in India and by his own sense of being uprooted and alienated from a culture, themes which do not appear to concern Ezekiel. A concern with the past, tradition and nostalgia for childhood tend to be characteristic of writers from Hindu families (Parthasarathy, Ramanujan, Mehrotra). Kamala Das has a similar nostalgia for family relations and her childhood. Writers such as Shiv Kumar, Kolatkar or Sharat Chandra may treat traditions sceptically or even satirically, but they are still conscious of them. *Rough Passage* does, I think, show that despite Parthasarathy's conscious search for a tradition and his attempt to graft himself on a Tamil tradition, a tradition of Indian English poetry has in fact developed from seeds planted by Ezekiel and, as shown by Parthasarathy and Ramanujan, it has some distinctive regional variations.

Arvind K. Mehrotra's 'The Emperor Has No Clothes', in *Chandrabhaga* (3, 1980, 12–28; and 7, Summer 1982, 1–32) raises objections to Parthasarathy's views on Indian poetry and the kind of style and imagery found in his *Rough Passage*. A particular criticism is of the generalized, unreverberant language and imagery of *Rough Passage*. Mehrotra wants a language of particulars, a poetry which embodies experience rather than distances it; by embodying its locale or context within it such poetry avoids self-conscious generalizing about experience. The crisis which Parthasarathy sees facing the Indian English poet does not exist for Mehrotra, who is instead concerned with the wider problem of the estrangement between poetic language and other forms of communication and experience in our age. While the argument is between two different notions of Indian poetry, its articulation by Mehrotra may be explained by the ages of the poets. As Brijraj Singh observes (*Chandrabhaga* 3, Summer 1980, pp. 49–74), Parthasarathy, born in 1934 and coming to maturity with national independence, feels caught between two cultures and his poem is a declaration of independence from British literature and the idealized colonial vision of England. Mehrotra, born in 1947 at independence, does not need to assert cultural nationalism; when he began writing poetry there already was a significant body of poetry by Indians in English.

A problem in discussing *Rough Passage*, beyond the road marked by Parthasarathy's own comments on his poem (in, for example, 'Notes on the Making of a Poem', *Studies in Indian Poetry in English*, ed. O. P. Bhatnagar, Jaipur, 1981), is that the work keeps changing. The second edition added two poems and offered slightly revised versions of a few others. The third edition will contain further poems. In that it will remain a work in progress throughout the poet's life it resembles Pound's *Cantos* and William Carlos William's *Patterson*—among other twentieth-century long poems created by continual editing and accumulating revisions. It is difficult to draw conclusions when the poem is not concluded. Those readers of Parthasarathy's essays who believed that he was giving up using English as the language of poetry and would in future write in Tamil concluded that the 'Homecoming' section was his farewell, his last words in English on the subject. Parthasarathy's subsequent English poems proved such a reading incorrect. A long poem written over fifteen years will in itself have inconsistencies, despite the author's attempt to stabilize it into a rigid manner; that is part of its richness.

Another problem is the poem's internal chronology, as the auto-biographical events do not follow each other in consecutive order. In 'Exile 1' the speaker is twenty-nine years old; by 'Trial 9' he is 'thirty odd years' and in 'Trial 16' he is forty-five; but later in 'Homecoming' he is only 'forty'.

Life abroad in the poem is limited to 'Exile 2', where we are told that by living in England the speaker's illusions were shattered. By 'Exile 3' the speaker has returned to Bombay which he does not like for its commercial interests, traffic and lack of personal warmth. Being unable to take root in Bombay or Goa the speaker in 'Exile 7' moves to Madras where, despite returning to Tamil Nadu, he remains alienated. The sea is 'tried', the language is 'skimmed', 'a shadow', the Tamil mind is now westernized:

> The hourglass of the Tamil mind
> is replaced by the exact chronometer
> of Europe.

The goddesses have been replaced by mannequins in shop win-dows. Parthasarathy blames colonialism for the westernization of India; the new ruling élite is a copy of the former colonizer:

> ... The clubs
> are there, complete with bar and golf-links.

> The impact of the West on India
> is still talked about,
> though the wogs have taken over.

The ironic use of 'wogs', the British insult for foreigners, to des-cribe the ruling Indian élite shows his own alienation, his sense of foreignness from the governing classes. It recognizes that his return to India might be futile; the human condition is universal, and does not change:

> ... What have I come
> here for from a thousand miles?

> The sky is no different.
> Beggars are the same everywhere.

The 'Exile' section of *Rough Passage* is as much about aliena-
tion and the problem of what to do with one's life as about the
results of colonialism. Studying abroad creates a crisis for
someone who had assumed that he would settle in England and
be an English poet. The disillusionment raises a consciousness of
being Indian; but after returning to India feelings of dissatisfac-
tion and exile remain as India seems no different from the West,
and he is exiled within his own country. Although alienated the
speaker implies he is the real India and that the modern India of
commerce, films, wristwatches, clothing shops is the rule of the
Indian 'wogs'. Such an attitude is typical of many who discover
their roots and become nationalists while studying abroad.
Usually it was dissatisfaction with life at home which drove them
abroad to begin with; returning home in search of an ideal they
find their alienation has increased and they are now even more
uprooted. Their dissatisfaction with their native land increases
with their heightened awareness of what is alien, what is ineffi-
cient and of the fact that others do not have the same nationalist
reforming concerns as themselves. In the last poem of 'Exile' the
poet 'has come full circle' during the past year; he has returned
only to find he is still an exile and still faces the problem of
responsibility for his life:

> I must give quality to the other half.
> I've forfeited the embarrassing gift
> innocence in my scramble to be man.

'Exile' is a self-contained section of *Rough Passage*, concerned
with an awareness at thirty that the poet's life has no direction, is
uprooted. The images of reality remain the same under any sky
because they are projections of the self, the way it sees life. Images
of mirrors, skies, water, walls, lamps, trees, smoke, stone, noise,
photographs, sleeps, ashes, dust, snow, children, traffic recur in
'Exile', linking the poems that comprise it. In London the fog is 'a
wall', the suburbs grey, the 'lanes full of smoke and litter': and
there are 'puddles of unwashed / English children'. The Thames
appears 'clogged' and the day is announced by the 'noises' of trains,
milkmen and newsboys. ('Exile 2') The streets of Bombay are noisy,
dusty ('Exile 3'), smoky, 'The sun burns to cigarette ash'. In the
suburbs there is 'noise', 'traffic' ('Exile 5'); in Madras the sky is grey;
there is also, as in London, a bridge; the women smell of 'cigarette

ash' while he shivers in 'dark alleys of the mind'; 'The ashes are all that's left' of his youth ('Exile 8'). Wherever he goes he is alone except for the women he loves.

The 'Trial' section expresses the attempt to overcome feelings of exile through love and the new responsibilities that begin with marriage. It covers approximately the next fifteen years, from the age of thirty to forty-five, picks up some of the previous imagery while giving more emphasis to the fingers, smell, taste, breast, tongue as symbols of the senses achieving oneness with another, the closeness missing in exile which he will seek in 'Homecoming' through a return to the culture and language of Tamil Nadu and the scenes of his childhood. While 'Trial' celebrates love as a means of overcoming exile it contrasts it to an awareness of death; both love and death are contrasted to poetry which is written while alone, and which is also threatened by death. 'Trial 2' shows the use Partha-sarathy made of Ramanujan's example of writing about memories of family:

> Over the family album, the other night,
> I shared your childhood:
> ...
> ... You rolled yourself
>
> into a ball the afternoon Father died.

The poem seems an example of how Parthasarathy aims at a language without reverberations, often through the use of clichés and dead metaphors: 'Over the family album', 'the other night', 'in the distance', 'a pretty kettle of fish', 'slaked your thirst', 'Hand on chin', 'turned the corner'. It is, however, difficult not to remember Andrew Marvell's 'To his Coy Mistress' in 'you rolled yourself / into a ball'.

In contrast to poems with grey, noisy but uneventful cities, those on love are filled with imagery of excitement ('Hours glowed to incandescence', 'live coals / blow on', 'A nipple hardens / on the tongue'). Whereas language lost colour, 'Touch brings the body into focus, / restores colour to inert hands'. In contrast to the union felt in love there are words 'no more than ripples / in the deep well of the throat'. Towards the end of 'Trial', however, tensions are acknowledged, 'The straw has come between us'; he lives his past through the writing of poetry:

> My past is an unperfect stone:

> the flaws show. I polish
> the stone, sharpen the lustre to a point.

He is now forty-five, has a son, and his life has settled into a routine which 'nibbles' at the passions still felt by his 'heart'.

'Homecoming' begins with a contrast between the poet's desire to give up English for Tamil and the corrupted condition of that language; 'Now, hooked on celluloid, you reel / down plush corridors'. The language of classical Tamil is dead, impotent, a symbol of its present culture; all the poet can do is 'Turn inward' to the past: 'perhaps, strike out a line for yourself / from the iron of life's ordinariness'. The sense of the past, as represented by his Brahmin childhood and by family relations, is sharpened by the now uncommon occurrence of a family reunion, representing continuity, union and security. A cousin with whom he climbed trees

> stood there, that day, forty years taller,
> her three daughters floating
> like safe planets near her.

Continuity is asserted when, watching the cremation of his father, he thinks 'I shall follow. And after me / my unborn son'.

Although far different in their nostalgic view of family and childhood the poems in 'Homecoming' often use situations and events found in Ramanujan's poems, such as memories of a girl cousin who has now grown up, a topic found in Ramanujan's ironic 'Looking for a Cousin on a Swing'. A comparison of the distanced irony of Ramanujan's 'Obituary' with Parthasarathy's assumption that he and his son will be cremated like his father with the family assembled at the burning ghat shows a difference in attitudes. Whereas in his poem on Madurai Ramanujan brings out the truth about the river, which seldom floods and when it does brings destruction, Parthasarathy laments 'No one has any use for Vaikai, / river, once, of this sweet city'.

After such pastoral scenes of family life and a once great, now decayed Tamil culture, 'Homecoming' returns to the present with the poet earning a living and writing, presumably, in Madras. He is again alone, exiled with his memories, choices and marriage. The decisions and illusions of the past are over. His task is now to shape a poem of his life: 'I have exchanged the world / for a table and chair. I shouldn't complain'. He is again walled in, like Keats looking through a window at unobtainable pleasure:

> I return home, tired,
> my face pressed against the window
> of expectation.

These poems are strangely devoid of children, his wife, love, others, events and sights except for abstract streets, traffic, his table and unopened letters representing his isolation as a writer living in his thoughts: 'Once in a way I light a cigarette. Follow / the smoke as though it were a private tour'.

The possible implication that the poet made the wrong choices has been answered by 'Exile 12' with its portrait of what he might have been if he had remained a university lecturer of English. 'He has spent his youth whoring / after English gods' in 'Exile 2' is echoed by:

> He went for the wrong gods from the start.
> And marriage made it worse.
>
> ...
>
> Now he teaches. Reviews verse
> written by others. Is invited to conferences ...
> ... he squats on the dungheap
> of old texts and obscure commentaries.

The images of gods, texts and commentaries are picked up in the succeeding poems which express fear of the silence towards which, according to Parthasarathy, poetry tends:

> I fear I have bungled again.
> That last refinement of speech
> terrifies me. The balloon
>
> of poetry has grown red in the face
> with repeated blowing. For scriptures
> I therefore recommend
>
> the humble newspaper: I find
> my prayers occasionally answered there.

The second edition of *Rough Passage* ends with acceptance of life as a 'bowl of milk', not cherries. In a series of plays on commonplace phrases and allusions to well-known literary passages he is the Joycean artist who, god-like, observes reality from a distance while he pares his nails, the Wallace Stevens poet who sees 'the world as it is'. God is far away and his poem is a prayer. It is time he stopped writing of himself ('wrung the handkerchief / of words dry') and became silent. Unlike the passionate lovers of Marvell's 'To his Coy Mistress'

> ... I've rolled my fate
> into a paper ball and tossed it

> out the window. I can now walk
> to the end of the marriage
> on my knees for my unspeaking sons.

While the starting point of *Rough Passage* is Parthasarathy's failure to take root in England and his attempt to overcome his sense of alienation in India through a rediscovery of his roots in Tamil culture and family relations, the dominant concern of the long poem is the consequences of his decision, the life he has made of himself in love, marriage, poetry. The more than fifteen years are the rough passage of manhood, between the end of youth and middle age, the period of being a father and a house-holder according to the traditional Indian view. The conventional idea of what is success is satirized in the teacher of literature in 'Exile 12'. Nor will the poet become a holy man and beggar. Rather than go to Benares, he will continue to 'the end of the marriage' and 'on my knees'. Another choice has been made; to continue as a res-ponsible husband and father, to be contented 'with the small change of uncertainties'.

It is unlikely that this low-keyed, ironic, self-deprecating accep-tance of greyness will be Parthasarathy's last word on the subject of his life. He moved from Madras to New Delhi and more recently he has been teaching in America while editing a classical Tamil text. In the American magazine *New Letters* (48:3 & 4, Spring / Summer 1982, pp. 82–4) he published three 'Delhi' poems which will probably appear in the next edition of *Rough Passage*. 'Delhi 3' concludes:

> Life, at forty-five
> is a breath of fresh air.
> The children are grown up...

> From afar shapes the poems
> till they become familiar as prayer.
> To be oneself, strike no postures,

> on rare occasions stumble upon
> the blessing of simplicity—
> I couldn't ask for more.

Adil Jussawalla's poems are preoccupied with alienation, with not being part of the society in which he lives and with the emotional need to be part of a community. In an article on 'The New Poetry' (*Readings in Commonwealth Literature*, ed. William Walsh, Oxford, 1973, pp. 75–90), Jussawalla says of his poems written abroad that he had 'tried to show the effect of living in lands I can never leave nor love properly to belong to'. Between 1957 and 1970 he studied and later tried to settle in England; his disillusionment is recorded in 'Indifference', an essay he contributed to *Disappointed Guests: Essays by African, Asian and West Indian Students* (ed. Henri Tajfel and John Dawson, Oxford University Press, London, 1965, pp. 128–35). He returned to India only to find himself out of place; meanwhile he had turned sympathetically to the Third World politics of the New Left. While the 'Missing Person' sequence was written during this period, its themes, although set within a larger political context, develop from his earlier *Land's End* poems (1962). 'Missing Person' contains similar feelings of alienation and cultural chaos, but suggests a Fanonite-Marxist rather than Christian explanation for their occurrence. As Jussawalla was educated at an Anglican school, although raised in a Zoroastrian family, the Christian vision of *Land's End* is an example of the continuing effects of colonialism with which 'Missing Person' is concerned.

'Seventeen', the first poem in *Land's End*, is in the tradition of Henry Vaughan, Thomas Traherne, Wordsworth and Dylan Thomas in contrasting the supposedly unified sensibility of a child, when all experiences are felt directly and vitally, with the decay of such feelings through maturation and a developing rationality:

> Time was short,
>   short time
>   when a boy
> lived each moment
>   anew,
>
> ...
>
> Now detached, the
>   water is spilled
>   killed
>   on rocks,
>   one by one
>   the lights are
>   snuffed.

'Seventeen' exhibits characteristics later found in 'Missing Person'. There are the short, abrupt lines, jagged rhymes (short / short time; spilled / killed), angular rhythms and a distanced reflectiveness even when describing the time when each moment was 'like a / birth of flames'.

'November Day', the second poem in *Land's End*, uses the seasonal fading and falling of leaves as symbolism for a similar mood of futility:

> As outside my window
> Leaves fall faded from tree
> So let me let fall my thoughts
> Gone yellow and dry.

'31st December '58', the third poem in the book, also records sterility.

Jussawalla imagines the past was once filled with vitality, belief, wonder, but such poems as 'The Moon and Cloud at Easter', 'The Suburb' and 'The Dolls' view modern life as sterile. The title poem, 'Land's End', contrasts the geographical place in England with its tourists to the older Christian belief in God's creation of the world and to the early Church which Peter founded. Published in the 1960s these poems of Jussawalla's are late examples of a mode established by T. S. Eliot, and used by such writers as Evelyn Waugh and Graham Greene, in which the banalities of modern life are juxtaposed with Christian symbols to show the vitality and superiority of a former sacred to a present secular culture. But behind the disillusionment is Jussawalla's own sense of exile, of alienation from a Europe, especially England, which has disappointed him and in which he feels rejected.

The symbolism of the wasteland reflects a personal sense of being a castaway, of having gone astray in England and Jussawalla's own estrangement there. It is the unhappiness which results from culture shock, from lack of friends, from youthful loneliness and aimlessness which has been sharpened by being in a strange country which one had earlier thought would be home, the promised land of those who sought the Eden of British literature. The Eliotics express an Anglo-Catholic religious phase Jussawalla was going through at the time, which was part of his crisis.

In 'A Letter for Bombay', written on turning twenty-one, Jussawalla tries a technique which he was later to develop in 'Missing Person', of juxtaposing autobiography with representative scenes from the life of an Indian middle-class intellectual. Starting with recording of the war years, the poem recalls fears, alienation and various feelings of treason:

> (Who's winning to-day? Are we on the side of the
>   Germans?)
> My enemy tongue to mark time silently while the rest spoke
>   treason.

It continues by referring, strangely, to such a past as 'those careless, gardened days', after which the poet began his wanderings abroad, and concludes with an appeal to Devi, used here as muse and goddess of Bombay, to bring coherence so he may return from his wandering:

> ... instruct me in my art,
> Lacking a legendary muse, give my chaos form.
> Should you refuse—the rack of your hovels raising your
>   voice
> Still further—demand nothing: touch me only as far
> As the parted psyche can stand: divided city, combine,
> And I shall return and pass beyond your storm.

Missing Person (1976) is concerned with the need to find coherence in an India from which Jussawalla feels alienated. But paradise is no longer a lost tradition or childhood; the poems are concerned with present problems and their solutions. The book is divided into three groups of poems: the 'Missing Person' sequence (mostly written in 1975), 'This Room and That' (poems written between 1962 and 1972) and 'Travelling Separately' (a group of songs written between 1965 and 1975). The increasing political content of his work can be seen in 'Karate', a poem about the love-hate relationship many blacks supposedly have towards whites and in 'Song of a Hired Man', 'Freedom Song' and 'Immigrant Song'. In these poems of the mid sixties the angularity of the earlier verse has become elliptical as Jussawalla increasingly compresses syntax to heighten juxtaposition. 'Sea Breeze, Bombay' mentions such varied problems of modern India as Partition and refugees from Tibet, to complain that the cooling sea breeze 'investigates nothing' and 'settles no one adrift of the mainland's histories'. Instead of accepting Indian life as it is, he asks, 'Restore us to fire'.

'Approaching Santa Cruz Airport, Bombay' (written in

1966–7 on a trip home) records not only his ambivalent feelings
on returning to India but also sets them within a general political
and social context, in which the slums he sees below are contras-
ted to the attitudes of the well-off passengers in the airplane:

> Economists enclosed in History's
> Chinese boxes, citing Chairman Mao,
> Know how a people nourished on decay
> Disintegrate or crash in civil war.
> Contrarily, the Indian diplomat,
> Flying with me, is confident the poor
> Will stay just as they are.

In 'Nine Poems on Arrival' a political and social consciousness
similarly arises directly from the concrete circumstances of his
life.

Jussawalla's increased radical social awareness, while resulting
from his personal concern as an alienated Indian intellectual, is, I
think, shaped by the familiarity he gained in London with the
black West Indian analysis of their middle class and the situation
of the intellectual in the Third World. While the *Land's End*
lyrics, written in England, express his sense of isolation, the 'Missing
Person' sequence explores his relation to India. The persona of a
typical middle-class Indian intellectual is created and then viewed
as a victim of colonialism, being seen ironically as representative
of the bourgeois romantic fated to be inconsequential and dissatis-
fied by circumstances, upbringing and an inability to understand the
contradiction between longings and what might be solutions. Not
only has Jussawalla's poetry become more politicized, it also has
become increasingly, on the surface at least, depersonalized. Masks,
impersonations, the creation of characters and the use of juxtaposed
ironies have become a means to guard the self. The castaway, land's
end, wasteland and sterile emotions felt in Europe are now located
within a political analysis.

The two sections of 'Missing Person' are an attempt to see
beyond the alienation of *Land's End*. Continuing to reject his
upper-middle-class Indian Parsi upbringing but no longer attempt-
ing to insert himself into an already dated European Catholic revi-
valism, Jussawalla now seeks unity of being by identifying with a
revolutionary process in which the peoples of the Third World will
create a new society. Until this happens, in the future, the intellec-

tual can only write with an historical awareness of his own situation as a representative of a decaying class soon to be replaced by forces of which he cannot be part. The resulting work will express his heightened consciousness of the causes of discontent and the difficulties in personally resolving them. Jussawalla's mode in 'Missing Person' is a version of romantic irony, the distancing of the self to see it from the outside. He uses techniques that create other perspectives to show contradictions, self-deceptions and causes of failure. To the already difficult, unstable mixture of an irony-laden zone of bourgeois consciousness and the non-narrative organization of modernist poetics, he uses post-modernist extreme fragmentation along with techniques of the cinema and a diction often borrowed from popular, mass culture.

The first part of the 'Missing Person' sequence is entitled 'Scenes from the Life' and consists of fourteen selections from a representative autobiography seen as cinema flashbacks, interspersed with various material which ironically places or comments upon the life:

> 'Believe, that's me on the screen—
> through the stuttering dust, through the burst-open door.'
> *The running dog runs but thy've put out its eyes.*
> 'Once I was whole, I was all.
> Believe, why don't you believe?'

After a section recalling the alienating effect of schooling and expatriation, 'Lost, running from acid to Marx', the Missing Person returns home still psychologically an exile. Although now recognizing that his privileges are based on the continuing injustices of capitalism and colonialism he is unable to rise above his situation as a bourgeois rebel:

> In the fist of a rioting people
> his rotting head.
> A mirror fires at him point blank
> and yells, 'Drop dead,
> colonial ape,
> back under an idealist spell.
> Yes, you've made it to some kind of hell,
> backslider, get liquidated'.

> 'Wait! you know whose side
> I'm on', he shouts,
> 'but the people, their teeth bright as axes

came after my stereo and cattle,
came after my bride'.

He is murdered, literally torn apart, by conflict, especially in section
I.14, by his 'tribe', family, 'bookdust' and 'Eng. Lt.'. In contrast to
his inability to break from his past, his fate predicts the future:

And here's an announcement:
Hope
which periodically triggers
some men to act
and looses the bonds of the earth,
has set a bright tide revolving inside me, a door.
Give up your seats and join the cast of thousands,
revolve about his pieces too
(brown slaves, black vamps, white faggots,
deceivers, women who rend and claw)

Some poems in the first section of 'Missing Person' are difficult to
understand because of the extreme fragmentation. The various bits
are pieces of an unintegrated character shaped by varied contra-
dictory cultural influences. The jerkiness, caused by juxtapositions,
ellipses, and the line movements of the poem, is meant to express
this. The shifts in voice and register suggest the uneasiness of a
middle-class, English-speaking Indian who has no authentic
character, voice and consistent tone or angle of perception.

The first part of 'Missing Person' has the feeling of a quick mov-
ing, roughly-cut movie with rapid shifts of focus, an abruptness
which is supported by a deliberately flat diction drawn from clichés,
advertising and mass culture. There is an audience watching a film of
the missing person, there is a school-room setting in which the
lasting effects of learning the English language are represented by
the letter A, which is contrasted to the child's giggly laughter at
learning about hieroglyphics and the languages of dead culture;
there is a shift (Part I, section 6) in which the missing person
appears to be a Third World black surrounded by and alienated
from the sexual deviants of a foreign metropolis, there are lines in
italics where it is difficult to say who is speaking. The unassimila-
ted melange of influences and pressures on the missing person
creates a chaos expressive of the personality, vision and culture of
a bourgeois colonial intellectual. The poem reveals the negative,
fragmented, passive quality of the missing person as a result of

colonialism, western mass culture, the English language, the attractions of a foreign metropolis, the East–West conflict, the bourgeois family and the potentially revolutionary situation in his homeland, of which he is unable to be part. He belongs to no place, he consists of bits and pieces. As in many of Jussawalla's poems internal and end rhymes occur closely together, creating a somewhat comic, ironic effect, an anti-poetry in which the overload of rhyme undermines dignity and contributes to the criticism of the missing person.

Although fragmentation is characteristic of the poem, which rapidly juxtaposes various perspectives, unidentified voices and kinds of material, there are places where Jussawalla steps in as a speaker or imposes coherence on the seeming chaos. The chaos is somewhat of an illusion; the varied voices, attitudes, advice and criticisms made throughout the poem either contribute to a critique of the missing person or are themselves misleading voices which advise him and themselves reflect the post-colonial situation. For example in Part II, section 5, the claim that Indians are the new Renaissance people is itself meant as ironic, and the critic is criticized. A problem is distinguishing between the voices and how to regard them, as there is often no guide as to who is speaking or how the voices may be wrong. But occasionally a controlling voice intervenes (as in Part I, sections 8 to 10) to contribute a perspective.

'Points of View', the second section, consists of seven poems which offer a critical portrait of the missing person as a representative of a class which, in Fanon's words, will accomplish nothing and is condemned to failure. There are various speakers in Part II, representing the attitudes of such different persons as a wife, a professor and an artist. They are the supposed audience of the film of the person's life shown in the first part of the sequence, and part of his context. As is seen by the missing person being ripped apart in I.14, he is surrounded by violence, the violence of his society and the violence of the various influences on him. He is weak, unable to participate in the violence because he does not care, because he is uninvolved, because he does not love. He cannot come to terms with this situation and what Jussawalla sees as the revolutionary forces of society. Rather than becoming a hero, or anti-hero, the missing person is negative, unable to solve the problems of his identity; being unable to act, feel or care is ultimately his personal damnation. The sequence concludes with the missing person

'Empty even of original sin', as representative of his class falling off
the pages of history,

> tumbling through cavities of space,
> your mind's gone,
> onwards, rocketing
> blind
> with unloving error.

Whereas Parthasarathy has sought to recover a lost Tamil–Hindu
past, Jussawalla hopes for involvement with the progressive forces
of historical development. Both poets, however, desire kinds of
organic communities, identification with some collectiveness, as a
means of overcoming personal alienation. While the themes and
concerns are indicative of problems faced by the Indian English
poet, they also represent two usual responses to the chaos and
unsatisfactoriness of the modern world—nostalgia for the supposed
authenticity of the past and faith in finding wholeness by involve-
ment with a revolutionary movement working towards a better
future.

Alienation, the lack of harmony with one's community, the
feeling of what others might consider inappropriate responses,
the sense of not belonging, is also noticeable in Indian poets who
have not lived abroad, such as Manohar Shetty and Keki Daruwalla,
and might be said to be part of the human condition. Parthasarathy
and Jussawalla are writing of the human condition, but treating it
within a specific historical context brought about by colonialism,
the role of the English language in India, the alienation of the edu-
cated urban Indian from the rural Hindu population, and their own
sense of unease both in England and in independent India. Such a
concern with alienation is a major theme of Indian English poetry.

As poetry in our time is not part of mass or popular culture, to
be a poet (in contrast to a song-writer) is to be alienated, regard-
less of what language is used or where one lives. While aspects of
alienation are part of the thematic repertoire of most poets, and a
central concern of some, to be a serious writer or intellectual
means that it is impossible to return to one's roots. This situation
is bound to be felt more intensely by an Indian English poet. Perhaps
all the poet can do is use the tension between writing and an ideal
to produce a new culture.

I earlier compared the poetry of Mehrotra, Chitre, Kolatkar and

Mahapatra for characteristics usually thought of as modern and post-modern writing. It is useful to compare Parthasarathy and Jussawalla in such terms. It should be understood, however, that my comments are descriptive, not evaluative. Parthasarathy's *Rough Passage*, as might be expected from someone influenced by T.S. Eliot, is in the tradition of modernist poetics. It has an alienated, aloof author who focuses on his memories. Reference to the material, historical world is slight: the emphasis is rather on the psychology of the self. Thematically the poem is hostile to the contemporary world of technology and modernization and solace is found in writing; after various disillusionments art becomes a way of life. *Rough Passage* is open-ended and given coherence through symbols and patterns of imagery and other devices, including suggestions of a story, which give it a formal structure.

'Missing Person' appears authorless. There are many voices but, as in most post-modern writing, none is identifiable as specifically the author's or his persona. The form is highly fragmented and without a structural centre. In places it reads as bits and pieces. Jussawalla's collage, montage and cinematographic techniques can be said to illustrate the post-modern tendency to imitate technology and mass culture. History is not a tradition to be regained, as it is for modernists, but an undesirable colonial past which has led to cultural chaos and present hopelessness. But unlike the postmodernists who refer to a continuing nothingness or those who focus on the self-reflective nature of the artistic creation, Jussawalla is closer to the Latin American writers who see the possibility of hope in raised political consciousness and revolution. The disorder and chaos of the poem is given sense by allusion to Fanon's views on the Third World bourgeois intellectual and the need to change one's situation through revolutionary actions and identification with an historical process. This might be described as another, later version of the modernist use of myth, in such works as *The Waste Land* and *Ulysses*, to provide a frame which gives coherence to the fragmentariness of the modern era. Despite their modernist or post-modernist styles, neither Parthasarathy nor Jussawalla is willing to allow the poem to be totally open and fragmented. Both authors provide comments or other materials, such as significant quotations, to impose a perspective; both poets retain more control of the reader's response than do Mahapatra, Mehrotra, Kolatkar or even Ramanujan. In this sense they are both inheritors of Ezekiel's early poetics with its situating of the personal within a larger cultural context, its emphasis on moral choice and its anxiety to communicate to the reader.

PART
2

CHAPTER FOURTEEN

The Diaspora

AGHA SHAHID ALI'S TRICULTURAL NOSTALGIA

In recent decades the older boundaries between the nation and the outside world have become fluid, even arbitrary, as cultural influences and people rapidly cross boundaries and languages. For many writers the choice between living in India and living as an exile now seems a product of a time before low-cost international travel, the internationalization of the economy and increased opportunities to study, live and work abroad. In such circumstances, when writers may be part of a large and increasing diaspora, the question of who is or is not an Indian poet is different from in the past when charges of being non-Indian were essentially attacks on writers who did not conform to some nationalist notion of what Indian culture and tradition should be. Whereas the nationalist finds in aspects of an idealized past useful, if arbitrary, symbols of identity, the writer of the diaspora is always faced by the need to give coherence to his or her life. If writing of the diaspora is marked by feelings of exile and loss, the better writer will find ways to transcend uprootedness and turn lamentation into a more encompassing vision.

There are now several generations of poets who travel regularly to and from India, poets who were born of Indian parents abroad or had a significant part of their childhood and education abroad, or who seem always on the move. Many teach in foreign universities or are married to non-Indians and live outside India. R. Parthasarathy and Saleem Peeradina now teach and live in the United States. Many Indian poets are also part of the new multiculturalism of the United States, Canada, Australia and England. An international literary market has also developed with the result that some Indian poets are better known abroad than in India. Agha Shahid Ali might be considered part of a diaspora, Indians who spent part of their youth abroad, returned to India, but settled elsewhere, and frequently visit India. Such lives have produced a different kind of poetry which, rather than being marginal to the contemporary literary scene abroad, is often central to it.

Agha Shahid Ali is one of the few Indian Muslim English-language poets (although the number is increasing), one of the few English-language poets from Kashmir (H. K. Kaul is another) and, now that he has been a long-time resident of the United States, one of the new American multicultural poets. Trilingual, tricultural, he is a product of many events—Indian Independence and the subcontinent's Partition and the subsequent migration of peoples—and influences—education in literary modernism, participation in contemporary literary styles—which make him 'post-colonial'. But his poems often make us question the applicability of generalizations about the post-colonial and post-modern. Rather than a poetry of fragments and fragmented experiences in which cultures incongruously conflict, Ali's poetry has become increasingly organized into meaningful structures, with inner narratives, suggestive of continuity.

While Ali is conscious of exile, of the way, especially in India, language and culture cause separations, differences, there is also awareness that multiculturalism, change, exile, difference, loss and nostalgia are common to the human condition as seen in the lives of his own family, his friends and the artists he admires. Loss is part of the passing of time, history, the earth's geography. Loss, whether of the protection of family, of friends, homelands or alternative futures, is normal, part of grown-up experience, rather than particularly the tragedy of exile or the result of cultural conflict. This sounds as much Islamic fatalism as post-modernism. Ali received part of his schooling in the United States, which might warn us against superficial generalizations.

Born in Delhi into a well-educated English-, Urdu- and Kashmiri-speaking family, Ali lived in Kashmir before attending the Burris School in Muncie, Indiana. The Burris School is affiliated to Ball State University—where Ali's father was earning the first Doctorate ever granted by Ball State as well as the first Doctorate in Education by a Kashmiri. Ali was well integrated in the school, was encouraged to write and is still remembered with affection by former classmates and teachers. Although Ali is part of the new wave of post-colonial immigrants to first world countries, his writing is more characterized by nostalgia for his various homes than by cultural conflict. Considering his family and personal history, a term such as 'new internationalism'—with its awareness of the spread of modernity, new technologies, international education and the international mobility of trained workers and professional elites—might be more useful than 'post-colonialism' with its emphasis on a fractured, resistant, national or cultural identity.

While Ali's poetry reveals exile blues, fantasies about roads not taken, longings for the securities of family and old friends, its idiom is often American and without the exile's defensive need for cultural assertion, revenge for humiliations or self-congratulation for having made it in a strange land. Rather, his poetry moves imaginatively across borders associating and examining experiences in a variety of lands and situations to establish relationships or to recall what has been lost. Loss or nostalgia can crop up in his poetry for parts of his American as well as Indian past. He has always been interested in what others have lost—whether it be the northern Indian culture of his mother or the American Indian past of Arizona where he for a time lived. His lyrical nostalgia provides continuity and a springboard for fantasy. If the poetry appears to accept the world as it is, such lyric sensitivity can be misread; the Urdu ghazal is by its nature elliptical, lyrical. While writing in modern English verse forms Ali is also influenced by the conventions of Persian and Urdu poetry, especially the ghazal with its concise use of repetitive images and phrases, to develop suggestions of symbolic narrative, its elliptical metaphors, imaginative leaps and reliance on the reader to bring together a diversity of unrelated couplets into a supposed metaphoric narrative. By convention there is greater significance in what its imagery implies than in what is actually said.

Although Ali writes in the manner of American poets, with their emphasis on the concrete, the specific, the here and now, their gestures towards transcendence (or the denial of transcendence) and the colloquial parodying of cultured sensibility, he also inherits a tradition of nuanced desire, of fatalism and separation, of imagining, of nostalgia for what cannot be, the poet's union with the divine. All experience, whether of family, friends, place or culture, is tinged with loss, nostalgia. Nostalgia, not for an ideal world, a place of origins or roots, but for something missed, a past or future, relationships that will not develop, lives unlived, histories the poet cannot share except by an extension of the self through desire and imagining.

Ali studied for a BA in the Humanities (1968) at the University of Kashmir; he then went to Delhi University for a Master's (1970) in English literature and taught there until 1975. He returned to the United States where he earned a Master's degree in English and wrote a doctoral thesis, which was later published as *T. S. Eliot as Editor* (1986). Having decided that his interest was primarily in poetry he read for a Master's in Fine Arts in Creative Writing at the University of Arizona. Arizona often appears in his poems where American and Islamic deserts are linked through memory. American Indians and even the changing geography of the American Southwest are part of a history which he may wish to know but can share only in the sense of the universal loss of the past.

Bone-Sculpture (1972), written and published in India, is the work of a promising young poet who has not yet assimilated influences or found a style. The echoes of T. S. Eliot, W. H. Auden and others are obvious. While the loneliness of youth and the uprooting from family and home brought about by travel and education contribute to expressions of cultural dislocation, many of Ali's personal obsessions are already present. These include memory, death, history, family, ancestors, nostalgia for a past he never knew, dreams, Hindu ceremonies, friendships and self-consciousness about being a poet. Alongside clichés of exile and biculturalism are stronger images. Bones are symbolic of a now dead world that will not reply to his interest. Ritual and ceremony seem wasted. Even as a participant 'in the Mohurrum / Procession' when Shiite Muslims flagellate themselves in memory of 'slaughtered martyrs' he feels alone. But his solitude is also that of Kashmir, 'this mosaic-world of silent graveyards'. In a poem called 'Dear Editor' (to an American) he claims 'I am a dealer in words / that mix cultures / and leave me rootless'. His dreams turn into nightmares 'and / I wake up in my dark room / alone with sweat'. There is also a wry sardonic humour. 'Cremation', which he later republished, is an epigrammatic four-line poem addressed to someone whose bones did not burn in the ritual funeral and who therefore is 'stubborn in death'. There are several other poems in this first book about funeral pyres and death. While the sentiments are a mixture of Islamic poetry and youthful confusion, these poems anticipate the surreal, somewhat grotesque lyricism found in the later verse. 'Share this death of another / time with me. Bury the bones of dreams in a river ... Ask the dream-skeleton / Is death worth dying?'

In Memory of Begum Akhtar (1979), while still nostalgic for Kashmir, focuses on Delhi, especially the old Muslim Delhi of the Moghuls. Ali was already starting to learn how to unify a volume of poems by place, symbol, images, themes and autobiography. There is, as in much Indian Islamic literature, an elegiac feeling of a lost rich past, of time as destroyer. In 'Painting a Kashmir Landscape' Ali writes, 'My colours could hold nothing ... the sunset ran through my fingers'; reality is often an inaccessible past which he cannot grasp. The great singers of the past become symbolic as bridges to a history he cannot experience and symbolic of Ali's poems in their attempt to find links and continuities. 'K. L. Saigal' is celebrated as such a link: 'Nostalgic for my father's youth,/ I make you return / his wasted generation ... You felt it all ... the ruins of decades.' In the title poem, 'In Memory of Begum Akhtar' (later reprinted), Ali writes an elegy for the great singer which has the oblique lyrical qualities of the ghazal. The way the feelings are expressed parabolically through images, the way statements are left standing on their own, the general feeling of delicacy, and the way the poem really is a song made up of lyric phrases show how instinctively Ali writes English-language poetry with the music and pattern of the ghazal in his ear.

We are so used to the clichés of modernism and post-modernism in which fracture is valued as critique that it is natural to misread the sophistication of the rich cultural tradition in which Ali participates and celebrates: 'You've finally polished catastrophe / the note you seasoned // with decades of Ghalib, / Mir, Faiz: // I innovate on a note-less raga.' Since Partition, however, Urdu culture has been in decline in India. Perhaps the only strong survival of the older poetic tradition is in the ghazals as sung in movies. 'Thumri for Rasoolan Bai' commemorates her voice, which is contrasted to her house, burned down during riots in 1969 in Ahmedabad: 'I ran from there./ The wind's blood-edge where / her songs had curled me in flames—// I could only preserve/ her breaking voice.' Ali sees himself in exile as an heir to the tradition of Rasoolan Bai and Begum Akhtar. Rasoolan was a Muslim but her style of singing was influenced by the Hindu Benares tradition. One loss, one nostalgia, is that of the pre-partition north of India with its rich Muslim culture that had taken Indian roots and developed as Indian culture with shared sources.

Many of Ali's poems are autobiographical and concern his exploration of origins, his condition of exile or his evolution and life as a poet. 'Introducing' traces his development as a poet from his mid-teens through his twenties. It begins with the interesting observation that English romantic poetry was not out of place in Kashmir with its changing seasons and natural beauty. Although the trees were different, Urdu poetry was often similar. At 18 an English professor (who read through his poems and wrote a detailed criticism) taught him about modern poetry, T. S. Eliot and 'discipline'. An increasing awareness of the contemporary world and its wars led to the use of a more supple language and an obsession with death which took the form of poems about bones and death. His poems became less simple as the pun on slant suggests 'Now I slant my way through rhymes,/ stumbling through my twenties.' Each of the four stanzas of eight lines approximates its theme in technique beginning with the 'easy' rhymes of 'easy / Shelley' and 'here / corner' to such slanting rhymes as 'day / death/ password'.

'Not Autobiographical I' and 'II' recount Ali's estrangement from Islam. His parents were modern and secular, read Freud and Marx, but his grandparents were observant. While we should not assume that all the family details are literally true rather than poetic truths, Ali's point is that he was raised in a family in which Islam and European thought existed alongside each other, although with each generation there was a rapid increase in westernization. One grandfather, an orthodox Muslim, prayed five times a day. A grandmother used the tale of Job to teach him that all things belong to the Lord. Ali wryly claims to have lost his faith when a servant's shoes were stolen at the mosque. Instead he became a devotee of poetry: 'My voice cracked on Ghalib / and my tongue forgot the texture of prayer.'

Ali looks backward to a supposedly unified culture and nation he has lost and which he tries to recapture in his imagination, friendships and verse. (Such nostalgia for a lost unified culture has been a feature of Indian Islamic writing since the mid-nineteenth century, when the British destroyed the social fabric of Delhi after the Mutiny.) The two versions of 'Learning Urdu' concern the divorce that Partition brought about between the past and the present. The revised version, 'After Partition', comments 'History broke the back // of poetry.' In Delhi the grandfather of a Hindu friend warns 'Those Muslim butchers ... they stab you in the back.' In another poem, 'The Jama Masjid Butcher', Ali buys from a butcher 'Urdu, bloody at his lips' who does not smile but 'We establish the bond of phrases,/ dressed in the couplets of Ghalib'. Bloody, hacking at ribs, a prayer book hung on a hook, using the language of Ghalib, there is 'a century's careful image' in the Butcher's tongue. Ali later revised this poem as the experience represented many of the conflicts within himself and his view of his past. The final poem in this volume, written in the United States, is 'The Editor Revisited' in which Ali's 'faint British accent' is contrasted to the violence on the streets. Marxists tell him he must learn to write in Hindi, Urdu, or Bengali if he is to be an Indian poet. A product of three cultures (Western,

Hindu and Muslim) and a 'foreign' language, he realizes that he is only paying lip service to Revolution. Instead he continues to study English literature and ironically observes that 'Shakespeare feeds my alienation'. Although Ali's politics are of the Left, he, like many writers, is aware of the absurd incongruities between actuality and political simplifications.

In 1987 he published two volumes of poetry which marked his emergence as someone with real achievements. They are rather different books, almost contrasting in manner, and, surprisingly, were mostly written over the same period of time. Both are related to Ali's continued residence in the United States and acceptance of his new home. The poems show an increase in verse technique, in polish, in fantasy and the ability to work within a larger range of reference. His life has become his mythology, his subject. *The Half-Inch Himalayas* partly looks back to the past and in structure follows his change of homes from India to the United States. It even republishes two of his earlier poems. *A Walk through the Yellow Pages*, as its title shows, is written directly in a modern, American, idiom.

The Half-Inch Himalayas consists of a prologue followed by four distinct sections which provide a loose imaginative narrative while being linked to each together through images, echoes and other patterns. To appreciate Ali's accomplishment it will be necessary to discuss the poems in more than usual detail. 'Postcard from Kashmir', the prologue, introduces the themes of the volume, exile, memory, loss of home and acceptance that you cannot go home again as you and it have both changed. All you can have is a shrunken image of a lost past: 'Kashmir shrinks into my mailbox,/ my home a neat four by six inches.// ... Now I hold/ the half-inch Himalayas in my hand.// This is home. And this the closest/ I'll ever be to home.' Decision, purpose, control and neatness are reinforced by the careful balance of syllables. The eight or nine syllables in each line of the first couplet and the way the first four lines are visually of equal length establishes a pattern which is varied as disturbed emotions are brought forward: '. . . My love / so overexposed.// And my memory will be a little / out of focus, in it.' The new technical assurance in the handling of line length and the way syntax and phrasing conform to line breaks are also seen in how well the emotions and meaning finds metaphoric expression in the picture postcard and the extension of the picture image in 'love ... overexposed' and 'memory . . out of focus ... negative ... still underdeveloped'.

Section I consists largely of fantasies or imaginings of his family history. In the first of the eight poems, 'A Lost Memory of Delhi', Ali

writes of the time immediately before and at his conception. Each of
the three-line stanzas develops the narrative around an image or place:
'I am not born / it is 1948 and the bus turns / onto a road without
name.' He desires to be part of his parents' earlier life; 'I want to tell
them I am their son / older much older than they are / I knock keep
knocking.' The poems imagine a past he never knew and which is
often fantastic. 'A Dream of Glass Bangles' imagines that his mother
would have worn such bangles. This links, in his fantasy, his parents
sleeping warmly in a quilt 'studded / with pieces of mirrors' to her
'bangles / like waves of frozen rivers' to a later winter when the family
house is covered with icicles which are used for torches.

The first section of *The Half-Inch Himalayas* is carefully planned.
The eight poems move from the Himalayas of ancestral and racial origins
and his father's Kashmir down to the plains of India of his mother's
side of the family, the plains of the great Urdu culture that preceded
Partition. 'The Season of the Plains' speaks of his mother's childhood
in Lucknow, the music and the seasons, especially the monsoons
(which do not occur in Kashmir). Memories within memories: within
the frame of the poet's fantasies and memories occur the memories his
mother might have had. History repeats itself even in her remembering
of the same records and music her son will later celebrate. Although
Lucknow was a centre of Islamic culture his mother remembers and
appreciates music about Krishna ('that invisible / blue god'). The
India of his imagination is the Muslim-Hindu India of northern India
before the Partition. There are also poems on his grandmother's life
and continuing religious belief, as represented by the 'Prayer Rug', and
the great crafts of the Indian past, as represented by 'The Dacca Gauzes',
destroyed by British colonialism and never again practised with quite
the same skill:

> In history we learned: the hands
> of weavers were amputated,
> the looms of Bengal silenced,
>
> and the cotton shipped raw
> by the British to England.

The eight poems in the second part are concerned primarily with
life, culture and history in Delhi and the plains. A bridge between
the last poem in the previous section and the first of the second is the
monsoon season and rain. 'A Monsoon Note on Old Age' also uses
the device of 'A Lost Memory of Delhi' of the poet imagining himself

in another time, here the future: 'This is fifty years later.' The overexposed photograph metaphor is also picked up from the Postcard prologue poem, 'I overexpose / your photograph.' This is followed by still another revision of 'A Butcher', the best of the three in print. Here 'Urdu,/ bloody at his fingertips,/ is still fine on his lips ... I smile and quote // a Ghalib line; he completes / the couplet, smiles,// quotes a Mir line. I complete / the couplet.' Ali's poem being in couplets continues the tradition the two Urdu-speaking Muslims share despite their differences.

A film about *King Lear* causes the poet to think about the distance between the former splendour of Delhi and its rulers during Moghul times and the poverty of the present: 'Beggars now live here in tombs / of unknown nobles and forgotten saints.' He recalls Zafar, a poet and emperor, whose sons were killed by the British and who was exiled to Burma. While this poem draws on and makes explicit the subtext of Islamic nationalist protest within the tradition of post-Mutiny Urdu literature with its nostalgia for the glories of Moghul Delhi, it also looks ahead to the concluding poem of this section, 'Homage to Faiz Ahmed Faiz' in which the modern Urdu revolutionary poet is seen as the heir of Ghalib. Faiz in Beirut 'two years before / the Sabra-Shatila massacres' is like Ghalib giving voice to the 30,000 men hanged by the British in Delhi during the summer of 1857 after the Mutiny.

Section III also consists of eight poems and begins by alluding in 'A Wrong Turn' to the massacre mentioned in the 'Homage to Faiz Ahmed Faiz' in the last poem of Section II: 'In my dream I'm always / in a massacred town.' But this dreamland is a nightmare of alienation, of bloody unexplained foreign revolutions and strange, dead gods rather than the dream of a renewed Urdu tradition and the hope of a revolution for social justice:

> I'm alone, walking among atrocities,
> guillotines blood-scorched,
> gods stabbed at their altars,
> dry wells piled up with bones,
> a curfew of ghosts.

The following poems are set in America. His life is uprooted; there are many references to airplanes, nights in bars and changing apartments. In the last part of 'A Wrong Turn' thoughts about the Indian Partition curiously appear to take the form of a deserted town where the speaker, alone, awaits another train—except that here he is stranded at the 'town's ghost station', the tracks are 'rusted' and the train is 'lost'. The scene is of exile someplace off the map among foreign bodies with no way out.

In the world of living death that follows, the idiom becomes increasingly American, the setting contemporary, but there is a thinning of poetic texture corresponding to the thinning of experience in a land of exile. Ali's sense of humour, however, is allowed to surface more, although the metaphor of life in exile as death now replaces the symbolic landscape of bones, tombs and monuments of the earlier poems. The landscape now is of an American life, being on the move, from apartment to apartment, airport to airport. There are no longer ancestral homes, historical monuments. This is not a land which remembers. In 'Vacating an Apartment' the cleaners 'burn my posters / (India and Heaven in flames), ... make everything new,/ clean as Death'. He does not know the new tenants of the apartment, but they are the future—the woman is pregnant—while he is 'moving out holding tombstones in my hands'. He begins moving into another apartment; there is an apparent repetition of cleaning walls and shelves, but Ali imagines 'The Previous Occupant' as a poetry lover, someone with the same horoscope as himself, and from this imagines a political prisoner, dying, blinded, a ghost he has constructed which will haunt him and 'never, never, move out of here'. The poems appear so obvious that the reader may not appreciate how much work is needed to achieve that air of natural simplicity. But there is more to it than that. Ali has learned an American poetic idiom, the poem as a direct image of the natural world, the surface, the moment as real, but he inhabits it like a hermit crab in the shell of another, bringing with it his exile's themes, personal obsessions, the dialectic between past and present, there and here, the heart and freedom. His poems mean more than they say, the actual world described is also metaphoric.

In this understated, economically composed book we are no sooner on the move in America and running freely from the past than images of the past begin to appear in unexpected places as preparation for a transition to the concluding section. On a 'Flight from Houston in January' the clouds are 'like cotton for quilts', there is a frozen runway, 'everwhite trees / found on Christmas cards' and other images such as dervishes suggestive of Kashmir in the earliest poems of the volume. Nothing has really changed, 'The Moon did not become the sun' (Kashmir did not become Texas), and the section ends with the loneliness and disillusion of 'Write to me'. The poem's title 'Stationery' includes the obvious pun on stationary with its double contrast between home and exile and the poet as stationary, his life having undergone no real change, despite his travels.

In the last section there are six dream-like poems of nostalgia for India written while in the United States. In 'Survivor' he imagines 'someone', himself if he remained or returned, in his home in Kashmir with Radio Kashmir and the voice of his mother. But in a grotesque final twist 'He is breathless to tell her tales / in which I was never found'. There is the obvious analogy to Radio Kashmir's announcement that the search has been abandoned for some climbers. The power of the poem is partly in the way the obvious parallel and mood of self-pity is distanced and disrupted by Ali shifting between an imagined continuity if he had not left home and imagining his other self commenting upon his present life as if Ali were someone else, someone lost who will never be found and return again. This awareness that one has changed and cannot return to the securities of childhood is a universal theme but one especially strong in Indian poetry because of the importance of family. It is elaborated in other poems, such as 'I Dream It is Afternoon When I Return to Delhi' where he imagines he will take up the past as it was. His friend Sunil is waiting for him with a cinema ticket, but at the end of the show Sunil is not there; 'The usher taps my shoulder, says / my ticket is ten years old.' The final poem, 'Houses', returns to the contrast between his act of imagining a home and the security of home:

> The man who buried his house in the sand
> and digs it up again, each evening,
> learns to put it together quickly
>
> and just as quickly to take it apart.
> My parents sleep like children in the dark.
> I am too far to hear them breathe

The Half-Inch Himalayas is remarkable for its individual poems and for its structural development and unity. It is a summing up and distillation of some fifteen years of writing poetry. Each poem invites comment on its technique, whether it is Ali's handling of the three-line stanza he seems to prefer, the ease with which he imagines metaphorically, the linkages between poems, the concise lyrical delicacy of movement, the creation of a narrative frame, the projection of an inner world of feeling into consistent images, or in the music of the lines.

A Walk through the Yellow Pages takes further the surreal world of nightmare, fantasy, absurd incongruity, wild humour and the grotesque that often appears in Ali's poetry. Besides the five 'Bell Telephone Hours' poems, there is a poem which slightly reworks an oriental food store's advertisement for Dim Sums, two poems called 'Language Games' based on Scrabble and Charades, a poem based on graffiti ('Poets on Bathroom Walls'), another telephone poem—this time significantly at Christmas, and three poems based on fairy tales. In these poems language and narrative reveal the insecurities and fears caused by homelessness, cultural displacement and personal isolation. Each of the 'Bell Telephone Hours' plays with a slogan used in the television advertisements ('Has anyone heard from you lately?', 'Call long distance: the next best thing to being there') and reveals an existential anxiety under the social loneliness: 'I only hear / the busy signals / of their nightmares.' The horror is, in the contemporary manner, displaced into humour. The slogan 'Today, talk is cheap. Call somebody' becomes the basis for dialling Heaven; but instead of the Angel of Love he gets the Angel of Death:

> He answered, 'God is busy.
> He never answers the living.
> He has no answers for the dead.
> Don't ever call again collect.'

The ways in which one becomes habituated to, even made comfortable by, recurring fears, so that they provide a home of a kind, concludes 'An Interview with Red Riding Hood, Now No Longer Little'. She, now rich and successful and no longer part of what actually was a demanding family, is asked whether she has any regrets:

> Yes.
> I lied when I said it was dark.
> Now I drive through the city,
> hearing wolves at every turn.
> How warm it was inside the wolf!

While it could be said that Ali's revisions of fairy tales are another return to childhood—although one influenced by the recent rediscovery of the terrors in the original Grimm's versions—'Hansel's Game' concerns the impossibility of such a return. Life is a narrative of various stages in which maturing and surviving means becoming similar to, in the process of mastering, the sources of one's fears. Here the narrative begins after the happy ending when Hansel's mother tells him 'the womb's no place for a big boy like you' and pushes him out into the world again on the route 'from the womb to the grave'. Wiser now, no longer innocent, he lives comfortably and keeps the witch in the basement. On special occasions instead of cake 'we take portions of her / to serve': 'And our old father washes / her blood from the dishes'. The young replace the old and build their own house? Might the witch be the fears that are turned into poetry? Would I be wrong to see that ice-box in the basement as not only the repressed but as representative of an American house and therefore imaginatively connected with becoming an adult by living abroad?

Ali's poetry about his insecurities has turned into a narrative which itself has become the subject of allegories that elaborate on the story through various metaphors, disguises and figures. Autobiography often starts in a golden age of childhood which is lost in growing up. The specificity of Ali's experience and emotions, his acceptance of difference, his feeling of being comfortable yet exiled, of missing something wherever he lives or goes, contribute strongly to the lyrical power of his poetry. The more sophisticated technique since his earlier poetry allows him to make use of varied associations, moving rapidly, often elliptically, between layers of feelings, while ordering the poems into a complex book.

The 104 pages of poetry in *A Nostalgist's Map of America* (1991) also have a significant organization with section leading to section, recapitulations of themes and images and underlying narratives. There is a prologue, 'Eurydice', which creates the tone and is followed by four sections. The first section is set in the Southwest United States and the five poems move from the personal to the mythic and anthropological. 'Beyond the Ash Rains' begins with an announcement of themes:

> When the desert refused my history,
> refused to acknowledge that I lived
> there with you, among a vanished tribe ...

The second poem is 'A Rehearsal of Loss'. India and America, the personal and the historical, loss and fantasy, merge in the last poem of the section, 'I Dream I return to Tucson in the Monsoons':

> Below me is a world without footprints
> I am alone I'm still alone
> and there's no trace anywhere of the drowned
>
> The sun is setting over
> what was once an ocean.

While Section II consists of only three poems, 'In Search of Evanescence' is itself a sequence of eleven poems. The theme of 'Evanescence' which unites the section comes from a poem of Emily Dickinson (which is quoted as a prologue to Section II). The poems are addressed to a friend living in Southern California who died of AIDS. 'It was a year of brilliant water', the second poem in the 'In Search of Evanescence' sequence, announces the structure of the section ('I'm driving away from that widow's house ... I don't know I've begun // Mapping America, the city limits / of Evanescence now everywhere') and looks forward to 'The Keeper of the Dead Hotel'.

Section III, a sequence of thirteen poems called 'From Another Desert' continues the motifs of loss and deserts (here an Islamic desert) and retells an Arabic love, story, common to Persian and Urdu literature, in which Majnoon, the possessed or mad one, who has sacrificed everything for love, can be understood as a rebel or revolutionary and the loved one as the revolutionary ideal. In Arabic or Islamic literature love poetry is usually understood to be about love of God, but Ali belongs to the more recent tradition where the significance is understood politically:

> ..... Will he bring a message
> from her eyes, so far away now, gazing
>
> at a dream in which the ghosts of prisons
> are shaking the bars till iron softens ...

The eight poems of Section IV return to the desert and such earlier themes and motifs as myth and water while providing a farewell. The concluding poem 'Snow on the Desert' begins '"Every ray of sunshine is seven minutes old" ... So when I look at the sky I see the past? ... especially on a clear day' and moves by various imagistic associations from New York to Tucson, New Delhi and Bangladesh. It is a time to 'recollect' :

> a time to think of everything the earth
> and I had lost, of all
>
> that I would lose,
> of all that I was losing.

Both Ali and Salman Rushdie are products of a partitioned India who, while receiving part of their education abroad and living a large part of their lives in the West, continue to have strong ties with Islamic Indian culture. Such writers are aware of and refer to distinct cultural traditions yet imagine a universal condition shared by all cultures, races and times; such universalism is formed by Western liberalism rather than by, say, Islamic universalism. As Ali is younger than Rushdie and as North American society is more fluid than British, there is in his writing less confusion about cultural identity, dislocation, anger, insult, humiliation, confrontation, resistance. This may be a matter of Ali's personality, personal circumstances or a difference of generations. This could also be a matter of the conventions of the literary genres. Both modern European and traditional Islamic poetry are lyrical and personal whereas the novel, based on mimesis and representation, focuses on the social and political. I have also suggested that Islamic fatalism—an acceptance of change which it is useless to resist and which is part of the divine will—might explain Ali's turning of loss into nostalgia and his universalizing loss as natural to the passing of time through history.

Ali is interested in actually knowing about the past of others and is able to assimilate the lacunae of foreign history with his own imagination. In *A Nostalgist's Map of America* his own exile is transformed and assimilated into the *topoi* of the travelling American, the American always on the road between places. The book of poems is his own version of the 'being on the road' novel or autobiography as he travels by car, airplane, train and imagination to friends, places, memories and the past. As in the American versions there are mentions of specific roads, exits, radio stations, places, people. Ali is often, literally, behind the wheel and on the road between one place and another. Whereas the American artist invests the here and now with everything, making experience the only value, Ali treats being on the road as a journey of the imagination, fancy and memory.

In Ali's poetry the imagination links past and present, America and India, Islamic and American deserts, American cities and former American Indian tribes, modern deserts and prehistoric oceans. Sometimes the linkage is a word such as 'Calcutta' or 'desert' that conjures up India as well as a place in the United States. Ali is conscious of the imagination as a playground and of poetry as a product of the playful. There are literary allusions, literary echoes and self-conscious intertextuality. Like that of many contemporary authors, his writing is self-referential in pointing to what it is doing and how, both alluding to its structures and creating a metapoetic that governs its conventions. *A Nostalgist's Map of America* is more than a title to a volume of poems.

The formal structuring of the poems in *A Nostalgist's Map of America* is paralleled by chains of linking images of earth, deserts, oceans, water, rain, mirrors, windows, reflections, diamonds, emeralds, turnpikes, expressways, stairs, trains, wings. Such images assimilate with images of dead seas, ghost towns, silver cities, silver fractures, green change, Chance Village, Ghost Ranch Cliffs, the mirrored continent, the ocean that evaporated. Although Ali's voice and most reported conversations are colloquial, there is a highly profiled language of colour, paradox, oxymoron and other means to lift the poems into the lyrical and fanciful. The poetry presents a world of mirrors in which each experience, object, person, place, time, has reflections in the past and present, the here and there, the near and faraway. If 'Each ray of sunshine is seven minutes old' then there are places and people that have already seen it or that will see it. All existence becomes the subject of nostalgia and probably has some link or similarity to its opposite. Former oceans have become deserts, cities in America have the same names as cities in India that Ali knew, a place to be visited has associations with a friend who died of AIDS. Or to cite the title of one of the poems: 'I see Chile in my Rearview Mirror'.

In this poem we are on the road and the structure is like a Robert Bly or James Wright poem of the 1960s or early 1970s in which the here and now is a starting point to build fanciful associations on top of each other. Prefaced by a quotation from a poem by James Merrill, it appears very American, yet it is a poem that probably could only have been written by an observant foreigner whose imagination was first formed by the 'bones' of Kashmir. What began as imaginings of an Indian past he never knew has become a continental New World, a contemporary Whitmanesque vision in which the continent is plagued by curfews, vanishing rain forests, wounded republics:

> What will the mirror try now? I'm driving
>
> still north, always followed by that country,
> its floors ice, its citizens so lovesick
> that the ground—sheer glass—of every city
> is torn up. They demand the republic
>
> give back, jeweled, their every reflection.
> They dig till dawn but find only corpses.
> He has returned to this dream for his bones.
> The waters darken. The continent vanishes.

Am I wrong to hear the translator of Faiz Ahmed Faiz in such lines? There is not only a nostalgist, there is a radical at heart on the road mapping America. Is Ali an Indian poet? An Islamic poet? A Kashmiri?

An American? The only reason to ask such questions is to understand how useless such distinctions have become in discussing the poetry of the diaspora and perhaps most recent poetry. It could even be argued that the awareness of being part of a culture and yet sharing in many cultures and their artistic traditions is characteristic of all good artists.

The re-categorizations of Agha Shahid Ali's poetry reflect many changes in recent literary history. By the time he was included in Arvind Krishna Mehrotra's *Oxford India Anthology of Twelve Modern Indian Poets* (1992), he was long resident in the United States and already becoming an American poet with *The Half-Inch Himalayas* (1987) and *A Nostalgist's Map of America* (1991). Now, according to the jacket of his *The Country without a Post Office* (1997), he is a Kashmiri-American. From the contents he could be the national poet of a future independent Kashmir, a land that the poems remind us has not been free since conquered centuries ago by the Moghul emperor, Akbar. Ali would probably deny a nationalistic intent and claim to be a humanist concerned with universal justice, which explains his references to Sarajevo, Armenia, even a Norwegian hostage killed by Kashmiri militants.

Perhaps his intense emotional involvement with Kashmir has led him to experiment with so many forms as a way of distancing his feelings. The poems create an evolving loose narrative with seeming digressions harmonizing with the main themes through repeating images and phrases. After a prologue there are five sections, each a small group of poems with its own characteristics, followed by a few notes. The prose poem 'The Blesséd Word: A Prologue' expands on a phrase from Mandelstam to imagine a time when Kashmir will be free. 'Farewell', the opening poem of the first section is in one-line stanzas. The note says, 'This poem at one—but only one—level is a plaintive love letter from a Kashmiri Muslim to a Kashmiri Pandit (the indigenous Hindus of Kashmir are called Pandits).' It might also be seen as expressive of a shared culture and history asserted throughout the volume: 'In the lake the arms of temples and mosques are locked in each other's reflections' [22]. There are villanelles, ghazals, even a proper ghazal in which the couplets, though each is independent in meaning, are linked by the initial couplet's AA rhyme word, 'Arabic', recurring as rhyme in the second line of each following stanza. Stanza 13 explains some allusions in Ali's poetry and the psychology that informs this work. 'They ask me to tell them what *Shahid* means—/ Listen: It means "The Belovéd" in Persian, "witness" in Arabic.' In the modern political fashion desire for and loss of communion with the beloved, God, is understood as part of the longing for home by the exiled and conquered.

While Ali brings an Islamic tradition of high lyricism into English, his diction can also be clipped, economic, the language of modern anxiety, as well as winged. Allusions range from the Koran and Greek mythology to Shakespeare, Emily Dickinson, G. M. Hopkins and Auden. During our time of rapid cross-pollinations of cultures and peoples, he blends the radically different tradition of Islamic poetry with that of Europe, renewing a former probable Islamic link in such Renaissance forms as the canzone, of which there are two in this volume. The concluding poem 'After the August Wedding in Lahore, Pakistan' consists of five 12-line stanzas and a 5-line envoi. While the five rhyme words are repeated in each stanza, they change places in each stanza as the concluding rhyme becomes the first rhyme in the following stanza, forming the linked sequence abaacaaddaee / eaeebeeccedd / deddaddbbdcc / cdcceccaacbb / bcbbdbbeebaa / abcde. As Agha Shahid Ali is increasingly a major poet it is perhaps unfair to contrast the variety of his forms, styles and tones with, say, H. K. Kaul's *Firdaus in Flames* (1995) which for all its ambition and epic length is stuffed with gods, philosophical discussions, wooden explanations and stiff language: 'Also, if the rules of our movement / were set in the valley, we would have / Drafted our own free agenda for freedom.'

The better poets of the diaspora bring out most clearly how Indian poetry in English is rooted in the time and place of the poet while being part of many overlapping cultural and literary traditions within India and abroad. When you closely examine the poetry of Agha Shahid Ali or A. K. Ramanujan it is often impossible to say what is distinctly Indian and what is foreign. The same is often true of such poets as Arvind Mehrotra and Jayanta Mahapatra who live in India and who at times are strongly influenced by Indian literary traditions. Perhaps the conventions of poetry, and other arts in many cultures are of a similar species and, for those with the right words and craft, interbreed with marvellous joy.

CHAPTER FIFTEEN

Publishing 1987–99

I.

The cultural status of modern Indian English-language poetry began to change for the better after 1986. Previously the poets fought an uphill battle for recognition and publication. Suddenly poetry societies were being formed in major cities, new magazines started, many new poets were coming into view and courses in modern Indian English poetry were being taught at universities abroad. Vikram Seth's *Golden Gate* (1986) showed that it was possible for a publisher to make money from Indian poetry. While other books were unlikely to be as commercially successful as *Golden Gate* or Dom Moraes' *Collected Poems* (1987), Indian poetry in English was no longer regarded as the poor, unprofitable, unwelcome relative of the literary world. It now had prestige, might well earn its keep, possibly even make a steady profit for a publisher. New Oxford University Press publications included Nissim Ezekiel's *Collected Poems* (1989), Imtiaz Dharker's *Purdah and Other Poems* (1989), and Gieve Patel's *Mirrored, Mirroring* (1991). Penguin / Viking, Disha, Praxis, Indus and Rupa began to publish books of poetry. For a time Praxis, with Adil Jussawalla giving editorial advice, continued the high selectivity that had been characteristic of Clearing House. While the quality was excellent Praxis suffered from problems of financing and distribution; it published in runs of 500 and once financing was withdrawn it collapsed.

After Oxford University Press the most prestigious poetry series has been the books published by Penguin India / Viking sometimes under one or both imprints. The Mumbai poets and those associated with them had naturally fed into the Oxford Poets and at first into the Penguin poets when David Davidar, formerly managing editor of *Gentleman*, became the CEO of Penguin India and moved from Mumbai to New Delhi. Davidar and Moraes were friends in Mumbai and the Penguin / Viking poetry programme began with Moraes,

Collected Poems, followed by Moraes' *Serendip* (1990). This was, in effect, the public return of Moraes to poetry after many years of silence except in prose where he has always been a larger-than-life personality. It is the poetry, however, which is his art. Davidar, who was doing a good job building the new Penguin / Viking publishing house into a major company which transformed the Indian publishing scene, was uncomfortable with publishing poetry. Himself a writer of prose he knew the poets and knew of the difficulties in selling books of poetry to a broad general market. Early on, he appears to have decided to approach poetry with caution and if possible stick to established names, such as Vikram Seth, likely to sell.

This changed somewhat for a few years when, during the early 1990s, there was a sudden discovery of modern Indian poetry in English by many newspapers, journals and publishers. Penguin brought out Jayanta Mahapatra's *A Whiteness of Bone* and began in 1992 publishing some younger writers such as Agha Shahid Ali, who was already established abroad, and Rukmini Bhaya Nair, who had a reputation as an essayist, intellectual and reviewer, and who had won the second All India Poetry Contest in 1989. *Gemini* (1992) was the first of two books, prefaced by Dom Moraes, each volume introducing two young poets, here Jeet Thayil and Vijay Nambisan. Thayil was already known in magazine circles. Vijay Nambisan had won the first All Indian Poetry Competition in 1988. The next year Penguin republished two books of poetry by Sujata Bhatt that had already been published in England and had been widely praised. This was followed by Imtiaz Dharker's *Postcards from God* (1994), her second book of poetry. Dharker was well known as a painter and filmmaker. *Gemini II* (1994) was divided between Jaithirth Rao and C. P. Surendran. Another young poet Penguin introduced was Vinay Dharwadker (b.1954) whose *Sunday at the Lodi Gardens* followed a string of publications in the USA. Dharwadker did his doctorate with A. K. Ramanujan who was singing his praises as an up and coming star and with whom he co-edited a major anthology of Indian poems from many languages. In 1994 Penguin published three more books of verse by Vikram Seth and Ruth Vanita's *A Play of Light*, which uses mythology to examine the roles of women. For the next five years Penguin only republished poets, like Seth, with reputations abroad. Penguin would return to publishing new poetry in 1999 with Rukmini Bhaya Nair's *The Ayodhya Cantos* and C. P. Surendran's *Posthumous Poems*. Future volumes were contracted by Vijay Nambisan and Tabish Khair, who had by now published three volumes of poetry and a novel elsewhere, as well as being awarded first prize for the 1996 All India Poetry Competition.

After some years of uncertainty Penguin has settled for publishing one or two volumes a year by younger poets who are already known to the reading public and therefore likely to sell. While the level of poetry is good and it is to be welcomed that many of the poets are young, Penguin with its immense resources and distribution network could invest more in poetry with the expectation that it will be worthwhile over a period of time, which, rather than in the short run, is how poetry rewards. American publishers expect a book every few years from a poet; otherwise the poet is not worth having since he or she is unlikely to develop a reputation and readership. It is a pity that Daruwalla keeps needing new publishers or that Kolatkar has hundreds of new unpublished poems or that de Souza's poems appear in small editions.

Beyond Oxford and Penguin the third most important commercial publisher of poetry was for a time Rupa. Rupa, with Ezekiel as advisor, during the early 1990s brought out a large number of volumes of new poets and in the process, along with Penguin, changed the poetry scene. Many new poets of the 1990s either published their first volumes or their first commercial volumes with Rupa, and Rupa also published an anthology to publicize them (Makarand Paranjape's *An Anthology of New Indian English Poetry* 1993). The start of The New Poetry from Rupa series was amazing; an advertisement was placed in the newspapers seeking manuscripts which brought in a number of new faces including one of the best, the previously unknown Tabish Khair. The books were inexpensive and nicely designed.

Disha, with Ezekiel also advising, published a few volumes of poetry, including Charmayne D'Souza's *A Spelling Guide to Women* (1990). At about the same time, HarperCollins also began to publish poetry. These were perhaps the best years for publishing poetry in India. Unfortunately, towards the end of the decade most commercial publishers withdrew from publishing poetry or kept a low profile.

With the increased interest in Indian English poetry many new anthologies were published with a shift in emphasis and preferences rather than a radically new canon. Vilas Sarang's *Indian Poetry since 1950* (1989) brought Moraes back into the canon, republished Chitre's *Ambulance Ride*, confirmed the importance of de Souza, Jussawalla, Shetty and Peeradina, implied that Mahapatra had become a world-class poet, and included Darius Cooper, Santan Rodrigues and Sarang.

Mehrotra's *The Oxford India Anthology of Twelve Modern Indian Poets* (1992) was more adventerous in ignoring Kamala Das, Parthasarathy, Shiv Kumar, Patel, and himself, to include Moraes, Chitre, de Souza, Jussawalla, Shetty, Agha Shahid Ali and Vikram Seth. In terms of space, Kolatkar and Moraes do best. Mehrotra mentions some interesting alternative possibilities including the older poets, such as Fredoon Kabraji, Berman Saklatvala, Ruskin Bond and L. P. Bantleman and such younger ones as Menka Shivdasani, Vijay Nambisan and Tabish Khair. I would have included some of the short lyrics Mehrotra had published during recent years. They are almost perfect distillations of poetry into pure anthology pieces, an aim he shared with Ramanujan—both writers being influenced by the great anthologies of nameless or almost nameless medieval poems in the Indian languages. Sarang and Mehrotra reveal a diminishing interest in Ezekiel as Indian poets examine other models and traditions.

Perhaps the most conscious attempt at modifying the canon of Indian poetry since Mehrotra's anthology was Eunice de Souza's *Nine Indian Women Poets: An Anthology* (1997) which besides reinstating Kamala Das includes Mamta Kalia, Melanie Silgardo, Imtiaz Dharker, Smita Agarwal, Sujata Bhatt, Charmayne D'Souza, Tara Patel and Eunice de Souza. Three of the poets are Goan Christians, one a Muslim educated abroad, one a Parsi, and another a Bengali living in Germany. Except Das and Kalia it appears mostly a post-colonial configuration, an elite of the marginalized. While this is perhaps to be expected at present— think of how many of the writers of contemporary England are immigrants or the children of immigrants—it does show why there will always be those unhappy with the idea of Indian poetry in English. Indian poetry in English is part of the continuing modernization of India, including the increasing independence of women.

Nine Indian Women Poets: An Anthology was obviously intended as a reply to A. K. Mehrotra's *Oxford India Anthology of Twelve Modern Indian Poets* which had reduced the representation of women writers to one, Eunice de Souza, and pointedly ignored Kamala Das. Mehrotra's expectations of high standards of technique, economy, a body of work, a preference for impersonality and imagist poetics, had worked against the inclusion of some Indian women writers who had been more casual and instinctive about craft. De Souza could meet Mehrotra's standards and tried to bring similar standards and ideas about poetry to her canon of women poets, although she was more concerned with the vigour and use of ordinary speech and the position of women in India. De Souza's anthology, however, seemed less assured, less convincing than it could have been. She included Smita Agarwal who had won an All India Poetry award but did not have a book in print, and Tara Patel who claimed she was not really a poet. De Souza included but was very critical of Sujata Bhatt, who has lived most of her life abroad and who seems more American than Indian. I can understand de Souza's inclusion of and reservations about Bhatt who while being the most published, recognized and professional of the new women poets can at times write about culture and language existing in the blood or sentimentally assume that there is some significant unspoken communication between humans and animals.

While de Souza seems not to have had enough major poets for an anthology she did return Mamta Kalia to readers of English-language poetry, a writer who never received the attention she deserved. This not only restored an historically important poet, but placed in the context of other women poets, brought out her strengths. Mamta Kalia can be a powerful poet with her strongly cadenced phrases and changing rhythms. There was the Sylvia Plath influence, but Kalia also has her own voice, a striking one: 'Who cares for you, Papa? / Who cares for your clean thoughts, clean words, clean teeth? / Who wants to be an angel like you? / Who wants it?' There were those great openings: 'I want to pick my nose / in a public place'; 'Looking at my navel / I'm reminded of you, Mama.' The range of tones and dramatic situations the reader overhears are impressive, and the speech, the situations, and personality are of the present, immediately there: 'After eight years of marriage,' 'Let us forget your death and mine'. It is a voice and tone that can still be heard in younger poets such as Mukta Sambrani.

Besides creating a way of regarding poets from Kalia through herself, Silgardo, and such poets as Tara Patel and Charmayne D'Souza, Eunice de Souza avoided the trap of making a larger anthology through those 'I, woman, am a victim, but proud' mantras which still fill anthologies of women's writings abroad and which can be found in Debjani Chatterjee's *I Was that Woman*: 'I was the woman, neurotic, torn / disowning my sex / I was the voluptuous, decorative drudge / I was the creature with will-power raped / I was that woman.'

It is depressing how often critics, especially academics, still want some nativistic Indian tradition in the arts. Depressing because demands for authenticity and purity rapidly translate into radical politics and have often become rallying cries for racial, ethnic, or religious murders. But also depressing because there is, no, never has been, such a pure past uncontaminated by alien otherness. As Arun Kolatkar points out:

Many poets in Marathi have used foreign forms such as the sonnet .... The Roman-
tics in Britain opened up a new area of poetry in India. It became possible to write
about a waterfall .... There are a lot of mythical birds and beasts in Indian poetry but
not ordinary things. Usually an ordinary thing appears only as a symbol of some
higher spiritual meaning. Sparrows and crows have rarely appeared in Marathi po-
etry, but it is full of mythical Sanskrit birds ... there is a gap between daily life and the
remote imagery used by some of the best poets. To the ordinary man this kind of
imagery is as remote as Greek imagery.

It is clear by now that while modern Indian poetry in English took
part in a worldwide change in literary tastes it was often influenced
by modernism and social changes in other Indian languages. Eunice
de Souza seeking the sources of the use of ordinary speech and formerly
forbidden topics in the poetry of Mamta Kalia is told 'I was already a
Hindi poet of the anti-poetic tradition. *Akavita* started with our efforts
.... My two dozen poems in an anthology in Hindi were shockers for
the Hindi reader.' Kolatkar and Mamta Kalia are among the ten poets
interviewed by Eunice de Souza in *Talking Poems: Conversations with
Poets* (1999), a book that usefully shows the many sources of and
pressures upon Indian poetry in English.

Indian poetry has become a global network of writers in many
countries. There is Sujata Bhatt in Germany (and the British literary
scene), Tabish Khair in Denmark, Agha Shahid Ali, Saleem Peeradina,
Meena Alexander, Jeet Thayil and Chitra Banerjee Divakaruni in the
United States, Melanie Silgardo in England and Vikram Seth and Sudeep
Sen going back and forth between India and England. Then there is
Imtiaz Dharker, from a British Muslim Pakistani family, who has become
an Indian poet. Marriage, jobs, education, opportunities, the desire for
adventure, chance, all come into it, but the fact is that Indian poetry is
no longer a poetry solely written by those living in India necessarily by
those born in India. It would also be a mistake to assume that every
writer with Indian origins is part of Indian literature. The children of
those who emigrated abroad are natives of their new country, at best
sentimental Indians. Identity is not in the blood.

If a characteristic of recent years is the number of good new women
poets, another characteristic is the large number of Indian poets,
especially women, living abroad. The days are over when a few years of
studying or adventuring abroad were followed by a return to India or a
good job at an American university that allowed one to specialize in
India and being Indian. There are now jet-setters who travel back and
forth and there are now Indian poets living in Denmark, Germany
and Australia as well as Canada, England and the USA. They tend to

publish where they live and their works may not be known in India. As can be seen from Agha Shahid Ali the question of nationality stops being straightforward. While Ali still thinks of himself as Indian and often returns to India, there are newer poets, such as Reetika Vazirani, who was raised in the USA, and who perhaps only sentimentally can still be thought Indian. Vijay Seshadri, who moved to the USA, when 5 years old, objects to such national or cultural classifications. Increasingly Indians will take root in other lands and no longer regard themselves as Indians in exile nostalgic for their origins.

The Spring 1995 'India, South Asia and the Diaspora' issue of *Wasafiri* (England) included sections on Canada, America, England and South East Asia / South Pacific, as well as the Caribbean and East and South Africa. The English section has poems by Ketaki Kushari Dyson, Debjani Chatterjee, Prabhu Guptara, Melanie Silgardo, Satyendra Srivastava, Sanjeev Richariya, Maya Chowdhury, and Shanta Acharya. Only Melanie Silgardo is likely to be known to readers of this book. Just as West Indians living in England went through a long period of writing about the Caribbean and the clash of cultures before a new English-born generation started to think of themselves as Black British, so we will soon see poets of Indian descent in England and other countries who are unquestionably a part of that national literature and have no or few ties with India itself. Too often, however, such poets are encouraged to remain part of the national 'other' as European nations try to come to terms with their new large multicultural immigrant populations.

Debjani Chatterjee, who has won poetry competitions in England and has at times been an advisor to the Arts Council in England, is another member of the diaspora who writes about India as if it were exotic, an escape from her actual life. In 'The Parrot Fortune-Teller' in *I was that Woman* (1989, 1997) she is aware of how she uses parts of her origins and the contrast between reality and her desires: 'how dare it / dream of raw chillies and chick-peas? It needs / to fly, you need to fly from silly games. / But that's why you go to the parrot / fortune-teller, isn't it?' This is a clever idea but it is prose, the comparisons are too obvious and drawn out. There is a similar problem with the rhythm. The regular ten syllables seem to be counted rather than poised to take flight.

There are too many lines in Chatterjee's poems that seem prose clichés strung together. 'The loneliness of city jungles / Shelters the reluctant immigrant / Amid skyscraper towers of silence. / I roam the mugger-stalked streets / Of Porno-Babel, an easy victim, / Unwelcome on the gold and tinsel pavement, / But free to go my way ... But on

annual pilgrimage / My jet hopping brings me back... In defining my
Indianness / I can only unravel the essential me.' And that is part of the
problem in such diaspora poetry—this obsession with an abstract no-
tion of Indianness and the lack of any real locality. In 'The Elephant'
she 'looked straight up at the eyes. / A storehouse of sorrow was locked
in its brain'. Even as prose this would be clichéd. In the new world of
First World liberal multiculturalism writers are encouraged towards
the expected cliché. Chatterjee knows this, 'Animal Regalia' is con-
cerned with it—'visas, arranged marriages, immigration ... I should be
used now to this phenomenon', but the very next poem, 'Primary Pur-
pose' sees the world from the same pigeonhole she complains about:
'All know you are an Asian woman. / No matter what your generation,
/ You will always be an immigrant.' In 'To the English Language' even
the cliché about dreaming in one language while speaking another is
resurrected although Chatterjee is apparently not at ease in Bengali:
'What has proficiency to do with it? / I know I dream it endlessly.' The
Bengali of her imagination is 'sweet and juicy with monsoon warmth/
rich and spicy with ancestral outpourings'. The expression to dream in
a language meant that it was the language in which a person was raised
at home and spoke in the community in contrast to the language taught
in schools and used at work or among an elite. Poets who claim to dream
in languages they do not know well do not even get the clichés right. I
find similar clichés in the work of a much better poet, Sujata Bhatt.

There is a demand by some official bodies and postcolonial critics for
politically correct sentiments. In such supposed multiculturalism the
immigrant is always understood to be a victim and desirous of a lost
'home', of people of the same colour, race, religion, and language. The
ways in which such emphasis on 'difference' rapidly turns into separatism
and a self-defeating reverse racism are well known. It is, however, not
the politics that concern me but the way such politics harm poetry.
Indian English poetry is the product of a complex, sophisticated, modern
society; it should reflect it. The best poets do. For diaspora poets to
treat India as some tribal Eden is absurd and rapidly becomes a
contemporary Indian version of the old black minstrel show for the
approval of 'postcolonial' metropolitan First World intellectuals.

If postcolonialism has come to mean a post-nationalist concern with
minority groups within a state in contrast to the dominant powers,
Indian poetry in English has always had an ambiguous relationship
with such power. Many of the writers have instinctively been part of
the liberal opposition to both Hindu fundamentalism and to a state-led

Socialism. Yet English has been a language of the non-political elite and modern poetry itself tends towards being an elite art form requiring extreme sensitivity towards language.

It is clear that those who have a mastery over English are going to be attracted to the better conditions and greater opportunities of work and life overseas, especially during this age of multiculturalism. More Indian poets will be diaspora poets and some will play up nostalgia for their origins or their 'difference' and this may not always be good for their poetry. There is, of course, another reason besides opportunities and a normal sense of adventure for those at home in English to leave India. The growth of religious fundamentalism and the political consequences of the regional-language nationalists have made more than one writer feel unwelcome. If postcolonial means the state being challenged by its parts, that does not always lead towards tolerance and modernization. With the lack of a centre, the parts of a nation—the various regions, castes, religions and language groups—increasingly come into conflict as they assert their independence, desire dominance or claim territories. The social and political changes that help develop—among other things—an English-language literature, feminist movements, single lives and open homosexuality are also likely to produce an opposing new fundamentalism, radical neo-traditionalism and micronationalisms.

As Dilip Chitre is not only a bilingual poet but has been closely involved with the original culture of his region and writes in *The Mountain: A Series of Poems* (1998) about his spiritual conversion at a local holy spot, it is a shock to learn that he feels a victim of regional-language and cultural nationalists. Chitre's Afterword to his *The Mountain* might be regarded as a dispatch from one of the front lines at this time:

I started writing poetry seriously in 1954 at the age of sixteen. I am now sixty years of age. When I started writing poetry forty-five years ago, I wrote both in my mother-tongue Marathi and my favourite 'other tongue'—English. This practice has survived so far and it will be my habit for a lifetime. These two languages are equally crucial to my self-expression in a chosen universe of awareness and action.

I have been a reasonably well-known Marathi poet. With the publication of *Ekoon Kavita-3*, the third and final volume of my collected poems in Marathi, every completed and available poem written by me from 1954 to 1998 is now accessible to the Marathi reader ....

My poetry in English had to accept the fate of all Indian poetry written in English. English is perceived by some Indian ideologues as a colonial vestige and therefore as a sign of continuing bondage. This confusion is shared by religious and cultural fundamentalists with Marxists and post-Marxists steeped in anti-colonial rhetoric. Champions of 'nativism' in Marathi attack a major bilingual poet such as Arun Kolatkar betraying a new kind of politically inspired cultural illiteracy. They come to the predetermined conclusion that Kolatkar's series of poems *Jejuri* that won him the Commonwealth Prize was written in bad faith because it was not written in his mother-tongue, Marathi, and was written for an English-speaking audience. ...

The present Indian nation-state is perceived by Hindu religious fundamentalists as a nation in which they are the privileged natives, and people practising other religions or no religion as 'outsiders'. One does not know how they could account for the innermost insiders, 'the first people' of India, the tribals. A five-thousand-year old, often successfully repressed, conflict is the dialectic underlying India's cultural evolution: the conflict between the Brahmanical model of the world and the non-Brahmanical reality that India is. During the last fifty years, Brahmanism has bitterly fought to change the egalitarian and libertarian aspects of the democratic constitution of the republican state of India. A further complexity was introduced in this situation when the constituent states of the Union of India were identified according to the language spoken by the regional majority. Thus the moral claim on land in any state of the Indian Union is justified by language and it is language that determines a person's nativity. This has deep and disturbing implications. Sindhi, Urdu, and English become India's leading stateless languages. Or, for instance, if you are an English-speaking Indian, you are a non-native in any state of India and only a second-class citizen everywhere, by implication. You are an 'alien' just as Muslims, Christians, Sikhs, Buddhists, and all others are simply 'others'. ...

My own Marathi citizenship and status as a poet is of no use to me when, as a bilingual poet writing in English, the nativist casts aspersions on my nativity. I do not cease to be a Marathi poet when I write poetry in English. The voice of poetry cannot be split by the language it does not speak; and the language it chooses to speak excludes no human ear.

II.

When *Modern Indian Poetry in English* (1987) was first published there was still no consensus about who were the significant poets or recognition of what had been accomplished. I came to Indian poetry by accident; I had read some good poems by good poets and I wanted to know more about them. This was mostly uncharted territory and I soon found myself mapping it as a way of learning about it. The book that resulted was favourably reviewed, but left me wanting to read and write about some of the poets in a more systematic way. I was troubled by not having found a way of organizing my book to discuss Moraes at length or to examine the Indian influences on Ramanujan. *Three Indian Poets* (1991) allowed me to have a second chance to discuss Ezekiel, Ramanujan and Moraes. I had also wanted to discuss the poetry of Agha Shahid Ali and Meena Alexander which I do here. *Gemini* (1992) by Vijay Nambisan and Jeet Thayil brought two new poets to notice. By 1994 recent developments included books by Menka Shivdasani, Tabish Khair, Bibhu Padhi and Imtiaz Dharker. There was new poetry awaiting critical discussion.

There were also excellent new translations into English including Agha Shahid Ali's version of Faiz Ahmed Faiz's Urdu poetry in *The Rebel's Silhouette*, Dilip Chitre's *Says Tuka: Selected Poetry of Tukaram*, and Arvind K. Mehrotra's *The Absent Traveller: Prakrit Love Poetry of the Gathasaptasati of Satvahana Hala*. R. Parthasarathy's *The Tale of an Anklet: An Epic of South India* was awarded many prizes. Ranjit Hoskote and Mangesh Kulkarni's translation of Vasant A. Dahake's *Yogabhrashtra: A Terrorist of the Spirit* brought a remarkable contemporary Marathi poet to light. Anju Makhija and Menka Shivdasani have brought to light many lost publications in their *Freedom and Fissures: An Anthology of Sindhi Partition Poetry*. Just as the translations have revealed many sophisticated traditions of older Indian poetry with their own highly codified conventions, genres and poetics, so translations from Oriya and Marathi have shown how European modernist poetics have influenced regional languages and developed in strikingly original ways in response to modern India. Influences include surrealism and T.S. Eliot's reduction of poetry to imagistic fragments musically organized. By comparison Indian poetry in English may seem traditional, conservative, more directly addressed to the reader. It is perhaps only in the poetry of Ramanujan, Chitre, Mamta Kalia and Jayanta Mahapatra or, more recently, Tabish Khair and Hoskote that some of the strengths of regional language poetry have infused poetry in English.

A major event was the publication of *The Oxford Anthology of Modern Indian Poetry* (1994), edited by Vinay Dharwadker and A.K. Ramanujan, including 125 poems by 67 authors from 15 languages including 20 poems from English. Besides selections from such newer authors as Agha Shahid Ali, Meena Alexander, Sujata Bhatt, Imtiaz Dharker, Vinay Dharwadker and Vikram Seth, the book concluded with a brilliant Afterword by Dharwadker commenting on various contexts of Indian poetry. These range from stylistic and ideological movements found in all the major Indian languages at approximately the same periods, through what is unique to the literatures of specific languages, and how each poet may be a product of personal histories, influences and taste. The anthology and Afterword show it would be wrong to view poetry in English in isolation from what was being written in other Indian languages, just as it would be wrong to assume that the story of each literature can be told without reference to Europe and the Americas, or that a critic knowing one or two Indian literatures can presume to speak for all. Dharwadker, who studied with Ramanujan, shares his characteristic clarity of mind, an ability to classify, make distinctions, yet create a frame for discussing a large complex changing world. Dharwadker, like Ramanujan, claims the world consists of change in which historical links fragment and are reformed in new ways. He sees recent Indian poetry as bound to be influenced by the passing of an older colonial India and its ways into mythology, while the younger poet, like the novelist, is likely to be attracted towards the rewards of an international English-language readership.

The first modern generation took decades to establish a poetic tradition and to debate basic questions. I speak of a generation because despite differences of age the poets were still a small group and there was a continuity through friendships and publications. Jayanta Mahapatra felt an outsider, and his poems were certainly different from those written by many of the other poets, but eventually they appeared in the same journals and anthologies. With Vikram Seth and Agha Shahid Ali things began to change. These poets lived abroad and were not part of local cultural and publishing circles. While some of the new poets of the early 1990s had a connection with Ezekiel, or now Eunice de Souza, through studying or living in Mumbai, others, such as Tabish Khair, were outsiders to the Mumbai poetry scene. *Skylark*, a minor provincial poetry magazine, was Khair's 'home'. His subject matter, or world, was life in the provinces. Many of the new poets were women who had been educated, lived or worked abroad, and they expressed the problems of the single career woman in urban India.

Rupa's entry into publishing poetry followed the formation of poetry societies during the mid- and late 1980s. Some of the changes in poetry during the 1990s began with the formation of the Poetry Society (India) in New Delhi in 1984. This was followed, two years later, by the Poetry Circle in Mumbai and other groups in many cities of India. The poetry societies bring together those interested in poetry beyond the circles of universities and journalists, often have annual contests and some sponsor magazines. The Poetry Circle in Mumbai began under the sponsorship of Dom Moraes and Nissim Ezekiel and among its founding members were Menka Shivdasani, Aroop Mitra and R. Raj Rao. It still meets twice a month and since 1992 has published *Poiesis*. In Bombay, now Mumbai, there are also often 'Loquations', weekly poetry readings held mainly at the Chauraha Sunken Garden.

The Bombay Poetry Circle contests, however, are not as well known and have not resulted in book publication in the same way as those held by the Poetry Society (India) in New Delhi which publishes an annual *Journal of the Poetry Society (India)* and beginning in 1988 the annual (with some gaps) All Indian Poetry Competition which the British Council co-sponsors. Although open to poems translated from any Indian language, almost all the entries and winners have been poems written in English. The best poems are then published in an annual *Poetry India* anthology edited by H. K. Kaul, the Secretary-General of the Poetry Society. The judges usually include such established Indian poets as Nissim Ezekiel, J. P. Das, Lakshmi Kannan, Sujatha Mathai, Keshav Malik, Eunice de Souza, Shiv Kumar, Keki Daruwalla, Jayanta Mahapatra, and Imtiaz Dharker with an annual visitor from England such as Alan Brownjohn, Anthony Thwaite, Michael Hulse, Jo Shapcott or Vicki Feaver.

The competition has been successful at discovering or bringing to notice many of the new poets who were to become part of the Indian poetry scene during the 1990s. The first competition was won by Vijay Nambisan for his now widely republished poem 'Madras Central'. Since then first prize winners have included Rukmini Bhaya Nair, Anju Makhija, Tabish Khair and Ranjit Hoskote. Other prizes have been won by Sudeep Sen, Smita Agarwal, and C. P. Serendran. Several of the winners soon published volumes with Penguin, Rupa or Har-Anand. Although the numbers of poets and entries vary from year to year, from 1500 to 2900 poets annually enter a total of 4000 to 8000 poems. The success of the competition led to an All India Competition among schoolchildren, with its own anthology *Poetry of the Young*—also edited by H. K. Kaul.

The new poets who appeared in the 1990s seemed like a new start. Some were from Mumbai, but after a long period in which a social and cultural network had been formed, there were suddenly a number of new faces whose books required attention and large numbers of poets coming forward for the All India Poetry Competition. A new generation had appeared. Rupa's New Poetry series included volumes by Makarand Paranjape, Hoshang Merchant, Rachna Joshi, Anna Sujatha Mathai, Sudeep Sen, Tara Patel, Tabish Khair, Bibhu Padhi and Sitakant Mahapatra. Several of these poets were not so new and had published with P. Lal's Writers Workshop or other small presses, but this was their first time with a commercial publisher with national distribution and sales. Rupa was not Penguin/ Viking or Oxford University Press but it had offices in Calcutta, Allahabad, Mumbai and Delhi, and its books could be purchased in London.

Makarand Paranjape's *An Anthology of New Indian English Poetry* (1993) was important in bringing together the new faces. Here were selections from Robin Ngangon's *Words and Silence* (Writers Workshop, 1988), Menka Shivdasani's *Nirvana at Ten Rupees* (Praxis 1990), Sudeep Sen's *The Lunar Visitations* (Rupa, 1991), Charmayne D'Souza's *A Spelling Guide to Women* (Orient Longman, 1990), E. V. Ramakrishnan's *Being Elsewhere in Myself* (Writers Workshop, 1990), Tabish Khair's *My World* (Rupa, 1991), Tara Patel's *Single Woman* (Rupa, 1991), Ranjit Hoskote's *Zones of Assault* (Rupa, 1991), Jeet Thayil's *Gemini* (Viking, 1992), Vijay Nambisan's *Gemini* (Viking, 1992), Rachna Joshi's *Configurations* (Rupa, 1993), Hoshang Merchant's *Stone to Fruit* (Writers Workshop, 1989), *Yusuf in Memphis* (Writers Workshop, 1991), *Hotel Golconda* (Writers Workshop, 1992), and *Flower to Flame* (Rupa, 1992) and Paranjape's own *The Serene Flame* (Rupa, 1991) and *Playing the Dark God* (Rupa, 1992). Suma Josson's *Poems and Plays* (Writers Workshop, 1982), and Bibhu Padhi's *Going to the Temple* (Indus, 1985) and *A Wound Elsewhere* (Rupa, 1992), and R. Raj Rao's *Alien* (Writers Workshop 1982) and *Slide Show* (Peepul Tree, 1993) were represented along with two poets who had not yet published a volume, Desmond Kharmawphland and Prabhanjan Mishra. Mishra had a manuscript awaiting publication by Rupa. Manohar Shetty, Sanjiv Bhatla and Rukmini Bhaya Nair did not want to be included. Vikram Seth and Sujata Bhatt were too expensive to include. Most of the poets had published their first books since 1990.

Paranjape's 'Preface' rightly observes that the poetry in his anthology is too varied to be said to represent a fashion or manifesto, but then he ruins it by making just such a claim:

Yet, I believe, that one thing is certain. Modernism is dead .... Modernism in Indian English poetry, with its notions of literary *avant garde*, its emotional restraint and repression, its preference for irony and scepticism over all other attitudes to life, its self-conscious and precious craftsmanship, its belief in the image as the supreme poetic device, its aloofness and alienation from India, its secular dogmatism, its outright rejection of the past, and above all, its arrogant narcissism and self-absorption is, thankfully, now passé.

This is an incredible statement as most of the poets he included in his anthology are ironic, sceptical and self-consciously artists (why else should they write poetry). Menka Shivdasani in 'Hinges' describes her body as a door: 'one hinge / was insecure, but the other / firm as iron.

(Iron is short/for ironic.)' Nor had any Indian modernist poet pro-
claimed an aloofness towards India, nor even a rejection of the past.
No Indian poet lived in an Ivory Tower, not even in an ivy-covered
cottage. Paranjape's Indian modernism did not and never did exist.
Academic literary criticism unfortunately often consists of such shadow
boxing with imagined opponents. There is a sub-text. Paranjape's critical
and cultural writing is attracted towards precisely the mysticism and
nativism that most of the poets reject, so, ironically, there is an ill-fit
between his new generation and his claims. There are still Indian poets,
such as Niranjan Mohanty, attracted towards local Hindu traditions
and cultural nationalism, or those, such as Shanta Acharya (*Not This,
Not That*, 1994) who have written attractive, understated lyrics expres-
sive of mysticism and spiritualism. Even Vivek Tandon's *Climbing the
Spiral* (1995), although meant as an answer to spiritualism, might be
regarded as a kind of mysticism. These, however, are not Paranjape's
new poets.

The manifesto might apply to Paranjape's own poetry. Besides being
interested in nativism, nationalism and spiritualism, he has also written
about postmodernism. Paranjape's postmodernism is little more than
a playful mixture of things real, fancied and mythic. His poetry is
autobiographical, at times embarrassingly so, but enlivened with
humour, supposed conversations, confessions, dialogues, the pretense
of acting mythic and some heavily self-conscious attempts at
self-reflective writing in which he highlights the conventions of his art.
The Serene Flame (1991) and *Playing the Dark God* (1992) recount his
relationship with his wife and some extra-marital affairs. *The Serene
Flame* begins with a jokey 'Invocation', followed by a 'Prologue' and
concludes with a 'PS: Venus Sernus' and 'Epilogue (As an old-fashioned
Homily)'. In between there are selected autobiographical moments
('College Days', 'The Seven Year Itch', 'In Love (At Thirty)') and some
fooling around (in more than one sense), such as the mini-sequence
'The Love Poem Unwritten', '[A Missing Poem]', 'In Lieu of the Missing
Poem' and the 'Muse's Gift'. Paranjape teaches English literature and
the two books show it in their many echoes, parodies and nods to
classroom topics:

> There are I take it, many texts in this post-structural age
> In which introductions become interminable
> Because, quite simply, there's nothing to introduce,
> No main body, no inner chamber, no sanctum designate,
> Nowhere to lead into, nowhere *intro ducere*:

Just mazes, passages, and entrances,
Decentred disseminations of difference.
So these poems may lead nowhere but back to myself,
Voices in my own consciousness seeking release and play.

This academic postmodern playfulness is elephantine. The eroticism
is even worse:

The privileged uptight seam
Eats into the warmth between your legs—
How will it feel
If I palm you gently there?
Will your thigh-stubble tickle?
You dress to tempt
to provoke undress:

It is difficult not to contrast this clumsiness with the seriousness,
precision, drama, and economy of Ezekiel's *The Unfinished Man*, another
sequence in which marriage, love outside marriage and commitment
to art and India are intertwined. O Dear Spirit of the Age, bring back
that out-of-date modernism and convince Paranjape that he is not a
postmodern Byron, not even a Don Juan!

While it is easy to mock Paranjape's poetry and criticism, the anthology
of new poets is another matter. Most of the poets were of some interest
and Menka Shivdasani, Charmayne D'Souza, Tara Patel, Tabish Khair,
Jeet Thayil and Vijay Nambisan were good. It had taken a long time
before there was general acceptance of Indian poetry in English and
awareness of who were the better poets. While those battles were being
fought a new generation was coming along. Paranjape's anthology
contributed to bring many of the newer poets forward.

With the growing national and international importance of English
to communication, entertainment, education, careers and travel, new
generations of poets seem to arrive in less than a decade. If the early
1990s saw the first publications of D'Souza, Ranjit Hoskote, Tabish
Khair, Vijay Nambisan, Tara Patel, Menka Shivdasani and Jeet Thayil,
the last years of the decade were a time when another generation was
beginning to gain attention. Although they had no publisher or pub-
lishing house, several had worked on *Debonair* or *Gentleman* in Mumbai.
Gayatri Majumdar's *The Brown Critique* or *TBC* was becoming a voice
for this new generation. Mukta Sambrani is the first of this generation
to have published a book.

There was a long span, beginning with the publication of the Oxford

University Press series, when the situation of Indian poetry appeared to be improving as new journals were started and publishers became interested in publishing poetry. This reached its peak in the early 1990s; since then the poetry market might be said to be in recession. After 1996 publishing books of English-language poetry in India once more became a problem as first Rupa, then Oxford, withdrew from poetry publishing. During 1999 Oxford University Press in England said that while publishing poetry did not lose money, it did not make enough and ended its Oxford Poetry series. OUP India followed. Penguin India has begun publishing poetry again but gradually, maybe a volume a year. Rupa no longer publishes poetry. Disha similarly lost interest. Ravi Dayal's list is very small and not widely known. HarperCollins is erratic. Other less well-known publishers include Firma KLM (Calcutta), D. C. Books (Kottayam, Kerala) and Writers Forum (Ranchi). The Writers Workshop continues to publish a wide range of books. There are some good poets, but they get lost among the many others in the haystack. Har-Anand (New Delhi) is a bit like the Writers Workshop in that poets are expected to purchase 75 copies of their books. Supposedly 500 copies are printed. While some copies are sold to libraries and available in book shops, they are not sent to reviewers (which is the responsibility of the author). Har-Anand, unlike the Writers Workshop, does send proofs to authors. There are good authors published by the small and subsidized presses, but they are swamped by those far less able and tend not to attract critical attention.

It is noticeable that during the final years of the century there were fewer important books of poetry published and that good younger poets were once more starting to print privately their own poems or turning to the Writers Workshop. As in any art, improvement comes from competition with the best, moving up to publishers with prestige and commercial distribution who pay royalties (rather than needing to be paid to publish), and the real test is in competition on an international scale. Whether the entry of Picador on the Indian scene will help poetry remains to be seen. There is money to be made as shown by the number of anthologies in progress, but how to make it on small books by one author? There are now a few more magazines and newspapers paying for the occasional poem as it is recognized that the readership that is interested in culture also reads poetry, but publishers still find it difficult to make profit from poetry unless the poet is well known and likely to be widely reviewed in the national press.

Indian poetry has started to gain some attention abroad, and some poets have been published in England, the USA, even Germany. As British and American poets complain about the lack of publishers and sales, even the small number of Indian poets published abroad is remarkable. It is noticeable that besides Vikram Seth, the international market appears mostly interested in female poets, possibly an indirect consequence of the feminist movement.

How might we explain the high quality of Indian English poetry? It is sometimes thought that art requires a long tradition and a stable society. This is true in the sense that an art form is a language with conventions which each artist and generation builds upon or reacts against. Even protest literature is created by rules, conventions and models. It is also true that stable societies are likely to provide the leisure and patronage necessary for the production of complex, lasting art. Stability, however, is relative. Life consists of growth and decay. The vitality of Indian poetry is an embodiment of change. The diversity of India, its many cultures, frustrations and conflicting desires are a rich source for a writer. The need to make sense of discontinuity and disjuncture—even acceptance of or amusement with incongruities— can fertilize art.

Literary form is itself the dominant language for a writer. A poet works within or reacts against the conventions of poetry. Each literary tradition has its own conventions, models, influences, but every literary tradition has been influenced by the conventions, forms and models of other traditions. Even the rebel is in rebellion against something. From a comparative perspective the similarities between the world's literary traditions are surprising; it is as if they shared a similar grammar of conventions and kinds, but at various times emphasized different usages. The vitality of Indian English poetry results from the constant, rapid adaptation of literary influences, whether from British, American, European or various Indian language poetries. Literary influence often involves the partial adoption or adaptation of a mentality, a way of seeing and conceptualizing the world. While such poets as Ramanujan, Mehrotra, Chitre, Ali, Mahapatra, Kolatkar, Parthasarathy, and Sarang are bi- or tri-lingual and imaginatively work within more than one literary tradition, good poets are always influenced by other cultures— whether the models and conventions are Greek, Latin, French, Tamil, Sanskrit or Persian.

An accurate discussion of Indian poetry would need to take into account the transnational and transcultural influences and the layering of many different kinds of mentalities and linguistic models, knowledge and abilities within a writer's imagination. English-language poetry exists in an entangled relationship with various dialects and other languages. Arvind Krishna Mehrotra's Introduction to *Twelve Modern Indian Poets* has a short but exceptionally acute discussion of multilingualism, including varieties of English. Mehrotra's view is that Indian poets writing in English have many different linguistic structures available without any one being more natural, authentic or national than any of the others and that the levels keep being shifted around; for a competent writer no one language or dialect is the base, other languages are not superstructural. Mehrotra's anthology is a reply to Parthasarathy's earlier *Ten Twentieth-Century Indian Poets* (1976). Parthasarathy was nostalgic for the Tamil culture of the past and discontent that English had become a literary language in India and that an Indian English had not yet appeared. Parthasarathy, who for a time gave up writing in English, is representative of a period when nationalism and cultural identity were confused with choosing between local and European languages.

I have written about Ezekiel's role in keeping modern Indian literary culture alive, but I doubt whether many readers who are not themselves writers have any notion of Adil Jussawalla's continuing role as an editor of anthologies, including the important Penguin *New Writing in India* (1974), and in such publishing houses as Praxis and Clearing House, and as an editor for *Debonair* and *The Times of India*, in promoting Indian writing in English and other languages. I sometimes have a feeling that a large part of Indian English-language culture, including what is available from other languages, results from the discoveries, enthusiasms, energy and judgement of Ezekiel, Jussawalla, Ramanujan, Mehrotra, Chitre, and to a lesser extent Mahapatra and Moraes.

III. POSTSCRIPT 1999

That India became a nuclear power, that its population crossed a billion, that Bangalore and Hyderabad emerged as centres of modern communications and science, and that Hindu nationalism threatened the stability of the country, seemed a fitting context for Indian poetry at the end of the century. It did not take much hindsight to see that Indian poetry in English was one of the seeds of European colonialism which hybridized, cross-bred, took on local characteristics and flourished as part of modernization in many places after national independence. Throughout the decolonized world the English learned by the former colonial elites was being transformed into a local language and culture which held nations together, and which became a necessary tool for large segments of the population as they entered the world of modern education and modern jobs.

English-language literature might be seen as an aspect of the new global economy. It is associated with rationalism, secularism, scepticism, tolerance, liberty, individualism, minorities, universalism and criticism of the status quo, even of itself. No wonder it has been regarded with distrust by the nationalists and by those who had a single-minded proprietorial view of the worker, the people or the truth. The poetry itself has been oddly unideological, apolitical, and has been criticized for its lack of public commitment and rhetoric on social justice although many of the poets were themselves social democrats or held a belief in a social liberalism in which freedom and liberty were thought to be the most important ideals. Pragmatism, empiricism and commitment to what they know and feel have made the poets avant garde, the real revolutionaries, pointing to a future that was already becoming part of India.

An era is passing, entering the pages of literary history. Ramanujan and Rayaprol are dead, Ezekiel is showing the effects of age and is the subject of a biography by R. Raj Rao. It is now obvious that Ramanujan was a giant, an extremely good poet, a great translator, an internationally famous scholar, and someone of powerful and broad intellectual and cultural interests; he had few equals in the quality of intelligence he brought to his many works and his range of achievements. Mehrotra, no longer the young rebel, has carried on some of Ramanujan's interests in older Indian literatures, languages and their conventions, and in his panoramic vision of Indian literature, and in his insistence on Indian cultures as both uniquely a product of specific times and places and yet part of the larger world.

CHAPTER SIXTEEN

Maturity

MORAES, PEERADINA, RAMANUJAN, PATEL, SHETTY,
MEHROTRA,DARUWALLA, DE SOUZA, ALEXANDER

The change from regarding Indian poetry in English as an unprofitable, eccentric minority interest began quietly with Vikram Seth's *The Humble Administrator's Garden* (1985) which was highly praised in London; the title poem, 'The Humble Administrator's Garden', was said by some critics to be a certain candidate for future anthologies of English poetry. Whereas previously Indian English poets appeared to be catching up with recent changes in style, Seth's book was itself part of a movement towards greater formalism and rhyme and away from the excesses of modernism and experimentalism, although its blend of amusement, witty allusions to artistic conventions and laid-back hedonism was itself characteristic of one stream of postmodernism at the time. Seth soon went beyond any other poet of the new style in his internationally successful novel in rhymed verse, *The Golden Gate*. While some Indians were still debating whether Indians could write good English poetry, Seth had conquered literary London and New York. Seth was the first Indian poet to have such a reputation since Dom Moraes, but whereas Moraes's success was in a style that had already been formed by poets of the previous generation, Seth was a leader among those who were changing the direction of English verse. Just as Salman Rushdie gave the Indian novel a prominent place on the international literary scene, so Seth brought Indian English poetry from the margins to the centre of English literature. On a smaller scale Agha Shahid Ali did something similar in the United States. *The Half-Inch Himalayas* (1987) sold remarkably well and was reprinted in a paperback edition. While he did not have Seth's grand success, Shahid Ali was rapidly recognized as one of the better young American poets, someone with an unusual range of language, sound, imagery and mastery of technique. His next volume of poetry was brought out by a well-known 'trade' publisher, rather than a university press. In the United States that means a poet has made it; few poets get that far. One of the signs of provinciality is not to recognize the exceptionally talented. Indian English poets were too often faced by such scepticism of why they were writing in English. Ramanujan's magnificent *Second Sight* (1986), perhaps the most interesting fusion so far of Indian and European literary traditions, was mostly ignored by Indian reviewers who apparently had not the least idea of what the volume of poetry was about. Seth and Ali published and gained recognition abroad where no one asked whether they were Indian but judged their books in comparison with other poets and found them outstanding.

That Seth and Ali first received recognition overseas is perhaps not surprising. Recognition of Indian English poetry had long been delayed by an older cultural nationalism which began in the late nineteenth century and which was once the source of the independence movement. Originally a force of vitality, liberation and rediscovery, it had outlived its utility and become repressive, a burden on a rapidly changing modern India. Even such concepts as the nation and national cultures have been challenged by the new internationalism and by the assertion of regional, ethnic, religious, gender and class differences within nations.

The publication of Dom Moraes's *Collected Poems: 1957–1987* and *Serendip* (1990) brought back to the local poetry scene its first major modern English-language poet, put its history and development into clearer perspective and offered an alternative to such influential models as Ezekiel and Mahapatra. *Collected Poems* sold well to the general public while the new, later, verse revealed a mature poet, somewhat difficult, at times even puzzling, but richer in interest than the romanticist that had made his reputation in England.

During the 1950s and mid-1960s Moraes was the darling of England. A craftsman who did tricks with traditional forms, a writer in love with writing, a poet whose verse paid echoing homage to English literature from Spenser to Auden, Moraes had over unusual mastery over the harmonies and rhythms of traditional English verse. He was romantic, witty, concerned with stanzaic form and rhyme. From the first there was something larger than life about his poetic personality. He had a voice, the poems struck poses, took attitudes. Before, during and after his years in England his poems were filled with an exile's blues. For personal reasons, having to do with his family and early life, he never felt at home any place. That was the point of *John Nobody* (1965). Moraes began as a romantic dreamer but by the mid-1960s his poems were haunted surreal nightmares, deliriums of private anxieties, memories of a troubled family history, fears about his own future; the imagined faerylands forlorn of his youthful desires were now populated by demons, self-destructive friends and his own lack of home or family. At some point the muse left him. She began slowly, uncertainly, to return with the privately published *Absences* (1983).

Collected Poems offers a few instances of Moraes during the museless decade experimenting with a colloquial, post-Hemingway realism, but the more recent major works at the end of the collection are not reader-friendly. Some of the allusions are very private and it is difficult to find a point of entrance into his world of personae, masques, myths and dramatic monologues with their formal tightness and labyrinth-like movement. Exile and withdrawal, the casting of a shell around one's life, is as likely to occur 'at home', if you are not really at home, as abroad. But then, as *Serendip* shows, exile, the living in a snail's shell while roaming the world of imagination, may result from the intensities of loving, from not having any children as heirs, and from an awareness that with age all the world is no longer before you while death approaches. Moraes was now building poetic enclosures in which the words densely guarded his feelings. This is very much a late style, a private world, a craftsman's art, admirable in its complexity, rather unique in manner, at times off-putting. Moraes condenses his images in startling ways. The expected connectives and transitions are not there, the place or scene is vague, shifts in time and focus help to dissolve the narrative. As the poems are tightly crafted, the dislocation between what is being said and poetic structure is disconcerting. From earlier versions it seems that Moraes begins with a more open, clear poem which as he revises becomes tight, complex and puzzling. He claims that he is not a difficult poet and that is true in the sense that you know what the poem is saying even if everything is refracted oddly.

Serendip consists of three sequences and eighteen 'Other Poems'. The title sequence of sonnets refers to an ancient name for Ceylon or Sri Lanka, where Moraes lived for a time as a child. Here myth, personal history and present horrors serendipitously intertwine. 'Steles' is also concerned with writing and death. 'Steles' is extremely layered in themes, 'Have we time to inscribe our steles? / And who will read them? / Whose are these great caped figures / Coming down, silent, from the floes?' 'Barrows', a sequence of monologues, written in five quatrains, each using a different persona, concludes with a long dead Swedish guard finding his identity through tourists: 'My tunic is still on flame/

Under my black suit.' Horrors, absences, the desire for comforting breasts, the way life is transformed into art and how art memorializes the dead are themes found throughout the volume. The language can be knotted, clotted, chiselled and hammered into unusual, even Jacobean, word order. At times it can be biblical, traditional, poetical. Yet it is an impressive show: 'All language is its own history, /... If it is reducible to a word, / Each one must find his own. / It is the destiny of a dynasty / To form a language from a language.'

Moraes has always been an outsider, only at ease among the cosmopolitan, the off-beat, the unlikely, only at home in language and poetry. Yet how Indian! Complex societies produce their own complexities, their own forms of alienation, their own relationships to other artistic traditions. If Moraes's late poems are laboured they work well at a subliminal level. It has sometimes been said that Moraes's identification with British and European poetry is a dead-end and would leave no poetic heirs. That might superficially be true, but poetry itself is a language and a nation; while Moraes's poetic heirs, such as Jeet Thayil, might not look like him, they are likely to have his complex relationship with India and also to see themselves in terms of world, especially European, poetry.

One poet who has continued to build upon the Ezekiel tradition is Saleem Peeradina. *Group Portrait* (1992) is a self-examination by someone who is now married, head of a family, a father, and responsible for himself and others. The poet is aware of the duties expected of a man at his stage of life and the poems are Sanskritic in their economy and the moral concern that infuses the narrative. There are the family portraits, introspective self-examinations and moral studies of friends and characters characteristic of such poets as Ezekiel, de Souza, Katrak, Parthasarathy and Rodrigues. Even the unity of the volume, the subsections and the pairing of poems, are methods used by Ezekiel, Ramanujan and Parthasarathy.

Peeradina's main concern appears to be the reconciliation or harmonizing of conflicting emotions through a social and ethical consciousness. Whereas Ezekiel's poems often treat marriage as a trap for the spiritual and moral self, Peeradina finds the fullest self-realization in the tight community and duties of family. The erotic, the public self, the creative, the affectionate and the moral find resolution in the familial. The conflict between the busy life of the householder and the poet's need for privacy and silence to nurture his emotional life as a writer is shown to be deceiving. While 'staying divided' is a condition for writing poetry, the attainment of 'equipoise' is necessary for the pleasures of fulfilment that come with being a man, a father, a husband in love with his wife. In 'Beginnings' Peeradina mentions a 'mentor' who schooled him 'in the exercise of his wit, / the fruits of meditation, critical self-judgement'. The mentor is Ezekiel. In *Group Portrait*, written by a Muslim Indian, using Hindu moral and social concepts, paying homage to a Jewish mentor, we can see how an Indian poetic tradition began by making use of English poetry, developed its own traditions, and all along had roots in the many sides of Indian culture.

With the publication of the *Collected Poems 1952–1988* (1989) of Ezekiel and the *Collected Poems* of Moraes, their long out-of-print writings are now available, and it became possible to see what had been published in those early decades and to trace the development of such major founding modern poets. Most of Daruwalla's volumes of poetry have also been republished and selections of Kamala Das are available, if rather erratically. Time was also having its effect. Ramanujan died on 13 July 1993 in a Chicago hospital after receiving anaesthesia in preparation for an operation that was supposedly without danger. His poetry often told of such grim incongruities; their amusing, wry ironies showed that life was filled with imagined anxieties and unexpected real dangers. The deaths absurdly reported in such poems as 'Obituary' and 'Madura' were attempts to distance the pain and apparent arbitrariness of ordinary existence. Rejecting the Hindu revivalism and mysticism of many nationalists, he still regarded the past as an influence on the present, although in such forms as memories, the unconscious and genetic inheritances, where the actual manifestations were likely to appear when least expected or desired.

Ramanujan early rejected notions of spiritual transcendence; his poetry shows that reality is in the particular, the specific, the individual experience. The lesson he drew from both *Upanishads* and science was that after a life of unsatisfied fantasies and self-destructive passions we return to nature but as part of the food chain. His later poems sometimes joke about Hindu-style ecology. In classical Indian writings he found a similar vision to that of modern science. Everything is unstable, changing, transitory, predatory, striving to survive. He welcomed modernity but his sensibility was shaped by a view of life as repetitive cycles which have the appearance of change. He practised Buddhist meditation as a way to stop anxieties and dissatisfactions.

While he was an excellent poet in three languages, and thought of himself primarily as a poet, Ramanujan's interests included linguistics, folklore, mythology, psychology, philosophy and literary theory. His translations of classical and medieval Tamil and Kannada poetry were the means by which many readers became aware of the older literary traditions of southern India.

Although his poetry is easy to read and appears personal and focused on the present, its seeming transparency is deceptive. It is filled with echoes, quiet allusions, ironic symbols and other enriching resonances that deepen, multiply and change its significance. Several radically different semiotic structures may be teasingly present in a poem. Trying to unpack the various strands is like being in a room full of trick mirrors; nothing is final, each image changes with the perspective. 'The Striders' is a short, imagistic description of the New England water bug, but for those who know Tamil poetic terms and myths concerning Siva the poem can be interpreted as an argument about Hindu philosophy which is taken up throughout his poems. Ramanujan spoke of the meaning of his poems as 'negotiations' between cultures and himself as the hyphen in Indian-American. As appearances are the effect of many hidden distant causes, interpretation will change according to the kinds of available knowledge. Such a 'poetic' is as applicable to national cultures, families, individuals, linguistic theory, psychology and religion as to literature. Perhaps its most concise statement is in such poems as 'Elements of Composition' and 'On the Death of a Poem' in *Second Sight* (1986).

If Ramanujan's accomplishment as a poet is not better known it is because he published slowly, wrote in three languages and few except himself had a similar range of immediate cultural references. There is also the problem of the kind of poem he wrote. He may have been the last major modernist, the last poet of the perfect, concise, imagistic lyric. The modernist movement had an earlier, stronger influence on several regional Indian-language literatures than on the Indian English poets. Among Ramanujan's early publications are translations from Kannada of the verse of Gopalkrishna Adiga, a poet he knew and admired. The *Collected Poems* Ramanujan was working on before his death were to include translations of his own writings in Kannada. Partly influenced by the modernists, partly by the conventions of Tamil and Kannada poetics, Ramanujan aimed at a toneless impersonality by revising through perhaps fifty versions over a decade. The ideal poem would be an anonymous lyric in an anthology. Such a poem would also be part of a carefully constructed sequence with developing themes and recurring images, punctuated by a few contrasting poems. The apparent openness of *Second Sight* is deceptive as it is his most carefully organized volume; here the seeming postmodernist flow of free associations and pretense at autobiography masks another, but different, set of classical Tamil poetic conventions governing longer poems, which he discussed in *Poems of Love and War*. I have discussed this in greater detail in *Three Indian Poets*. His verse was never free; it was shaped by complicated rhymes, disguised stanzaic forms and conventions of prosody which owe as much to Indian as Western literary traditions.

As Ramanujan died while preparing his collected poems, they were published after his death in a *Collected Poems* largely the work of his former pupil Vinay Dharwadker, but with help from Molly Daniels-Ramanujan, Krittika Ramanujan and others. *The Collected Poems* includes 60 new poems issued under the collective title of *The Black Hen*, a selection compiled by a committee of eight people from 148 new poems Ramanujan had left on computer disks. Besides a Preface by Krittika and a long useful Introduction by Vinay Dharwadker there is a concluding 'Note on *The Black Hen* and After' by Molly Daniels-Ramanujan. While *The Black Hen* poems and Dharwadker's Introduction emphasize Ramanujan's concern with the body in relation to time and death, and the way everything is related while remaining distinct, the fact remains that the selection and arrangement are not by Ramanujan. This is a different *Collected Poems* from the one he had in mind. I remember having several conversations with him in which he spoke of including translations of his poems from other languages but felt that he had to write new poems in the spirit of the originals. I imagine that they and the poems not selected for *The Black Hen* will eventually appear in a volume of uncollected poems. If so I hope it will include those early uncollected poems and early versions of his poems which help illuminate the vision and methods behind his volumes of poetry. The present *Collected Poems* is not a Complete Poems; it republishes the first three volumes along with the *Black Hen* selection, nothing else.

The Black Hen takes its title from the first poem in the selection, in which the coming of 'it', presumably poetry or the poetic image but also philosophical insight and death, is something that must come naturally from growth over a period of time the way leaves appear on a tree. By now there are a number of poems in which the mysterious coming of 'it' is understood to be inspiration and Ramanujan's poem is a reply to such a romantic aesthetic; here 'it comes sometimes / as the black hen / with the red round eye'. This might seem a lovely image, even a suggestion of fertility and life, but the black fowl with its red eye is also disturbingly suggestive of anxieties and perhaps of death: 'the black hen stares / with its round red eye // and you're afraid.' These three themes—poetic inspiration, anxieties and death—will recur through-out the volume along with the idea that all history is linked in often untraceable causes and effects and that birth is the start of death and the eventual return to nature from which a person will be recycled in other forms. There is a concise amusing version of this vision in 'A Taste' from the 'Images' sequence:

> Mothers smear bitter neem
> paste on their nipples
> to ween greedy babies
>
> and give them an inexplicable
> taste for bitter gourd
> late in life

The poems in the volume were clearly meant to be understood as linked and returning to parts of a larger view of life. 'It', for example, takes up that 'It' with which the selection begins:

> I see it out there like a small
> tree with two broken branches
> between two gnarled oaks lifting
> their full head of leaves
> into the rain,

but, 'I hear it / running like an underground Ganges / under my feet, over my head ... always running from me.' As the many comparisons that I have not quoted in the poem and the various scenes he mentions show, 'it' is life and death intertwined in all existence, and therefore all existence is a possible subject for poetry as a possible image of such a reality.

The Black Hen poems seem less complete, less worked over, less pol-ished, less complicated, less a house of mirrors, than Ramanujan's earlier poetry. He normally punctuated lightly but few of these poems have any punctuation. It may well be that this is a conscious later manner, but the foregrounding of the philosophical vision of his work simplifies it. In Ramanujan's previous poems his philosophical themes developed from an image and some concrete situation, here ideas seem to predomi-nate. There are some lovely poems like 'In Toyland' with its live chame-leon mimicking rubber toy ones and its amusing paradoxical child-like rhyming conclusion worthy of any Hindu or Buddhist philosopher :

> If you think you see
> nothing on a tree, then it's
> a chameleon you see.

There are, however, poems such as 'Night's Day' which must be unfinished or else something has been miscopied. The second stanza makes little sense as printed:

> Walking, dancers need crutches
> deafmutes and eunuchs
> in mafia harems
> and piranhas savour cats' flesh.

Speaking of Ramanujan's philosophical vision, while true, can be misleading in emphasizing a totalizing interpretation over the particulars of life that are the subject matter of the poems. Many of the poems appear autobiographical and treat life as sexual desire, the longings of the flesh, and especially of his divorce from his wife and his continual longing for her and his family, along with implied other affairs. The trouble is that while each poem can be read on its own they inevitably lead the reader to other poems with similar ideas, phrases or images. Using the conventions of medieval Tamil poetry, conventions still found in other Asian poetries, any mention of the scene can carry a fixed significance; even the mention of a colour is meant to act like a symbol. So each poem should properly be seen as part of the volume, often in paradoxical and ironic, even amusing, ways. Six of the poems are titled 'Love' and the way they and other poems are linked to each other, in imitation of the linkages between past and present, can be gathered from the tree, leaves and colour images of 'LOVE 6: winter'; 'Green leaves on a grey tree / look almost like flowers, sudden smiles on a chickenpox / face, or an accidental/ touch between quarrels.' Someone with an extremely successful career, Ramanujan felt that his domestic life was a failure; he was surprisingly lonely although he had many close friends. This personal side of his life is in the poems, often distanced by irony or humour, and it would be a mistake to neglect the autobiographical for the larger, philosophical and psychological themes. There is no satisfactory way around the problems raised by a work that an author left unfinished and *The Black Hen* must be regarded as unfinished as a volume of poetry despite the quality of many of the poems.

It is significant of how poetry in English was moving from the margins to the centre of Indian culture that Gieve Patel's first two books were published by Ezekiel and Clearing House while his third was published by Oxford University Press as an Oxford paperback. With his poetry, plays and paintings Patel is very much part of the culture of Bombay. While his *Mirrored, Mirroring* (1991) carries further the movement towards even greater economy, compression, understatement and irony in his poetry—a tendency also noticeable in new volumes by Mehrotra, Ramanujan and de Souza—what at first appears surprising is its sudden avowal of spirituality. The initial poem, 'The Difficulty' begins

> In the beginning
> it is difficult
> even to say,
> 'God',

and the volume concludes 'Embattled mind, settle down so / to sweet quietude.' Patel's emphasis on the physical, on the body's suffering, his awareness of the world's violence, and of such conflicting emotions within the self as the co-presence of love and violence in sexuality, or of compassion and hate towards the wounded, and of his own inner conflicts along with a crisis in his life led him to an ashram and a quest for inner peace. The poems in *Mirrored, Mirroring* form moments from a narrative, 'God or / something like that / shot / through each part of you.' Some of the story is alluded to in de Souza's *Talking Poems: Conversations with Poets.*

Patel is not a confessional poet and the details are vague, but it seems that his sexual desires were part of what made him seek spiritual peace. In 'Hill Station', 'Each ecstatic thrust is/ Freely contaminate with an appetite for lice.' In 'My Affections': 'Such odour, such rioting—/ The eroticism of twelve lives / Crowded into one, now / At a stroke thinned.' God becomes his new love, someone with whom he is having an affair. The ashram, being away from the grime and noise and bad air of the city, make access to his new love possible. He uses such images to describe his new condition as life without the burdens of the past, such as the image of a donkey and building a new house. These are of course the kind of simple metaphoric analogies that are so effective in the seventeenth-century religious poetry of George Herbert's *The Temple*, and in such a poem as 'In Just Two Years, Said the Dream' the model is Herbert's great poem 'Love' with the imagery of Christ's sacrifice being recalled in the Eucharist communion within His church. It is possible Patel's models were also Indian, such as Akho, the Gujarati mystic he translated. I am not so concerned with Patel's 'source' (although it should be remembered that poetry is a language learned by imitation) as by his turning to a religious poet as part of the discipline he feels he needs. To imitate a poem can also mean trying to imitate the state of mind in the poem. Herbert's conversations with his God have become one example or exercise of a universal meditative technique which, stripped of its doctrinal specifics, crosses boundaries and can be found in most cultures and religions.

Reading Manohar Shetty's *Domestic Creatures* (1994) I am struck by how personal life is the same throughout the world—change a few names and allusions, and the poems could have been written in any country; they have the universality of the personal, of feelings that are a recognizable part of life. They are as the volume's title says 'domestic'. In 'Dialogue with a child' there is passing of time, pain, memories of the ideal, and the relationship of time, pain and memory to the making of art, relationships that are natural to living. The details of life convey the truth.

> Yes, that's a pretty scene.
> It's pressed into the page
> By a hot iron.

> And inside that glass
> Paperweight the flowers
> Are frozen.

> No, they're not rings
> In the tree stump
> But my footprints.

I like a title like *Domestic Creatures*. It does not begin with an idea of Indianness or an ideology; its quality comes from its concentration on the personal, the known, the genuinely observed and what it really means. It is different from yet as specific as the stripped-down poetry of Mehrotra and de Souza. It is too often assumed that Indian poetry, or any national literature, must be unique, must have some special attribute, such as spirituality or dialect. That, however, is a false, politicized, notion of authenticity which results in stereotypes and dishonesty of intellect and emotions. The novelist Amit Chaudhuri observed ('Lure of the Hybrid'; *Times Literary Supplement*, September 1999: 5–6):

One of the subtlest ways, indeed, in which the multilingual imagination enters an Indian text has to do with the use of English words—not transmuted or 'appropriated and subverted for the post-colonial's own ends', as the current dogma has it, but estrangingly, in their ordinary and standard forms; yet this is a practice whose import has been insufficiently acknowledged or studied. The peculiar excitement of the poetry that Ramanujan, Arvind Mehrotra or Dom Moraes (to take only three examples) wrote in the 1960s and 70s derived not so much from their, to use Rushdie's word, 'chutnification' of the language, but, in part, from the way they used ordinary English words like 'door', 'window', 'bus', 'doctor', 'dentist', 'station', to suggest a way of life. This was, and continues to be, more challenging than it may first appear; as a young reader, I remember being slightly repelled by the India of post-offices and railway compartments I found in these poems; for I didn't think the India I lived in a fit subject for poetry. The poets I have mentioned appeared to make no overt attempts to 'appropriate' or 'subvert' the language, because the English language was already theirs, linked not so much to the colonizer as to their sense of self and history; these poets' use of language had less to do with the colonizer than with the modern Indian's exploration, and rewriting of himself.

Shetty has given examples of how a poem may begin with an image of a fruitless avocado tree, a cauliflower, a brinjal, or his daughter's asthma. The image in itself is an empty picture which needs to be linked to reality, brought into a wider human canvas, shaped by language and emotion, made into a 'meaningful metaphor' with an identity of its own ('Writer at Work', *Gentleman*, July 1997: 117).

The concentration on the self, on the place, on reality itself, even the reality of the imaginings, has always been at the heart of what Arvind Krishna Mehrotra learned from Ezra Pound's imagism and from W. C. Williams' insistence on locality. Here is Mehrotra's 'Approaching Fifty' in *The Transfiguring Places* (1998); he is no longer the young rebel, experimentalist and formalist, but instead a mature poet who has polished his craft to a classic minimalism:

> Sometimes,
> In unwiped bathroom mirrors,
> He sees all three faces
> Looking at him:
>
> His own,
> The grey-haired man's
> Whose life policy has matured,
> And the mocking youth's
> Who paid the first premium.

I have quoted the complete poem. And it is marvellous. It seems so easy to write such verse, but it could provide subject matter for an essay in itself with its patterning of 's' and nasal sounds at the line ends, its compressed imagery and symbolism, its internal rhymes and harmonies, even its descent and difference from and relationship to such A. K.

Ramanujan poems as 'Self-Portrait' and 'Instead of a Farewell'. There is now a tradition behind such a poem; not a tradition of conscious Indianness, rather of poets learning from each other and their own previous work how to write about themselves and what they experience. It is not a tradition that shuts out foreign literatures, but somewhere along the line the building blocks, the models, the intertexuality, started having mostly Indian rather than foreign sources as the poetry developed its own history.

Contemporary culture values youth and newness, but there is something to be said for maturing as a poet. As with wines the passage of time may polish off those rough edges and better bring out the essential flavour. The verse and diction of Keki Daruwalla's *A Summer of Tigers* (1995) is smoother than in the earlier poems, the manner and matter more reflective. There is the same tough common sense, along with a distrust of ideologies, and a puzzlement at how history repeats itself without people learning from it. The first poem in the volume begins 'Players change, but not the crime, / dagger-moment, word and deed.' First there is the betrayal and killing of Julius Caesar by Brutus in ancient Rome 'On the abacus of time / history rearranges beads; ... nothing can reverse the tide.' The second half of the poem tells of an assassination in modern Argentina of a gaucho by his grandson—'He dies, not knowing he has died, / to re-enact a Roman scene.' Later in the volume Daruwalla addresses the famous South American Communist poet Pablo Neruda, 'Pablo, as you must have known, / they always fall in their metaphoric togas. / (Caesar, of course, fell/ with the real one on his back.)' Throughout history there are betrayals and killings in the name of some revolutionary justice:

> We don't know whom to believe; each one
> turns the tourniquet when he gets the chance.
> The ones who dined on the revolution
> for fifty years were no different.
> Ceausescu was a bigger bastard
> than any dictator on your continent.
>
> You talked of the bombs
> and the 'murdering gas' in Vietnam,
> but not a word on the Prague of 1968
> not a word on the Budapest of 1956,
> as if the Soviets never had a tank.

In the next poem Daruwalla mocks both Neruda's blindness to
Communist atrocities and the blindness of those intellectuals who,
while proclaiming non-alignment and socialism, were sympathetic
to the Soviets during the Cold War. He imagines Neruda in India:

> And you would have
> enjoyed talking to Nehru.
> He would have given you such a dose
> on non-alignment and non-violence and socialism
> that who knows, you'd have stayed on and perhaps accepted
> a Visiting Professorship at JNU.

Daruwalla's technique may at first seem that of free verse, but despite
the way the lines break there are many scattered end and internal
rhymes ('you', 'Nehru', 'you', 'who', 'you'd', 'JNU') and the rhythm
feels like an iambic pentameter that has been strung over the line
breaks and generally been loosened to resemble colloquial speech. In
many ways such poems recall such great satirists as Dryden, Johnson
and Auden in their compressed metaphors ('dined on the revolution'),
subtle barbs ('He would have given you such a dose') and unexpected
endings. In 'History', Daruwalla retells the teaching at school of the
usual heroic story of Aryan horsemen invading India from the north
and then settling down, which he contrasts with the beauties, ironies
and injustices of real life. 'This too was history / though no one ever
wrote of it.' Daruwalla's poetry is often concerned with such history.

It would be a mistake, however, to see Daruwalla's poetry as only
concerned with society and politics; they are for him part of a larger
problem, how we give meaning to life. His view of life is existentialist.
There is a scepticism towards large ideas whether religious, political
or intellectual. He can be amazed by, and write impressively of, those
who willingly suffer for their beliefs. He sees life as a void that needs to
be given significance. 'Writing is more than mere self-expression. It is
also an attempt at transcendence of sorts.' 'The seed of the void is within
us all .... With age this little pocket of emptiness expands. Writing
helps me erect battlements against the expanding void' ('Writer at Work',
Gentleman, August 1997: 116).

Kamala Das was the first modern woman poet to create a name for
herself and a body of recognizable work, but it was difficult for others
with less flamboyant personalities to build upon her achievement. A
breakthrough came with Eunice de Souza's *Fix* which was almost the
opposite of Kamala Das's poetics in its carefully crafted social portraits,

ironic memories and economy. While de Souza is still best known for those quietly angry yet somehow compassionate portraits of the society in which she was raised, her writing has moved on. De Souza's *Women in Dutch Painting* (1988) contrasts ideals of feminine quiet and calm assurance with the poet's personal disquiet and questing. There is a marvellously ironic comparison of herself with Kali as she, self-conscious of her appearance, stands before her bank manager: 'I look striking in red and black / and a necklace of skulls.' Rather than self-dramatizing and trustful of her own voice, de Souza is often epigrammatic and distanced.

Although it could be argued that she writes well-edited, personal reflections in what I think of as the manner of the Mumbai poets influenced by Ezekiel, she also shows another, more extreme, idea of poetry. She eliminates most of the usual attractive characteristics of verse and this results in a distinctly new style, a minimalism. This poetic in which tone, sound and the bare thing said in the fewest of possible words is extreme, but related to a similar economy and conscious self-limitation in Arvind Mehrotra's later poetry. Such a poetics of a minimalist imagism was at times shared by Ramanujan, and might be thought of as a school or movement of poetry on its own. I know of poets in other countries who write that way; indeed it is tempting for any artist to ask what are the essential bare bones of my art, but that three major Indian poets, de Souza, Mehrotra and Ramanujan, share such an aesthetic makes them a movement.

While de Souza's *Ways of Belonging: Selected Poems* (1990) and *Selected and New Poems* (1994) differ somewhat in their selection, the *New Poems* come closest to the purity of the poetic which has increasingly governed her poetry. Here is the complete 'It's Time to Find a Place', a poem which alludes to its own conventions:

> It's time to find a place
> to be silent with each other.
> I have prattled endlessly
> in staff-rooms, corridors, restaurants.
> When you are not around
> I carry on conversations in my head.
> Even this poem
> has forty-eight words too many.

Through economy, clarity, avoidance of ornamentation and metaphor, an appearance of detachment and the dampening down of emotions, de Souza packs a lot of hidden feelings into a small package. This seems like making prose do the work of poetry. But wait a minute, where does that rhythm come from? The poem hovers around, departing from and returning to an eight-syllable line. It consists of four two-line statements. There are such echoing patterns as 'time', 'find', 'silent', 'forty', 'many', 'to find' 'to be', 'too many'. And what about those final two lines, especially as the poem is not 48 words but only 42 without the title; do they not create a striking complication in which the poem itself becomes a metaphor for the 'prattle'. One result of such an analogy is that the poem itself becomes its aesthetic which necessarily creates a second level of interpretation with the poem being about writing poetry as well as being a supposedly factual statement about a relationship with some person. I say supposedly because suddenly we might wonder if there really was a personal relationship and whether the poem might not always have been about writing poetry. And why does she need to find a place for silence? Silent places are for prayer, perhaps assignations, maybe a silent place for a silent poem without words? The more I look at those 42 words the more poetry they become. This is the kind of minimalism de Souza, Mehrotra and A. K. Ramanujan share and while it develops from imagism there are plenty of precedents for it in older Indian poetry, especially in some of the poetry Ramanujan and Mehrotra have translated, although the conventions in the past were different.

Meena Alexander, in contrast to Eunice de Souza, is inclined towards poetry that is incantatory and meditational. Memories, desires and fiction merge as she examines the construction of her identity and its relationship to family history, actuality, being a woman and writing poetry. Although she has written some very good individual poems, her writing seems more a world of process than de Souza's fixity. Alexander's power comes from poems resonating upon each other within a volume or as her work is followed from book to book. She has written about phenomenology and women in Romanticism; her poetry is similarly concerned with the creation of the self, especially the feminine self and what it means to be Indian if you live abroad.

House of a Thousand Doors (1988) mixes verse and prose to form a self-contained, private emotional world of images, symbols and obsessions. Houses represent fixity, shelter, rootedness and in Alexander's poetry, like that of Kamala Das, are associated with a maternal family house in Kerala. Alexander recalls two grandmothers, one political, the other domestic. The former stands for her feminist consciousness, the latter presents her own longing for roots after a life spread across India,

Africa, England and now the United States. Many of the memories in the book are false, imaginings created by desire including, seemingly, the political grandmother. The problem of how to combine the two sides of her desires is temporarily solved by the creation of literature, which is also the creation of herself in a world in which she feels 'abandoned'.

Alexander introduces *The Storm: A Poem in Five Parts* (1989) by comparing it to one of those fans made by folding a sheet of paper. Reading her poem is like watching the scenes on such a fan, the narrative comes in bits and pieces. Instead of unity there is the act of reading, an ordering which Alexander sees as similar to 'parts of the feminine world'. *Night-Scene, the Garden* (1992) is a ten-part poetic, dramatic sequence in several voices which has been performed in New York. It also recalls her maternal home in Kerala and the fate of several women associated with her childhood. Although meant for performance the sequence is basically a meditation in which one of the starting points is an experience in a garden when Alexander felt that she could only possess the world through being a poet. Her poetry resembles that of Jayanta Mahapatra in the way her writing foregrounds the provisional creation of the self through writing, in her use of abstract symbols (sky, star, sun), and in its focus on the mind, its obsessions, desires, and essential loneliness. She has been writing for decades, living in different countries ranging from Sudan and England to India and the United States where she now lives. Her poetry still reveals a tendency towards the abstract high lyricism found in her early French verse written in Sudan, and she remains influenced by a phenomenological approach to the existence of the self and its expression in art, a topic examined in the doctorate she wrote in England. As a university professor living in New York she tends to be influenced by literary and intellectual fashions. During a time when postcolonialism is the discourse of the month and when there is excitement in mixing literary genres, and when there is a fashion for autobiographies, especially by those thought minorities and multicultural, it is perhaps not surprising that her *The Shock of Arrival: Reflections on Post-Colonial Experience* (1997) should intermingle selections from her verse with autobiographical prose. This appearance of keeping up with intellectual fashions can be misleading. She has always been a restless writer and the nature of her vision of reality means that it must always change and should never be fixed since the inner core is always the search for self-articulation and definition in a world of changing situations.

CHAPTER SEVENTEEN

New Women Poets

SHIVDASANI, PATEL, D'SOUZA, SAMBRANI, DHARKER,
DIVAKARUNI, BHATT

Poetry in English by Indian women has been seen at odds with traditional culture. This is another issue overtaken by modern society in which what is supposedly traditional is often a guise for gaining or keeping power when faced with the liberating effects of democracy, education and urbanization. According to traditionalists Sita should be the model for women, but, of course, there are many versions of the *Ramayana*, some of which might be thought feminist. Traditions are what you make of them; there are always other versions available, as can be seen in Ruth Vanita's *A Play of Light* (1994) which contrasts images of Sita the dominated with Saraswati, the unmarried goddess. In Menka Shivdasani's *Nirvana at Ten Rupees* (1990) social conventions and cultural myths are enemies of the repressed, angry, imaginative self. A poem titled 'Protein-rich' concludes: 'The egg yolks choke in the freezer, / and I, stiff as a refrigerator, / pride of place in a middle-class home.' Watching the *Ramayana* on television 'like yet another nightmare. Somebody's / crying as usual, tomato ketchup / oozing past a knife. And here, something else / coagulates beneath my eyelash ... I want to stick my fangs into Sita, / but she vanishes just as I strike.'

Whereas previously the existence of a woman poet inevitably led to questions about her relationship with the feminist movement, now that the feminists have helped free women from being expected to express a narrow range of opinions, feminist ideology has taken its place within a broad spectrum of topics including the complications of a single life, problems of marriage and life abroad. Women have more education, more exposure and are more financially independent than ever before. Poetry in English by women is part of the modernization of Indian society including its participation in a global system of education and economics which has replaced the older colonial and imperial networks.

For urban middle class women, this means education at good schools and universities, some experience of a liberated life, time abroad, careers, and either a single life or a marriage in which both husband and wife work. It is very different from being raised among women followed by a traditional marriage and serving one's husband.

Menka Shivdasani's *Nirvana at Ten Rupees* (1990) was one of a very small number of books published in an edition of 500 under the supervision of Adil Jussawalla by Praxis. A careful selection spanning twelve years' work, it remains one of the best first books of poetry to appear during the 1990s. Some of the poems were written when Shivdasani was still at school, others soon after. They are obviously the work of a young poet using as models poets studied in classes. They show the progress of a young woman from a student through the early stages of a career to a mother.

Shivdasani, a well-travelled journalist who worked for a year in Hong Kong, was one of the founding members of the Bombay Poetry Circle in 1986. In her poetry, she anticipated many of the new characteristics of Bombay poetry as it would develop during the 1990s. There was the inclusion of the filth, power shortages, bugs, noise and other disagreeable aspects of the city's life. There were the horrors and temptations of living alone in a small flat, the anxieties of a 'single' life, which were complicated by being a woman. While her poetry alludes to a world of drugs, sex, bad food, broken relationships and sleepless nights, there is also wit, irony, knowingness, and a marvellous imagination. Shivdasani can use vulgar speech, make expressionist and confessional remarks, but the poetry is always highly imaged, clever, surprising, amusing and self-mocking.

Her poetry holds together a private world of chaotic emotions through its logical development and its strikingly imaginative images. 'Hinges' begins 'I found my body / hinged like any other door' and concludes, 'Now I'm building / another body for myself.' The opening metaphoric statement and its logical development could be from one of those seventeenth-century George Herbert religious lyrics about the self and God. 'Today's Fairy Tale' begins 'Hold me, octopus. / Your eight arms are not enough.' and similarly develops logically though several shifts in tone and direction to a self-analytical observation but almost surreal image: 'Were you really there or did I / only imagine your tentacles / sprouting from my scalp?' These appear to be early poems as is the witty 'Schoolgirl No More': 'I learnt the mechanics / of bird-flying in Biology / but did not possess the wings.' Her poems are

often continuous metaphors making use of puns, refer to body parts
and result in unusual scenes. 'Spring-Cleaning' begins strikingly: 'That
was your skull on the bottom shelf, / staring socketless at my ankle'
and develops:

> Carelessly draped on a hanger, I found an arm
> leaning bonily towards the perfumes;
> in another corner, a dislocated knee.
> Did you run away so fast, you broke your leg?
> I wish you'd wipe that foolish
> toothless grin off your stupid face.
> You needn't be embarrassed about letting
> me down. Other men have too, and they
> didn't disintegrate like you.

This is like Jacobean 'metaphysical' poetry of wit, with its mixture of
opposites; there is even a similar use of the grotesque and macabre.
    The title of the volume comes from 'Loser, Loser, Addict', another
poem about the disappointments of a love affair:

> When you are happy, only clichés
> come to mind—the sky is blue,
> grass is green, butterflies are free.
> Then something happens, and solitary
> as a murderer, you twist the knife
> and stalk the streets, your brain
> being crushed to powder like the contents
> of a vial of smack. Nirvana at ten rupees
> is cheap, but the sky has a silvery tinge
> you would rather perceive as grey,
> the butterflies are pinned, heads down,
> their backs to the wall, like you.

The drama, compression, rapid development, logic and narrative are
impressive as is the use of rhyme or the significant repetitions of 'you'
which moves from the second word of line one to the middle of line
five, is echoed in 'your' in line six, renews its importance at the start
of line ten and then strongly concludes the stanza as the final word.
This is very much a poem about the self as 'you'—someone observed,
analysed and judged—not a complaining 'I'.
    The highly metaphoric, at times almost surreal, imagination and
the logical development found in such early poems as 'Hinges' are still

characteristic of the later 'Repair Job' about a more mature woman alienated from the expected conventions of social life, strongly aware of her sexuality and mental unrest, her inner and outer life at odds. It begins powerfully: 'Yesterday I slit a jugular / That strayed into a corner of my brain.' No one notices; 'they said: "See the roses in her cheeks!"' After some marvellous sexual imagery (read the poem for yourself, don't expect it all here) she 'stuck the slits together with gum. / Nobody notices what happened; / the businessman—he smiled and proposed.'

A poem about having a carpenter build a table contrasts the poet as a self-conscious social being ('anxious hostess') and her real self angry with the world, bothered by the noise of the carpenter's work, tempted by men she has recently met, and thinking of her own modern version of being in love with what Keats termed easeful death. 'I would gladly drink potassium cyanide, / innocuous in a lovely frosted glass, / a cherry sinking gently to the bottom.' The volume has its own implied autobiographical narrative as it moves chronologically beyond the schoolgirl and the working woman alone in a flat to a home owner and mother. Real life remains stifling, far from the desires of the imagination and urges of the body.

Shivdasani mocks the easy but destructive Nirvana of smack at ten rupees, but at the heart of the volume is a similar urge for a paradise or a nirvana, something better than the anxieties, dishonesties, repression, false needs and basic ugliness of ordinary life. In 'Four Walls' she feels like a fly trapped in a spider's web, she has lost her freedom through being drugged by 'garbage': 'Somewhere in those trapped / gauze wings is a freedom born of shit, buzzing / self-satisfied after a meal of garbage.'

Tara Patel's one book, *Single Woman* (1991), assumes that being a woman is in itself a perspective on life. Using a simple vocabulary and an elementary sense of versification, craft and rhyme, Patel manages to create forceful images and poems that have a personal voice and tell a continuing story, a story which gains from being recognizable. The title of her volume is itself significant of a modern woman living alone without the securities of family and a husband about which other women complain. 'I cannot live like you mother .... I cannot be a dutiful daughter.' Her world is that of a modern woman with the illusions and pains of love, education, being on one's own. Violence, domination and neglect are lesser problems than the experience of pain and the wish to avoid what can hurt. She does not have the alienation from her feelings, the hiding of what one feels and thinks that Imtiaz Dharker writes about; rather there is anger at the way 'A woman's life is a reaction

/ to the crack of a whip. / She learns to dodge it as it whistles around her.' The poems which follow concern the effects of such reaction on memory and in the isolation from others, 'You want to talk to someone.' 'You feel trapped in your dreams.' There is the collective common wisdom of women: 'If you catch a man by his balls / his heart and mind will follow.' Patel, like many women Indian poets, has a directness and frankness about sexual matters seldom found among the males. 'Even a one-night stand is luxury ... He is another woman's man.' She refuses to go to bed with an American she met on a Goan beach, but: 'For weeks I can brood of nothing else. / He is a growing regret.'

Although the poems complain about the treatment of women by men they are the opposite of misandry. The speaker wants a man, wants companionship, wants love, but throughout the volume there is a feeling of having missed out, and of the costs and price of easy sex, of casual affairs, of being outside the easy joys and conquests of life. 'Sometimes for old times sake / you should look me up. / Have lunch with me, I'll pay the bill. ... I miss you most when I'm eating alone.' There is the awareness of age and death, of the lowering of expectations, 'You can go blind looking for the choice / tidbits of love. ... But unfed and unbanked hungers / can kill you, / you cannot kill them.' There are affairs with married men, with older men, 'This city breeds homelessness / in women, in me.' 'Time passes even when unemployed. ... Unemployed people try to sleep at any / time of day.'

The power of *Single Woman* is in the larger story rather than in individual poems; here is the pain that can follow rebellion, living by one's self, failing at making a romantic marriage, dreary jobs, urban loneliness, living in hostels, growing old. It is a story about being an older single woman, but also about the modern condition and the disappointments of freedom. This is a poetry of failure, which in itself is remarkable. Art, no matter how much about tragedy or even if about victims, usually ends in victories, triumphs, affirmation, heaven, dignity. Patel simply ignores such expectations and conventions. She has written a book of poems about life's disasters without pretending it really is not so bad after all.

By now there are a number of subjects that are known as likely to be found in poems by women. There are poems to their mothers (whom they have probably defied, rebelled against and left), poems to their grandmothers (likely to be associated with traditions, an older feminism or an alternative home), and poems about motherhood and poems about successful artists or women who in some way have been heroic. Security is attractive, but is also a trap, a falseness to oneself, a purdah. Charmayne D'Souza often writes of the attractions of insecurity, the fun of anxieties. She can be witty about risks and satirical towards those who do not take risks. 'A Maiden's Prayer' amusingly contrasts real desires with the supposed peace of a night alone 'without a man'. Hugging a pillow the maiden desires what she lacks: 'Security / from the vagaries of love / can only offer me / its own cares.' In 'White Line Down the Road in Minnesota', the line painted in the middle of the road to separate traffic going in different directions becomes a symbol with many meanings including: 'a life-line for those moving on, / a strait-jacket / for those yet unborn.'

It is easy to neglect her short poems with their short lines and simple rhymes, especially as many of them preach, make obvious points, even rant about social issues. How can someone who wrote 'Subway Vigilante', 'God's Will' or 'Train of Thought II' be a poet? She is, however. Her *A Spelling Guide to Woman* (1991) was introduced by Ezekiel and there are selections from it in both Eunice de Souza's and Paranjape's anthologies. She is capable of such amazing imagery as 'Shark fins / swim through snowdrifts, / then leer past you / as mere rocks' in 'Winter in South Dakota', a poem in which she, like thousands of previous and future poets, seeks new and interesting ways to describe the way a heavy snowfall can make the world seem pure and innocent as it covers everything with whiteness. Then there is 'Strange Bedfellows', a perverse poem about the relationship that can exist between desire, sexuality, violence and death. It is a poem which can be interpreted in several different ways, and gains some of its power from the way the language itself moves from the incantation of 'Seven time around / the fire of my shots', through the weaving speech rhythms of 'What I have done / is done / for all my unborn sons', to the double vision of hanging and sexual penetration in 'and a swift sharp / erection / into death.' There is the macabre humour of 'When God First Made a Whore':

> One day,
> God will ask for this sweaty body
> of mine,
> but, like all the rest,
> He will have to stand in line.
>
> So said the whore,
> as they asked for more.

Her poems appear easy, but often they take unexpected directions and the attitude is baffling. 'I Would Like to Have a Movie Cowboy for a Husband' is a jokey title, but the description of 'Our lovemaking ... our orgasms' with its 'crisp certainty / of death' is disturbing. The amusing parody cowboy life of 'fried bread, beans and hash' takes a twist with the 'guarantee' that it will only last a few years,

> that our marriage could be
> deliciously wiped out,
> like an Indian tribe,
> forever.

The idea of the male is desirable for a time as is sex and security—then it is time to move on. But 'deliciously wiped out' has that same perversity and love of risk noticeable elsewhere, even in the connection between orgasms and death, while the reminder of the extinction of the Indians makes clear that she knows that her imagination is playing with danger and violence. D'Souza is a poet of risks, of strange bedfellows.

Even nice young women from middle-class Hindu families are writing poetry in English, cursing their fathers and moving to America. Mukta Sambrani's *The Woman in this Room Isn't Lonely* (1997) is a book of surprising intensity and imagination. Sanbrani has a lyricism and fanciful imagination seldom seen in English-language poetry in recent decades. (It is at times made even more surreal by the usual Writers Workshop misprints.) The titles of the poems, pointing to their basic source in the anxieties of a young female, are similar to the themes found in other women poets although her poems develop very differently—'Idea of Freedom', 'Idea of a Wife', 'The Colour of Desire', 'Birthing', 'Bastard Poem', 'Dear Father', 'An Apple for Mother', 'Her Mother's House', 'He Asks', 'That Is Not My Name', and 'Female Ancestor'. Want an unusual feminist love–hate poem?

> The man with the plastic heart
> unhooks his heart-lung machine
> and bends down to kiss
>
> ....
>
> She opens her breast pocket,
> finds the heart-shaped candy,
> chews it into gum
> and spits after him.
> Her heart dissolves.
> Streaks of blood die downstream.

As with many of Sambrani's poems, while the literal meaning is clear, I am uncertain how to explicate the metaphoric meaning of each image and that is part of their attraction.

She shares with Mahapatra and Chitre an instinct towards suggesting a world of multiple significances. There is a surreal characteristic of different kinds of realms of being interpenetrating so that the familiar suddenly involves the unexpected and becomes almost magical. A poem about a man and woman in bed is anything but sentimental. Sambrani's economy, independence of mind, hard-headedness and irony combine into a rapidly dramatic scene which within twelve lines becomes grotesquely comic :

> The idea of a wife
> begins to nudge
> at his bed-side.
>
> Maybe she will
> make two-a.m. soups
> for his whim and him.
>
> He turns to the woman.
> 'Let's', he says.
> 'Fuck', she says.
>
> They share a tall glass of water.
> Then there is a knock on the door.
> 'That must be your wife', she says.

There is the contrast between the simple diction and the surprisingly rich pattern of sounds ('wife', 'begins', 'side', 'will', 'soups', 'whim', 'him', 'women', 'says', 'says', 'water', 'door', 'says'). There are the dramatic ambiguities. Is 'Fuck' what is on her mind, what she wants, what she will be able to do more of in marriage, or is it her rejection of his thoughts of getting married and being taken care of? There is that 'tall glass of water' with its ironies of being both a cliché and an understated way of suggesting reflection, the cooling of passion (is this afterwards or instead of?). Is the wife interrupting their love-making a grotesque future produced by the imagination or perhaps his real wife? The wife has swiftly evolved from the start of an idea to that knock on the door ending the love-making.

By now there is a tradition in Indian poems of the coming of poetry as something mysterious. Sambrani's version is totally unexpected. Her 'Bastard poem' comes directly after a poem titled 'Birthing' ('I call, I break / the window. / I hear voices under the sea.'); it

... will rush home to me
like men to their wives.
It will come on scraps borrowed from strangers,
from someone else's ink
and I will love it
like my blood.
It will be mine.
My bastard child.

This is an amusing, or imaginative description of intertextuality, an intertextuality that the poem itself demonstrates by its use of topics and phrases common to other poems to produce 'My bastard child'.

The situation develops a few poems later with 'Dear father ... I always wanted to come home happy ... and I wanted to place your grandchild on your lap' which suddenly erupts into

Time's up father.
Yours and mine.
All my friends have finished having babies
and your friends finished taking them for strolls.
Don't ask me father what I have done with it
like I asked you
for the doll you had forgotten to buy me.
I am sorry father, I forgot.

This is a marvellously dramatic poem with its many shifts in attitudes and tones and its hard-hitting yet low-profiled contrasts and repetitions ('yours', 'mine', 'my friends', 'your friends', 'finished', 'finished', 'you had forgotten', 'I forgot'). What seems at first an apologetic or indifferent poem contains a strong assertion of independence shown by the concluding pronouns—'you' 'me' 'I' 'I'.

The next poem in the volume is 'An Apple for Mother' about women living only to give birth to a child and then dying:

and mother had a seven pound baby girl
who grew into an apple-eating woman
who says 'Mother, kiss me and you'll die happy'.

The poem contrasts the innocent apple of a supposedly pastoral past when women existed to become mothers with the apple of sexual knowledge and personal choices; its ironic conclusion is shocking in its contrast between the language of tenderness and hatred. Urban, single, irreligious, from a middle-class Hindu family, part of the Mumbai poetry scene during the late 1990s, Mukta Sambrani, who recently moved to the United States, is heir to Mamta Kalia, Adrienne Rich (her favourite poet) and the fragmentation of the traditional family that is noticeable, especially in the larger cities, as India modernizes and more people have a secular education in English and qualifications they can use in the modern world.

Imtiaz Dharker's *Purdah* (1989) introduced a major new voice, someone as distinctive in her own way as Mamta Kalia, Kamala Das and Eunice de Souza. Dharker brought to Indian poetry a different background and a sense of political commitment. One of the few poets from a Muslim background, she was raised in Scotland and broke with her Pakistani family to marry an Indian and move to India. Her poetry is consciously feminist, consciously political, consciously that of a multiple outsider, someone who knows her own mind, rather than someone full of doubt and liberal ironies. She has a poet's instinctive talent for cadence, the sounds of words and rhyme. Although she appears to write free verse her lines are rhythmic, and despite differing lengths often have a strong iambic feel. There are linkages of sound in the end words of lines: 'said', 'shame', ' safety', 'skin', 'in', 'sin'. As a painter and film-maker she has an instinct for images. Her poems have both an argumentative and dramatic structure; in examining the personal she becomes universal. 'Purdah I' takes its setting from specifics of Muslim culture, specifics that are criticized, but it is also a metaphor for the way women retreat into shells to be safe from disapproval and harm; it is a condition of the mind under social pressure and stress where eventually one loses a sense of being true to oneself:

> One day they said
> she was old enough to learn some shame.
> She found it came quite naturally.
>
> Purdah is a kind of safety.
> The body finds a place to hide.
> The cloth fans out against the skin
> much like the earth that falls
> on coffins after they put the dead men in.

Purdah is an alienation from one's own self, a doing of what is expected rather than what one feels. And this, in Dharker's view, results from the shame women are taught early on about their gender and sexuality:

> She half-remembers things
> from someone else's life,
> perhaps from yours, or mine—
> carefully carrying what we do not own:
> between the thighs, a sense of sin.

'Purdah II' interweaves Dharker's own conflicts between the comforts of a Muslim identity, based on how she was raised, and the actuality of studying the Koran: 'nudging words into your head;/words unsoiled by sense, / pure rhythm on the tongue.' Even in studying the Koran there was sexuality. 'The new Hajji .... There was nothing holy in his look. / Hands that prayed at Mecca / dropped a sly flower on your Book.' There is a powerful criticism of Muslim treatment of women and especially of ways such customs are intensified within the diaspora. While women are viewed as slaves and commodities the worst effect is on the spirit, the falseness between what women feel and what they are allowed to show, the distance between them and their social selves.

At the heart of the problem, according to the analysis suggested by Dharker's poems, is female sexuality. Culture uses shame to repress female sexuality and the independence of spirit which is a part of it.

> They have all been sold and bought,
> the girls I knew,
> unwilling virgins who had been taught,
> especially in this strangers' land, to bind
> their brightness tightly round,
> whatever they might wear,
> in the purdah of the mind.

Custom, tradition, religious and ethnic history reinforce such mental purdah, and such a tradition and sense of history is used by diasporas to keep control of their women by telling them that their customs are superior to those of the foreigner:

> A horde of dead men
> held up your head,
> above the mean temptations
> of those alien hands.
> You answered to your race.

Her poetry can transcend the personal to become that of a community, especially the diaspora of Muslim women in England:

There are so many of me.
I have met them, meet them every day,
recognise their shadows on the streets.
I know their past and future
in the cautious way they place their feet.
I can see behind their veils,
and before they speak
I know their tongues, thick
with the burr of Birmingham
or Leeds.

Purdah had four distinct sections—Purdah, The Haunted House, The Child Sings, Borderlines—each section grouping together poems around a basic theme. The opening Purdah section includes 'Purdah I', 'Purdah II', 'Grace', 'Prayer' and 'Sacrifice', poems which specifically use Islamic religious teachings and rituals as settings or analogies. In 'Grace' the title provides an ironic contrast between God's mercy (and the graciousness of the architecture of a mosque) and the ungraciousness of those who see women, especially during her period, as defiling. 'He does not look at you. / Instead ... "She trails the month behind her./We are defiled."' The Haunted House is about the social tensions of home, whether being a foreigner living in England, conflicts whether or not to leave home and social resentments towards those who have apparently made good, including enjoyment at their failures of assimilation:

It was easy to hate, from the tenements,
the ones in the house on the hill.
'They'll come to no good,
daughter's higher-educated, mixing
with "belaiti" boys. They 'll regret it.'

Yes, they will.
Their heads come rolling down the hill.

The Child Sings section has poems about children, motherhood, being a wife, such as 'A Woman's Place': 'If occasionally you need to scream, do it / alone but in front of a mirror/ where you can see the strange shape the mouth makes / before you wipe it off.' The sequence ends not with emphasis on the husband bringing another woman home (although that happens), but on the way the wife has herself become 'Another Woman' from what she was after years of shopping for food in the market, counting 'her coins out carefully', cooking, facing her hostile mother-in-law, waiting for and on her husband, being alone. Society, religion and her culture have given her no options, no other possibilities, 'it was the only choice / that she had ever known.' This leads to 'Choice' which concludes 'Mother, I find you staring back at me. // When did my body agree / to wear your face?' Women try to escape the fate of their mothers and the way mothers attempt to mould them, but eventually, with age, the rebellious woman herself becomes a mother and recapitulates the ways and attitudes of her own mother.

So it is not only religion or Islamic culture, it is also relationships, love, marriage, motherhood, ageing, which wear a woman down into submission, into being false to herself, into mental purdah. Life consists of dangerous borderlines. The self is distinct yet involved in a battle of the sexes; love, indeed all identity, is confining. In 'Battle-line' the two lovers have been brought together by desire, but after sex they remain distinct, distrustful of each other, sleeping back to back like two different countries. Making love is like war, an attack. There are borders between people, checkpoints at which to halt before being allowed to go through to the other country:

> Checkpoint:
> The place in the throat
> where words are halted,
> not allowed to pass,
> where questions form
> and are not asked.

Relationships, love, marriages, are constant struggles in which people may as much grow apart as together. Small irritations become signs of great differences, of larger failures, of ageing and life catching up, so that even the rebel, even the woman who chooses freedom, is never really free. There is no return to paradise:

> You come into a room;
> strangers haggle over trivial things—
> a grey hair curls in a comb.
> Someone tugs sadly at your sleeve.
> But no one screams.
>
> Because leaving home,
> you call yourself free.

Because, behind you
barbed wire grows
where you once
had planted a tree.

The title *Postcards from God* (1994) is ironic; it assumes that God is
a visitor looking at a world which he does not recognize or approve.
He distrusts his 'interpreters'. He is 'nothing but a space / that some-
one has to fill'. People fill the empty space with the images they cre-
ate. The volume has three major sections, Postcards from God, Nam-
ing the Angels and Bombay: The Name of God. As in *Purdah* the
sections can be read as sequences and the volume as a structure be-
ginning with a general discussion and definition which leads, by the
end of the volume, to the specific and more personal. Two poems
have dates for titles. '6 December 1992' and '8 January 1993', while
a third is simply titled '1993'. The poems concern politics and com-
munal rioting. In 'Seats of Power' she writes: 'Here, in this quiet, civil
room / permission has been given / for the carnage to begin;' in '6
December 1992': ' Outside, / blood runs;' in '8 January 1993': 'A match
is struck and thrown. / The burning has begun. // Afterwards / the
bodies are removed / one by one.' In '1993' she writes of 'these days /
crusted with hate and prejudice.'

Postcards from God is in comparison to *Purdah* less rich in imagery,
allusions and implications. The central notion of God as an absence
which people fill with their desires runs the risk of becoming talky, an
idea. Political poetry is especially difficult to write. Dharker, however,
enriches the poems with other implied dimensions as the way the title
'Seats of Power' coming after the angel sequence makes an ironic
contrast, or the way she images the communal violence as like breaking
glass which of course calls to mind the 'crystal night' when the Nazis
attacked the Jews during Hitler's rise to power. This is committed poetry,
committed to the politics of truth and humanity rather than party or
ideology:

It's not Bombay that burns,
but this specific child
screaming behind a bolted door;
the particular man on fire
trapped inside his locked car.

In 'Minority', in speaking of herself she speaks for most of us:

I was born a foreigner.
I carried on from there
to become a foreigner everywhere
I went, even in the place planted with my relatives

A documentary filmmaker concerned with political injustice, Dharker suggests that it is through working with the problems of craft, or getting art right, that one comes to find one's true self and in doing so an artist will communicate with others. God, others, oneself, Dharker, all are strangers, all outcastes.

until, one day, you meet
the stranger sidling down your street,
realize you know the face
simplified to bone,
look into its outcast eyes
and recognize it as your own.

Postcards from God can be seen as an extension of the themes raised in *Purdah*. Although each book has its own specific subject matter, and the general feel is different, *Postcards* takes up the idea of how people use ideas of religion and culture to gain and enforce power and how violence against others (whether women or those of other religions) is central to society. Dharker is a powerful poet who uses her own situation in society, whether in England or India, to create poetry which examines large social problems. Her two books so far have begun with what might be considered the root of the problem, the origins of how and why ideas of authority are formed. They then take the theme through stages until concluding by focusing it within the self. Some of the individual poems are strong and musical, others may be thought thin and weak, but the scope and ambition are impressive. The poetry of commitment and politics is seldom as successful. Dharker is a painter and both volumes were meant to have accompanying drawings. Unfortunately the 1989 Oxford University Press edition of *Purdah* did not include her drawings which can be found in the Bloodaxe 1997 edition which published both her books together.

Many women poets have lived abroad at some time in their lives, some as children. Meena Alexander lived in Sudan, Sujata Bhatt in the USA, Imtiaz Dharker in Scotland and Tara Patel in Malaysia. Others, including Eunice de Souza and R. B. Nair, have had some of their education abroad. Menka Shivdasani has worked in Hong Kong,

Charmayne D'Souza in the United States. Alexander lives in New York, Bhatt in Bremen. With the increasing number of women living abroad the same question applies as to men: at what point do they stop being part of a diaspora and become, instead, American, British, or of whatever country they are citizens?

Chitra Banerjee Divakaruni and her husband are both Indians, often return to India from the United States, and she writes about India and Indian lives, yet she is one of several Indians who are part of the American literary and cultural scene and are not published in India itself. Best known as a novelist, she began with and continues to write poetry. Her *Leaving Yuba City* (1997), a volume of new and selected older poems, consists of a few poems about the author, such as 'How I Became a Writer' and 'Blackout: Calcutta, 1971' (at the time of the liberation of Bangladesh), intertwined with groups of poems, many from her *Black Candle: Poems about Women from India, Pakistan and Bangladesh* (1991).

Divakaruni has a novelist's sense of movement, narrative economy, point of view and use of memories. The groups of poems range from being raised by Irish nuns in a section titled 'Growing up in Darjeeling' to poems at the end about Indian immigrants in the United States where she becomes a 'we' speaking about the contrast between aspirations and reality. The volume, however, does not constitute a simple biography of selected moments from a life. There are groups of poems about Rajasthan (including the eye-opening 'At the Sati Temple, Bikaner', a poem made powerful by treating its subject with composure), about babies, Indian miniatures, Indian films, touring Europe and Yuba City (an Indian community in Northern California created early in the century by Punjabi farmers who until the 1940s, because of racial laws, were unable to bring brides to the United States). Although varied, the poems suggest two intertwined themes found in the opening and concluding poems of the volume. The first tells of her mother teaching her each morning to read and write before her dominating father awakes; the last is about Indians in New Jersey gathering to see a film and their sense of community temporarily overcoming the feelings of humiliation and exile from living in the United States.

Chitra Banerjee Divakaruni has a remarkable ability to notice what is significant. 'Villagers Visiting Jodhpur Enjoy Iced Sweet' begins 'In their own village they would never dare it, / these five men, sitting on the grainy grey sand / by the roadside tea stall licking at ices.' At home, 'heads of households', they beat their children and wives and get drunk. Losing their fields they will try to keep their pride as men by going to whorehouses:

> But for now,
> held within these frozen orange crystals,
> silent, sucking,
> they have forgotten to be men
> and are, briefly, real.

The movement of the lines and the placement of the words is effective, each line focusing on a part of the narrative and argument. Such a poem has its connection with the opening poem, contrasting writing as a female activity with the father. It even brings sympathy to the men who are prisoners of an expected role and likely victims of economics, class and caste. Indians migrate to leave the limitations of such a world, enjoy wider horizons, but find themselves uprooted, nostalgic, and perhaps discriminated against abroad. Moreover, in taking their culture with them they also bring its problems. Individuals cannot be free of community. *Leaving Yuba City* is a subtle, multifaceted portrait of India and Indians in which the links and contrasts are mostly left unstated.

Sujata Bhatt is perhaps the most ambitious and controversial of the female poets of the diaspora in her technique, especially when she uses Gujarati along with English. She was brought by her parents to the United States while young, studied at the Iowa Writers Workshop, and, now married, she lives in Germany. *Brunizem* (1988) was awarded the Commonwealth Poetry prize for Asia and *Monkey Shadows* (1991) was a Poetry Book Society Recommendation in England. *The Stinking Rose* (1995) was followed by *Point No Point* (1997), a selection from the first three books introduced by one new poem, the title poem. While Bhatt has written poems concerning the position of women in society, and while her expression of female sexuality might be thought feminist, the lives of women, gender and the relations between the sexes are not central to her work. It is possible to be of two minds about her poetry. The problem partly arises from the ways in which she identifies with India, but that is a more obvious expression of the ways she implies connections and insights only superficially found in the poems.

It is unfortunate that she raises the question of her bilingualism and its significance, but as it is foregrounded in each of her volumes it has become a topic of critical discussion. In *Brunizem* Bhatt claims that a person's mother tongue is one's real language of expression. In

'Search for My Tongue' the punning claim 'I can't hold on to my tongue. / It's slippery like the lizard's tail / I try to grip / but the lizard darts away' is followed by Devnagari Gujarati script, the words in Roman script and a translation into the English. The process continues throughout the poem. Bhatt claims that although she is losing her mother tongue as she lives in a foreign place, it returns to her in dreams; it is the language of night rather than, as is English, the language of day. Many of Bhatt's poems make a similar point. 'Marie Curie to Her Husband' concludes 'But at night, I still count in Polish.' While Bhatt's nostalgia for her origins is understandable, especially as she sometimes works as a translator from Gujarati, she naturally writes in English for a non-Gujarati readership and her treatment of India can be embarrassingly sentimental and exotic. It is the diaspora poet who, in 'A Different History', writes such sentimental clichés as 'Great Pan is not dead / he simply emigrated / to India. / Here, the gods roam freely, disguised as snakes or monkeys.' In some poems Bhatt claims language and culture are instinctive, which is not always true.

In *Nine Indian Women Poets* Eunice de Souza has pointed to the now hackneyed convention of postcolonial and diaspora authors using two or more languages in a work as crude evidence of cultural conflict. The basis of incorporating a non-European language is the claim that it is the real tongue of the author, the language one dreams and expresses oneself in. The assumptions are foolish, and seldom true. (Arvind Krishna Mehrotra offers a more theoretically sophisticated and practical view of language in his Oxford anthology.) Bhatt does not write well in her supposed mother tongue, Gujarati, so the display of Gujarati, Sanskrit, and various scripts in her poems is foolish. Many of her poems are about the language and culture of her blood. You can say that you are more at ease or more competent in a language, but not that it is in your blood; that is a form of racism.

The formative period of Bhatt's life was in the USA and her poetry feels American. When interviewed by Cecile Sandten ('Interview', *Kunapipi*, XXI.1, 1999:110–8) Bhatt spoke of her Americanness, her closeness to the British literary scene, and how her feeling of Indianness was originally a response to being raised in America, a feeling that has become less strong over the years. Now that she lives in Germany she can see her Americanness. While that makes her neither a better nor worse poet, Bhatt is as likely to write of Canadian Indians as the Indians of India or being an Indian abroad.

Bhatt is one of the many people of the modern world who, having moved from country to country and having the opportunity to travel to other countries, cannot really be said to have a nationality or national identity in contrast to citizenship. After a time you stop being part of a diaspora and become a traveller, a permanent expatriate, a citizen of the world. You carry memories with you, you retain assumptions from youth, but your world is where you live at present.

Once these objections are acknowledged there remain many good poems in each of her volumes. She has a poet's ability to suggest more than she actually says. While *Brunizem's* 'The Peacock', with its implication of art and insight as given resulting from an inner receptiveness; it is not something you can get by specifically looking for it: 'Something has broken your attention; / and if you look up in time / you might see the peacock / turning away as he gathers in his tail.' This poem, with its various shifts in focus from the external world into the relaxed but concentrated self and then illumination follows the pattern of the romantic ode in its Americanized version as found in the 'surreal' poems of Robert Bly and James Wright. Her long, fluid free-verse lines, the way she invests the physical world with significance, and the way her imagination will suddenly leap from the physical to some indefinable epiphany are also characteristic of much American lyrical poetry during our time. The poems do not seem to develop from social or personal relations; they are poems of the Self experiencing and defining itself.

The title poem of *Point No Point* begins:

> Why name a place Point No Point?
>
> Does it means we are nowhere
> when we reach it?
>
> Does it mean that we lose our sense
> of meaning, our sense of direction
> when we stop at Point No Point?

Many of her poems are versions of 'road' poems, and have the same tendency found in Agha Shahid Ali's poetry to use a particular trip as a metaphor for life's journey, and which a critic might interpret as being part of the Indian diaspora, although here, in Bhatt's poem, the journey towards 'the Juan de Fuca Strait' appears to be part of her relationship with the person she is addressing and has to do with the renewal of the physical and instinctual. This hovering near profundity results in Bhatt's writing appearing to take off into the marvellously poetic and symbolic while the conclusions can seem contrived, meandering, even faked.

In a few poems, such as 'The One Who Goes Away', which opens *The Stinking Rose,* the road poem and lyric of self-definition are blended with her Indian identity theme, but the lyricism of 'I am the one / who always goes away' / with its wide range of possible significances, and the suggestive reflections:

> Sometimes I'm asked if
> I were searching for a place
> that can keep my soul
> from wandering
> a place where I can stay
> without wanting to leave

concludes tritely with:

> I am the one
> who always goes
> away with my home
> which can only stay inside
> in my blood—my home which does not fit
> with any geography.

Compare the power of those first lines with the tongue-twisting contrivance of the final lines, which fall flatly into poor prose with their unsayable rhythm and such a clanger as 'can only stay inside / in my' where the poem loses to an idea about what it should be saying about identity. 'I am the one / who always goes / away' would carry enough suggestiveness about being an Indian journeying through the world without her needing to explain.

Bhatt can write powerfully about sexual and maternal instincts. In 'Udaylee': 'so I remember fistfuls of torn seaweed / rising with the foam ,/ rising. Then falling, falling on the sand / strewn over newly laid turtle eggs.' In *Monkey Shadows* there is the powerful invocation of female sexual desire in 'White Asparagus'.

Her books are arranged in sections, each of which has some central theme or topic such as the stinking rose section about garlic which gives *The Stinking Rose* its title. The first third of *Monkey Shadows,* The Way to Maninagar, consists mostly of memories of the years she lived in India. India, however, provides a text for wondering about what she does not know. Monkeys appear in several poems and she wonders what monkeys feel. A child looks a monkey in the face and she wonders what they both feel. There is a mixture of sentimentality and honesty.

'The children feel closer / to the monkeys, although they never / really play together, although the monkeys / probably hate the children'. This leads to thoughts about Hanuman, the monkey god, in a poem which concludes:

> Some people have monkeys
> in their dreams, monkeys in their nightmares,
> monkeys crossing their shadows
> long after they stopped being children
> long after they have left such a garden.

And that is the trouble. Too many of her poems imply there are significances, 'monkeys', whenever she starts writing on a topic. Nature, elephants and freak waves are like garlic, subjects about which to think, puzzle and write. Her lyrics make grand gestures without the drama being clear; they are modern romantic odes, with all their attractiveness and vagueness.

CHAPTER EIGHTEEN

New Poets, Styles and Feelings

HOSKOTE, THAYIL, SURENDRAN, NAMBISAN, MERCHANT,
RAO, PADHI, KHAIR, PRASAD, RAMAKRISHNAN

From the mid-1980s a new generation of poets began to appear with new sensibilities and new themes. Previously poets had to argue that English was an Indian language; they positioned themselves against notions of Indian culture as spiritualist, Sanskritic, pastoral, and the cultural politics that claimed the peasant as the real India. A few poets were experimentalists exploring the range of poetic styles available; most, however, wrote in some version of the dry commonsensical manner that had been a major part of English-language poetry for most of the twentieth century and which was being reasserted as the main tradition during the 1950s and 1960s. The flamboyance of Kamala Das, the economy of de Souza, the romanticism of Moraes, the disillusioned toughness of Daruwalla, were not that different from Ezekiel's commonsensical approach in speaking directly and openly to his readers. Even Ramanujan, who was writing a more complex poetry, appeared to do the same. The result was, at times, a thinness of texture, an unwillingness to take chances, an avoidance of lyricism, obscurity, the wild, the political, the deviant. The poets who followed would explore these regions. They were not always as serious or successful as the earlier poets but they widened the range of emotions and areas of Indian life that were the subject of poetry.

For the Rupa new poetry series Ezekiel wrote inflated blurbs, only justified by his need to promote his fledgling authors, but even then it is surprising to read 'Ranjit Hoskote's *Zones of Assault* is probably the most complex first book in the history of Indo-English'. It is a very uneven book which, while having some magnificent lines, has few totally successful poems and, unfortunately, some of the best poems suddenly go off track and conclude in rant, obscurity or clichés. If Daruwalla's endings can be too pat, Hoskote's endings are often chaotic.

Zones of Assault (1991) is, however, a daring book in all that is attempted. Hoskote has an historical sense, is influenced by the surreal, experiments with metrics and has a complex sense of the political. His poems are linked in sequences by theme and by such techniques as repeating an image or even a colour. An art critic, he makes much use of landscapes, the sky and allusions to paintings. His main theme, as seen in 'The Acrobat', is life as intricate, complicated, revolutionary movements in time; however, time eventually brings stasis and betrays as in '1917' where the Russian revolution ends in 'slavery'. We live in a world of flux which requires violence for liberation, but history shows that violence itself turns into oppression and death. Wild dreams and hopes are often drugged imaginings in contrast to reality. Artists, revolutionaries and friends die unfulfilled; all that remains is art which immortalizes ambitions, dreams, challenges and deaths.

Hoskote's treatment of violence as both liberator and tyrant is romantic and dangerous, and gives his poetry some of the explosiveness sometimes found in the modern literature of such regional languages as Marathi. Often Hoskote appears to be following G.M. Hopkins and Dylan Thomas in imitating the former's 'sprung rhythms' and in the invention of metaphoric compound words such as, 'sky-sealed', 'swaying-sacred', 'scarab-earth' or 'starblood'. This can be enriching, but too often in the later poems of *Zones of Assault* such words clot the thought and movement of the stanza and create needless obscurity. While most of the poems begin with a clear argument, many end in obscure word play.

A complaint sometimes made against Indian English poetry is that it lacks the rich texture of writing in England or the West Indies. Verse in England is filled with social tones, ironies, self-awareness; a Caribbean writer may move through many registers and kinds of English including dialect. By contrast Indian poets seemed to distrust excess and remained wedded to the aesthetics of imagism or to the understated manner of the British Movement poets. Eunice de Souza's later poems display an extreme minimalism, a paring down of the poem as far as it can go. One of the surprises in recent years was Jeet Thayil's *Apocalypso* (1997) with its surreal humour and dense texture of sound and echoes of other poems. Thayil responds to the literature of other lands as if it were his own, writing about, for example, the American poet John Berryman or the Russian Osip Mandelstam. He exhibits a literary cosmopolitanism. He can mix the satiric narrative of West Indian calypso with the intensities of Christian apocalypse. Unlike some Indian poets who feel

insecure writing metric verse and either stay rigidly on the beat or escape
to free verse, Thayil enjoys a natural relationship between his voice and
what he writes. English is his language and he uses metre without feeling
bound to a form such as lines of a particular length:

> In America the angels rot young.
> their cheeks are hollow
> blowing out forest fires.
> They carry marks of past beauty
> on earlobe, nipple, bicep, nostril.
> They are skinny always, bearded sometimes,
> their eyes, haunted by waking dreams,
> have slipped over the edge,
> looked into the void and returned for now.
> They carry tiny gold-spoons of half razors
> dangling from the end of neck-chains.
> American angels live alone with their pets.

In *Gemini* (1992) Thayil introduced new areas of emotions to Indian
poetry. Beginning with a quotation saying that many people seek
after pain rather than pleasure, Thayil's half of the volume is concerned
with the attractions of drugs, drink, sex and even death as the dark
side of life rather than as liberating pleasures. 'A Morning Prayer'
contrasts 'two hungers ... A certain hunger of the flesh, / the other
disembodied, pure, / both softened for a moment as / the needle
mounts its bite of love.' There are such obvious poems of addiction
as 'The Alcoholic at Dawn' and 'A Nod for Burroughs': 'I slide in the
tip, / a red flower blooms / in my glass syringe.' This is different from
the romanticism of Keats and the hippy counterculture. Love is pain,
destructive, addiction to the flesh; or to cite 'Deadman's Whore': 'The
hangman's beautiful daughter / brings me thick-lipped house flowers /
fed on her own fetid juice.' Obviously it never lasts. There is little in
the usual streams of English poetry concerning attractions of pain
and self-destructiveness, even Keats writes of easeful death as if it
were a pleasurable state of being; the emotions Thayil explores are
more likely to be found in continental European literature. There is
the disgust with the flesh and desire in 'Hymn to Him' (the title
ironic in its clashing sounds and the implication that it is about the
divine):

> Oh put him out some perfect how
> I can't support his heaviness

> this hairy beast from down below
> his nonstop howls for food and flesh.

The selections in *Gemini* move towards the concluding 'A Circular Song', more about the poet's persona than India, in which there is senseless repetition instead of salvation. The poem begins beautifully 'What demon stalks this arid land, / how can you live here my poor soul?', but ends with the horror of:

> Slipping in semen, blotting his snot,
> what demon stalks this arid land?
> Slot in the slip, slip in the slot,
> even the sun steps like a thief.

The poems in the two halves of *Apocalypso* are more accomplished, wittier, less dependent on their place within a sequence than those in *Gemini*, but have the same concern with life as corruption, and with corruption as a source of art as well as life. Several of Thayil's poems have children disgusted at the sound of their parents having sex. Many of the poems are literary in recalling the deaths of poets or including an element of literary parody. 'Other People's Deaths' mocks the deaths of several American poets. 'Trout Fishing At Night' concludes 'There is a fat silvery trout dangling out of his fly.' A well-known poem by Arvind Mehrotra is the source of Thayil's 'Where This One Came From':

> Tonight the poem walks abroad,
> In moonlight, ravening for a thing
> That cannot easily be named, tonight.

> The poem does not promenade tonight,
> Utterly not, it skulks with the furtive
> Air of a body-thief or soul-robber.

Although from a Syrian Christian family, Thayil can seem like one of those Roman Catholic writers who finds the sinner closer to salvation than those whose horizons are limited to the ordinary secular world. Hell and Heaven are closer to each other than either to Limbo. Thayil's uncle translated Baudelaire, the great French poet of decadence, into Malayalam and introduced Jeet to such poetry. The temptations of decadence along with the Bible are basic influences on his poetry, appearing side by side, hand in hand, rather than always as conflicting opposites.

While Thayil is a special case, someone intensely exploring the emotional terrain where pain and pleasure meet, he shares the new range of subject matter, tones and revelations of Indian poetry in the 1990s. Dom Moraes has alluded to the urban quality in modern Indian poetry. There is certainly a big-city feel about many of the newer poets who appear cut off from family, alienated from religion, living on their own, part of the general disillusionment and disquiet which can accompany freedom, scepticism and individualism. Sometimes life appears to consist mostly of drink, drugs and lust, without even Thayil's fascination with and pleasure in the darker aspects of such emotions.

C. P. Surendran's poems first appeared in his half of *Gemini II* (1994) where he was introduced by Dom Moraes as fiery, raw, and filled with loneliness, alienation and anger. A journalist, he brought a hard-boiled scepticism and disillusioned tough-guyism to the poetry scene. His half of the *Gemini II* volume begins with a reply to Wallace Stevens's famous poem 'Sunday Morning'. In Surendran's version there is only flesh as opposed to the earth on which it lives. The first and third stanzas conclude 'This bed. Perhaps this bed is all.' There is a purposeful ambiguity throughout the poem; its subject may be the speaker's vision of the world as physical, a place of flesh and lust, but the poem could also be about a violent relationship with a woman. The poem is apparently both a reply to Stevens's hedonism of the imagination and also itself a metaphor in which man's violence towards nature shares in his relationship with the feminine. In the first stanza there is a pun on sole / soul (which will reappear later in the volume). 'Heel in my hand, / I outstare the sole of the beast / Twisting in my fist.' The implication is that the soul is where we touch the earth (the bed), there is only the flesh upon the physical.

Many of the poems ironically use religious titles—'Renunciation', 'Annunciation', 'Whisky Priest' (alluding to Graham Greene's novel *The Power and the Glory*), 'First Signs, Last Rites', 'Requiem of the Rose', 'Lazarus'. They offer a portrait of someone with a Roman Catholic background and familiar with the classics of modern literature living by himself with his cat after the break up of his relationship with a woman whom he still desires. Life feels meaningless to him; religion and notions of the spirit are no longer believable, yet human relations have failed and he is left with his anger at the lack of significance of life. In 'Surprise' 'I'm leaving, she says' and 'The day falls from the cross / Dies on the floor.' His salvation and redemption from life have died when she leaves. He drinks too much; making meals for himself (and his cat) is a disagreeable feature of his life; and he knows that eventually he will die. In 'Renunciation' he wakes up to 'Breakfast for one. Beer and wine .... Lunch is a conceit of three, My cat, / Your snapshot, and me. Secret rum / in mint tea.' He often speaks of himself as dead or imagines his death or that like Lazarus he will return to the world, although those he meets will not know that he is already dead. He cannot be like those in the past who lived among large families and as they grew old accepted their role as elders to be cared for. Seeing old people he knows, in 'Geriatrics, Geriatricks', that he does not want the humiliations of age with its 'Meekness without remission .... The emptying avenues of flesh and bone .... Denture and glasses .... I do not want to be there .... Take me, dear Lord, / before my time.' Weekends alone are hell. In 'Saturday Poems', he 'sits, wishing / Monday were here.' He watches TV, gets drunk, 'remains / Bedridden, thinking of her thighs'. He 'wants Monday like a woman'. These are poems of the anguish of modern urban secular life with its expectations of fulfilment and experience of dissatisfaction with one's personal reality and with the universe. This is the world of unrest that Hindu and Buddhist spirituality aim to avoid.

Surendran's solution is, rather romantically, in poetry. He has made clear his poetic, social context, purpose ('therapeutic') and assumed readership. 'The dangerously funny thing about arty-farty writing is that it is not meant for your consumer: the salaried man or woman who is pretending to have a good time in the big bleak cities of India, but is unable to make sense of his huge spatial and temporal dislocation; the urban alien unable to make sense of his migrant middle-class situation which makes survival possible but not its near-nostalgic vivid promises.' 'I am seeking a whole new constituency of readership.' 'You write so you remain sane .... You write so you can come to terms with your life ... in an increasingly urban India, alienation will reach mass neurosis levels. My poetry understands and respects that I write to heal, not impress. Poetry as prophylactic.' ('Writer at Work', *Gentleman*, August 1999: 94) His manner is aggressive, attention getting and the argument minimal, but Surendran has a clear notion of what he is doing in his poetry.

The ironically titled *Posthumous Poems* (1999) is prefaced by Surendran's explanation of the poems being 'posthumous' to the break up of his marriage, the collapse of Communism, the failure of the Naxalites and the betrayal of revolution by his friends who have chosen to go abroad and earn money. There is an inconsistency here since Surendran claims that he was always sceptical of politics, ideas and life, so such betrayals should not have shocked him; they should, if anything, have confirmed the correctness of his scepticism. Surendran's poetry tires less through sensationalism than the continual use of a heightened voice and a style in which many sentences are fragments intended as images or in which an extremely abbreviated kind of speech conveys macho knowingness. Economy is one thing, repetition of telegraphese can be as artificial as any older poetic diction. Surendran's Introduction to *Posthumous Poems* claims that 'all tragedies are trite; there's no grief death cannot resolve', which is itself, depending on how you read it, trite or false. In the face of such a disillusioning world he claims that only poetry is true, absolute, 'like dead men talking'.

It is easy to be put off by C. P. Surendran's manner. The Introduction to *Posthumous Poems* is a digressive attack on everything: 'If Christ were to swim on the cross again, how many of us would watch Him without a remote in hand? The question applies to Catholics as well.' Even the title of the volume, justifiable in itself, has an element of sensationalism. Surendran is very much alive; what has died is a former marriage, his belief (which he claims to have never really had) in ideas and politics, and in the radicalism (which he supposedly never shared) of his friends.

There is posturing here, but also much lyrical poetry. Often the two are found together. In the first poem, a five-liner, Surendran explains that he is trying to 'get one word right .... But death doesn't matter. / It's metaphor.' There is not only metaphor, there is also rhyme and harmonization. The 'metaphor' of the concluding line rhymes with the unusual 'Ms Christopher' in the first line and with 'matter' in line four; the 'r' sound is also in the 'right' at the end of line three. This is lyric poetry disguising itself as popular tabloid sensationalism. The second poem is 'Goal Keeper' which uses the problems of an athlete as a metaphor for man in the universe. Consisting of five stanzas of five lines, it ranges from the powerful Eliotic 'Implosion of all time in a moment's dare / And miss; a whiff of eternal loss' to the inflated banalities of 'I relapse into vigil-crystal, gaze at my goal, / Ice-emblazoned solitude to future and resolve.'

Surendran the metaphorist can be good, strikingly original even when dealing with such commonplaces as the relationship of nightmares to how we see the world upon waking. Here is the complete third poem:

> In my sleep the tree whirled
> And leaf by leaf light emptied.
> When I awoke everything I liked
> Looked alike.

This, alas, is immediately followed by the existential bathos of:

> The old fear of being
> Nothingness, and perhaps seeing
> Little more, very little more,
> To it than being himself, or
> The slow swelling fear of air
> And water and fire of others
> Leaving him untouched like smoke on water.

This one goes on and on. It is only a 30-line poem but feels longer.

Later poems in the volume become more specific and concrete, but that is not always an improvement although it provides a sense of autobiographical narrative. Surendran's use of images from modern culture is striking, but not always effective. Television provides some good original images, but also some dead lines. He combines the characteristics of modern urban life with the eternal problems of being human and our relationship with the world in which we live. *Posthumous Poems* claims that in a world of nothingness, disillusionments, boredom, failures and death there can be no answer except to tell the truth in poetry which challenges erasure. While such an answer to death has been offered by other artists I wonder why it is more true than, say, Camus's claim that we should challenge the world's lack of purpose by living intensely or Sartre's flirtation with going beyond the self in commitments to Others? That Surendran's poetry raises such questions is impressive, but I wish he had turned more of the prosy verse into those metaphoric poems. The sequence, however, improves with re-reading. Surendran is an acquired taste. There is more to this journalist's self-pitying poems than at first meets the eye.

The two *Gemini* volumes published by Penguin make use of a contrast between a shocking and a quiet poet. Vijay Nambisan, who shares his volume with Thayil, often adopts the manners of a poet from the past, but his poems conclude with modern ironies. In 'The Miracle of the Pomegranate' the natural world is a force 'changing the shape of the tree', a power that cuts through our desire for social order, bringing 'Unwanted things coming again and again to birth, / Ignoring the fact that the gardener's due tomorrow'. So far the poem appeals to our liberal and romantic sympathies for the natural against the artificial, the sexual against the repressed, even the cyclical and changing in contrast to the static. It is on the side of life, where even the gardener says 'Nothing useless nothing wasted': 'But the tree's grown so tall that half its prizes /

Will only come to the wasteful bats and thieving / Squirrels, then be left to lose their colours, rotting.' This is a rather different conclusion about nature as wasteful, excessive, a world of decay as well as fruition. The very precision of Nambisan's language and use of a regular form provides an additional irony.

In 'Madras Central' there is the contrast between the speaker's precise care for his possessions, his awareness of life as a continuing journey, and his knowledge that 'we're not wanted / And carry our unwanted-ness somewhere else.' Again a cliché, one of the basic tropes of poetry, life as a journey, is quietly subverted and existence is found to be as unwelcoming as in Surendran's more explicit despair. Both poems use five-line stanzas, with longish lines that tend towards twelve syllables. There is the subtle use of occasional rhyme, and a strange rather invo-luted syntax that both appears certain of what it is saying and yet leaves the reader disoriented as the poem works its way towards its revelation at the end.

If Thayil and Surendran speak of the pleasures and pains of desire, Nambisan warns against such concern with the self and its wants. His half of *Gemini* is prefaced by a quotation from Anand Coomaraswamy concerning 'joy without exultation' and 'passion without loss of serenity'. The poems themselves have a tone that avoids emotion while the topics are often about the foolishness of any extreme feeling. In 'Reflections on May Day' the speaker begins by mocking the shopkeeper, wholesaler and producer, 'Counting coins is no pursuit for a brave man. / Rather he should count the heads of his enemies / With a meataxe.' But there seems to be no place left for such primitive romanticism; and he wonders 'where my enemies are'. 'Paranoia / paranoia' has someone fleeing the safety of the city for the isolation of the wilderness, where she can face her paranoia, but, ironically, 'Safety has followed you from the city / And you do not know where else you can go.' 'Diary of the Expedition' once more mocks romantic notions of life as a difficult quest towards some great authentic experience. Here the old colonial trope of an explorer in a savage land concludes with everyone dead or dying and having 'reached the valley of our seeking / I see no signs of Gold'. After such pain there are 'no treasures that can now gladden my heart'. The many ironies of an affair between a man and woman in 'Ill Met by Moonlight' conclude even more ironically with 'When my time comes to be possessed, I know / I shall play my part well, after long study.' Nambisan sticks to that long line, usually of eleven or twelve syllables, often uses a five-line stanza, and depends on the ending of the poem to create the correct, ironic, perspective on what has been shown and said. 'The Garden Variety Show' ends with:

> Family relationships
> Are not as complicated as they're made out to be,
> I write in my notebook. It's doing as you would be done by
> That saps the strength. I do what is expected of me.

The concluding poems of the volume themselves seem critical of such acceptance and attempted calm. 'Narcissus in the Drought' returns to the imagery of previous poems, but instead of the water which brings growth to the tree here is a wasteland where the speaker has 'A need for more than water, a thirst / That water cannot assuage, but water must.' He has 'great thirst, / A prayer to the shadow to move a little more / Towards a vision I know possessed me there before.' His poems reveal a poet with an unusual personality and perspective whom it is difficult to pin down to specific ideas, but who is obviously distrustful of the kinds of excess displayed in the work of such writers as Thayil, Surendran and R. Raj Rao.

If Indian poetry in English is postcolonial in the sense of giving expression to women, and to such minorities as Jews, Christians, Goans, Parsis and those of mixed marriages, it has also started to make use of former taboo topics. Homosexuality is a theme of Hoshang Merchant's *The Home, the Friend and the World* (1995), *Love's Permissions* (1996), *The Heart in Hiding* (1996) *The Birdless Cage* (1997) and his many other volumes, as it sometimes is in the writings of R. Raj Rao. Vikram Seth has at times alluded to it. I am not aware of much Indian poetry in English that treats lesbianism. Perhaps the publications have not come to my attention. Suniti Namjoshi published with Writers Workshop such books as *Poems* (1967) and *More Poems* (1971), but only became more widely known after her openly lesbian short stories and fables were published in England, followed by a Penguin edition in India combining two of her previous books of prose. Namjoshi, who taught in Canada and resides in England, claimed that she could not live or write openly as a lesbian in India. Family pressures alone would have forbidden it.

One writer who goes beyond Thayil in using a vocabulary of the grotesque is R. Raj Rao. Rao, otherwise a respectable university teacher, dramatist and man of letters, appears to have gone out of his way to be shocking in *Slide Show* (1992), a Swiftian satire on just about everything. Besides 'Masturbation' and 'Confessions of a Boy Lover' there is a revolting sequence of 'Garbage' poems including 'Shit Like Food'. The title of the volume comes from a poem which treats life as a series of horrid yet ironic scenes: 'Twelve. Brain, blood, gut, all spilled on the road, / Feet impaled on the spokes of his wheel, / A cyclist lies limp as the people look on.' There is even a mocking, disgusting 'Self-Portrait':

> 'I have protruding teeth, a fungoid groin.
> I smell like a horse.
> My nails with which I sometimes scratch my verses
> Are grown and black and twisted out of shape.
> There are holes in my teeth that let out slime.

Besides being Swiftian satires such poems have the vitality, earthiness and lack of decorum sometimes found in the common speech and literature in Hindi and the regional languages. That Rao is also a dramatist contributes to his sense of a poem as dramatized speech, a show in which it is necessary to keep his audience's attention by not only letting it all hang out, but also waving it about. Rao's mixture of Swiftian satire and gay activism is unsettling and meant to be. While much of this grotesquerie is meant to amuse by showing that life is like a freak show at a circus, the rhetoric of being disgusting is, purposely, excessive. It lacks the humour, imaginative fantasy and wit that such a perspective requires. 'When I open the book again, / Each word is a blob of shit.' My views, however, might be generational prejudices as contemporary culture seems not only to accept but prize the display of bad taste. The art of each age must change, and in modern culture the change usually involves being shocking and making art out of what were previously considered materials outside the pale of high culture. Rao's poems share in the culture of shock that can be found elsewhere in the international success of Jim Rose's Circus and in the fame of the Sensation art exhibition in London and New York or in many recent films. Perhaps a levelling egalitarian culture of excrement, decay, growths and disabilities is our democratic equivalence to the aristocratic airs and anti-bourgeois decadence of the late nineteenth century?

In contrast to the cosmopolitanism of Jeet Thayil, the urbanized nightmares of C. P. Surendran and R. Raj Rao's Circus of Disgust, there is Bibhu Padhi's Cuttack, Orissa, where little happens, slowly and unchangingly at that. Occasionally, Padhi admits that the main road in Cuttack—a road that I know from a couple of visits can require Tabish

Khair's amusing 'Tips on Crossing a Street'—is noisily crowded with cars, but otherwise he shuts out modern phenomena except, as with power failures, to indicate the unchanging, hopeless, nature of his life and of the community. What might have been the subject matter for a novel, 'Our small town has been filled with / rural migrants in search of small jobs' is rapidly passed over for a litany of 'rheumatism and migraine. / The cycle starts all over again'.

Jayanta Mahapatra has also made a poetry of boredom about Orissa, in which besides the predicability of the sun rising after sleepless nights, and the rains which provide a subject for many poems, he is an outsider watching the world of believers with their customs and rituals. In Mahapatra's poetry the nationalists' eternal India becomes highly localized and seen through the eyes of a misplaced modern who wishes he were one of the faithful, but instead writes poems about the difficulty of expressing perceptions and yearnings. This has resulted in a large body of work of uneven quality which at its best is extremely good in its richness of imagery and in the range of possible significances raised as the mind meditates upon the world. Mahapatra combines the current interests of the intellectual avant garde with a literature celebrating Orissa and he manages to do it in a manner which is both puzzlingly abstract and yet conveys a feeling of locality without detail.

Padhi has learned from Mahapatra how to make poetry of waiting, of silence, of monotony, of place:

> It is raining in Cuttack once again.
> The rain that arrives so gently
> that it can scarcely be heard.

It is a poetry of the interior life, in which little is said, there is little communication between people and much of what is felt is barely articulated as it is somehow beyond the reach of the words that are being used to locate and define it: 'Words are sometimes faintly heard,/ or just remembered from a distant year / when I was small. Modest words'. This is a highly subjective poetry, stripped of the pleasures of lyricism. 'I write this line / I could've written another line.' The manner, voice, tone and treatment of subject are flat, uncoloured. In Padhi's verse, like Mahapatra's, English is used without much change in stress or pitch, while accents fall regularly in equal time:

> I could've kept my line
> invisible, secret, ...
> I admit though that such lines

> do appear on the page, but only when
> I am not writing, or only planning
> to remember the missing line.

In Padhi's world life drones from day to day. This can be as bad a
fate as the chaos and fears of urbanization. In the title poem of *A
Wound Elsewhere* (1992), a poem with more flare ups of excitement
than most, he, like Mahapatra, addresses himself as if he were another,
someone who could not understand what he feels:

> Not here, not here, not this, not here.
> It is one of so many things that
> you've failed to locate this year.
> You face questions about your
> declining health, from anxious lips;
> the answers remain ordinary, familiar.
> Not this, not here, not this, not here.

The manner is distinctive with its contrast between the poetic (the
end rhymes, the old-fashioned diction of 'anxious lips', the repetitions),
and the flat clichés ('one of so many things', 'failed to locate', 'declining
health'). There are similar contrasts between the specificity of what is
denied as the subject of the poem and the vagueness of what is: 'It
isn't the migraine that you get ... nor the wish to lie / in bed, face in
the pillow .... It isn't because ....' The poem concludes with a triumphal
hopelessness: 'No one knows, no one need know. / It is always some
other place—/ the hurt stealing into the night from there.'

If Padhi's poems can at times appear a parody of his own manner, so
can any poet with a strong characteristic style and body of work that
often, and sometimes foolishly, repeats itself: 'No one comes, and you
celebrate / the loss of a day, every following / day, with a mere look on
your face.' Padhi, however, is not Mahapatra, and those Mahapatra-like
lyrics of waiting and watching are not Padhi's strength. He is not an
outsider, he is a Brahmin, an insider. A friend tells him: "'You who live
in Cuttack / will never see the world. Even if you leave / for another town
or choose a wife from another place /'" because someone from Cuttack
will return to the crowds, filth, flies and mosquitoes. Padhi does not
reply, but thinks:

> ... I've been here since the time
> I was born a good thirty-five years ago,
> in this town encircled by three rivers

and with the superstitious clouds
of my town's forefathers
still hanging about my eyes in a loving stupor.

A Wound Elsewhere and *Lines from a Legend* (1993) reveal a small narrow society of close yet often strained and impoverished relationships that is almost novelistic. It is a provincial society in which the annual rise of the river, another power failure and the coming of the rainy season are events. A father dies, is remembered, becomes almost a ghost haunting the poet; there are memories of his grandmother; a child is born; there are Brahmin rituals; Padhi feels he seldom speaks with his wife the way he did in the past; a friend's son moves away; Padhi wonders why he continues to live in his father's house, then has another house built, they move in; Padhi and Mahapatra grow apart, Mahapatra retreats into some mood and Padhi recalls a time when they could speak without being falsely polite. It is this small society of births, deaths, anniversaries, illnesses, misunderstandings, wounded friendships, friends' children, within the small world of Orissa that eventually emerges from Padhi's poems and which make his poetic world different from Mahapatra's.

Ezekiel created the poem of modern Indian cities; Padhi in his own way has created poetry about the provinces, the places where there are no single career women and from which your best friends and their children depart for higher education and better jobs elsewhere. It is a lower middle class perspective of those who stay at home, teach at the local college, and for whom nothing changes, or changes slowly, while others move on to the problems of life in the big cities or abroad. As with any poet there are the hours of waiting for the poem to come, but here the waiting for inspiration and a subject becomes analogous to life itself.

One of the those who did leave the provinces for the wider world is Tabish Khair. He is also one of an increasing number of Indian poets from Muslim backgrounds, including Peeradina, Agha Shahid Ali and Imtiaz Dharker. It may be significant that Ali and Peeradina live and teach in the United States, Khair lives and teaches in Denmark and Dharker has come to India from England. Unlike the fundamentalists who seem to dominate politics, the Muslim poets are from the liberal, acculturating, modernizing, secular side of Islam. Those who modernize in such a context are also likely to have or have had a radical streak with progressive ideas and social involvement. Each of the four writers has written poems concerned with social justice. Khair's sympathies can be seen in 'The Streets of My Poems':

> In all my poems I simply walk the streets of my town once
> again;
> Unable to leave behind men and women pitching tar
> On the hot roads, muscles straining in the sun;
> Unable to forget that old beggar sleeping in the shade.

My World (1991) mostly concerns 'home' and homes, the world he
knew which keeps recurring in his imagination. The ugliness of the
scene is a projection of the speaker's dissatisfactions with his society.
Images of the morning (it feels like mourning) enter his consciousness
'like water from the dry, sputtering tap outside'. An aged former sailor
has been drinking all night 'And still lies huddled in the ordure'. There
is a little child sleeping under a lamp-post:

> Old Mr Rao comes out into his patched and peeling porch
> With a brush between toothless gums
> And stands lost in memories of lost passion.
> His son, after studying till four last night,
> Splutters and coughs like a goat in his sleep.

This is a more critical portrait of India than the one found in Padhi's
poems. The poetry is also more formal with each of the five lines of
each stanza conforming to normal syntactical units, and repetition of
words and alliteration.

Khair, unlike Padhi, is looking at such a society more analytically.
He has thought about what kinds of English and rhythms might be
appropriate for writing about Bihar. There is a curious use of slightly
uncolloquial older diction 'ordure', 'whilst', which suggests that this
place is lost in time, a meaning which would make sense in terms of
the poem's conclusion which speaks of the images as a mirror of
'Yesterday and the days before'. There is also the implication about
such diction that English is a literary language to these people, a
language likely to be learned from books rather than spoken. Although
the poem is strongly rhythmic, the rhythms are unusual as if Khair
were purposefully departing from Anglo-Indian speech. His poetry
will often have an off-centred tone and manner as if he were aiming
for some region- or class-specific Indian characteristic that is more
subtle than the usual ways that writers characterize Indian English.

The India of decay and the past in which nothing happens is not
always bad. It has a rootedness in contrast to the modern world which
replaces it. In 'House with the Grey Gate', the gate is useless being 'off
one hinge and always open', while an old woman on the porch looks

up whenever the gate creaks in the wind 'Expecting someone; though no one comes, nor has for years'. In the garden 'shrubbery has spread, refusing to be weeded out' which serves as an analogy for 'the old man and the old woman and an old pattern of life—/ refusing to be weeded out from this skyscraping street'. This contrasts with the next poem where the speaker and his friend sit in a café discussing Durkheim's *Le Suicide* and that night his friend commits suicide. The subtext implies that the suicide results from the anomy of modern urban life, a condition shown in the next poem, 'After Work', where the speaker has 'nothing to look forward to', the streets seem 'endless', the faces are those of strangers, and his apartment and heart are empty. Khair uses the usual techniques of early modernist literature, such as projection of subjective emotions upon the external world to show loneliness and lack of a sense of community for the urban office and factory worker.

Other poems in *My World* speak of recurring communal tensions and proclaim a private world of the 'weak' that exists alongside the road 'As you drive to office, five days a week'.

> The Walls of my world are made of clay and straw.
> Water trickles in from a rent in its roof, mixing with my food;
> But, on clear and calm nights, the stars come visiting me.
>
> (I know all my little stars, each by its name,
> Though you have probably never heard of them—
> They are so small, they would be lost in your world.)

This world of the weak and poor who are close to nature and can see the stars will last, like those weeds of an older way of life, long after the ruins of the regimented impersonal 'prouder worlds, larger worlds'.

Many of the short poems in 'My India Diary' concern memories of the pains, limitations and continuing influence of home: 'to tear away your roots / wrench free / I will have to take myself apart / brick by brick.' The villages are places from where 'all roads lead out // except during elections', but for those who leave such communities: 'where did the aloneness end / and loneliness start'.

Khair writes from the perspective of an atheist influenced by Marxist materialism. He sees life as a short period of existence before nothingness. There is, however, an existentialist influence in seeing such a reality as leaving us fearful with the need to make something of our lives. Writing is his solution. *A Reporter's Diary* (1993) takes up the idea of a diary from *My World*, but has death, rather than

home, as its central theme. In 'To Gyanendara' he recalls his dead
friend:

> I shall be true to us. I shall believe your death.
> We knew heads are shaven in vain, graves contain emptiness.
> That there is no soul to start with and no flesh after a month,
> And all that might remain of us will be a piece of bone.

The common poetic trope of returning to nature, a view consistent
with Hinduism and Buddhism, is treated with irony: 'The dead will
live in bits and pieces scattered over the land. / The living will die in
bits and pieces in the slush and sand.' The next poem 'The Young
and the Old' continues the theme 'They find out too late, / Death is
too much a part of our life.' An awareness of the lack of transcendence
or comfort in death results from experience. Life is found to be like
an onion peeled to the core: 'At the end, there was nothing to hold,
to show .... / Except, of course, the inevitable tears in the eyes.'

Many of these poems are small narrative allegories of life as seen
from a materialist perspective. A broad range of religious, cultural and
scientific references are drawn upon for images. 'Only the dead stay in
one place. / The living are condemned to movement.' 'This, perhaps,
was the curse of Adam and Eve—/ Having left home once, never to
find home again.' Life, especially after having left home, consists of
anxieties. 'Fear' is a recurring word and there are two sonnets on Fear.
'I fear the second when this-All may end, / The darkness, sudden as a
power-cut, / that shall leave me un-done, without a friend / In a
meaningless flux.' Writing is a way of seeking refuge from the fear of
nothingness where we are 'hurled / from sense to senselessness'. In 'When
Someone Dies' Khair returns to the deaths of his two friends, Lata and
Gyan. In contrast to art 'Off stage when someone suddenly dies, / There's
blood and screaming despite the lies.' There are no peaceful deaths,
there is always 'blood and screaming inside the head'. The concluding
poem claims that 'Happiness is a word scribbled on sand' but if you
can ignore the way the tide erases happiness there are blue skies and a
wide beach on which to write a future. Khair's imagery could be seen as
ironic or perhaps there is a suggestion here of a revolutionary future.

There is a variety of moods in Khair's poetry ranging from the
depressive and various kinds of irony to the comic. His vocabulary is
simple and easy to read, yet there is a coherent intellectual vision. He
also has an instinct for light verse, the subjects of which are sometimes,
not always, related to his serious poetry. In the ironically titled *The*

Book of Heroes: A Collection of Light Verse and Much Worse (1995),
politics include "The Caangrassman" whose 'men adore him; they
are paid to, / And if you don't agree they'll "convince" you!' 'The Ball-ad
of Elections' mocks the paradoxes of democracies and the governments
they produce:

> That someone may rule us for our own good,
> Tell us to grow crops, and export our food,
> Tether us, flatter us and then milk us dry;
> That is why we need elections. That is why.

Many of the poems make fun of the pretenses of the professional classes.
There is the paradox of the 'The Dentist, Ah!' who 'tortures you like
no one can,/ and gets a hefty fee'. And the newspaper editor who 'just
a week after each tragedy ... warned against it prophetically'. The variety
of forms Khair uses, the range of his subjects, and the thought that has
gone into his volumes suggests someone likely to keep developing.

One new poet who uses conventions of light verse for serious themes
is the critic and academic G.J.V. Prasad. While accepting English as an
Indian literary language, Khair is uncomfortable with its elite basis and
he wants writing that is closer to regional and class use without
descending to humiliating comic dialects and pidgin Indian English.
Khair claims that the many people who speak English in India usually
do so in a limited number of contexts and speak it well. Prasad, however,
tries for a popular poetry which does reflect the bleeding of other
languages into Indian English and the way mistakes in English usage
result from interference of the conventions of other languages. Such
poems might be said to take Ezekiel's Indian English poems further in
that the conflict between languages is an expression of conflicting world
views. In 'Cross Talk in Kaliyugam':

> Why you girls are being anti-sati
> it is being great honour to dying with sati
> laugh not so my English not being good
> I am only used to cooking food
> but what is being use of good education
> if you are learning this mem's liberation

Criticism of the treatment of women and of sati is one of the recurring
themes of G.J.V. Prasad's *In Delhi without a Visa* (1996), a book which
opens with three poems specifically on the subject. Many of the poems
are based on real events covered by newspapers and television. 'Sati I'

begins: 'When anything went wrong / her grandmother would say / like me a woman born.' In a society in which widows have no place sati logically follows as, ironically, 'her only chance / for a place in the sun'. 'Sati II' picks up the paradoxical irony. This is told from the perspective of a merchant who sells camphor, sweets, flowers and pictures of goddesses and who 'left for the village at once / for a killing was to be made / at the sati stall'. The poem concludes 'the sati had done more for our religion / and region than all the sadhus in action / just look at the money we made.'

The next poem is spoken by a woman reporter from a big city who mocks the village and its assumptions—'who could have trusted the water there?'—in an era of liberation. Rather than seeing the woman's acceptance of sati as a result of indoctrination concerning her place in the social order and lack of other choices, the reporter claims she was 'forced' and is told that is a 'sacrilege'. She calls this 'an angry assertion of identity' and is told to mind her own business. Interviewing the local swami she becomes subject to sexist comments, and is told that women are unequal, sati 'solves the problems of widows'. Returning home her story and interview is a newspaper scoop for only a few days before being lost among other stories concerning the ill-treatment of women: 'dowry deaths ... and the rape of lower class girls'. Her parents, who are trying to marry her off, turn out to be sympathetic to sati and claim she has 'lost touch with our country/ that's the trouble with education'. In a final irony the reporter herself agrees to an arranged marriage: 'if you can't make it to the ceremony / come tomorrow anyhow to see the sarees / and the jewellery.'

Other poems treat communal violence, religious and caste intolerance, regional nationalism, the Emergency, the immense distance between the middle class and the poor, and the corrupt and undemocratic ways of politicians. *In Delhi without a Visa* is a satirical portrait of a country, but the presentation is often amusing, the tone can even be jaunty: 'after the floods / the drought. // You either die with water/ or you die without.'

On first reading Prasad, I wondered about his history. Why does he write such poems as 'Desperately Seeking India':

> In Delhi
> without a visa
> in Madras
> an Aryan spy.
>
> ...

> In Bombay
> I'm an invader
> in Assam
> an exploiting trader.

From the various poems towards the end of the volume, such as 'Tamil-indians' and 'Family Poem II', it appears that Prasad's family were middle-class Brahmins in rural Tamil Nadu and fled first to Madras and then further afield as a result of caste and class violence: 'we had no land as tatha put it / being true Tamilians driven out / into the desert sands of Delhi / the anti-brahmin sentiment grown out of hand.' 'Immigrants in our motherland / emigrants from our homeland / reserved out of state / and reduced to mere madrasis .... Oh you don't look a madrasi / would say acquaintances':

> But you said anna interrupted wisely
> something about us not being hindus

> You have to be a Pakistani to be that
> appa relied you have to live near the Indus
> so in Delhi you are a Jamun.

Although claiming to be a perpetual outsider within India, Prasad writes poems from deep within society. Except that the underlying issues are as likely to result in class and caste violence as in social snobberies, the social comedy could be part of Vikram's Seth's *A Suitable Boy:*

> he is from Vadarkadu they're not brahmins there
> and he's no hindu.

> Spoken like a terkattiya appa laughed
> she equates wealth with brahmins
> we are suffering you can see for whose sins.

> But we are hindus anna interjected
> a future communist almost naxalite
> you might as well be Gangas or Cauveries
> or better still Ganya Cauveries appa replied

Prasad brought over into poetry many of the ways of mapping and representing India found by such novelists as Rushdie and Seth. These are regional or class stereotypes and might be seen as part of the general movement in recent poetry away from dense textures and imagism to a more accessible verse, easy to understand and suitable for public readings. Such poetry is more oral, more performance oriented, than poetry in the past. This is in keeping with contemporary literary fashion as narrative replaces spatial and musical organization; critical theories are more likely to be concerned with prose, representation, and story-telling than poetry and the image. In the process, if intensity has been lost, there is a gain in the creation of a wider audience.

While it is doubtful that E. V. Ramakrishnan's *A Python in a Snake Park* (1994) is an example of the general improvement of poetry during the past decade, he is an example of someone who writes poems that are likely to be ignored as he is neither a major poet nor does he fit into an obvious category that can easily be discussed. Ramakrishnan (b.1949) is a university professor who teaches and writes about English literature. He has published a book about American poets and a book about modernism in the poetry of several Indian languages. He was included in Paranjape's anthology of new poets and his *A Python in a Snake Park* was one of the books published by Rupa. *A Python in a Snake Park* includes several good poems including the amusing 'A Speech Heard at a Feminist Seminar in Payyannur' which begins with the speaker admitting that he does not know anything about the topic, 'women writers of Kerala', he is supposed to discuss. He then mentions how his two wives have betrayed him and his child, and just as we are about to laugh at his knowledge of women as their victim (itself a humorous irony at a feminist seminar), he starts talking about his directing plays and the perspective changes again:

> ... I also sleep with the main actress.
> For each new play I insist on a new actress
> for the lead role. Now I am directing my
> twenty-first play. I hope some day I will know
> enough of women writers of Kerala
> to speak to an august audience like this.

The above might be a cousin of Ezekiel's poems in Indian English. It has a similar multiple perspective and uncertainty whether to laugh at or with the speaker, a complexity rooted in its somewhat stilted English which allows more than one view of the speaker's treatment of his subject matter and the way we should respond. And what is he saying in those closing lines, especially as 'know' can have a sexual meaning?

There are other good poems in the volume, including 'The Unwritten Sequence' and 'Rain'. Ramakrishnan's better poems are different from each other, but they often take something ordinary and rapidly make it seem significant. There are more such poems and poets around than there were a few decades ago in India. They are unlikely to become the subject of critical attention or be studied in courses, but to come across them in a magazine or anthology is a pleasure. By now to argue about the appropriateness of English language poetry in India is like arguing whether monsoons are Indian.

Chronology of Significant Publications, Journals and Events, 1947–99

THE FOLLOWING ABBREVIATIONS ARE USED:

A (anthology), D (drama), E (event), J (journal), P (prose), Tr (translation), V (verse).

B (Bombay), C (Calcutta), M (Madras), ND (New Delhi).

AH (Arnold-Heinemann), CH (Clearing House), NG (Newground), OUP (Oxford University Press), UW (United Writers), WW (Writers Workshop).

1947

E. C. R. Mandy appointed editor of *The Illustrated Weekly of India*, B, 1947–59.

1948

J. *Thought* (ND, 1948–75). Keshav Malik, first literary editor; second Richard Bartholomew, then Rakshat Puri. Malik again editor 1959–75.

E. Kamala Das publishes in *P.E.N.* (edited by Sophia Wadia).

E. Nissim Ezekiel goes to London until 1952.

1950

J. *Chakra* (M, 1951–4).

J. *Illustrated Weekly* begins publishing poetry.

E. Keshav Malik travels in Europe and the USA until 1958.

1952

V. Nissim Ezekiel (b. 1924), *A Time to Change*, London: Fortune Press.

J. *The Literary Criterion* started, Mysore.
E. Nissim Ezekiel assistant editor of *Illustrated Weekly* (1952–4).

1953–1954

V. Nissim Ezekiel, *Sixty Poems*, B.
J. *Atlantic Monthly*, USA, October: A Perspective of India.
E. Dom Moraes and Gieve Patel publish in *Illustrated Weekly*.
E. K. Katrak, Srinivas Rayaprol and R. Bartholomew publish in *Illustrated Weekly*.
E. P. Lal writes weekly column for *Thought*, publishes some poets, 1954–7.
E. Dom Moraes meets Stephen Spender in B.
E. Sahitya Akademi founded.

1955

V. R. de L. Furtado (1922–83), *The Centre*, Toronto: Cromlech Press.
J. *Orient Review and Literary Digest* (C, 1955–9). Editors Alfred Schenkman and P. Lal.
J. *Quest* (B, 1955–77) founded. Nissim Ezekiel editor 1955–7.
J. *Shabda* (Marathi, 1955–6, 1960). Editors include Kolatkar and Chitre. Stencilled.
E. Dom Moraes leaves for England.

1956

J. *East and West* (Secunderabad, 1956–60). Editor Srinivas Rayaprol.

1957

V. Dom Moraes (b. 1938), *A Beginning*, London: Parton Press.
J. *Indian Literature*, founded (ND: Sahitya Akademi).
E. Adil Jussawalla goes to England, returns 1970.

1958

A. A. V. Rajeswara Rau (ed.), *Modern Indian Poetry: an anthology*, ND: Kavita.

E. Dom Moraes wins Hawthornden Prize in England for *A Beginning*.
E. Writers Workshop started in C.

1959

V. Nissim Ezekiel, *The Third*, B: Strand Bookshop.
V. K. Malik (b. 1928), *The Lake Surface and Other Poems*, ND: Surge Publications (reprinted 1961).
V. Robert Perlongo, *The Lamp is Low*, C: WW (first WW publication).
A. P. Lal and K. R. Rao (ed.), *Modern Indo-Anglian Poetry*, ND: Kavita.
J. *Opinion* founded (B, 1959–83).
J. *Poetry* (Chicago), Indian poetry issue, January.
E. K. R. Srinivasa Iyengar Visiting Professor of Indo-Anglian Literature, University of Leeds, England.
E. Writers Workshop begins publications.

1960

V. Deb Kumar Das (b. 1936), *Night Before Us*, C: WW.
V. Nissim Ezekiel, *The Unfinished Man* (repub. 1965, Student edition 1969), C: WW.
V. R. de L. Furtado, *The Oleanders*, C: WW.
V. P. Lal (b. 1928), *The Parrot's Death and Other Poems*, C: WW.
V. K. Malik, *Rippled Shadows*, ND: Surge Publications.
V. Dom Moraes, *Poems*, London: Eyre and Spottiswode.
J. *Indian Journal of English Studies* founded.
J. *The Literary Half-Yearly* founded, Bangalore, Mysore, ed. H. H. Anniah Gowda.
J. *Miscellany* founded, C: WW, ed. P. Lal.
J. *Poet* founded, M, ed. Krishna Srinivas.
E. Dilip Chitre teaches at a school in Ethiopia, 1960–3.
E. A. K. Ramanujan, Fulbright scholar in USA, 1960–2.
E. Sahitya Akademi awards in Indian English literature begin.
E. Writers Workshop registered.

1961

J. *Imprint* founded, B. Nissim Ezekiel associate editor 1961–7.

J. *Mirror.*
J. *Osmania Journal of English Studies* founded, Hyderabad.
    Editors Shiv Kumar and V. A. Shahane.
E. Malay Roy Choudhury and Bengali 'Hungries' begin publica-
    tion, C.
E. Nissim Ezekiel appointed Professor of English in Mithibhai
    College of Arts, B.

1962

V. Lawrence Bantleman (b. 1942), *Graffiti*, C: WW.
V. Adil Jussawalla (b. 1940), *Land's End*, C: WW.
V. Monika Varma (b. 1946), *Dragonflies Draw Flame*, C: WW.
A. *Penguin Modern Poetry 2* (Dom Moraes, Kingsley Amis and
    Peter Porter).
.J. *The Century* (ND 1962–7).
P. K. R. Srinivasa Iyengar, *Indian Writing in English*, B: Asia
    Publishing House.
E. Allen Ginsberg in India.
E. A. K. Ramanujan appointed to University of Chicago.

1963

A. Margaret O'Donnell (ed.), *An Anthology of Commonwealth
    Verse*, London: Blackie and Son.
J. *Opinion* starts publishing poetry. (K. D. Katrak poetry
    advisor, 1963–73.)
E. R. Parthasarathy British Council scholar at University of
    Leeds, England, 1963–4.

1964

V. Lawrence Bantleman, *Man's Fall and Woman's Fall-Out*, C:
    WW.
Tr. A. K. Ramanujan, *Fifteen Tamil Love Poems*, C: WW.
J. *Bombay Duck* (B, 1964–5, 2 issues). Eds. S. V. Pradhan and R.
    Parthasarathy.
J. Lawrence Bantleman literary editor of *The Century* (ND),
    1964–7.
E. Kamala Das, Poetry Award, Asian PEN, Manila, Philippine
    Centre.
E. Nissim Ezekiel Visiting Professor, University of Leeds. Teaches
    course on Indian literature.

E. Writers Workshop group in ND, 1964–7, led by L. Bantleman.

196ɔ

V. Deb Kumar Das, *Through a Glass Darkly*, C: WW.
V. Kamala Das (b. 1934), *Summer in Calcutta*, BD: Rajinder Paul.
V. Nissim Ezekiel, *The Exact Name*, C: WW.
V. Dom Moraes, *John Nobody*, London: Eyre and Spottiswode.
V. P. K. Saha (b. 1932), *Poems from the Fifties*, C: WW.
A. P. L. Brent (ed.), *Young Commonwealth Poets*, London: Heinemann.
J. *damn you: a magazine of the arts* (Allahabad, 1965–8, 6 issues, stencilled). Founded by Arvind Krishna Mehrotra, Amit Rai and Alok Rai.
J. *Dionysius* (B, 2 issues), ed. S. V. Pradhan and A. S. Benjamin.
E. H. O. Nazareth moves to London.

1966

V. P. Lal, *'Change!' They Said*, C: WW.
V. Arvind Krishna Mehrotra (b. 1947), *bharatmata: a prayer*, Ezra-Fakir editions, B (stencilled).
V. Dom Moraes, *Poems 1955–1965*, New York: Macmillan.
V. Gieve Patel (b. 1940), *Poems*, B: Nissim Ezekiel.
V. A. K. Ramanujan (b. 1929), *The Striders*, London: OUP. (Recommended by the Poetry Book Society).
V. Monika Varma, *Gita Govinda and Other Poems*, C: WW.
A. Abu Sayeed Ayyub & Amlan Datta (eds.), *Ten Years of Quest*, B: Manaktalas.
J. *Contra 66* (ND, 4 issues, 1966–7). Editor, J. Swaminathan.
J. *Literature East and West*, vol. x, nos. 1 & 2, Indian Literature issue, State University College, New Paltz, NY, USA.
J. *Poetry India* (B, 1966–7, 6 issues), Ed. Nissim Ezekiel.
P. Rajeev Taranath and Meena Belliappa, *The Poetry of Nissim Ezekiel*, C: WW.
E. R. Parthasarathy, Ulka Poetry Prize of *Poetry India*.
    Amit Rai (b. 1948), poet and co-editor of *damn you*, dies.

1967

V. Lawrence Bantleman, *Kanchanjanga*, C: WW.
V. Lawrence Bantleman, *New Poems*, C: WW.
V. Ashok Chopra, *Town Poems*, B: Ezra-Fakir Press, stencilled.

V. Kamala Das, *The Descendants*, C: WW.

V. P. Lal, *Draupadi & Jayadratha*, C: WW.

V. Arvind Krishna Mehrotra, *Concrete Poetry*, B: Fakir Press, stencilled, 66–8?

V. Arvind Krishna Mehrotra, *Woodcuts on Paper*, London: Gallery Number Ten. (Some reprinted in ICA Bulletin, Aug.-Sept. 1967).

V. Pritish Nandy (b. 1947), *Of Gods and Olives*, C: WW.

V. R. Parthasarathy, *The First Step, Poems 1955–56* (stencilled, privately circulated).

A. Howard Sergeant (ed.), *Commonwealth Poets of Today*, London: John Murray.

Tr. Dilip Chitre (ed.), *An Anthology of Marathi Poetry*, B: Nirmala Sadanand.

Tr. A. K. Ramanujan, *The Interior Landscape*, Indiana University Press.

J. *Blunt* (B, 2 issues). Eds. R. Parthasarathy, S. Rege, I. Jayakar, K. Shri Kumar.

J. *Ezra: an imagiste magazine* founded (Allahabad, 1967–71, 5 issues, stencilled). Editor Arvind Mehrotra.

J. *Indian Writing Today* (B, 1967–70, 12 issues).

J. 'npw', English section of *Kruti*, edited by Pavan Kumar Jain, 1967–8.

J. *Poetry East West*, ed. Syed Amanuddin, Hyderabad / Sumter, South Carolina, USA.

J. *Sameeksa*, Indian Renaissance Number, M.

J. *Tornado* (B, 1967–70, 6 issues, stencilled). Editor Pavan Kumar Jain.

E. Nissim Ezekiel's first LSD trip (24 in 1967–72).

1968

V. Deb Kumar Das, *The Eyes of Autumn*, C: WW.

V. Gauri Deshpande (b. 1942), *Between Births*, C: WW.

V. Paul Jacob (b. 1940), *Sonnets*, C: WW.

V. K. D. Katrak (b. 1936), *A Journal of the Way*, C: WW.

V. Dom Moraes, *Bedlam and Others*, London: Turret Press.

V. Pritish Nandy, *I Hand You in Turn My Nebbuk Wreath*, C: Dialogue Publications.

V. Pritish Nandy, *On Either Side of Arrogance*, C: WW.

V. Rakshat Puri (b. 1925), *Poems*, C: WW.

V. Srinivas Rayaprol (b. 1925), *Bones and Distances*, C: WW (second edition, 1975).

V. F. Stanley Rajiva (F. R. Stanley), *The Permanent Element*, C: WW.

V. G. S. Sharat Chandra (b. 1938), *Bharata Natyam Dancer and Other Poems*, C: WW (second edition, 1975).

A. Howard Sergeant (ed.), *New Voices of the Commonwealth*, London: Evans.

J. *Dialogue Calcutta* (C, 1968–70, 19 issues, restarted 1972–5 as *Dialogue India*). Editor Pritish Nandy.

J. *Fakir* i, B: Ezra Fakir editions. (Dilip Chitre's translation of Tukaram.)

J. *Intrepid* (no. 10), Buffalo, New York, 'New Prose and Poetry from India'.

P. Devindra Kohli, *Virgin Whiteness: The Poetry of Kamala Das*, C: WW.

P. Dom Moraes, *My Son's Father*, London: Secker & Warburg.

P. M. K. Naik, *et al.*, *Critical Essays on Indian Writing in English*, Dharwar: Karnatak University, repub. 1972, 1977.

P. Shankar Mokashi-Punekar, *P. Lal, An Appreciation*, C: WW.

E. A. K. Ramanujan, Gold Medal of Tamil Writers Association for *Interior Landscape*.

1969

V. Nissim Ezekiel, *The Unfinished Man*, (1960, 1965). Student edition with notes by Eunice de Souza, C: WW.

V. Paul Jacob, *Alter Sonnets*, C: WW.

V. K. D. Katrak, *Diversions by the Wayside: Poems*, C: WW.

V. P. Lal, *Yakshi from Didarganj*, C: WW.

V. Pritish Nandy, *From the Outer Bank of the Brahmaputra*, New York: New Rivers Press.

V. Anil Saari, *an odd thing*, damn you press, stencilled.

VD. Pritish Nandy, *Rites for a Plebeian Statue*, C: WW.

A. Daisy Alden (ed.), *Poems From India*, New York: Thomas Crowell.

A. P. Lal (ed.), *Modern Indian Poetry in English: An Anthology and a Credo*, C: WW (second edition, 1971).

D. Nissim Ezekiel, *Three Plays*, C: WW.

J.   Ivar Ivask (ed.), *Books Abroad*, Oklahoma, USA, vol. 43, no. 4, on Indian Literature.

J.   *Banasthali Patrika*: issues on Indo-English Literature.

J.   *Vrishchik* (Baroda, 1969–73, 48 numbers). Editors Gulam Sheikh and Bhupen Khakhar.

P.   Sukanta Chaudhuri, *Bantleman's 'Kanchanjanga': A Critical Monograph*, C: WW.

P.   David McCutchion, *Indian Writing in English*, C: WW. (Reprint, 1973).

E.   Nissim Ezekiel poetry editor, *Illustrated Weekly*, 1969–71.

1970

V.   K. N. Daruwalla (b. 1937), *Under Orion*, C: WW.

V.   Deb Kumar Das, *The Fire Canto*, C: WW.

V.   Gauri Deshpande, *Lost Love*, C: WW.

V.   Mamta Kalia (b. 1940), *Tribute to Papa*, C: WW.

V.   Suresh Kohli (b. 1947), *Death's Epicure*, C: WW.

V.   Shiv Kumar (b. 1921), *Articulate Silences*, C: WW.

V.   Keshav Malik, *Poems*, C: WW.

V.   Pritish Nandy, *Masks to be Interpreted in Terms of Messages*, C: WW.

V.   Monika Varma, *Green Leaves and Gold*, C: WW.

A.   V. K. Gokak (ed.), *The Golden Treasury of Indo-Anglian Poetry*, ND: Sahitya Akademi (Reprint 1978, 1983).

A.   Howard Sergeant (ed.), *Pergamon Poets 9: Poetry from India*, Oxford: Pergamon Press (Ramanujan, Parthasarathy, Ezekiel, Deb Kumar Das).

J.   *Indian Literature*, vol. 13, no. 1, special number on Indian writing in English.

J.   *Kamadhenu*, founded (USA, 1970–8, 16 issues). Ed. G. S. Sharat Chandra.

J.   *Quadrant*, vol. xiv, no. 6 (Nov.-Dec. 1970), Asia 1971, Special Issue, Sydney, Australia.

J.   *Rupambara*, vol. 1, no. 6, International Poetry Number, C.

J.   *Skylark* founded (Aligarh). Editor Baldeu Mirza.

P.   H. M. Williams, *Indo-Anglian Literature 1800–1970*, B: Orient Longman.

1971

V.   K. N. Daruwalla, *Apparition in April*, C: WW.

V. Deb Kumar Das, *The Labyrinths*, C: WW.

V. Gopal Honnalgere (b. 1942), *A Wad of Poems*, C: WW.

V. Jayanta Mahapatra (b. 1928), *Close the Sky, Ten by Ten*, C: Dialogue publication.

V. Jayanta Mahapatra, *Svayamara and Other Poems*, C: WW.

V. K. Malik, *Poems*, C: WW.

V. Arvind Krishna Mehrotra, *Pomes/Poemes/Poemas*, Baroda: Vrishchik publication.

V. Pritish Nandy, *Madness is the Second Stroke*, C: Dialogue Publications.

V. Gauri Pant (b. 1920), *Weeping Season*, C: WW.

V. A. K. Ramanujan, *Relations*, London, OUP.

V. G. S. Sharat Chandra, *April in Nanjangud*, London: London Magazine Edition.

V. Monika Varma, *Quartered Questions and Queries*, C: WW.

A. Shiv Kumar (ed.), *Indian Verse in English*, C: WW.

A. P. Lal (ed.), *Modern Indian Poetry in English: An Anthology and a Credo*, C: WW. Expanded edition.

V. Pritish Nandy, *Bangla Desh: A Voice of a New Nation*, C: Dialogue.

Tr. Pritish Nandy, *The Prose Poems of Lokenath Bhattacharya*, C: Dialogue.

J. *India Horizons*, N. D.

J. *Poetry Time*, ed. Laxmi Narayan Mahapatra, Berhampur.

P. Usha Katrak and Kersey Katrak, *Five Little Sermons Went to Market*, C: WW.

E. Kamala Das poetry editor, *Illustrated Weekly*, 1971–2.

E. Arvind Mehrotra Visiting Writer, University of Iowa International Writing Program, 1971–3.

E. R. Parthasarathy joins OUP, M, moves to ND, 1978.

E. Saleem Peeradina student in USA, 1971–4.

1972

V. Agha Shahid Ali (b. 1949), *Bone-Sculpture*, C: WW.

V. Richard Bartholomew, *Story of Siddhartha's Release*, C: WW.

V. Ruskin Bond (b. 1934), *It Isn't Time That's Passing*, C: WW.

V. Dilip Chitre (b. 1938), *Ambulance Ride*, B: self-published.

V. Gauri Deshpande, *Beyond the Slaughterhouse*, C: Dialogue Publications.

V. Gopal Honnalgere, *A Gesture of Fleshless Sound*, C: WW.

V. Suresh Kohli, *Target for a Kiss*, C: Dialogue Publication.

V. P. Lal, *Love's The First*, C: WW.

V. Arvind Krishna Mehrotra, *Twelve Poems from the Good Surrealist*, B: Ezra-Fakir Editions (stencilled).

V. Gauri Pant, *Voodoo*, C: WW.

V. Rakshat Puri, *Nineteen Poems*, C: WW.

V. Srinivas Rayaprol, *Married Love and Other Poems*, C: WW.

V. Subhas C. Saha (b. 1946), *Insights*, C: WW.

V. Monika Varma, *Past Imperative*, C: WW.

A. Pritish Nandy (ed.), *Indian Poetry in English: 1947–1972*, ND: Oxford and IBH Publishing Company.

A. Saleem Peeradina (ed.), *Contemporary Poetry in English; An Assessment and Selection*, *Quest* 74 (January) and B: Macmillan (Reprint 1977).

J. *Debonair* founded, B. Poetry editor Imtiaz Dharker.

J. *Dialogue-India* (C, 1972–5, 18–20 issues). Ed. Pritish Nandy.

J. *Gray Book* (Cuttack, 1972–3, 3 issues). Associate Editor Jayanta Mahapatra.

J. Howard McCord, (ed.), *Young Poets of India, Measure 3*, Bowling Green, Ohio: Tribal Press.

J. *Youth Times* (ND, 1972–9). Poetry Editor Keshav Malik, 1973–6.

E. Daruwalla's *Appartion in April* (1971) receives Uttar Pradesh State Award.

E. Nissim Ezekiel appointed Reader (subsequently Professor) of American Literature, University of Bombay.

1973

V. Richard Bartholomew, *Poems*, C: WW.

V. Kamala Das, *The Old Playhouse and Other Poems*, M: Orient Longman.

V. Gopal Honnalgere, *Zen Tree and Wild Innocents*, Cuttack: Gray Book Publications.

V. Paul Jacob, *Swedish Exercises*, C: WW.

V. Pritish Nandy, *The Poetry of Pritish Nandy*, C: Oxford and IBH.

V. Gauri Pant, *Staircase*, C: WW.

V. S. Santhi (b. 1934), *Angetral*, ND: AH.

V. Monika Varma, *Alakananda*, C: WW.

A. David Cevert (ed.), *The Shell and the Rain: Poems from New India*, London: Allen & Unwin.

A. Pritish Nandy (ed.), *Indian Poetry in English Today*, ND: Sterling.

Tr. Arvind K. Mehrotra, *Three: Poems by Bogomil Gjuzel*, Allahabad and Iowa City, Ezra-Fakir Press.

Tr. Soubhagya Kumar Misra, *Countermeasures*, translations by Jayanta Mahapatra, C: Dialogue Publications.

Tr. A. K. Ramanujan, *Speaking of Siva*, Harmondsworth: Penguin.

J. *Indian Verse* (C, 1973–8, 24 issues). Editor Pranab Bandyopadhyay.

J. *The Journal of Indian Writing in English* founded, editor G. S. Balarama Gupta, Gulbarga University.

J. *Minimax* (ND, 1973–6). Ed. Durgadas Mukhopadhyay.

J. *Poetry from Bombay* (B, Siddharth College of Arts and Sciences, also 1975).

J. *The Probitas* (1973–6, 5 issues). Editor H. P. P. Patnaik.

J. *Soliloquy* (ND, St Stephen's College, 1973–6).

J. *South and West* (Arkansas, USA), vol. 11, no. 4, special Indian issue, ed. Jayanta Mahapatra.

J. *Vagartha* (ND, 1973–9, 25 issues). Ed. Meenakshi Mukherjee, Joshi Foundation.

P. Monika Varma, *Facing Four* (Kamala Das, Gauri Deshpande, Suniti Namjoshi, Bharati Sarabhai), C: WW. 1973.

E. Arnold Heinemann Indian Poetry series starts.

1974

V. Lakshmi Kannan (b. 1947), *Impressions*, C: WW.

V. Shiv Kumar, *Cobwebs in the Sun*, ND: Tata McGraw-Hill.

V. P. Lal, *The Man of Dharma and the Rasa of Silence*, C: WW.

V. Ashok Mahajan (b. 1940), *The Garden of Fand*, C: WW.

V. Pritish Nandy, *Dhritarashtra Downtown:* Zero, C: Dialogue Publications.

V. Tejaswini Niranjana (b. 1958), *Liquid Sapphire*, Bangalore, Christ College (second revised edition 1978).

V. P. K. Saha, *Blue Magic*, C: WW.

V. G. S. Sharat Chandra, *Once or Twice*, Sutton, England: Hippoppotammus Press.

A. Gauri Deshpande (ed.), *An Anthology of Indo-English Poetry*, ND: Hind Pocketbooks.

A. Adil Jussawalla (ed.), *New Writing in India* (verse and prose), Harmondsworth: Penguin.

Tr. Nissim Ezekiel with Vrinda Nabar, *Snakeskin and Other*

Poems (translations from Marathi of Indira Sant), B: Popular Prakashan.

J. *Opinion Literary Quarterly* (B, four issues). Eds. K. Katrak and Gauri Deshpande.

J. *Volume* (B, 5 issues). Ed. Niteen Gupte.

P. Chetan Karnani, *Nissim Ezekiel*, ND: A H.

E. A. K. Ramanujan's *Speaking of Siva* nominated for National Book Award in USA.

1975

V. Pranab Bandyopadhyay (b. 1925), *Wherever You Go*, C: Oxford and IBH.

V. Ruskin Bond, *Long Fox Dancing*, C: WW.

V. Pritish Nandy, *Lonesong Street*, C. Poets Press and AH.

V. Pritish Nandy, *Riding the Midnight River: Selected Poems*, ND: AH.

V. Ami (tava) Ray (b. 1952), *Apocalypso*, C: WW.

V. G. S. Sharat Chandra, *Offsprings of Servagna*, C: WW.

A. Pranab Bandyopadhyay (ed.), *The Voice of the Indian Poets: An Anthology of Indian Poetry*, C: UW.

J. Distractions (Hyderabad). Ed. Srinivas Rayaprol.

J. *Fulcrum* (B, 1975–6, 12 issues). Ed. Yogi Agrawal, poetry editor Gieve Patel.

J. *Littcrit* founded (Kerala). Editor P. K. Rajan (Published poetry 1975–8).

J. *Poetry* (C, later Berhampur). Ed. N. Mohanty.

J. *Spark*, C, 1975–6.

P. Devindra Kohli, *Kamala Das*, ND: AH.

E. Dilip Chitre member of International Writers program, University of Iowa. Remains in USA until 1977.

E. Emergency rule 1975–7. Many journals cease publication.

E. Jayanta Mahapatra, Jacob Glatstein Memorial Award (Chicago).

1976

V. Meena Alexander (b. 1951), *The Bird's Bright Ring*, C: WW.

V. K. N. Daruwalla, *Crossing of Rivers*, ND: OUP.

V. Deb Kumar Das, *The Winterbird Walks*, C: WW.

V. Nissim Ezekiel, *Hymns in Darkness*, ND: OUP.

V. Adil Jussawalla, *Missing Person*, B: CH.

V. Lakshmi Kanan, *The Glow and the Grey*, C: WW.

V. Randhir Khare (b. 1951), *Hunger*, C: WW.
V. Arun Kolatkar (b. 1932), *Jejuri*, B: CH.
V. Shiv Kumar, *Subterfuges*, ND: OUP.
V. Jayanta Mahapatra, *A Father's Hours*, C: UW.
V. Jayanta Mahapatra, *A Rain of Rites*, U. of Georgia Press, USA.
V. Arvind Krishna Mehrotra, *Nine Enclosures*, B: CH.
V. Pritish Nandy, *In Secret Anarchy*, C: UW.
V. Pritish Nandy, *A Stranger Called I*, ND: AH and Poets Press (Revised version, ND: AH and Kavita, also 1976).
V. Gieve Patel, *How Do You Withstand, Body*, B: CH.
V. Rakshat Puri, *The Year Like a Fuse*, C: WW.
V. A. K. Ramanujan, *Selected Poems*, ND: OUP.
V. Santan Rodrigues (b. 1948), *I Exist*, C: WW.
A. R. Parthasarathy (ed.), *Ten Twentieth Century Indian Poets*, ND OUP.
J. *Art and Poetry* (ND, 1976–82, 20 issues). Editor Keshav Malik.
J. *The Book Review* founded, ND.
J. *Commonwealth Quarterly* founded, Mysore.
J. *Indian Book Chronicle* founded, ND.
J. Inder N. Kher (ed.), *Journal of South Asian Literature*, vol. 11, 3–4, Nissim Ezekiel Issue.
J. *Kavi* founded (B, 1976–7, 5 issues, unregistered). Editors, Santan Rodrigues, Aroop Mitra, Ivan Kostka and Rajiv Rao. Becomes *Kavi-India*, 1978. Editor Santan Rodrigues, consulting editor Nissim Ezekiel.
J. *The Literary Criterion*, XII, no. 2–3, Indian Writing in English.
P. Kamala Das, *Alphabet of Lust*, ND: Orient paperback.
P. Kamala Das, *My Story*, ND: Sterling (Reprinted 1977).
P.' Subhoranjan Dasgupta, *Pritish Nandy*, ND: AH.
P. Adil Jussawalla and Eunice de Souza (eds.), *Statements: An Anthology of Indian Prose in English*, B: Orient Longman.
E. Clearing House begins.
E. Nissim Ezekiel poetry editor, *Illustrated Weekly*.
E. Kolatkar's *Jejuri* awarded Commonwealth Poetry Prize.
E. Jayanta Mahapatra member of International Writers program, University of Iowa.
E. Oxford University Press New Poetry in India series begins.

1977

V. Meena Alexander, *Without Place*, C: WW.

V. Meena Alexander, *I Root My Name*, C: WW.

V. P. Lal, *Calcutta: A Long Poem*, C: WW.

V. P. Lal, *Collected Poems*, C: WW.

V. Niranjan Mohanty (b. 1953), *Silencing the Words*, C: UW.

V. Pritish Nandy, *Nowhere Man*, ND: AH.

V. R. Parthasarathy (b. 1934), *Rough Passage*, ND: OUP.

A. Roger Weaver and Joseph Bruchac (eds.), *Aftermath*, Green-field Review Press, New York.

A. Syed Ameeruddin (ed.), *Indian Verse in English: A Contemporary Anthology*, M. Poets Press.

A. Pritish Nandy (ed.), *Strangertime: An Anthology of Indian Poetry in English*, ND: Hind Pocket Books.

J. *New Quest*, Poona.

J. *Osmania Journal of English Studies*, vol. 13, no. 1, on Contemporary Indian Poetry in English.

P. Meenakshi Mukherjee (ed.), *Considerations: Twelve Studies of Indo-Anglian Writing*, ND: Allied Publishers.

E. Emergency ends.

1978

V. Gopal Honnalgere, *Nudist Camp*, Dharwad: Release Publications.

V. K. R. Srinivasa Iyengar (b. 1908), *Cosmographica Poetica*, C: WW.

V. Sunita Jain (b. 1941), *Man of My Desires*, C: WW.

V. Suresh Kohli, *Since Decay Impairs*, ND: Indian Literary Review Editions.

V. Pritish Nandy, *Pritish Nandy 30*, ND: Kavita and AH.

V. Tejaswini Niranjana, *Burnt Smoke and Wood Ash*, Bangalore, Christ College.

V. Rakshat Puri, *In the Chronicle*, ND: Paraj Prakashan.

V. G. S. Sharat Chandra, *The Ghost of Meaning*, Lewis Clark College, Lewiston, Idaho: Conference Press.

V. *Three Poets*: Melanie Silgardo (b. 1956), Raul D'Gama Rose, Santan Rodrigues, B: NG.

A. Mary Ann Dasgupta (ed.), *Hers: An Anthology of Poetry in English by Indian Women*, C: WW.

A. P. Lal (ed.), *New English Poetry by Indian Men*, C: WW.

J. *The Indian Literary Review* (ND, 1978–9, 13 issues). Ed. Suresh Kohli. Restarted 1984.

J. *Kavi-India* founded, B. Editor Santan Rodrigues; consulting editor Nissim Ezekiel.

J. *Lyric* (ND, St Stephen's College, 1978–82).

E. Nissim Ezekiel reads at Rotterdam International Poetry Festival.

E. Shiv Kumar Commonwealth Visiting Professor, University of Kent, England. Elected Fellow of Royal Society of Literature.

E. Shiv Kumar poetry editor, *Illustrated Weekly*.

E. Jayanta Mahapatra at Writers Week, Adelaide, Australia, Festival of Arts.
Newground begins.

E. R. Parthasarathy member of International Writers program, University of Iowa, 1978–9.

1979

V. Agha Shahid Ali, *In Memory of Begum Akhtar*, C: WW.

V. Kamala Das and Pritish Nandy, *Tonight, This Savage Rite*, ND: AH.

V. Eunice de Souza (b. 1940), *Fix*, B: NG.

V. K. R. Srinivasa Iyengar, *Leaves from a Log*, ND: AH.

V. Sunita Jain, *Beneath the Frost*, ND: Indian Literary Review edition.

V. Sunita Jain, *Between You and God*, C: WW.

V. Mamta Kalia, *Poems '78*, C: WW.

V. K. D. Katrak, *Underworld*, C: WW.

V. H. K. Kaul (b. 1941), *A New Journey*, ND: AH.

V. Randhir Khare, *13 Poems*, Silver Cord Publishers.

V. Shiv Kumar, *Woodpeckers*, London: Sidgwick & Jackson.

V. Jayanta Mahapatra, *Waiting*, ND: Samkaleen Prakashan.

V. Pritish Nandy, *Anywhere is Another Place*, ND: AH.

V. Pritish Nandy, *The Selected Poems*, ed. Krishna Srinivas, M: Poets Press India.

V. Shreela Ray, *The Passion of Draupadi*, C: WW.

J. *Chandrabhaga* (Cuttack, 1979–85, 14 issues). Ed. Jayanta Mahapatra.

J. *ETC.* (C, 1979–80). Director Pranab Bandyopadhyay.

J. *Expression India* (Cuttack, 1 issue). Ed. Bijoy K. Sahoo, advisory editor Jayanta Mahapatra.

J. *The Humanities Review*, (ND). Editor Chaman Nahal.

J. *Tenor* (Hyderabad, 1979–80, 4 issues).

P. S. Z. H. Abidi, *Studies in Indo-Anglian Poetry*, Bareilly: Prakash Book Depot.

P. Arnab Bandyopadhyay (ed.), *Interpretations* (of Pranab Bandyopadhyay), C: WW.

P. K. N. Daruwalla, *Sword and Abyss: A Collection of Short Stories*, ND: Vikas (reprinted 1982).

P. A. N. Dwivedi, *Indo-Anglian Poetry*, Allahabad: Kitab Mahal.

1980

V. Meena Alexander, *Stone Roots*, ND: AH.

V. Dilip Chitre, *Travelling in a Cage*, B: CH.

V. K. N. Daruwalla, *Winter Poems*, B: Allied Publishers.

V. Pria Devi, *In Tensities: Selected Verse, 1970–75*, ND: Samkaleen Prakashan.

V. Gopal Honnalgere, *The Fifth*, Hyderabad: Broomstick Publications.

V. Sunita Jain, *Love Time*, ND: AH.

V. Ashok Mahajan, *Vivisections*, C: WW.

V. Jayanta Mahapatra, *The False Start*, B: CH.

V. Jayanta Mahapatra, *Relationship*, Greenfield Review Press, New York (Indian edition, Cuttack 1982).

V. Saleem Peeradina (b. 1944), *First Offence*, B: NG.

A. O. P. Bhatnagar and Vikramraj (eds.), *New Dimensions in Indo-English Poetry*, Mysore: Commonwealth Quarterly.

A. K. N. Daruwalla, *Two Decades of Indian Poetry: 1960–1980*, ND: Vikas.

A. A. N. Dwivedi (ed.), *Indian Poetry in English*, ND: AH.

Tr. Sitakant Mahapatra, *The Song of Kubja and Other Poems*, translated by Jayanta Mahapatra, ND: Samkaleen Prakashan.

J. *Cygnus* (Lucknow), vol. ii, no. 1, on Indian Writing in English.

J. *Ekestasis*, ND.

J. *Freedom First* (B, 1980–3). Ed. Nissim Ezekiel.

P. Chirantan Kulshrestha (ed.), *Contemporary Indian Verse: an Evaluation*, ND: AH.

P. Amitava Ray, *Baby Tiger*, Glebe, Australia and Los Angeles: Wild and Woolley.

P. V. A. Shahane and M. Sivaramkrishna (eds.), *Indian Poetry in English: A Critical Assessment*, ND; Macmillan.

1981

V. Keshav Malik, *26 Poems*, ND: Malik.

V. Pritish Nandy, *The Rainbow Last Night*, ND: AH.

V. Donald T. Nigli, *Sattvanti*, C: WW.

V. Manohar Shetty (b. 1953), *A Guarded Space*, B: NG.

A. Guy Amirthanayagam and S. C. Harrex (eds.), *Only Connect*, Centre for Research in the New Literatures in English, Adelaide and Honolulu.

A. Keshav Malik and Manohar Banjopadhyay (eds.), *19 Poets: An Anthology*, ND: Pachi Prakashan.

Tr. A. K. Ramanujan, *Hymns for the Drowning*, Princeton Univ. Press, USA.

J. *Journal of Literature and Aesthetics*, Quilon, Kerala.

P. O. P. Bhatnagar (ed.), *Studies in Indian Poetry in English*, Jaipur: Rachana Prakashan.

P. Pritish Nandy, *Some Friends: Stories*, ND: AH.

P. Anisur Rahman, *Expressive Form in the Poetry of Kamala Das*, ND: Abhinav Publications.

P. Anisur Rehman, *Form and Value in the Poetry of Nissim Ezekiel*, ND: Abhinav Publications.

E. Film of Pritish Nandy, *Lonesong Street*.

E. Jayanta Mahapatra, Sahitya Akademi award for *Relationship*.

E. Arvind Mehrotra, Homi Bhabha Fellowship.

1982

V. K. N. Daruwalla, *The Keeper of the Dead*, ND: OUP.

V. Bob D'Costa (b. 1960), *A Brutal Sunset*, C: WW.

V. Nissim Ezekiel, *Latter-Day Psalms*, ND: OUP.

V. Sunita Jain, *Silences*, ND: National Publishing House.

V. Jayanta Mahapatra, *Relationship* (1980), Indian edition, Cuttack: Chandrabhaga Society.

V. Keshav Malik, *Negatives*, Berhampur: Poetry Time Publications.

V. Arvind Krishna Mehrotra, *Distance in Statute Miles*, B: CH.

V. *Poems of Gitanjali*, (1961–1977), Stocksfield, England: Oriel Press.

V. Vikram Seth (b. 1952), *Mappings*, C: WW.

V. G. S. Sharat Chandra, *Heirloom*, ND: OUP.

V. Man Mohan Singh, *Village Poems*, ND: AH.

J. *Journal of Literature and Aesthetics*, vol. 2, no. 4 (Quilon, Kerala), special number: 'Aesthetics of Irony in Indian Poetry in English'.

J. *Keynote* (B, 1982–3, 6 issues). Editor Manohar Shetty; assistant editor Melanie Silgardo.

J. *New Letters*, David Ray (ed.), vol. 48, no. 3–4, Kansas City, USA, special Indian issue.

J. *Orbit*, ed. Hari Mohan Prasad, Gaya.

P. Bijay Kumar Das, *Modern Indo-English Poetry*, Bareilly: Prakash Book Depot.

P. M. K. Naik, *A History of Indian English Literature*, ND: Sahitya Akademi.

1983

V. Jayanta Mahapatra, *Life Signs*, ND: OUP.

V. Aroop Mitra (b. 1955), *Displacing the Sunlight*, B: Wildhorse Press.

V. Dom Moraes, *Absences*, B: Dom Moraes.

V. Rajiv Rao (b. 1950) and Rafique Baghdadi (b. 1947), *45 RPM*, B: The Hack Writers' Cooperative.

A. J. O. Perry (ed.), *Voices of Emergency*, B: Popular Prakashan.

J. *Ariel* (Canada), vol. 14, no. 4, Indian issue.

J. *Opinion* ceases publication.

P. A. N. Dwivedi, *Kamala Das and Her Poetry*, ND: Doaba House.

P. Bijay Kumar Das (ed.), *Perspectives on the Poetry of R. Partha-sarathy*, Bareilly: Prakash Book Depot.

P. Shiv Kumar, *Nude Before God*, New York: Vanguard.

P. E. N. Lall, *The Poetry of Encounter: Dom Moraes, A. K. Rama-nujan and Nissim Ezekiel*, ND: Sterling.

P. K. R. Srinivasa Iyengar, *Indian Writing in English*, third, enlarged edition, ND: Sterling.

P. Vikram Seth, *From Heaven Lake: Travels through Sinkiang and Tibet*, London: Chatto & Windus/Hogarth Press.

E. Nissim Ezekiel general editor of Bibliography of Indian Writing in English series, ND: Concept Publishing Company.

E. Nissim Ezekiel, Sahitya Akademi award for *Latter-Day Psalms*.

E. A. K. Ramanujan, MacArthur Fellow, 1983–8.

1984

V. Kamala Das, *Collected Poems*, vol. 1, Trivandrum: Navakerala Printers.

V. Patrick Fernando (Sri Lankan poet 1931–1982), *Selected Poems*, ND: OUP.

V. Sunita Jain, *Find Me With Rain*, ND: Amrit Publications.

V. K. D. Katrak, *Purgatory*, ND: AH.

V. Arun Kolatkar, *Jejuri*: Zweisprachige Ausgabe (German translation by Giovanni Bandini), Freiburg, Germany: Verlag Wolf Mersch.

V. Jayanta Mahapatra, *Dispossessed Nests: The 1984 Poems*, Jaipur: Nirala Publications.

V. Arvind Krishna Mehrotra, *Middle Earth*, ND: OUP.

V. H. O. Nazareth (b. 1944), *Lobo*, B: CH.

V. Yuyutsu R. D. (b. 1960), *A Prayer in Daylight*, Jaipur: Nirala.

A. Keshav Malik (ed.), *Centre and Circumference*, ND: Authors Guild of India.

J. *Choice*, ND.

J. *Helix* (Melbourne, Australia), no. 19–20, 'Ten Contemporary Indian Poets', ed. Bibhu Padhi, pp. 35–53.

J. *Kaiser-E-Hind* supersedes *Opinion*.

P. K. R. Srinivasa Iyengar, *Indian Writing in English*, fourth edition, ND: Sterling.

P. M. K. Naik (ed.), *Perspectives on Indian Poetry in English*, ND: Abhinav Publications.

E. Keshav Malik retires as editor of *Indian Literature*. S. Balu Rao becomes editor.

E. K. N. Daruwalla, Sahitya Akademi award for *The Keeper of the Dead* (1982).

E. Pritish Nandy, E. M. Forster Award.

1985

V. Deb Kumar Das, *Through a Glass Darkly*, C: WW.

V. Lakshmi Kanaan, *Exiled Gods*, ND: AH.

V. H. K. Kaul, *On the Waves: Poems*, ND: AH.

V. Keshav Malik, *Between Nobody and Steps*, ND: Abhinov Publications.

V. Keshav Malik, *Shapes in Peeling Plaster*, ND: AH.

V. Vikram Seth, *The Humble Administrator's Garden*, Manchester, England: Carcanet Press.

V.   Melanie Silgardo, *Skies of Design*, London: The College Press.

Tr.   A. K. Ramanujan, *Poems of Love and War*, New York: Columbia University Press/ND: OUP.

J.   *India Literary Review*, restarted, ND. Editor Devindra Kohli.

E.   Kamala Das, Sahitya Akademi award for *Collected Poems*, vol. 1 (1984).

E.   Poetry Society of India, ND, Keshav Malik Chairman, H. K. Kaul Secretary. *TPS Bulletin* begins.

E.   Nissim Ezekiel retires as Professor of English, University of Bombay.

E.   Vikram Seth awarded the Commonwealth Poetry Prize for Asia for *The Humble Administrator's Garden*.

1986

V.   K. B. Basant, *Ellipses*, C: WW.

V.   *Kamala Das: A Selection with Essays on Her Works.* Editors: S. C. Harrex and Vincent O'Sullivan. Adelaide: Centre for Research in the New Literatures in English.

V.   Sunita Jain, *Till I Find Myself*, ND: Sterling.

V.   Shiv K. Kumar, *Trapfalls in the Sky*, M: Macmillan.

V.   A. K. Ramanujan, *Second Sight*, ND: OUP.

V.   Vikram Seth, *The Golden Gate*, New York: Random House and London: Faber. (ND: OUP, 1987)

J.   *Delhi-London Poetry Quarterly*, Starts, Richmond, Surrey. Editor Gopi Warrier.

J.   Special Nissim Ezekiel issue of *The Journal of Indian Writing in English*, vol. 14, no. 2. (Guest editor, Hanovi Anklesaria)

J.   Special Bombay poetry issue, *The Literary Endeavour*, vol. 8, nos. 1–2 (1986–87). (Guest editor, R. Raj Rao). Hyderabad.

P.   Jayanta Mahapatra, *Orissa*, ND: Lustre Press.

P.   Madhusudan Prasad (ed.), *The Poetry of Jayanta Mahapatra*, ND: Sterling.

P.   A.K. Ramanujan and Stuart Blackburn (eds), *Another Harmony: new essays on the folklore of India*, Berkeley: University of California

E.   Poetry Circle, B. Secretary: Menka Shivdasani.

E.   Film on Nissim Ezekiel, by Jane Swany, 1986–87.

E.   Nissim Ezekiel, Chair of international panel of judges for Commonwealth International Poetry Award. Eunice de Souza, judge. Vikram Seth's *Golden Gate* co-winner of award.

E. Nissim Ezekiel, Kamala Das, Adil Jussawalla at International Book Fair, Frankfurt.
E. Jayanta Mahapatra at Cultural Center, Rockfeller Foundation, Bellagio, Italy.
E. Vikram Seth, Guggenheim Fellowship.
E. Vikram Seth, return to India.

1987

V. Agha Shadid Ali, *The Half-Inch Himalayas*, Middletown, Connecticut: Wesleyan University Press.
V. Agha Shadid Ali, *A Walk through the Yellow Pages*, Tuscon, Arizona: SUN-Gemini Press.
V. K. N. Daruwalla, *Landscapes*, ND:OUP.
V. Chitra Banerjee Divakaruni (b. 1956), *Dark Like the River*, C:WW.
V. Gopal Honnalgere, *Internodes*, ND: Samakaleen Prakashan.
V. Jayanta Mahapatra, *Selected Poems*, ND: OUP.
V. Dom Moraes, *Collected Poems: 1957–1987*, ND: Penguin.
J. *Chelesea*, 46, New York. Commonwealth issue.
P. Bruce King, *Modern Indian Poetry in English*, ND: OUP.
P. Devinder Mohan, *Jayanta Mahapatra*, ND: AH.
E. K. N. Daruwalla, Asian Region Commonwealth Poetry Prize for *Landscapes*.
E. Nissim Ezekiel in Canada: Conference on India Forty Years after Independence.
E. Adil Jussawalla literary editor of *Debonair*.
E. Lakshmi Kannan, Iowa International Writers Workshop.
E. Shiv K. Kumar, Sahitya Akademi award for *Trapfalls in the Sky*.
E. Manohar Shetty, editor of *Goa Today* until 1993.

1988

VP. Meena Alexander, *House of a Thousand Doors*, Washington, D.C.: Three Continents Press.
V. Sujata Bhatt (b. 1956), *Brunizem*, Manchester: Carcanet.
V. Eunice de Souza, *Women in Dutch Painting*, B.: Praxis.
V. Tabish Khair (b.1966), *Twilight Thoughts*, Aligarh: SL [Skylark] Publications.
V. Jayanta Mahapatra, *Burden of Waves and Fruit*, Washington, D.C.: Three Continents Press.
V. Robin Ngangom (b. 1959), *Words and Silence*, C: WW.

V.   Bibhu Padhi (b. 1951), *Going to the Temple*, ND: Indus Publishing Company.

V.   Manohar Shetty, *Borrowed Time*, B: Praxis.

A.   Vilas Sarang (ed.), *Indian English Poetry Since 1950*, B: Orient Longman.

D.   Gieve Patel, *Mister Behram*, B: Praxis. (Originally staged 1987.)

J.   *Bahuvachan: An Occasional of the Arts and Ideas*, Bhopal.

J.   *Kavya Bharati: A Review of Indian Poetry* (Madurai: American College). Ed. Jayanta Mahapatra.

J.   *Nimrod*. Special Indian issue, Tulsa, Oklahoma.

P.   Makarand Paranjape, *Mysticism in Indian English Poetry*, ND: B.R. Publishers.

E.   Meena Alexander, *Night Scene, the Garden* (pub 1992) produced as play, New York.

E.   All India Poetry Competition, sponsored by Poetry Society (India) and the British Council. Vijay Nambisan awarded first prize.

E.   Nissim Ezekiel, Padma Shri Award by the President of India for contribution to literature in English.

E.   Nissim Ezekiel at Adelaide, Australia and Wellington, New Zealand Arts Festivals.

E.   Gopal Honnalgere, first prize, Poetry Circle, B.

E.   Saleem Peeradina moves to the United States in 1988.

E.   Melanie Silgardo, editor, Virago publishers, London, until 1995.

1989

V.   Meena Alexander, *The Storm*, New York: Red Dust.

V.   Debjani Chatterjee (b.1952), *I Was That Woman*, England: Hippopotamus Press.

V.   Imtiaz Dharker (b. 1954), *Purdah and Other Poems*, ND: OUP.

V.   Nissim Ezekiel, *Collected Poems: 1952–1988*, ND: OUP.

V.   Jayanta Mahapatra, *Temple*, Mundelstrup, Denmark: Dangaroo Press.

V.   Hoshang Merchant (b.1947), *Stone to Fruit*, C: WW.

VP.   Suniti Namjoshi, *Because of India: Selected Poems and Fables*, London: Onlywomen Press.

A.   H. K. Kaul (ed.), *Poetry India: Voices in the Making*, ND: Arnold.

J.   *The Bombay Review* (ed.), Vilas Sarang, Five issues 1989-91.

J.   *The Journal of the Poetry Society of India*, ND.

P.   Meena Alexander, *Women in Romanticism*, London: Macmillan.

P.   Madhusudan Prasad (ed.), *Living Indian-English Poets: An Anthology of Critical Essays*, ND: Sterling
E.   Rukmini Bhaya Nair, first prize, All India Poetry Competion.
E.   Menka Shivdasani works for *South China Morning Post*, Hong Kong.

1990

V.   Sanjiv Bhatla (b.1956), *Looking Back*, B: Disha, Orient Longman.
V.   Eunice de Souza, *Ways of Belonging*, Edinburgh: Polygon. [Poetry Book Society recommendation.]
V.   Chitra Banerjee Divakaruni (b. 1956), *The Reason for Nasturtiums*, Berkeley, California: Berkeley Poets Workshop Press .
V.   Charmayne D'Souza (b. 1955), *A Spelling Guide to Woman*, B: Disha, Orient Longman.
V.   Dom Moraes, *Serendip*, ND: Penguin.
V.   Vikram Seth, *All You Who Sleep Tonight*, ND: Viking/Penguin.
V.   Menka Shivdasani (b. 1961), *Nirvana at Ten Rupees*, B: Praxis.
J.   Special Shiv Kumar issue of *Journal of South Asian Literature*, XXV.2 (Summer, Fall).
A.   Kaiser Haq (ed.), *Contemporary Indian Poetry*, Columbus: Ohio State University Press.
A.   Arvind Krishna Mehrotra (ed.), *Twenty Indian Poems*, ND: OUP.
P.   Hoshang Merchant, *In-Discretions: Anais Nin*, C: WW.
E.   K. N. Daruwalla returns from government service in England.
E.   Imtiaz Dharker, 'Borderlines' (exhibition of drawings) B & D.
E.   'New Poetry from Rupa' begins with Nissim Ezekiel as consultant.

1991

V.   Agha Shahid Ali, *A Nostalgist's Map of America*, New York: Norton.
V.   Sujata Bhatt, *Monkey Shadows*, Manchester: Carcanet. [Poetry Book Society recommendation.]
V.   K. N. Daruwalla, *Crossing of Rivers and The Keeper of the Dead*, ND: OUP. [rept. of 1976 & 1982.]
V.   K. N. Daruwalla, *Under Orion*, ND: Indus/HarperCollins. [1970, revised.]
V.   K. N. Daruwalla, *Winter Poems*, ND: Indus/HarperCollins. [1980, revised.]
V.   Kamala Das, *The Best of Kamala Das*, Kozhikode: Bodhi.
V.   Chitra Banerjee Divakaruni, *Black Candle: Poems about Women from India, Pakistan and Bangladesh*, Corvallis, Oregon: Calyx Books.

V.   Ranjit Hoskote (b. 1969), *Zones of Assault*, ND: Rupa.
V.   Tabish Khair, *My World*, ND: Rupa.
V.   Anna Sujatha Mathai, *The Attic of Night*, ND: Rupa.
V.   Hoshang Merchant, *Yusuf in Memphis*, C: WW.
V.   Makarand Paranjape (b. 1960), *The Serene Flame*, ND: Rupa.
V.   Gieve Patel, *Mirrored, Mirroring*, ND: OUP.
V.   Tara Patel (b. 1949), *Single Woman*, ND: Rupa.
V.   Sudeep Sen (b. 1964), *Lunar Visitations*, ND: Rupa.
A.   K. Ayyappa Paniker (ed.), *Modern Indian Poetry in English*, ND: Sahitya Akademi.
Tr. Agha Shahid Ali, *The Rebel's Silhouette*, ND: OUP. (Faiz Ahmed Faiz's Urdu poetry).
Tr. Dilip Chitre, *Says Tuka: Selected Poetry of Tukaram*, ND: Penguin. (From Marathi.)
Tr. Arvind K. Mehrotra, *The Absent Traveller: Prakrit Love Poetry of the Gathasaptasati of Satvahana Hala*, ND: Ravi Dayal.
P.   Meena Alexander, *Nampally Road*, New York: Mercury House.
P.   F. A. Inamdar (ed.), *Critical Spectrum: The Poetry of Keki N. Daruwalla*, ND: Mittal.
P.   Bruce King, *Three Indian Poets: Nissim Ezekiel, A. K. Ramanujan, Dom Moraes*, M: OUP.
P.   Shiv Kumar (ed.), *Contemporary Indian Short Stories in English*, ND: Sahitya Akademi.
P.   R. Raj Rao, *Ten Indian Writers in Interview*, C: WW.
E.   Sujata Bhatt, Cholmondeley Award
E.   All India Poetry Competition, Rajlukshmee Debee Bhattacharya awarded first prize.

1992

V.   Agha Shahid Ali, *The Belovéd Witness: Selected Poems*, ND: Viking/Penguin.
V.   Meena Alexander, *Night-Scene, The Garden*, New York: Red Dust.
V.   Jayantha Mahapatra, *A Whiteness of Bone*, ND: Viking/Penguin.
V.   Hoshang Merchant, *Flower to Flame*, C: Rupa.
V.   Hoshang Merchant, *Hotel Golkonda: Poems 1991*. C:WW.
V.   Rukmini Bhaya Nair (b. 1952), *The Hyoid Bone*, ND: Viking/Penguin.
V.   Vijay Nambisan (b.1963) and Jeet Thayil (b.1959) *Gemini*, ND: Viking/Penguin.
V.   Bibhu Padhi, *Lines from a Legend*, Leeds: Peepal Tree.

V. Bibhu Padhi, *A Wound Elsewhere*, ND: Rupa.
V. Makarand Paranjape, *Playing the Dark God*, ND: Rupa.
V. Saleem Peeradina, *Group Portrait*, ND: OUP.
V. R. Raj Rao (b. 1955), *Slide Show*, Leeds: Peepal Tree.
V. Sudeep Sen, *Kali in Ottava Rima*, London: Paramount.
V. Vikram Seth, *Beastly Tales from Here and There*, ND: Viking/ Penguin.
A. Keith Fernandes and Eunice de Souza, *Bequest*, B: Department of English, St. Xavier's College.
A. Arvind Krishna Mehrotra, *The Oxford India Anthology of Twelve Modern Indian Poets*, ND: OUP.
A. H. K. Kaul (ed.), *Poetry India: Emerging Voices*, ND: Hind Pocket Books.
A. R. K. Singh (ed.), *Recent Indian English Poets: Expressions and Beliefs*, ND: Bahri.
J. *Poiesis*, Journal of Poetry Circle, Bombay.
Tr. Ranjit Hoskote and Mangesh Kulkarni, *Yogabhrashtra: A Terrorist of the Spirit* (from Vasant A. Dahake's Marathi), ND: HarperCollins.
Tr. Vikram Seth, *Three Chinese Poets*, ND: Viking/Penguin.
P. Nissim Ezekiel, *Selected Prose*, ND: OUP.
P. Dom Moraes, *Never at Home*, ND: Viking/Penguin.
P. John Oliver Perry, *Absent Authority: Issues in Contemporary Indian English Criticism*, ND: Sterling.
E. Imtiaz Dharker, 'Living Spaces' (exhibition of drawings), B.
E. Imtiaz Dharker, All India Artists' Association: Balraj Sahni Award for Art.
E. Gieve Patel translates Akho, 17th-century Gujarati mystic, at University of Chicago on Rockefeller fellowship.
E. Tabish Khair moves to Denmark.

1993

V. Agha Shahid Ali, *A Nostalgist's Map of America*, NY: Norton. [Rept of 1991.]
V. Agha Shahid Ali, *The Half-Inch Himalayas*, ND: OUP. [Rept of 1987.]
V. Jimmy Avasia, *The Man in Dark Glasses*, B: English Department, St. Xavier's College.
V. Sanjiv Bhatla, *Haiku My Friend*, ND: Rupa.
V. Sujata Bhatt, *Brunizen*, ND:Penguin. [Rept of 1988.]
V. Sujata Bhatt, *Monkey Shadows*, ND: Penguin. [Rept of 1991.]

V.   Rachna Joshi, *Configurations*, C: Rupa.
V.   Tabish Khair, *A Reporter's Diary*, ND: Rupa.
V.   Prabhanjan K. Mishra (b.1952), *Vigil*, ND: Rupa.
V.   Sudeep Sen, *New York Times*, London: The Many Press.
V.   G. S. Sharat Chandra, *Family of Mirrors*, University of Missouri-Kansas City, Mo.: Book Mark Press.
V.   G. S. Sharat Chandra, *Immigrants of Loss*, Hippopotamus Press.
V.   Eunice de Souza, *Selected and New Poems*, B: Department of English, St. Xavier's College.
A.   H. K. Kaul (ed.), *Poetry India: Voices for the Future*, ND: Virgo.
A.   Makarand Paranjape (ed.), *An Anthology of New Indian English Poetry*, ND: Rupa.
A.   Makarand Paranjape (ed.), *Indian Poetry in English*, M: Macmillan.
A.   Arlene Zidé and Aruna Sitesh (eds.), *In Their Own Voice: Women Poets from India*, ND: Penguin.
D.   Nissim Ezekiel, *Don't Call it Suicide*, M: Macmillan.
Tr.   Arvind Krishna Mehrota (with Daniel Weissbort) , *Periplus: Poetry in Translation*, ND: OUP.
Tr.   Pritish Nandy, *Untamed Heart: A Selection of Love Lyrics of Bhartrihari*, C: Rupa.
Tr.   R. Parthasarathy, *The Tale of an Anklet: An Epic of South India*, NY: Columbia University Press. (Various awards including Sahitya Akademi Prize for Translation into English, 1995.)
Tr.   A. K. Ramanujan, *Hymns for the Drowning, Poems for Visnu*, ND: Viking/Penguin. [Rept of 1981.]
Tr.   A. K. Ramanujan, Velcheru Narayana Rao and David Shulman, *When God is a Customer: Telugu Courtesan Songs by Ksetrayya and Others*, University of California Press.
J.   *The Indian Review of Books*, August-September, 'Ramanujan's Legacy'.
J.   *Kavita '93*, ND: Virgo.
J.   *Poetry Review* (London), vol. 83, no. 1 (Spring 1993), 'In Search of Kavita: Poetry from the Indian Subcontinent and Beyond'.
P.   Meena Alexander, *Fault Lines: A Memoir*, ND: Viking/Penguin.
P.   Vrinda Nabar, *Endless Female Hungers: A Study of Kamala Das*, ND: Sterling.
P.   K. R. Ramachandran Nair, *The Poetry of Kamala Das*, ND: Reliance.
P.   Makarand Paranjape, *Decolonization and Development: Hind Swaraj Revisioned*, ND: Sage.

P.   G. J. V. Prasad, *A Clean Breast*, ND:Rupa.
P.   Vikram Seth, *A Suitable Boy*, ND: Viking/Penguin.
E.   Janet Beck and Melanie Silagardo (eds.), *Virago New Poets*, London: Virago.
E.   All India Poetry Competition. Shampa Sinha awarded first prize.

1994

V.   Shanta Acharya, *Not This, Not That*, ND: Rupa.
V.   Sujata Bhatt, *Monkey Shadows*, Manchester: Carcanet.
V.   Imtiaz Dharker, *Postcards From God*, ND: Viking/Penguin.
V.   Vinay Dharwadker (b.1954), *Sunday at the Lodi Gardens*, ND: Viking/Penguin.
V.   Suma Josson (b. 1951), *A Harvest of Light*, Bombay: Orient Longman.
V.   Niranjan Mohanty, *Prayers to Lord Jagannath*, ND: Harper Collins.
V.   Robin Ngangon, *Time's Crossroads*, Hyderabad: Orient Longman.
V.   Jaithirth Rao (b.1952) and C. P. Surendran (b.1959), *Gemimi II*, ND: Viking/Penguin.
V.   E. V. Ramakrishnan, *A Python in a Snake Park*, ND: Rupa.
V.   Amitava Ray, *Blue Ponies*, C: Renaissance.
V.   Sudeep Sen, *South African Woodcuts*, London: Peepal Tree & NY: White Swan.
V.   Vikram Seth, *Arion and the Dolphin: A Libretto*, ND: Viking/Penguin.
V.   Vikram Seth, *Mappings*, ND: Viking/Penguin. [Rept. of 1981.]
V.   Vikram Seth, *The Humble Administrator's Garden*, ND: Viking/Penguin. [Rept of 1985.]
V.   G. S. Sharat Chandra, *Immigrants of Loss*, UK: Hippopotamus Press.
V.   Manohar Shetty, *Domestic Creatures: Poems*, ND: OUP.
V.   Ruth Vanita, *A Play of Light*, ND: Viking/Penguin.
J.   *Indian Literature*, 162, 'Remembering A. K. Ramanujan'.
A.   Aditya Behi and David Nicholls (eds.) *The Penguin New Writing in India*, ND: Penugin.
A.   Vinay Dharwadker and A. K. Ramanujan (eds), *The Oxford Anthology of Modern Indian Poetry*, ND: OUP.
A.   A. K. Ramanujan (ed.), *Folk tales from India: A Selection of Oral Tales from Twenty-two Languages*, ND: Penguin.
Tr.   Shiv K. Kumar, *Selected Poems of Faiz Ahmed Faiz*, ND: Viking/Penguin.

Tr.   Jayanta Mahapatra, [trans. of Shakti Chattopadhyay from Bengali], *I Can, But Why Should I?*, ND: Sahitya Akademi.

Tr.   A. K. Ramanujan, *Speaking of Shiva*, ND: Penguin. [Rept of 1972.]

Tr.   A. K. Ramanujan, *The Interior Landscape: Love Poems from a Classical Tamil Anthology*, ND: OUP. [Rept of 1967.]

P.   Suma Josson, *Circumferences*, ND:Penguin.

P.   Makarand Paranjape, *This Time I Promise It'll Be Different: Short Stories*, ND: UBS Publishers.

P.   T. R. Sharma (ed.) *Essays on Nissim Ezekiel*, Meerut: Shalabh Prakashan.

E.   All India Poetry Competition, Anju Makhija awarded first prize.

E.   Dilip Chitre, Sahitya Akademi award for first volume of his collected poems, *Ekoon Kavita-I* in Mararthi and the translation award for *Says Tuka*.

E .   Imtiaz Dharker, 'Postcards from God' (art exhibition), B, M, Bangalore.

E.   Arvind Krishna Mehrotra, *Gettysburg Review Award*, USA.

E.   Dom Moraes invited to the Institute for the Translation of Hebrew Literature, Israel.

1995

V.   Shanta Acharya, *Numbering Our Days' Illusions*, Herts:Rockingham Press.

V.   Meena Alexander, *River and Bridge*, ND: Rupa.

V.   Sujata Bhatt, *The Stinking Rose*, Manchester: Carcanet.

V.   Keki N. Daruwalla, *A Summer of Tigers*, ND: Indus (HarperCollins).

V.   H. K. Kaul, *Firdaus in Flames*, ND: Virgo.

V.   Tabish Khair, *The Book of Heroes*, ND: Rupa.

V.   Anju Makhija, *View from the Web*, ND: Har-Anand Publications.

V.   Hoshang Merchant, *Jonah and the Whale*, C: WW.

V.   Hoshang Merchant, *The Home, the Friend and the World*, C: WW.

V.   Donald T. Nigli, *When We Speak*, C: WW

V.   A. K. Ramanujan, *The Collected Poems*, ND: OUP.

V.   Srinivas Rayaprol, *Selected Poems*, C: WW.

V.   Sudeep Sen, *Mount Vesuvius in Eight Frames*, Leeds: Peepal Tree.

V.   Sudeep Sen, *New York Times and Kali in Ottava Rima*, ND: Rupa. [Rept 1993.]

V.   Sudeep Sen, *Twisted Hands*, Leeds: Peepal Tree.

V.   Vikram Seth, *The Poems 1981–1994*, ND: Viking/Penguin.

V.   Vivek Tandon (b. 1962), *Climbing the Spiral*, ND: Har-Anand.

A.   H. K. Kaul (ed.), *Poetry India: Voices in Time*, ND: Virgo.

J.   *Kavya Bharati 7*, Madurai:The Study Centre for Indian Litera-
     ture in English and Translation, American College. [Focus on
     Meena Alexander.]

J.   *The Brown Critique* founded by Gayatri Majumdar, B. then moves
     to C.

J.   *Wasafiri* (England), no. 21, Spring 1995. 'India, South Asia &
     the Diaspora'. Guest editor: Sudeep Sen.

P.   Kamala Das, *The Sandal Trees and Other Stories* (translated from
     Malayalam), Hyderabad: Longman Disha.

P.   Bijay Kumar Das, *The Poetry of Jayanta Mahapatra*, ND: Atlantic
     Publishers.

P.   Bijay Kumar Das, *The Horizon of Nissim Ezekiel's Poetry*, ND:
     B. R. Publishing Corporation.

P.   Chitra Banerjee Divakaruni, *Arranged Marriage*, NY: Doubleday.

P.   A. N. Dwivedi, *The Poetic Art of A. K. Ramanujan*, ND: B.R.
     Publishing Corporation.

P.   Iqbal Kaur (ed.), *Perspectives on Kamala Das's Fiction*, ND: Intel-
     lectual Book Corner.

P.   Makarand Paranjape, *The Narrator: A Novel*, ND: Rupa.

P.   R. Raj Rao, *One Day I Locked My Flat in Soul City*, ND: Rupa.

P.   P. K. Rajan (ed.), *Changing Traditions in Indian English Litera-
     ture*, ND: Creative Books.

P.   E. V. Ramakrishnan, *Making It New: Modernism in Malayalam,
     Marathi and Hindi*, Shimla: Indian Institute of Advanced Study.

P.   C. R. Yaravintelimath, et al. (eds.), *New Perspectives in Indian
     Literature in English*, ND: Sterling.

E.   K. N. Daruwalla retires as Chairman, Joint Intelligence Com-
     mittee,

E.   Jeet Thayil, editor of literary section of *Gentleman*, 1995–8.

E.   All India Poetry Competition among Schoolchildren. Vishnu
     Prabhakar awarded first prize.

E.   Ranjit Hoskote at Iowa Writers Workshop

1996

[Note: from 1996 M for Mumbai (Bombay), Ch for Chennai (Madras)]

V.   Kamala Das, *Only the Soul Knows How to Sing*, Kottayam: D.C.
     Books.

V.   Randhir Khare, *Swimming into the Dark and Other Poems*, ND:
     Har-Anand Publications.

V.   Keshav Malik, *Ozone Layer: Selected Poems*, ND: Abhinav Publications.

V.   Jayanta Mahapatra, *The Best of Jayanta Mahapatra*, Calicut: Bodhi Books.

V.   Hoshang Merchant, *Love's Permission*, C: WW.

V.   Hoshang Merchant, *The Heart in Hiding*, C: WW.

V.   G. J. V. Prasad (b. 1955), *In Delhi without a Visa*, ND: Har-Anand Publications.

A.   H. K. Kaul (ed.), *Poetry India: Voices from Within*, ND: Virgo.

D.   R. Raj Rao, *The Wisest Fool on Earth and Other Plays*, Kalyan, Maharashtra: The Brown Critique.

J.   *Lines Review*, 138, September 1996, Midlothian, Scotland. 'Twelve Modern Young Indian Poets, Guest editor: Sudeep Sen.

J.   *Metverse Muse* (ed.), Tulsi Naidu.

Tr. Dilip Chitre, *Shri Jnandev's 'Anubhavamrut/The Immortal Experience of Being'*, ND: Sahitya Akademi. (From Marathi.)

P.   Shirish Chindhade, *Five Indian English Poets: Nissim Ezekiel, A. K. Ramanujan, Arun Kolatkar, Dilip Chitre, R. Parthasarathy*, ND: Atlantic Publishers.

P.   Keki Daruwalla, *The Minister for Permanent Unrest and Other Stories*, ND: Ravi Dayal.

P.   Kwame Dawes (ed.), *Sudeep Sen: A Bio-Bibliographical Sourcebook*, Sumter: University of South Carolina.

P.   Chitra Banerjee Divakaruni, *The Mistress of Spices*, NY: Doubleday.

P.   Tabish Khair, *An Angel in Pyjamas*, ND: HarperCollins.

P.   Jeet Thayil (ed.) *Vox: New Indian Fiction*, M: Sterling.

E.   All India Poetry Competition, Tabish Khair awarded first prize.

E.   All India Poetry Competition among Schoolchildren. Ambika Nair awarded first prize.

E.   K. N. Daruwalla, PEN International, Freemantle, Australia

E.   Imtiaz Dharker, 'Random Blue' art exhibition, M.

E.   R. Raj Rao, International Writing Program, University of Iowa.

E.   C. P. Surendran, journalism fellow at Cambridge University.

1997

VP. Meena Alexander, *The Shock of Arrival: Reflections on Post-Colonial Experience*, Boston: South End.

V.   Agha Shahid Ali, *The Country without a Post Office*, New York: Norton.

V.   Sujata Bhatt, *Point No Point: Selected Poems*, Manchester: Carcanet.

V. Debjani Chatterjee, *I Was That Woman*, C: WW. [Rept 1989.]

V. Imtiaz Dharker, *Postcards from God*, Newcastle upon Tyne: Bloodaxe. [Includes *Purdah* and *Postcards from God* and art.]

V. Chitra Banerjee Divakaruni, *Leaving Yuba City*, NY: Anchor.

V. Jayanta Mahapatra, *Shadow Space*, Kottayam: D.C. Books.

V. Hoshang Merchant, *Talking to the Djinns*, C: WW.

V. Hoshang Merchant, *The Birdless Cage*, C: WW.

V. Moin Qazi, *The Real Face*, C: WW.

V. Moin Qazi, *Voices from a Tinctured Heart*, Ranchi: Writers Forum.

V. Mukta Sambrani (b. 1975), *The Woman in This Poem Isn't Lonely*, C: WW.

V. Sudeep Sen, *Postmarked India: New & Selected Poems*, ND: HarperCollins.

V. Jeet Thayil, *Apocalypso*, London: Aark Arts.

A. Eunice de Souza, *Nine Indian Women Poets: An Anthology*, ND: OUP.

Tr. A. K. Ramanujan, *A Flowering Tree and Other Oral Tales from India*, (eds), Stuart Blackburn and Alan Dundes, ND: Viking/Penguin.

J. *London Magazine*, vol. 37, nos. 5–6 (August–September), special Indian issue.

P. Meena Alexander, *Manhattan Music*, San Francisco: Mercury House.

P. Gauri Deshpande, *The Lackadaisical Sweeper*, Ch: EastWest Books.

P. Jayanta Mahapatra, *The Green Gardener*, Hyderabad: Orient Longman.

P. Rukmini Bhaya Nair (with Ramnik Bajaj and Ankur Meattle), *Technobrat: Culture in a Cybernetic Classroom*, ND: HarperCollins.

P. Makarand Paranjape (ed.), *Nativism: Essays in Literary Criticism*, ND: Sahitya Akademi.

P. Jeet Thayil (ed.), *Vox 2: The Gentleman Collection of New Fiction*, M: Sterling.

E. Imtiaz Dharker, art exhibition, London.

E. Vijay Nambisan, *Gentleman* poetry prize.

E. All India Poetry Competition. First prize awarded to Ranjit Hoskote.

1998

V. Sujata Bhatt, *Nothing is Black, Really Nothing*, Hanover: Wehrhahn Verlag. [Bilingual English-German edition]

V.   Debjani Chatterjee, *Albino Gecko*, Salzburg: University of Salzburg.

V.   Dilip Chitre, *The Mountain*. Pune: Vijaya Chitre.

V.   Shiv K. Kumar, *Woolgathering*, ND: Disha/Orient Longman.

V.   Keshav Malik, *Outer Reaches*, ND: Sterling.

V.   Keshav Malik, *Under Pressure*, ND: Samkaleen Prakashan.

V.   Arvind Krishna Mehrotra, *The Transfiguring Places*, ND: Ravi Dayal.

V.   Aroop Mitra, *Awakening*, privately printed.

V.   Shaul Bassi (ed.), *Poet: Indiani del Novecento di lingua inglese*, Venice: Supermova.

A.   H. K. Kaul (ed.), *Poetry India: Voices of Silence*, ND: Virgo.

Tr.   Anju Makhija and Menka Shivdasani with Arjan Mirchandani, *Freedom and Fissures: An Anthology of Sindhi Partition Poetry*, ND: Sahitya Akademi.

Tr.   Dom Moraes, *A Chance beyond Bombs*, ND: Penguin. [Antholgy of Modern Hebrew Peace Poems, selected by Haya Hoffman]

J.   *Kavya Bharati*, vol. 10, Madurai: The Study Centre for Indian Literature in English and Translation, American College. Tenth Anniversary Issue.

P.   Nilufer Bharucha and Vrinda Nabar (eds.), *Postcolonial Indian Literature in English: Essays in Honour of Nissim Ezekiel*, ND: Vision.

P.   Shiv Kumar, *A River with Three Banks—The Partition of India: Agony and Ecstasy*, ND: UBS Publishers.

P.   Manohar Shetty, *Ferry Crossing: Short Stories from Goa*, ND: Penguin.

E.   Kamala Das receives Valayar Award and Sahitya Parishad Award.

E.   Sudeep Sen, 1998 Hawthornden Fellowship for Poetry.

E.   Jeet Thayil moves to the USA.

E.   Kalpana Swaminathan and Inshrat Syed (as 'Kalpish Ratna') begin editing *Sunday Observer* 'Books and Ideas' section, Mumbai.

1999

V.   Rukmini Bhaya Nair, *The Ayodhya Cantos*, ND: Penguin.

V.   Bibhu Padhi, *Painting the House*, Hyderabad: Disha/Orient Longman.

V.   C. P. Surendran, *Posthumous Poems*, ND: Penguin.

V.   Tenzin Tsundue (b. 1973?), *Crossing the Border*, M: Self published.

V.   Gopi Warrier, *Lament of JC: Poems*, London: The Delhi London Poetry Society.

A.   H. K. Kaul (ed.), *Poetry India: Voices of Many Worlds*, ND: Virgo.

P.   Chitra Banerjee Divakaruni, *Sister of My Heart*, NY: Doubleday.

P.   Hoshang Merchant (ed.) *Yaarana: Gay Writing from India*, ND: Penguin.

P.   Randhir Khare, *The Dangs: Journeys into the Heartland*, ND: HarperCollins.

P.   Randhir Khare, *Notebook of a Footsoldier and Other Stories*, ND: HarperCollins.

P.   S. Mokashi-Punekar, *Post-Independence Indo-English Poetry (1947–1977)*, C:WW.

P.   G. J. V. Prasad, *Continuities in Indian English Poetry: Nation Language, Form*, ND: Pencraft International.

P.   A. K. Ramanujan, *The Collected Essays*, edited by V. Dharwadker, ND: OUP. [Dated 2000.]

P.   Cecile Sandten, *Broken Mirrors. Interkulturalität am Beispiel der indischen Lyrikerin Sujata Bhatt*, New York: Peter Lang.

P.   Vikram Seth, *An Equal Music*, London: Phoenix House.

P.   Eunice de Souza (ed.), *Talking Poems—Conversations with Poets*, ND: OUP

E.   All India Poetry Competition. K. Sri Lata awarded first prize.

E.   Sahitya Akademi seminar by ten poets at University of Hyderabad, March. (Keki Daruwalla, Shiv Kumar, Arvind Mehrotra, R. B. Nair, Bibhu Padhi, Makarand Paranjape, R. Raj Rao, Menka Shivdasani, Eunice de Souza.)

E.   UGC conference on 'Trends and Techniques in Contemporary Indian English Poetry', Osmania University, December.

E.   Mukta Sambrani studies in the USA.

A detailed annual bibliography, complied by Shymala Narayan, can be found in the *Journal of Commonwealth Literature*.

Chart 1: Life and Career Details of Some Poets

Name	Shiv Kumar	Nissim Ezekiel	Srinivas Rayaprol	Keshav Malik
Date of birth	1921	1924	1925	1926
Place of birth	Lahore	Bombay	Secunderabad	Miani (Pakistan)
Where raised	Lahore	Bombay	Secunderabad	Srinagar, Delhi, Calcutta
Father's religion	Hindu	Judaism	Hindu	Reformed Hindu, Arya Samajist
Mother's religion	Hindu	Judaism	Hindu	Reformed Hindu
Languages spoken at home	English, Hindi	English, Marathi		English, Punjabi
Father's occupation	Headmaster	Professor of Botany & Zoology	Professor of Telugu	Advocate
Mother's occupation		Principal of Marathi primary school		Painter, writer, translator
Main school or college		A Catholic school, Bombay	Nizam College, Hyderabad	DAV, Delhi/ St Joseph's, Calcutta
BA	A.S. Govt College, Lahore	Wilson College, (English)	Benares University	Amar Singh College, Srinagar (politics, history)
MA	Foreman Christian College	Wilson College	M.S., Stanford, USA (civil engineering)	
Ph.D.	Cambridge University, England			
Career(s)	Professor of English	Professor of English	Engineer	Editor, critic
Travel abroad	Yes	Yes	Yes	Yes
Began writing	In college, then at age 49	In college	At the age of 18	At the age of 21
Discovered modern poetry	In college	In college	In USA	At the age of 22
Multilingual writer	No	No	Telugu	No
Translator from Indian languages	No	Marathi	Telugu	Yes
Other arts	Novelist	Dramatist, Critic of art, music, dance		Art critic
Now lives in	Hyderabad	Bombay	Secunderabad	Delhi
First significant publication	*Illustrated Weekly*	*Illustrated Weekly*	*Illustrated Weekly*	*Illustrated Weekly Quest, Thought*

Chart 1 (*contd.*)

Name	P. Lal	Jayanta Mahapatra	A.K. Ramanujan	Arun Kolatkar
Date of birth	1928	1928	1929	1932
Place of birth	Kapurthala, Punjab	Cuttack, Orissa	Mysore	Kohlapur, Maharashtra
Where raised	Calcutta	Cuttack	Mysore	Kohlapur
Father's religion	Hindu	Christian	Srivaisnava Brahmin	Hindu
Mother's religion	Hindu	Christian	Srivaisnava Brahmin	Hindu
Languages spoken at home	English, Punjabi, Hindi, Bengali	English, Oriya	English, Tamil, Kannada	Marathi
Father's occupation	Homeopathic doctor	School Inspector	Professor of Mathematics	Educational administrator
Mother's occupation				
Main school or college	St Xavier's, Calcutta	Stewart European School	Mysore	Bilingual Marathi/English
BA	St. Xavier's, Calcutta (English)	B.Sc., Ravenshaw College (Physics)	Mysore University (English)	Art diploma, Bombay
MA	St Xavier's Calcutta	M.Sc. Science College, Patna	Mysore University (English)	
Ph.D.			Indiana University, USA (Linguistics)	
Career(s)	Professor of English	College physics teacher	Professor of Linguistics	Graphic designer
Travel abroad	Yes	Not until older	Yes	No
Began writing	1946	At the age of 38	At the age of 15	Around the age of 16-17, seriously at 21
Discovered modern poetry	1947	At the age of 38	At the age of 18	In the 1950s
Multilingual writer	No	Oriya	Kannada	Marathi
Translator from Indian languages	Yes, Sanskrit, Hindi, Punjabi, Bengali	Oriya	Kannada, Tamil	Marathi
Other arts	Calligraphy	Short story		Painting
Now lives in	Calcutta	Cuttack	Chicago	Bombay
First significant publication	*Illustrated Weekly, Thought*	*Illustrated Weekly, Levant*	*Illustrated Weekly*	*Quest*

Chart 1 (*contd.*)

Name	Kamala Das	Rajgopal Parthasarathy	K.D. Katrak	K.N. Daruwalla
Date of birth	1934	1934	1936	1937
Place of birth	Punnayurkulam, Kerala	Tirupparaitturai, Tamil Nadu	Bombay	Lahore
Where raised	Calcutta	Srirangam, Bombay	Bombay	Various places
Father's religion	Hindu	Srivaisnavism	Zoroastrian	Zoroastrian
Mother's religion	Hindu	Srivaisnavism	Zoroastrian	Zoroastrian
Languages spoken at home	English, Malayalam	Tamil, Sanskrit, English	English, Gujarati	English, Gujarati
Father's occupation	Salesman	Accountant	Businessman	Professor of English
Mother's occupation	Poet			
Main school or college	Various, including Catholic boarding school	Dom Bosco, Bombay	Cathedral Anglican School	Various
BA		Siddharth College, Bombay University (English)	Started at St Xavier's, Bombay	In English, History and Political Science
MA		Bombay University (English) Diploma in English Studies, Leeds, UK		University of Punjab (English)
Ph.D.				
Career(s)	Writer	Lecturer in English, editor	Advertising	Police, government
Travel abroad	No	Yes	Yes	Yes, later
Began writing	Very young	At the age of 16	At the age of 16	At university
Discovered modern poetry		At the age of 20	At the age of 16	At university
Multilingual writer	Malayalam	Tamil	No	No
Translator from Indian languages		Tamil, Sanskrit	No	Yes, started recently
Other arts	Fiction, Journalism	Music, film, theatre, painting	Theatre, acting	Short story
Now lives in	Trivandrum	New York State, USA	Bombay	Delhi
First significant publication	PEN	Quest	Illustrated Weekly	Quest

Chart 1 (*contd.*)

Name	Dilip Chitre	Dom Moraes	G. S. Sharat Chandra	Eunice de Souza
Date of birth	1938	1938	1938	1940
Place of birth	Baroda	Bombay	Nanjangud, Mysore	Poona
Where raised	Bombay	Bombay, Ceylon, Australia	Mysore, Bangalore	Poona
Father's religion	Hindu agnostic	Roman Catholic	Lingayat	Roman Catholic
Mother's religion	Hindu atheist	Roman Catholic	Hindu, Naidu	Roman Catholic
Languages spoken at home	Marathi, some English	English	English, Kannada	English, Konkani
Father's occupation	Editor, publisher	Journalist, editor	Attorney, Advocate-General	Teacher, school inspector
Mother's occupation	Editor	Pathologist		School teacher
Main school or college	Many	Various Catholic schools		Jesus & St Mary's, Poona
BA	Bombay University (English)	Oxford, England (English)	Maharaja's College, Mysore	Sophia College, Bombay (English)
MA	Started in English		Law colleges, Poona and Bangalore	Marquette University, USA (English)
			MFA Univ. of Iowa, USA (Writing)	
Ph.D.				
Career(s)	Teaching, advertising, etc.	Writer, editor	Professor of English	University lecturer in English
Travel abroad	Yes	Yes	Yes	Yes
Began writing	At the age of 14	At the age of 10	In school	At the age of 30
Discovered modern poetry	At the age of 10	Early	In late teens	
Multilingual writer	Marathi	No	No	No
Translator from Indian languages	Marathi	No	Yes, Kannada, Sanskrit	No
Other arts	Film maker, Painter	No	Short story	Columnist, drama
Now lives in	Bhopal, Poona	Bombay	Kansas City, Missouri, USA	Bombay
First significant publication	First in Marathi; In English: *damn you, Dionysius, Blunt*	*Illustrated Weekly*	*Literary Half-Yearly*	*Quest*

Chart 1 (*contd.*)

Name	Adil Jussawalla	Gieve Patel	Gauri Deshpande	Gopal Honnalgere
Date of birth	1940	1940	1942	1942
Place of birth	Bombay	Bombay	Poona	Bijapur
Where raised	Bombay	Bombay	Poona	Mysore, Bangalore
Father's religion	Zoroastrian	Zoroastrian	None	Hindu
Mother's religion	Zoroastrian	Zoroastrian	Hindu	Hindu
Languages spoken at home	English, Gujarati	English, Gujarati	English, Marathi, German	Tamil, Kannada
Father's occupation	Nature physician	Dental suregeon	Professor of Chemistry	Engineer
Mother's occupation			Professor of **Anthropology**	
Main school or college	Cathedral Anglican, Bombay	St Xavier's, Bombay	Ahilyadevi High School for Girls and Fergusson College	
BA	Oxford, England (English)	B.Sc., St Xavier's	Fergusson College (English)	B.Sc.
MA		Medical degrees	Poona University	
Ph.D.			Poona University (English)	
Career(s)	Editor, teacher of English	Medical doctor	Journalist, Lecturer in English	Art teacher, book seller
Travel abroad	Yes	Later	Yes	
Began writing	In 1954	At the age of 18	At the age of 22	In school
Discovered modern poetry	In school		In Marathi, at school: in English, at college	
Multilingual writer	No	No	Yes, Marathi	Yes, Kannada
Translator from Indian languages	Yes	Yes, Gujarati	Yes, Marathi	
Other arts		Painter, actor, playwright	Short stories	Theatre
Now lives in	Bombay	Bombay	Phaltan, Maharashtra and abroad	Panchgani
First significant publication	Miscellany	Quest	Opinion	Miscellany, Thought

Chart 1 (*contd.*)

Name	H. O. Nazareth	Saleem Peeradina	Arvind Krishna Mehrotra	Pritish Nandy
Date of birth	1944	1944	1947	1947
Place of birth	Bombay	Bombay	Lahore	Calcutta
Where raised	Bombay	Bombay	Allahabad	Calcutta
Father's religion	Roman Catholic	Islam	Hindu	Christian
Mother's religion	Roman Catholic	Islam	Hindu	Christian
Languages spoken at home	English, Konkani	English, Hindi, Gujarati	English, Hindi	Bengali
Father's occupation	Businessman	Homeopathic doctor	Dentist	Teacher
Mother's occupation				Teacher
Main school or college	Dr Antonio D'Silva, Bombay	Catholic high school		Left after one year
BA	University of Kent, England (philosophy and politics)	St Savier's, Bombay	Allahabad University (English)	
MA		University of Bombay (English) Wake Forest University, USA	Bombay University (English)	
Ph.D.				
Career(s)	Barrister, Computer programmer	Teacher, Advertising, Editor, Administrator	University lecturer in English	Advertising, Editor, Photographer
Travel abroad	Yes	Yes	Yes	Yes
Began writing	At the age of 15	In 1966	At the age of 17	At the age of 16
Discovered modern poetry	At the age of 16	In 1965	At the age of 17	At the age of 16–17?
Multilingual writer	No	No	No	No
Translator from Indian languages	No	Hindi and Gujarati	Yes, Hindi	Yes, Bengali, Urdu
Other arts	Film maker, drama	Painting and singing		Photography
Now lives in	London	Bombay	Allahabad	Bombay
First significant publication	*Poetry India*	*Poetry India*	*damn you, Miscellany*	*Quest, Miscellany*

Chart 1 (*contd.*)

Name	Santan Rodrigues	Agha Shahid Ali	Darius Cooper	Meena Alexander
Date of birth	1948	1949	1949	1951
Place of birth	Loutulim, Goa	Delhi	Poona	Allahabad
Where raised	Goa and Bombay	Kashmir	Poona, Bombay	Various
Father's religion	Roman Catholic	Islam	Zoroastrian	Syrian Christian
Mother's religion	Roman Catholic	Islam	Zoroastrian	Syrian Christian
Languages spoken at home	English, Konkani	English, Urdu, Kashmiri	English	English,
Father's occupation	Tailor	Professor of Education, Education Commissioner	Engineer	Meteorologist
Mother's occupation		Principal of training college		
Main school or college	Holy Name & St Mary's, Bombay	Various	Poona	Various
BA	K.C. College, Bombay (English)	University of Kashmir	St Xavier s, Bombay (English)	Khartoum University, Sudan (English and French)
MA	St Xavier's College, Bombay (English)	University of Delhi (English) Penn State University, USA (English)	University of Bombay (English) University of Southern California (English)	
Ph.D.		Penn State, USA	Southern California, USA (English and film)	University of Nottingham, England (English)
Career(s)	Public relations	University teacher of English	University teacher, English and film	University teacher Professor of English
Travel abroad		Yes	Yes	Yes
Began writing	In 1961	At the age of 12	Around time of BA	At the age of 13
Discovered modern poetry	In 1961	During BA course	Around time of BA	At the age of 13
Multilingual writer	No	No	No	In French
Translator from Indian languages	Yes, Konkani, Marathi, Gujarati	Yes, Urdu	No	No
Other arts			Film	
Now lives in	Bombay	Hamilton, NY, USA	Los Angeles, USA	New York, USA
First significant publication	Illustrated Weekly, Quest	Thought, Levant First poems, Miscellany	Fulcrum, PEN	

Chart 1 (*contd.*)

Name	Bibhu Padhi	Vikram Seth	Manohar Shetty	Melanie Silgardo
Date of birth	1951	1952	1953	1956
Place of birth	Cuttack, Orissa	Calcutta	Bombay	Bombay
Where raised	Cuttack	Patna, Delhi	Baroda, Panchgani	Bombay
Father's religion	Hindu	Hindu	Hindu	Roman Catholic
Mother's religion	Hindu	Hindu	Hindu	Roman Catholic
Language spoken at home	English, Oriya	English, Hindi	Tulu	English
Father's occupation	Lawyer	Business consultant	MNC employee	Pharmaceutical company executive
Mother's occupation		Lawyer, judge		School teacher
Main school or college		Doon School, Tonbridge School, UK	St Peter's, Panchgani	St Xavier's, Bombay
BA	Utkal University, Ravenshaw College (English)	Corpus Christi College, Oxford UK Philosophy, Politics & Economics	B.Com, University of Bombay	St Xavier's, Bombay (English)
MA	Utkal University, Ravenshaw College (English)	Nanjin University, China Stanford University, USA, Economics	Started in English, University of Bombay	University of Bombay (English)
Ph.D.		Stanford University (in progress)		
Career(s)	University teacher of English	Editor, Stanford University Press	Journalist, editor	Publishing, editor
Travel abroad	No	Yes	No	Yes
Began writing	At the age of 18		At the age of 19	In school
Discovered modern poetry	In school		At the age of 19	At the age of 18
Multilingual writer	Yes	No	No	No
Translator from Indian language	Yes	Yes, Urdu, Hindi	No	No
Other arts		Hindustani classical singing	Short story	Photography
Now lives in	Cuttack	New Delhi	Goa	London
First significant publication	*Dialogue-India*	*Writers Workshop*	*Illustrated Weekly*	*Kavi*

Chart 2: Anthologies, Publishers and Awards

Poets	Three major anthologies			Three significant publishers			Other significant publishers and awards	Other publishers and anthologies					
	Peeradina	Parthasarathy	Daruwalla	OUP	Clearing House	Newground		Arnold-Heinemann	Writers Workshop	Gauri Deshpande	P. Nandy 1972	P. Nandy 1973	P. Nandy 1977
N. Ezekiel	X	X	X	X			Fortune Press Pergamon Poets, Ezekiel issue of JSAL, Sahitya Akademi Award		X	X	X	X	X
Ramanujan	X	X	X	X			Pergamon Poets. OUP, England		X		X	X	X
K. Das	X	X	X				Orient-Longman, New Writing in India, PEN Philippines award	X	X	X	X	X	X
Daruwalla	X	X	X	X			Sahitya Akademi Award		X	X	X	X	X
Mehrotra	X	X	X	X	X		New Writing in India				X	X	
Patel	X	X	X		X		Ezekiel Publications New Writing in India			X	X	X	X
S. Kumar		X	X	X			Tata McGraw-Hill Sidgwick and Jackson		X				X
Parthasarathy	X	X	X¹	X			Poetry India Prize Pergamon Poets			X	X	X	
Mahapatra		X	X	X	X		U. of Georgia Press Poetry Chicago Award Greenfield Review Press Sahitya Akademi Award	X	X	X	X	X	X
Kolatkar	X	X	X			X	Commonwealth Poetry Prize, New Writing in India						
Jussawalla	X		X			X			X	X	X	X	X
Chitre			X			X	New Writing in India						X
de Souza			X			X							

Poets	Three major anthologies			Three significant publishers			Other significant publishers and awards	Other publishers and anthologies					
	Peeradina	Parthasarathy	Daruwalla	OUP	Clearing House	Newground		Arnold-Heinemann	Writers Workshop	Gauri Deshpande	P. Nandy 1972	P. Nandy 1973	P. Nandy 1977
Peeradina	X		X			X				X			
Katrak	X		X					X	X	X	X	X	X
Sharat Chandra			X	X			London Magazine edition		X				
Deshpande	X		X					X	X	X	X		
M. Kalia	X								X	X			
Patnaik			X								X	X	X
H.O. Nazareth					X								
Shetty						X							
Rodrigues						X			X				
P. Lal	X²								X		X	X	
Nandy								X	X	X	X	X	X
Silgardo						X							
Moraes							Hawthornden Prize Eyre & Spottiswode, etc.			X			
Rakshat Puri									X	X	X	X	X

¹Would have been included if he had answered letters from editor
²Included but treated severely

Chart 3: Important Anthologized Poems

	P. Lal	Peeradina	P. Nandy 1972	P. Nandy 1973	Gauri Deshpande	Parthasarathy	P. Nandy 1977	Daruwalla	Dwivedi	Golden Treasury	Ten Years of Quest	Books	Other
Daruwalla, 'The Epileptic'		X			X	X		X				*Under Orion*	
Daruwalla, 'Routine'						X		X				*Apparition in April*	
Daruwalla, 'Death of a Bird'					X	X						*Crossing of Rivers*	
Daruwalla, 'Haranag'			X		X							*Crossing of Rivers*	*Opinion*
K. Das, 'The Dance of the Eunuchs'	X							X	X	X		*Summer in Calcutta*	
K. Das, 'An Introduction'	X							X	X	X		*The Old Playhouse*	*Hers*
K. Das, 'Summer in Calcutta	X										X	*Summer in Calcutta, The Old Playhouse, Tonight, This Savage Rite*	*Hers*
K. Das, 'The Freaks'		X				X		X				*Summer in Calcutta, The Old Playhouse Tonight, This Savage Rite*	
K. Das, 'The Fancy Dress Show'			X		X				X				*Hers, Opinion*
K. Das, 'My Son's Teacher'			X	X	X		X						*Hers: A Book of Verse for Children (OUP, 1975)*
K. Das, 'A Man is a Season'			X	X			X					*Tonight, This Savage Rite*	
K. Das, 'Madness is a Country'			X	X			X						

Chart 3 (*contd.*)

	P. Lal	Peeradina	P. Nandy 1972	P. Nandy 1973	Gauri Deshpande	Parthasarathy	P. Nandy 1977	Daruwalla	Dwivedi	Golden Treasury	Ten Years of Quest	Books	Other
K. Das, 'Forest Fire			X	X			X					*Summer in Calcutta, The Old Playhouse, Tonight, This Savage Rite*	
Deshpande, 'Family Portraits'			X	X				X					
Deshpande, 'Migraine'					X			X					*Hers, Opinion*
Deshpande, *The Female of the Species*		X						X					
Ezekiel, 'Enterprise'	X	X				X		X	X	X	X	*Unfinished Man, Latter-Day Psalms*	*Quest*
Ezekiel, 'Night of the Scorpion'	X	X				X		X	X	X		*Exact Name, Latter-Day Psalms*	*Quest*
Ezekiel, 'Poet, Lover, Bird-watcher'		X				X		X			X	*Exact Name, Latter-Day Psalms*	
Ezekiel, 'Marriage'	X							X	X			*Unfinished Man, Latter-Day Psalms*	
Ezekiel, 'Philosophy'	X					X		X				*Exact Name, Latter-Day Psalms*	
Ezekiel, 'Background, Casually'		X	X			X						*Hymns in Darkness*	
Ezekiel, 'Very Indian Poem' (The Patriot)		X						X				*Exact Name, Latter-Day Psalms*	*Illustrated Weekly*
Ezekiel, 'Good-by Party for Miss Pushpa'					X	X						*Hymns in Darkness*	
Jussawalla, 'Sea Breeze, Bombay'		X	X	X			X					*Missing Person*	
Jussawalla, 'Approaching Santa Cruz'		X			X		X					*Missing Person*	*Illustrated Weekly*
Jussawalla, 'Nine Poems on Arrival'			X	X	X							*Missing Person*	*Illustrated Weekly*

Chart 3 (*contd.*)

	P. Lal	Peeradina	P. Nandy 1972	P. Nandy 1973	Gauri Deshpande	Parthasarathy	P. Nandy 1977	Daruwalla	Dwivedi	Golden Treasury	Ten Years of Quest	Books	Other
Jussawalla, 'The Raising of Lazarus'			X	X				X				*Missing Person*	
Kolatkar, 'the boatride'		X				X							*damn you*
Kolatkar, 'The Bus'						X	X	X				*Jejuri*	*Opinion Literary Quarterly*
Kolatkar, 'An Old Woman'						X		X				*Jejuri*	*Opinion Literary Quarterly*
Shiv Kumar, 'Indian Women'						X		X				*Cobwebs, Suberfuges*	
P. Lal, 'Because Her Speech is Excellent'	X								X	X		*Love's The First, Collected Poems*	
Mehrotra, 'The Sale'		X				X						*Nine Enclosures, Middle Earth*	*Penguin New Writing*
Mehrotra, 'Continuities'				X		X		X				*Middle Earth, Nine Enclosures*	
Mehrotra, 'Remarks of an Early Biographer'						X		X				*Nine Enclosures*	
Mehrotra, 'Between Bricks, Madness'		X						X				*Nine Enclosures*	
Nandy, 'Near Deshapriya Park'			X	X	X							*Poetry of P. Nandy, Selected Poems, Madness is the Second Stroke*	
Nandy' 'Calcutta if you must exile me'			X	X	X							*Poetry of P. Nandy, Selected Poems, Madness is the Second Stroke*	*Indian Verse in English 1977*
Nandy, 'What shall we do with these memories'			X	X							X	*Poetry of P. Nandy, Selected Poems, Madness is the Second Stroke*	

Chart 3 (contd.)

	P. Lal	Peeradina	P. Nandy 1972	P. Nandy 1973	Gauri Deshpande	Parthasarathy	P. Nandy 1977	Daruwalla	Dwivedi	Golden Treasury	Ten Years of Quest	Books	Other
Parthasarathy, 'This Business'			X	X	X								*Opinion*
Parthasarathy, Exile 8: 'A Grey Sky'		X	X			X						*Rough Passage*	
Parthasarathy, Trial 2: 'Over the family album'		X				X						*Rough Passage*	
Parthasarathy, Trial 7: 'It is the night'			X	X	X	X						*Rough Passage*	
Parthasarathy, Homecoming 8: 'With paper boats'		X				X						*Rough Passage*	
Parthasarathy, Homecoming 10: 'The street'		X				X						*Rough Passage*	
Patel, 'On Killing a Tree'			X			X	X	X				*Poems*	*Quest*
Patel, 'Servants'		X				X						*Poems*	
Patel, 'Nargol'		X	X			X	X					*Poems*	
Patel, 'Dilwadi'		X						X				*How Do You Withstand Body*	
Patel, 'University'				X		X		X				*How Do You Withstand Body*	*Penguin New Writing Illustrated Weekly*
Patel, 'The Ambiguous Fate'		X	X	X				X	X	X		*How Do You Withstand Body*	
Ramanujan, 'Still Another View of Grace'		X	X	X				X	X	X		*The Striders, Selected Poems*	*Indian Verse in English,* 1977
Ramanujan, 'The Gnomes'	X		X	X					X				*Indian Verse in English,* 1977
Ramanujan, 'A River'		X				X						*The Striders, Selected Poems*	

Index